THE HISTORY OF THE UNITED STATES

History 8 for Young Catholics

SETON PRESS
FRONT ROYAL, VA

Seton Home Study School
1350 Progress Drive
Front Royal, VA 22630
540-636-9990
540-636-1602 fax

For more information, visit us on the Web at www.setonhome.org.
Contact us by e-mail at info@setonhome.org.

ISBN: 978-1-60704-078-1

Cover: Stained Glass Window of St. John Neumann at the Shrine of St. John Neumann

DEDICATED TO THE SACRED HEART OF JESUS

THE HISTORY OF THE UNITED STATES
TABLE OF CONTENTS

INTRODUCTION

Our country today is in many ways, the greatest nation that has ever existed. However, the United States is not a Catholic country. It never has been nor is it likely that it ever will be. This does not mean that the United States is not a great country and that American Catholics should not be justly proud of the United States. The French historian, Alexis de Tocqueville, who traveled through America during the first part of the nineteenth century, observed that "America is great because she is good." Throughout our history, there have been many great Catholics who loved America and helped make it great. In this history, we will meet some of them.

You will learn how our nation grew from a handful of settlers on the eastern shore of America, to become one of the most populous nations on earth. These early settlers and the countless others who journeyed to these shores came to America seeking freedom. Many gave their lives in search of that freedom. In many ways the history of the United States is the story of the greatest freedom-loving people in the world.

When the Founding Fathers wrote the Constitution, they wrote it to guarantee freedom. From that day on, Americans have fought and died to preserve freedom, not only in America, but around the world. During the twentieth Century, the United States stood up to the two great evils of that century: Nazism and Communism. These sinister beliefs threatened the freedom of the world and the existence of the Catholic Church. Hundreds of thousands of Americans gave their lives to defeat these evil forces.

Today, America again is a nation under attack. We are attacked both from enemies without and from enemies within. These enemies hate America because it stands for Freedom. President Ronald Reagan once said that the "heart of America is strong; it's good and true."

The United States is different from other nations. Today, we look at other nations and see that the heads of many governments are elected. However, this was not always true. In the beginning, the leaders of the Chosen People, the Hebrews, were selected by God. Other peoples were usually led by the man who was the best general. He was able to take power by force. Often he forced other nations to join his kingdom by the power of his army.

In ancient times, when a king died, his son would often become the new king. The throne was thus passed down as an inheritance from father to son. However, often a stronger man would take the throne through the power of the sword.

During the Middle Ages, Kings passed the throne to their first born sons who then passed it on to their sons. This created a degree of stability in the land. However, if a king died without a son, there might be a war to decide who would rule.

When the Pilgrims and the other colonists came to America, they decided to try an experiment: government by the people. The colonists would elect their own rulers. This was a bold idea. It had been tried before in Greece and Rome, but not on the scale that these pioneers would try it.

Freedom and Democracy are the reasons that America is under attack today. It is because Americans dream great dreams. Ronald Reagan once declared that "America is too great for small dreams. The American people said, 'Let us look to the future with confidence both at home and abroad. Let us give freedom a chance.'"

In this book we will see the role that Catholics played in making America strong and free. Too often, history books neglect the role that Catholics played in building America. We will not do that. We will learn why these Catholic men and women always believed that they could be both good Americans and good Catholics at the same time. We will study about some of the first explorers of this land who were French and Spanish priests. We will learn about the first bishops and priests in the United States. As the United States grew, so did the Church.

From the thirteen colonies hugging the Atlantic Ocean, pioneers expanded westward. Over the next decades, Americans moved first to the Mississippi River, then to the Pacific. In time, they would tame the Wild West. The pioneering spirit that brought men and women to these shores would drive them to build roads, then railroads, then interstate highways. Finally, an American would be the first man to walk on the moon.

Our story will eventually take us into the 20th century. This was a century of challenge for both America and the Church. Both were tested. America fought two terrible wars. She faced the threat of Communism. Because generations of Americans were willing to work, and if necessary, to fight for their freedom, America prevailed.

Finally, we will bring our story up to the present. We will remember a day in September, when once again America was attacked. Once again, we will recall the price of freedom that Americans have paid for so many decades.

It is our hope that the Catholic students who read this book will come to love America. However, loving America does not mean that Catholics should ever ignore the mistakes that America has made in her history.

In Catholic teaching, the State and the Church have specific complementary functions in society. The primary purpose of the State is to serve the common good and create a society that allows the Church to minister to the people. The role of the Church is to lead people to the Supreme Good: God. The Church performs her role through teaching and administering the sacraments. Her work is to prepare us for the Eternal Life to come. Both the State and the Church should labor to encourage people to live virtuous lives. "Thou shalt not kill" and "Thou shalt not steal" are God's commandments. They are also laws. When laws legalize vice, society is in need of correction. As Catholics, we need to call attention to these laws and oppose them.

Over the next years, the boys and girls who read this book will go on to high school. Many will continue on to college. Then they will take their places in the world as workers, business men and women, mothers and fathers, priests and nuns, teachers, or any of countless honorable jobs. They will also be voters. They will have the chance to make this a better nation. It is hoped that in reading about the Americans who have built and preserved this nation, that they will be inspired. That a new generation of Catholic Americans will go forth as Catholics and as Americans to dream great dreams and to accomplish great things. Look to the future with hope and confidence. Look to the future with pride as an American.

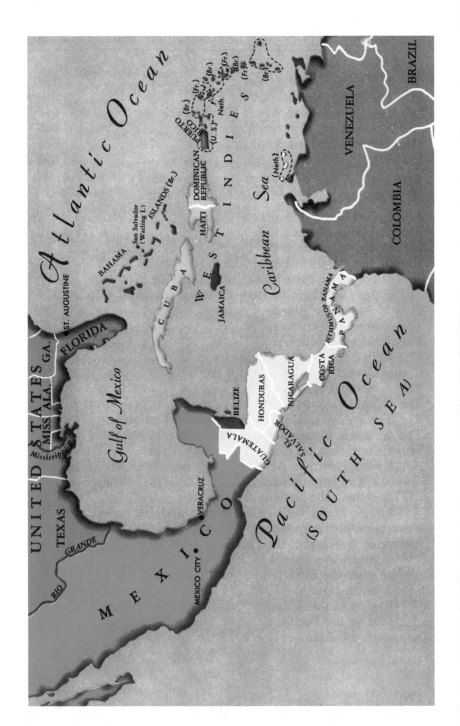

The Beginnings of our Nation

Columbus Discovers America

The Story Starts...

    The story of the United States of America begins almost five hundred years before Christopher Columbus came to America. It begins in the Old World, where for centuries our forefathers lived. It begins in Norway, Sweden, and Denmark. It has chapters in Portugal, Spain, Italy, France, and England. The story first begins in the ninth century when Viking warriors sought adventure, conquest, and plunder. The story of the beginnings of America is one of daring explorers. It is a tale of the sacrifice of priests and missionaries. It is a story of how men suffered and struggled and labored in their search for new lands, new markets, and new souls to save. It is a tale of discovery.

The Viking Explorations

Our story starts with the Vikings. These men were marauding seamen from Norway, Denmark, and Sweden. For nearly three centuries, their snake-shaped or dragon-modeled ships raided the coasts of Europe from the British Isles in the north to the shores of Italy in the south and to Constantinople in the east. These pirates killed, burned, robbed, and terrorized wherever they went.

About the year 874, the Vikings reached Iceland, an island in the North Atlantic ocean on which Irish monks had previously settled. Here the Vikings established a colony. A century later, the Viking, Eric the Red, sailed west from Iceland to Greenland where he founded another colony. The son of Eric the Red, Leif Ericson, left Greenland to return to Norway, where he became a Catholic. Then, at the request of the king, who also had become a Catholic, Leif went back to Greenland as a missionary. On this return voyage, about the year 1000, heavy storms forced Leif off course. Norse sagas tell that he touched the shores of what is now Labrador, Newfoundland, and Nova Scotia. He may have sailed and explored as far west as the Great Lakes. This land was covered with vines, and Leif called it Vinland. However, he did not establish a permanent settlement there. As a result, this land was forgotten for almost five hundred years.

The Vikings discovered Vinland.

The Crusades

To the Catholics of Europe, the Holy Land was sacred. It was the land sanctified by Our Blessed Lord Himself. This is where Jesus had been born, had lived, had taught, and had died. All the places and things associated with the life and death of Christ were in the Holy Land: Nazareth, Jerusalem, the Mount of Olives, the Tomb of Christ, and Calvary.

In 1071, at the Battle of Manzikert, the Turks won a decisive battle over the Eastern Empire. Though the capital of the Eastern Empire at Constantinople would not fall for another four hundred years, the loss of this battle spelled the end for the Eastern Empire. The Turks then moved on and captured the Holy Land. Jerusalem fell to the Turks in 1077. When news reached Europe of the capture of Jerusalem by the Turks, Catholics felt not only great sorrow but also righteous anger.

By the end of the eleventh century, conditions were at their worst. Catholics were denied the right to visit Jerusalem and the other sacred places. When they did go to the Holy Land, they were robbed and beaten. Many were killed. The safety of Constantinople also was threatened. For these reasons, the Eastern emperor, Alexius, appealed for help to Pope Urban II. So it was that in 1095, the pope called for volunteers to drive the Turks from the Holy Land and to recover the places made sacred by Christ.

Common people and knights answered his plea with a cry of "God wills it." Large bands of devoted men gathered and traveled by land and sea eastward to rescue the Holy Land. These expeditions were called the Crusades. Those who took part in them were known as Crusaders. For two hundred years, eight major Crusades were organized. However, of all these, only the First Crusade was truly successful. Jerusalem was captured and a Christian kingdom was set up. Later, however, the Muslims again captured the Holy Land. All further efforts to regain the Christian kingdom failed. The Crusades ended in defeat.

The Results of the Crusades

Although their original purpose was never gained, the Crusades did much to awaken the interest of Europe in the Holy Land and the East. Mostly, the Crusades proved to Europeans the value of trade with the Orient. The returning Crusaders produced in the people of Europe an intense interest in the products of the East and the desire for those products. Among the Eastern goods were pepper, spices, sugar, coffee, tea, drugs, perfumes, gems, pearls, rugs, and silks from the East. The desire to obtain these items stimulated trade and commerce. Merchants and traders began to import these goods in large quantities. European trade flourished.

The port cities of Genoa and Venice in Italy were well located. They became the shipping and distributing centers for trade between the East and northern and central Europe. As a result, both of these cities grew rich and independent. All Europe became anxious to share in the trade that contributed to the wealth and independence of these two great cities.

The Crusades also created a new interest in geography and travel. The thrilling tales of adventure told by the Crusaders and the daring exploits of the traders made people think about the Far East. More and more interest was focused on finding new trade routes to the fabulous lands of the East.

After the invention of the compass and the astrolabe, sea captains were able to find their way on the high seas. The compass told them in what direction to steer their ship. The astrolabe enabled them to tell the longitude of the ship and its approximate distance from land. These were great advantages. They gave the sailors ability to sail uncharted seas. Thus, the way was prepared for the discovery of America.

Spot Check

1. Who were the Vikings?
2. What were the Crusades?
3. Which pope called the First Crusade?
4. Name two results of the Crusades.

Marco Polo Describes the Riches of the East

From 1271 to 1295, Marco Polo, a Venetian, traveled in Asia. For a time, he served the emperor of China, Kublai Khan. He saw the wealth and culture of Asia. When he returned to Venice, Italy, he wrote a book about what he had seen and done. Although the book was written before the invention of the printing press and had to be copied by hand, many copies were made. The book was widely read all over Europe. It caused an increased interest in the Far East.

Why Men Searched for a Route to the East

As time went on, rivalry for the Eastern trade increased. So, too, did the expense and the length of time involved in moving goods between the East and the West. More and more it became necessary for the merchants to protect their caravans from robbers and hostile tribes along the routes. Warehouses and trading posts had to be built. Costly treaties had to be made with the various tribes whose land the routes crossed. This meant that eventually the cost of delivering the products became almost too expensive.

In 1453, the Turks captured Constantinople. This made it more difficult and expensive to transport goods overland. Hence it became important to look for a new route. Only an all-water route would solve the problems of transportation and at the same time reduce the cost of delivering the goods.

Portugal's Search

Portugal is a small nation on the western coast of the Iberian (Spanish) peninsula. It began the search for a new route to eastern trade. Portugal was in a good position to do this, since its entire coastline faced the Atlantic Ocean, the only alternate route to the Mediterranean Sea. One of Portugal's princes was so enthusiastic about exploration and navigation that he was known as Henry the Navigator.

Christopher Columbus

One of the people who had read Marco's Polo's book with great interest was Christopher Columbus. Columbus was born in the port city of Genoa, Italy. Growing up, he had heard the stirring tales of seamen and was determined to become a sailor. Therefore, at an early age, he entered upon a seagoing career. He sailed to all parts of the Mediterranean and on one voyage reached Portugal. There he became acquainted with the pupils and followers of Prince Henry the Navigator.

As a student of geography, astronomy, and travel, Columbus, together with the learned geographers, knew that the earth is round. However, he was mistaken in his belief as to the size of the world. His mistake was compounded when the most highly regarded geographer and mapmaker of the time, the Italian Toscanelli, said that China was only 5000 nautical miles from Europe by sea. (In fact, it is more than twice that far.) Toscanelli encouraged Columbus in his belief that the East could best be reached by sailing west. As a result, Columbus decided to make a voyage to prove that this was true. He hoped not only to find wealth for himself and those who aided him, but also to bring the teachings of Christ to the peoples of the Far East.

Getting a Nation to Help

Columbus was poor and could not carry out his idea without financial help. He vainly sought aid from Portugal, Venice, and Genoa.

Finally, through the influence of Father Perez, who had formerly been the confessor of Queen Isabella of Spain, he obtained help from that good queen. He obtained three small vessels: the *Niña*, the *Pinta*, and the *Santa Maria*. With these ships, Columbus prepared to sail from Palos, Spain. Before starting the voyage on August 3, 1492, Columbus and his crew attended Mass celebrated by Father Perez.

Christopher Columbus

In 1492, Columbus Sailed the Ocean Blue

Columbus' first stop was at the Canary Islands, where some time was spent repairing one of the ships. Then, as the three ships sailed on day after day without any sight of land, fear and anxiety grew. Again and again, the men begged Columbus to turn back. Their food was running low and the sailors lost hope. They even threatened to mutiny, to kill Columbus, and to take control of the ships. However, Columbus persuaded them to keep going.

At last, early on the morning of October 12, 1492, land was sighted. Columbus called the land San Salvador, which means "Holy Savior." Thinking that he had arrived in the East Indies, he called the natives, Indians. He came ashore, knelt down, gave thanks, and planted a cross claiming the new land for Spain.

Replicas of the *Niña, Pinta,* and *Santa Maria*

Columbus died in 1506 without knowing that he had discovered a new world. Up to the time of his death, he believed that he had reached islands off the coast of Asia. Yet he was puzzled and confused. If he had reached the East, where were the riches and the great civilization described by Marco Polo and other travelers to the Orient?

Sadly, Columbus died feeling that he had failed. However, he had made the most memorable voyage in history. After his death, the Spanish people, who had ridiculed him as the "Italian adventurer" and "idle dreamer," joined in paying tribute to him. They came to realize the importance of his discovery. The king of Spain erected a monument over his grave on which were inscribed the famous words, "To Castile and Leon, Columbus gave a New World."

Amerigo Vespucci

History failed to give Columbus the credit he was due. The land he discovered rightly should have been named Columbia. However, it is not the name of Columbus, but the name of Amerigo Vespucci, another Italian, that was given to the New World. It appears that Vespucci made voyages across the Atlantic in the employment first of Spain and then of Portugal. This second expedition carried him south along the coast of what is now Brazil. His fame rests upon the fact that he wrote a letter in which he told of the lands, peoples, and animals he had seen and in which he expressed his belief that this was a new world. Some years later, this account came to the attention of a German mapmaker, Martin Waldseemueller. Waldseemueller suggested that the "new part of the world" be called "America" in honor of Amerigo Vespucci, who, he believed, had discovered it. At first, the name was given only to what is now South America. However, it gradually came to be applied to the entire New World. As a result, we live in the United States of America, not the United States of Columbia.

Spot Check

1. Who was Marco Polo?
2. Why was a new trade route to the East needed?
3. What mistake did Columbus make about the earth?
4. Who was Amerigo Vespucci?

CHAPTER REVIEW

1. Who was the Viking leader who may have come to North America?
2. What was the purpose of the Crusades?
3. Why was Marco Polo important?
4. What early inventions were particularly helpful to sailors?
5. How did the capture of Constantinople by the Turks help bring about the discovery of America?
6. Why was Prince Henry of Portugal called the "Navigator"?
7. Which European country was the first to find an all-water route to the East?
8. What did Columbus study to learn that the earth is round?
9. Who was Amerigo Vespucci?
10. What date did Columbus discover America? Where did he land?

EXPLORING THE AMERICAS

De Soto Discovers the Mississippi River

SPAIN IN THE NEW WORLD

Settlements Are Made

The discovery of the New World caused the nations of Europe to dream of new empires. Even before the death of Columbus, the lands he had discovered became centers of Spanish life, for from the start Spain sought to establish a colonial empire and to convert the natives. The first settlements were made on the islands in the West Indies discovered by Columbus. These became stepping-stones for further colonization in the Americas. Little by little, the New World was opened up to settlement. Missionaries brought the Catholic Faith to people worshipping pagan gods.

Balboa and the Pacific Ocean

Among the Spaniards living in the West Indies in 1510, there was a daring young nobleman named Vasco de Balboa. He lived lavishly and, as a result, found himself heavily in debt. To escape his creditors, he had himself smuggled aboard a ship bound for the Isthmus of Panama. When he arrived there, he heard the natives tell of a great body of water south of the mountains. They also described a country so rich that its people ate and drank from golden cups and plates.

These stories aroused Balboa's curiosity. In 1513, with a group of followers, he set out to find the great body of water beyond the mountains. For twenty days, he tramped and cut his way through the jungle on the isthmus. At last, from the top of a mountain, he discovered the Pacific Ocean. He called it the South Sea because it lay to his south. He set up a cross on the shore and took possession of the sea in the name of Spain.

Balboa did not find the gold of which the natives had spoken. However, he proved that the new land was, as Vespucci had claimed, a separate continent.

Ponce de Leon and the Fountain of Youth

In 1513, the same year that Balboa discovered the Pacific, Ponce de Leon, the governor of Puerto Rico, discovered Florida. He had heard the Indians tell of a fountain in a land north of Cuba that would restore youth to even the oldest person. With high hopes and strong resolve, he set out in search of this magic fountain. In addition to searching for the fountain, he also desired to explore the new land and claim it for Spain. On Easter Sunday, 1513, he reached land. He called the land Florida, in honor of the Spanish name for Easter, Pascua Florida, "the Feast of Flowers."

Ponce de Leon's search for the fountain was in vain. There is no such thing as a fountain of youth. Instead of the fountain of youth, he found savage and unfriendly natives. They prevented him from establishing a settlement. However, he was able to explore much of the area around Florida. His voyage gave Spain a foothold in North America. A half century later, in 1565, this claim to territory in Florida was strengthened when the Spanish explorer, Menendez, founded St. Augustine in Florida. It is the oldest town in the United States.

Magellan Sails Around the World

In 1519, Ferdinand Magellan began what has been described as "the greatest single human achievement on the sea." On September 20, he left Spain with a fleet of five ships in search of a new route to the East. He sailed across the Atlantic to South America. By early December, they arrived in South America. The ships began to sail down the eastern coast of South America entering each river that they found. Finally the little fleet passed through the narrow, stormy strait at the southern tip of the continent, now called the Strait of Magellan.

When Magellan entered the ocean to the west of South America, the sea was so calm and peaceful that he named it the Pacific. Sailing westward, he crossed the waters discovered by Balboa. Finally, on March 16, 1521, he reached the Philippine Islands. By the time Magellan reached these islands, one ship had deserted and one had been wrecked.

In April, Magellan's ships sailed to Cebu, one of the Philippine Islands. There he met the King and Queen of Cebu. After trading gifts with the two monarchs, he told them of the Catholic Faith. They both saw the truth of the Faith and asked to be baptized along with several hundred of their subjects. Magellan presented the queen with a statue of the Infant Jesus as a gift for her baptism. However, tragedy soon followed this happy moment.

Chief Lapu-Lapu of a nearby island, Mactan, was an enemy of the King of Cebu. The king asked Magellan for help defeating his enemy. Magellan was eager to show his new friend the value of an alliance with the Spanish, so he agreed. On the morning of April 27, Magellan sailed to Mactan Island with about sixty of his men. They landed on the beach of Mactan, but were faced by a force of over 1,500 enraged natives. Magellan fought valiantly but was killed.

Despite the death of its leader, the expedition continued. Of the three ships left to the Spanish, one had to be burned before leaving the Philippines. Another ship was lost in a storm at sea. So it was that on September 6, 1522, only one ship returned to Spain. This ship, called the *Victoria*, which means victory, was well named. Its journey around the world had lasted three years, from beginning to end. Of the crew of two hundred forty-three men that set out from Spain, only eighteen returned. However, its cargo of cloves that it had picked up in the Spice Islands more than paid for the entire voyage. The dream of Columbus had been realized. Men had sailed around the world.

Hernan Cortez in Mexico: the Conquest of Darkness

In history, there have been primitive societies that sometimes practiced human sacrifice. None practiced them on the scale of the Aztecs in Mexico. The total number of humans killed was at least 50,000 per year. In 1487, a huge new pyramid was dedicated in the Aztec capital. On this occasion, 80,000 people were sacrificed to the Aztec "gods" over a period of four days.

However, there is even more evidence of the Satanic nature of the Aztec society. The Aztecs had two main "gods." One was known as the Lover of Hearts and the Drinker of Blood. The other was known as the Lord of the Dark. Nowhere else in history has Satan so institutionalized and formalized his worship than in the Aztec empire.

In the same year that Magellan set sail from Spain, 1519, Hernan Cortes landed on the coast of Mexico with about five hundred men. Since he had landed on Good Friday, he named the beach where he landed Vera Cruz, the True Cross. When the Aztecs learned he was there, ambassadors from the Aztec emperor, Montezuma II, came to greet him. In August, after spending several months learning all he could about the Aztec empire, he marched inland to its capital. He was quite literally marching into the mouth of Hell.

On November 8, after fighting a few battles, Cortes and his men arrived in the capital. There they saw the temples and the bodies of the victims. Montezuma came to meet them. He treated the Spanish well and housed them in the city near the temple. On November 13, after going to Mass, Cortes and his men climbed to the top of the pyramid temple where they saw the horrors therein.

Two days later, Cortes took Montezuma prisoner. Cortes feared that any minute the Aztecs would attack them. He hoped that with their emperor as his prisoner, an attack was less likely. However, this was not the case. In June 1520, a mob of Aztecs attacked. Cortes brought out Montezuma to try and quiet the mob, but his own people killed the emperor with a stone. The Spanish had to flee the city. As Cortes fought his way out of the city on June 30, he lost half of his men. Those that were captured were killed in sacrifice to the Aztec "gods."

Cortes was a brave soldier. His ancestors had fought 770 years to free Spain from the Muslims. He would fight to free Mexico from Satan. Over the next several months, he regrouped his army. He found allies among the enemies of the Aztecs. In February 1521, he marched on the Aztec capital. As Cortes won victories, more native people joined his army. From May to August, the Spanish and their allies fought the Aztecs for the city. On August 13, the Spanish captured the new emperor, bringing the city under their control.

The Satanic empire of the Aztecs was ended. The Catholic Faith could now come to Mexico. It would come in a most spectacular fashion. In December 1531, Our Blessed Lady appeared to Juan Diego at Tepeyac hill near Mexico City. Less than a decade after her apparition, virtually all of Mexico had become Catholic.

From Mexico, Spanish expeditions went forth to explore. They traveled northward to the Rio Grande and westward to the Pacific. Spanish colonists settled at various points in the more attractive parts of the country. With them traveled Spanish priests to teach Christ Crucified and to convert the Indians to the Catholic Faith.

Pizarro in Peru

History has painted the Spanish conquistadors as ruthless plunderers and killers. As we have seen, Hernan Cortes was not this kind of person. Sadly, other Spaniards did not live up to his noble ideals. Such a man was Francisco Pizarro. Pizarro had been born and raised in terrible poverty. Consequently, as an adult, he was interested only in becoming wealthy.

Prompted by the stories of a vast and wealthy kingdom to the south of Mexico, Francisco Pizarro, with about two hundred followers, decided to look for wealth there. In January 1531, Pizarro and his men landed in Ecuador. For the next year and a half, they tramped through the jungles of South America. Finally, in May 1532, he learned the location of the fabulous empire he sought. He headed to Peru. The natives of Peru were a highly civilized tribe known as Incas. Unlike the Aztecs, the Incas ruled a peaceful empire with little or no human sacrifices.

Pizarro seized the Inca emperor.

Pizarro's plan of conquest was simple and brutal. Just one day after his arrival, he asked to meet with the Inca emperor Atahualpa. Pizarro promised him that no harm would come to him. In the midst of the welcoming ceremonies, he abruptly seized the Inca leader in the middle of the town square. In the panic that followed, the Spanish soldiers attacked the mostly unarmed crowd. Thousands were killed. The emperor was taken as a hostage.

Seeing a chance to obtain a great deal of gold and silver, Pizarro encouraged the Incas to pay ransom. He asked that a room be filled with gold. However, after the Incas had filled the room with gold, the treacherous Pizarro killed the emperor. The Spaniards soon captured the capital city, Cuzco. Spanish rule, with little Catholic charity in it, extended over all Peru. This gave to Spain her richest possession in the New World.

De Soto and the Mississippi

Hernando De Soto had served under Cortes and Pizarro. He had seen the fabulous wealth of the Incas. He had heard that gold and great riches could be found in the Florida territory. With this hope in mind, he set out to conquer and settle this unknown land.

De Soto and his men tramped on and on. Instead of gold, the men found swamps, marshes, and jungles. The humid, insect-infested lowlands proved to be the breeding place of fever and disease. Food ran low. The men endured great hardship and suffering. The natives repeatedly attacked De Soto and his men, killing many. It is not surprising, therefore, that some of the men became discouraged and begged De Soto to turn back. Yet De Soto was determined to find gold. He refused to let suffering and even death stand in his way.

De Soto and his men kept up their weary trek from Florida through what are now Georgia, Alabama, Mississippi, and Tennessee. At last, in 1541, they came to the Mississippi River, just below where the city of Memphis is now located. Driven on by the lure of riches, they crossed the mighty river. The band of men made their way into the present states of Arkansas and Oklahoma. There, however, they found only thickets and lowlands.

In despair, De Soto and his men turned back. Discouraged and weakened by the hardships of the expedition, De Soto became ill and died. To prevent the natives from learning about the loss of their leader, his men sank his body in the muddy waters of the Mississippi, the great river that he had discovered. Then, they quickly built seven frail boats. They sailed down the Mississippi and through the Gulf of Mexico to a Spanish settlement in Mexico.

Coronado Explores the Southwest

While De Soto was struggling with hostile natives and suffering from hardships and disease, another Spaniard, Francisco Coronado, left Mexico and started northward in search of a land of legend. Like most of the other Spanish explorers, Coronado was enticed by stories of riches and wealth. Indians had told him of seven cities of gold. The expedition traveled as far north as the River Platte and explored what is now the southwest of the United States. Some of his men discovered the Grand Canyon. However, the fabled wealth was never found. There were only great plains, tepee villages, pueblos, and huge herds of buffalo that roamed the land. At last, tired and discouraged, Coronado returned to Mexico in 1542.

Spanish Missionaries in the New World

During the four hundred years of rule in the Americas, Spain became the richest country in Europe. However, it was not interested only in the gaining of wealth. Spain also desired to convert the natives and to civilize them. In establishing settlements, Spain founded missions and built schools to promote Spanish culture.

Spanish missionaries founded missions from southern California to Chile. Among these missionaries were Franciscans, Dominicans, Jesuits, and Carmelites. Priests and brothers came to the New World to preach and to teach the Faith. They came ready to endure any hardship and to suffer a martyr's death, if need be, in order to convert the natives.

Of all the missions, those founded in California by Franciscan Father Junipero Serra are the most famous. In all, he established nine of the twenty-one Franciscan missions that stretched from San Diego to San Francisco. Father Serra achieved this from 1769 to 1784, the year in which he died. He is not only an important figure in the history of California, but he is also remembered as a great and holy priest. He died in 1784 at Mission San Carlos Borromeo where he is buried. Pope John Paul II beatified him in 1988.

Mission Carmel

Besides converting the natives, the missionaries established schools where children were taught to read and write and sing. The boys were taught how to be farmers, carpenters, blacksmiths, shoemakers, and other trades. The girls were taught handcrafts, sewing, and cooking.

Two Great Schools

Spanish priests founded the first schools of higher learning in the Americas. In 1551, the University of San Marcos in Lima, Peru, was established. Two years later, the University of Mexico City was founded. These two great schools were established more than seventy-five years before Harvard College was founded. Another school, the College of Santa Cruz, was founded nearly two decades earlier in 1536. However, it no longer exists. It was closed at the beginning of the nineteenth century.

Spot Check

1. What did Balboa discover?
2. What did Ponce de Leon explore?
3. Where did Magellan die?
4. What was unusual about Aztec civilization?
5. Who conquered the Aztec empire?
6. Who was Francisco Pizarro?
7. What did Hernando De Soto explore?
8. What were the first two universities established in the New World?

FRANCE IN THE NEW WORLD

The Early French Explorers

Giovanni Verrazano, an Italian seaman, was the first explorer sent out by France to find a new route to India. Early in 1524, he reached the North American coast. He probably explored as far north as Newfoundland. Though he did not establish any settlements, he gave France a claim to territory in the New World.

The next sailor France sent out to search for a new route to India was Jacques Cartier. In 1535, about ten years after Verrazano's voyage, he discovered the great St. Lawrence River. A year later, he returned to the St. Lawrence and established settlements at Quebec and Montreal. However, the French colonists were not prepared to resist the bitter cold of a Canadian winter. Many of them died. Both settlements were abandoned the following spring. Despite this difficulty, Cartier gave France her claim to the valley of the St. Lawrence River.

The First French Settlers

It was not until more than seventy years after Cartier's explorations that the French became serious about settling Canada. In 1608, Samuel de Champlain established the first permanent French settlement at Quebec. This was the first French settlement in North America and the start of

New France. Like the Spanish explorers, Champlain wished to have the Gospel preached to the natives. Therefore, he brought missionaries to Canada to teach the native peoples and to help them become Christians.

The explorations of Champlain took him as far west as Lake Michigan. He discovered Lakes Ontario and Huron. He found the lake that bears his name, Lake Champlain, in upstate New York. Truly he can be called the "Father of New France."

Statue of Samuel de Champlain

Father Marquette and Joliet

Perhaps the most famous of the missionaries who came to New France was the French Jesuit Jacques Marquette. In 1673, he and Louis Joliet, a fur trader, set out to explore a great river that the natives called the "Father of Waters." They wanted to learn whether this river, the Mississippi, flowed into the Atlantic, the Pacific, or the Gulf of Mexico. They hoped it was the long sought passage to India.

Accompanied by five French fur trappers, they paddled up the Fox River from Green Bay, Wisconsin. Then they carried their canoes over the divide into the Wisconsin River at a place now called Portage. Returning their canoes to the river, they paddled down that stream to the Mississippi. They traveled down the "Father of Waters" to the mouth of the Arkansas River. There Marquette and Joliet learned from the natives that the great river emptied into the Gulf of Mexico and not into the Pacific Ocean. With this news, they turned back.

On the return voyage, they proceeded by way of the Illinois River to Lake Michigan. From there, they journeyed up the western shore to the mission of St. Francis Xavier. Here Marquette remained while Joliet traveled to Quebec to report the results of their trip. The next winter, Marquette returned to preach to the Indians in Illinois. However, hardship and overwork had broken his health. Within two years after his Mississippi expedition, he died. He gave his life working for the conversion of the natives. His remains lie at St. Ignace in the Upper Peninsula of Michigan.

Robert de La Salle

In 1682, Robert de La Salle explored the Mississippi River to the Gulf of Mexico. He and his band of twenty men started their journey from a point near the present city of Chicago. They sailed down the Chicago and Illinois Rivers until they reached the Mississippi. Then they sailed down the mighty river to its mouth. La Salle claimed the vast territory beyond both banks of the Mississippi in the name of France. He called the country Louisiana in honor of the king of France, Louis XIV.

After returning to Quebec, La Salle went to France to persuade the French king to establish a colony at the mouth of the Mississippi. The French king agreed and sent La Salle back to America in 1684 with four ships. The king knew the importance of controlling the Mississippi River if France were to hold on to her claim to the territory of Louisiana. Sadly, La Salle's efforts to found a colony failed. He could not find the mouth of the river. The ships landed at what is now Matagorda Bay in Texas. While attempting to reach the Mississippi by traveling over-land, some of his own men killed him.

Father Louis Hennepin

Franciscan priest Louis Hennepin was a close friend and companion of La Salle's. He accompanied La Salle on his famous trip, traveling as far as the present city of Peoria. There the two separated. With two companions, Father Hennepin voyaged down the Illinois River to the Mississippi, which the trio then explored upstream. On this journey, they reached the present site of Minneapolis in Minnesota. Here Father Hennepin discovered and named the Falls of St. Anthony. Shortly after this discovery, the Sioux Indians captured the trio. The Sioux forced the three men to travel with them. Thankfully, Father Hennepin was later rescued, and he returned to Quebec and then to France.

The North American Martyrs

On the Mohawk River in New York state, some forty miles northwest of Albany, the state capital, stands a huge shrine. It is dedicated to the first canonized saints of North America. The shrine is located in the little town of Auriesville. Auriesville was once the home of the Iroquois Indians. The Iroquois were a fierce tribe. They lived in what is now upper New York state. Being excellent fighters, they subdued the tribes from the St. Lawrence to Tennessee and from Maine to Michigan.

Of the eight Jesuit martyrs of North America, six were priests and two were brothers. The Iroquois martyred Father Isaac Jogues and his companions Rene Goupil and John Lalande at Auriesville. The Iroquois also tortured and murdered Jean de Brebeuf and Gabriel Lalemant, who were doing missionary work on the shores of the Great

Shrine of the North American Martyrs, Auriesville, New York

Lakes. The others were martyred in the West, where they were laboring among the Hurons. This devoted band of Jesuit martyrs was canonized June 29, 1930. The feast of these saints is celebrated on October 19th. It is called the "Feast of the North American Martyrs."

Spot Check

1. Who discovered the St. Lawrence River?
2. Who established the first permanent French settlement at Quebec?
3. Who is the Father of New France?
4. What did Robert de La Salle explore?
5. Why is Louis Hennepin famous?
6. Name three of the North American martyrs.

ENGLAND IN THE NEW WORLD

The First English Explorers

The Cabots, John and his son Sebastian, were England's first explorers. In 1497, John Cabot, an Italian sailor working for the English king, set sail from the ancient port of Bristol in search of a new route to the East. He landed on what is probably Cape Bonavista. He claimed the country for England, believing that he had reached parts of Asia. When he returned to England, King Henry VII was so happy that he made him an admiral.

The next year, 1498, John Cabot and his son undertook another voyage. It is not exactly clear what they explored on this voyage. However, they probably explored the coast of North America as far south as Delaware. Even though the Cabots gave England her original claims to North America, their voyages were not considered successful. They had failed to bring back gold and riches from the newly discovered lands. They had failed also to find a new trade route to the East. For these reasons, King Henry VII lost interest in their discoveries. As a result, nearly seventy years passed before England sought to re-establish her claims in the New World.

Later Explorers

The stories of the gold and silver found in Mexico and Peru renewed English interest in the New World. Filled with a desire for some of the wealth that made Spain the richest nation in Europe, seamen began to search for a new route to the Orient. They hoped to find a northwest passage to Asia.

Among these seamen was the unsavory Martin Frobisher. He had engaged in the slave trade and had visited the Spanish colonies in Central America. There he had seen the treasure ships of Spain laden with silver and gold. He decided that it was easier to steal gold than to find it, so he became a pirate. He captured some of the Spanish treasure ships. Thus

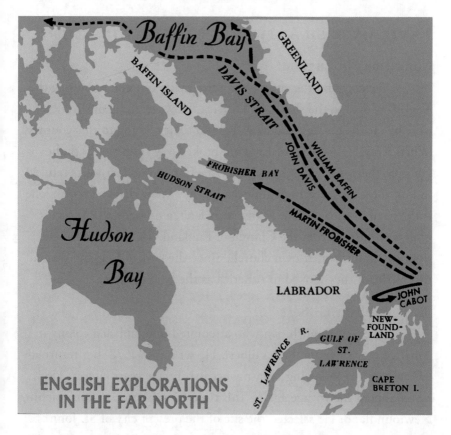

ENGLISH EXPLORATIONS IN THE FAR NORTH

began a practice that later led to widespread piracy among the English seamen.

Frobisher never did find a northwest passage. However, his travels took him to the great bay that is now called Hudson Bay. Other seamen continued the search, but they too failed. Of these, William Baffin and John Davis are the best known. They succeeded in exploring the northern coast of North America and in so doing, greatly strengthened England's claim to the New World. Though none of these explorers found a northwest route, the memory of their adventures lives today in such names as Frobisher Bay, Baffin Island, and Davis Strait.

EARLY ENGLISH ATTEMPTS TO SETTLE IN AMERICA

Conditions in England

Poverty and the chance for a better life did much to drive the English people to the shores of America. However, religious troubles were by far the greatest influence behind their coming to this country. When King Henry VIII of England broke away from the Catholic Church, there was widespread dissatisfaction. Good Catholics refused to join the Church of England because they knew that the pope alone is the head of the Church. Many years later, a number of Protestant groups withdrew from the Church of England. They demanded the right to establish their own church. Since the laws of England denied this to them, they looked to America as the land of hope.

Sir Humphrey Gilbert

The first Englishman who attempted to establish a colony in America was Sir Humphrey Gilbert. He set sail in 1578, but returned to England the following year, unsuccessful. Five years later in 1583, he attempted the voyage again. This time he was successful in reaching Newfoundland. He selected the site of the present city of St. John's for his colony. Then he explored the coast southward. At last he had to turn back for home. Sadly, he never reached his destination. The little ship on which he sailed was lost during a storm.

Sir Walter Raleigh

Sir Humphrey's failure to establish a colony in America did not discourage his half brother, Sir Walter Raleigh. Raleigh believed that the warmer climate farther south in the New World would make that area much more suitable for colonization. He asked Queen Elizabeth to grant him the right to establish a settlement there. This she did.

Thus, in 1585, Raleigh sent out about one hundred settlers to found an English colony. They landed on Roanoke Island off the coast of North Carolina. For a little while all went well. However, the venture ended in failure. There was not enough food. Most of the colonists became homesick and went home to England.

In 1587, Raleigh fitted out a larger expedition. This group of nearly one hundred fifty persons, under the leadership of John White, landed at Roanoke. This settlement did not last long. Once again, the settlers began to run out of food. White went back to England for more. During his absence, the colony was destroyed. No trace of the settlers was ever found. The Roanoke colony has become known in history as the Lost Colony. It is possible that the colonists were attacked and killed by the natives. However, they may have left the colony of their own free will and become part of a friendly native tribe.

Sir Walter Raleigh

THE DUTCH IN THE NEW WORLD

Henry Hudson

The Dutch, like other European people, were eager to share in the rich trade of the Orient. They wanted to find a short route to India. However, it was not until 1609 that the *Half Moon*, a little Dutch ship commanded by Henry Hudson, sailed into what is now New York Harbor. Henry Hudson was an Englishman employed by the Dutch East India Company.

When Hudson entered the great broad river that now bears his name and made his way through the rocky cliffs called the Palisades, he thought he had found a new route to the East. He went up the river as far as the present city of Albany. There he turned back. He had failed to find a short route to the Orient. However, Hudson gave the Dutch a claim to the Hudson River valley and laid the foundation for an extensive fur trade with the Indians.

A Replica of Henry Hudson's Ship, the *Half Moon*

Dutch Settlements

In 1624, the Dutch West India Company founded the first permanent Dutch settlement in the territory that Hudson had claimed. They built their settlement on the south end of Manhattan Island. They called it New Amsterdam. Today it is known as New York City. A colony was established also at Albany. It was then called Fort Orange. These settlements were basically trading posts where the Dutch companies engaged in fur trade with the natives.

To hasten settlement of the land bordering the Hudson River, the Dutch West India Company offered to give large sections of land to anyone who would bring fifty adult settlers to America. Under this plan, thousands of acres of land on both sides of the Hudson were settled. Later, the entire area from the Delaware River to the Connecticut River was known as New Netherland.

Spot Check

1. Who were England's first explorers in the New World?
2. What was the main reason England colonists came to the New World?
3. Where did Walter Raleigh establish a colony? What happened to it?

CHAPTER REVIEW

1. What did Balboa's discovery of the Pacific Ocean prove?
2. Why was Magellan's expedition of great historical importance?
3. Who was the conqueror of the Aztec empire?
4. Give two examples of the Satanic nature of the Aztec empire.
5. Who was the conqueror of the Inca empire?
6. Where and when were the first two universities in the Americas founded?
7. Whose explorations gave France a claim to Canada?
8. Who was called the "Father of New France"?
9. When and where was the first permanent French settlement in America established?
10. Who were England's first explorers in the New World?
11. What was the main reason that English people left England and settled in America?
12. Which explorer gave the Dutch their claims to the Hudson River valley?

THE SOUTHERN ENGLISH COLONIES ARE ESTABLISHED

The statue of John Smith stands watch over the harbor at Jamestown.

VIRGINIA

Trading Companies

At the beginning of the seventeenth century, there was a wealthy merchant class in England. These men always were looking for new ways in which to invest their money. One such venture was the trading company. A trading company allowed them to invest their money, but did not require them to run the business. One very successful trading company was the East India Company. It had been granted a charter and monopoly for trade with India. This suggested to investors the possibility of developing a colonial trade with the New World. America was known to be rich in natural resources. It was thought that exploiting these resources would pay for the cost of sending and equipping expeditions for establishing colonies.

Some English merchants, in order to carry on trade with the New World, formed two companies: the London Company and the Plymouth Company. Each company appealed to King James I to grant a charter that would give the company legal claim to the land in America. The king agreed to the requests. Under these charters, the London Company was leased land along the southern section of the Atlantic coast. The Plymouth Company was granted territory along the northern section.

The Settlement of Jamestown

The London Company established the first permanent English settlement in America. Like Christopher Columbus, the English colonists came to the New World in three little boats: the *Susan Constant*, the *Godspeed*, and the *Discovery*. The London Company sent a band of about one hundred men to Virginia to mine gold. The company thought gold was plentiful in the New World. The company also hoped that the men would discover a passage across the American continent to Asia.

With these goals in mind, the colonists sailed into what is now called Chesapeake Bay. They sailed slowly up a river (the James) to a low marshy peninsula about thirty miles inland. Here, in 1607, they established their settlement, which they named Jamestown in honor of the king. However, it was a poor tribute to the king. In their eagerness to begin searching for gold, the colonists paid little attention to the building of homes. They built only a few crude huts, some tents, and an occasional log house. This lack of proper shelter and the dampness of the lowlands caused many of the settlers to become victims of malaria, a serious illness. Supplies and food ran low, and the colony was in serious trouble. Had it not been for the leadership of Captain John Smith, the colony probably would have been abandoned.

Captain John Smith

Captain John Smith was an experienced soldier. He knew how to meet and solve difficult problems. He realized more than anyone else that only hard work and sacrifice would allow the colony to survive. Therefore, he made a rule: "He that will not work shall not eat." He saw to it that the rule was kept. Through the sheer force of his leadership, the colonists went to work. This hard-handed policy and Smith's friendship with the Indians held the little band of colonists together. In the spring of 1609, some four hundred additional settlers arrived. However, they were no more motivated than the original group.

"The Starving Time"

Unfortunately, Smith met with an accident in a gunpowder explosion and returned to England for medical care. Jamestown was left without a leader. The situation became worse. The men refused to work. The Indians turned against them and food became scarce. All this happened during the winter following Smith's departure. This period is known in the history of Virginia as "the starving time." Most of the colonists died during these months. The few who survived prepared to return to England. However, as they were sailing down the James River for England, they met a ship. It brought a load of new colonists, supplies, and a new governor. This timely arrival was providential. It saved the colony.

The Colony Begins to Prosper

The leader of the new band of colonists was Lord de la Warr. However, he remained in Jamestown less than a year before ill health caused him to return to England. His replacement was Sir Thomas Dale. He was forced to rule with an iron hand, as sternness was necessary because so many of the colonists were useless. The system of having a common storehouse was abandoned, and each settler was given a small farm. Instead of paying for the use of this land, each settler gave two and a half barrels of corn to the London Company every year. Everything else that he produced on the farm belonged to him. Hard working colonists liked this plan because of the possible profit they would be able to make on surplus crops. Lazy settlers knew that they would either work or starve. The settlers soon found that it paid to work, and the Virginia colony began to prosper.

The soil of Virginia was especially good for growing tobacco. Within ten years after the founding of Jamestown, tobacco had become its chief crop. England was a ready market, and the news of this success prompted ambitious farmers to immigrate to Virginia to share in the fortunes of the tobacco growers. Virginia continued to be a leading producer of tobacco.

The Beginning of Slavery

In 1619, the Dutch ship, *The White Lion*, arrived in Virginia. It carried twenty African slaves. (Sadly, at this time, African slavery was widely practiced in Latin America and the Caribbean.) The English needed workers and the Dutch needed supplies, so the Africans were traded to the English tobacco growers. The growers used them to work on their plantations. Over time, other traders brought Africans to Virginia and sold them to the colonists who needed laborers for their ever-expanding tobacco crops. This marked the beginning of slavery in the United States. It would result in serious problems for the nation.

Spot Check

1. When was Jamestown established?
2. What leader of Jamestown is remembered for the rule "He that will not work shall not eat"?
3. How and when did slavery come to Virginia?

The Beginning of Self-government

The year 1619 is memorable for another happier reason. It marked the beginning of self-government in the colonies. The London Company's Charter had promised the colonists the same rights as those enjoyed by Englishmen in England. However, the setters had not been given a voice in the government of Virginia. They now demanded representative government.

The House of Burgesses

The House of Burgesses was the name of the first legislature in Virginia. It was composed of representatives called "burgesses." They were elected from each of the districts into which Virginia was divided. They met for the first time on July 30, 1619, in a small church in Jamestown to write the laws of Virginia. However, their power was limited. No act passed by the burgesses could become law without the governor's approval. Even so, this was the beginning of self-government and of representative government in America.

The King Takes Back Virginia

King James began to receive negative reports from Virginia. He accused the London Company of bad management. He pointed out that the Colony had not been properly protected from the Indians. Therefore, he took away its charter. He made Virginia a royal colony with a governor and council appointed by him. However, he did not stop the meetings of the House of Burgesses. The burgesses continued to meet and demand self-government.

MARYLAND

Seventeenth Century England

During the seventeenth century, Catholics in England suffered many hardships. They were forbidden to attend Mass or to provide for the education of their children. It was against the law for a priest to celebrate Mass. Catholics were forbidden to hold office or even to enter the city of London. In fact, many things including torture were done to force them to join the Church of England. However, England had been a Catholic country for almost nine hundred years. It was impossible to destroy the Faith of all the people. Good Catholics refused to join the Church of England.

A Refuge for Catholics in America

Due to the severe laws in England, Catholics looked to the New World as a place to practice their Faith and raise their children. George Calvert, the first Lord Baltimore, was a Catholic. He understood their problems and desires. Hence, he planned to found a settlement in America that would be a safe refuge for the persecuted Catholics in England.

Fortunately, Charles I had given Lord Baltimore a grant of land in America. This land would make an ideal refuge. It extended from the Potomac River and Chesapeake Bay to the place where Philadelphia is located today. It was named Maryland, in honor of the king's Catholic wife, Henrietta Maria. Lord Baltimore planned to make this colony a place where Catholics and Protestants could live in peace and harmony. However, he died before he was able to carry out his plans. The work then fell to his son, Cecil Calvert, the second Lord Baltimore.

St. Mary's Settlement

In 1634, two small ships, the *Ark* and the *Dove*, brought the first settlers to Maryland; two English Jesuits, Father White and Father Altham, accompanied by about two hundred colonists. Leonard Calvert was the first governor of the colony. The group landed on the site that was later called St. Mary's. Here, on the Feast of the Annunciation, March 25, 1634, Father White celebrated the first Mass in the English-speaking New World. Here, too, a cross was planted as a symbol of belief in Christ. In describing this event, Father White wrote: "We raised a great cross as a trophy to Christ, Our Savior." Thus began the story of Maryland and St. Mary's.

Cecil Calvert and His Grandson

The colonists, Catholics and Protestants, lived at peace not only with one another but also with the Indians. The Indians showed the settlers how to plant corn and how to make corn meal and corn bread. With their help, the colonists did not go through a "starving time" as the settlers in Virginia had. In fact, the first crop of corn was so large that they were able to supply Massachusetts with a whole shipload. From the beginning, the Indians were interested in the Catholic Faith. Many became converts.

The Toleration Act

Among the first settlers of Maryland, there were no arguments over religious differences. Catholics and Protestants lived peacefully together. However, as the colony grew, Catholics feared persecution. More Protestants than Catholics were coming into the colony. Thus, it was decided to make freedom of religion part of the law in Maryland. In 1649, such a law was passed. The law stated that all Christians should enjoy religious freedom. It is, therefore, known as the Toleration Act.

This was the first law of its kind in the colonies. Sadly, it did not remain the law in Maryland. Five years later, when the Puritans came into power, they repealed the Toleration Act. This caused many abuses. Catholics were forbidden to hold public office. Churches were destroyed and the Jesuits were forced to leave the colony. Nearly ten years passed before the persecution of Catholics ended. Finally, in 1658, Lord Baltimore regained control of the colony. He restored religious freedom to the people of Maryland.

Spot Check

1. What assembly was the beginning of self-government in America in 1619?
2. Where did it first meet?
3. Where and when was the first Mass celebrated by an English priest in the New World?

THE CAROLINAS

The Early Settlers

In 1653, long before Carolina became an English colony, frontiersmen from Virginia moved south. They settled near what is now Albemarle Sound. Some of these people had come in search of religious freedom. Some came because of the tobacco, corn, and other crops that could be produced for trade. Even the fur trader found opportunity in this land. Clearly the land was quite valuable.

In 1663, King Charles II gave eight of his friends, all English nobles, the authority to establish a colony in the Carolina country. News of the commercial possibilities there made the land very attractive. The king's friends pointed out that the land south of Virginia might be taken over by Spain and annexed to the colony in Florida. The king did not want to lose this valuable land to Spain. Thus, he gave the grant land to his eight friends. The land included in this grant was called "Carolina" to honor Charles ("Carolus" in Latin).

Division into Two Colonies

It was evident from the beginning that it was not practical to try to organize these colonies under one governor. The people in the northern colony came mostly from Pennsylvania and New England. The population of the southern colony was made up chiefly of English and French Protestants. The occupations of these two groups differed. Farming, weaving, and lace-making were the occupations of the north. Lumber, pitch, and tar were their chief products. In general, small working class farmers owned the land. In the south, however, planters owned large estates and lived in comparative luxury. They delegated the care of their estates to an overseer. He, in turn, depended on slaves to do the work. Rice and indigo (a blue dye made from the indigo plant) were among the main products.

Thus, in Carolina, there were two distinct, widely separated settlements. One was located near Albemarle Sound and the other was located farther south in Charleston, which had been settled in 1670. There were few roads and little communication between the two major settlements. The settlers in the north found it easier to deal with Virginia. Those in the south looked to England for their trade. Therefore, when Carolina became a royal colony in 1729, it was only natural for the king to divide it into two parts. The northern section received the name North Carolina. The southern part became known as South Carolina. Each colony had its own governor and assembly.

Georgia

Georgia was the last English colony to be settled. In 1732, 125 years after the founding of Jamestown, King George II gave the land between the present-day Savannah River and Florida to James Oglethorpe. This grant of land was intended to serve two purposes. First, it was to be a buffer against the Spanish Catholics in Florida. Second, it was to be a refuge for inmates of the English debtor prisons.

Oglethorpe's Plan

Though Oglethorpe realized the importance of using Georgia as an outpost against Florida, he was more interested in the good that could be done for the poor English debtors. At that time, the English prisons were crowded with people who had been thrown into prison and punished for failing to pay their debts. The law stated that they were to be kept in prison until their debts were paid or until the creditors withdrew their claims. This method seems quite unjust, if not absurd. As prisoners, these debtors could earn no money. Therefore, they had no real hope of obtaining their release from prison. Oglethorpe asked the king to allow him to take some of these men to America where they could start new lives. The king agreed.

Although the plan had been to take mostly prisoners, over time Oglethorpe sought out the deserving poor both in and out of prison. In 1733, Oglethorpe established a colony at the mouth of the Savannah River. The colony was called Georgia in honor of King George II.

Oglethorpe and twenty other trustees governed Georgia. During the few years Oglethorpe was present in Georgia, the colony prospered. He made allies of the neighboring Indians. He was able to fix the boundary between Georgia and Florida to the advantage of England. However, when he returned to England in 1743, the trustees, who were all in England, neglected the colony. They imposed many harsh rules upon the colonists. Finally, in 1752, the colony was taken over by the king and made a royal province.

Unfortunately, Catholics never enjoyed freedom in Georgia. They were not allowed to vote or hold public office. They were even denied freedom of worship. In fact, there were raids by the Protestants in Georgia against the Catholic Indian settlements in Florida.

Statue of James Oglethorpe

Spot Check
1. Why was the colony of Carolina divided into North Carolina and South Carolina?
2. What were James Oglethorpe's two reasons for establishing the colony of Georgia?

CHAPTER REVIEW
1. When and where was the first permanent English settlement made?
2. What did John Smith do to make Jamestown succeed?
3. How did slavery start in Virginia? What year did it start?
4. What was the House of Burgesses?
5. Who founded Maryland?
6. What was the first settlement started in Maryland?
7. What was the Maryland Toleration Act of 1649?
8. Why was Carolina divided into two colonies?
9. Why was Georgia founded?

THE NEW ENGLAND AND MIDDLE ENGLISH COLONIES ARE ESTABLISHED

Mayflower lies at anchor on Cape Cod, Massachusetts, in 1620.

THE NEW ENGLAND COLONIES

Religious Conditions in England

While Elizabeth was Queen of England (1558-1603), Protestantism became the official religion of England. The English law forced people to become members of the Church of England. Everyone was required to attend that church whether they believed in it or not. Everyone was required to help support it. Those who refused were subject to persecution and death.

There was opposition on the part of both Catholics and some Protestants to these laws. Some of the Protestants refused to belong to the Church of England or to support it. They believed that they should not be subject to the authority of the state church. They claimed that they had the right to separate and establish a church of their own. For this reason, they called themselves Separatists or Independents.

41

The English government bitterly opposed the Separatists. Their leaders were punished. In some cases, they were heavily fined and imprisoned. Whenever possible, their meetings were broken up.

As a result of the persecutions, some of the Separatists left England seeking freedom of religion. They went to Holland, where they lived and worked. However, when they saw their children acquiring Dutch customs, they became alarmed because they wanted them to remain English. For this reason, in 1620, they decided to leave Holland and go to America. They hoped that in America, they would preserve not only English customs for their children but also the opportunity to enjoy religious freedom. Due to their wanderings, these people were called "Pilgrims."

The Pilgrims leave Plymouth, England, for Holland.

MASSACHUSETTS

The Pilgrims in America

Ships have played a vital role in the story of the discovery and settlement of our country. The story of Columbus and his discovery of the New World would be lacking without his three caravels: the *Niña*, the *Pinta*, and the *Santa Maria*. The settlement of Jamestown could hardly be told without reference to the *Susan Constant*, the *Godspeed*, and the *Discovery*. The *Ark* and the *Dove* were central parts of the story of the founding of Maryland. So, too, the story of the Pilgrims would be incomplete without their tiny ship, the historic *Mayflower*.

The westward journey of the *Mayflower*, with its one-hundred-and-two hardy souls, was difficult. For sixty-seven days, the little ship tossed about on a stormy sea. The creaking timbers and noisy rigging often caused the Pilgrims to wonder whether they would ever reach their destination. Finally, on November 21, 1620, the ship dropped anchor in the quiet harbor of present-day Provincetown on Cape Cod in Massachusetts.

Before setting sail for America, the Pilgrims had agreed to settle on land owned by the London Company. However, their landing at Cape Cod was north of their intended goal. It was beyond the London Company's territory. Nevertheless, they searched the coast of the bay for a suitable spot to make a permanent settlement. On December 21, 1620, their exploring party made the historic first landing at a spot later named Plymouth, after Plymouth in England.

The Pilgrims' plan of government was based on an agreement that all the men had signed on board the *Mayflower* while it was still anchored in Provincetown Harbor. This agreement is known as the Mayflower Compact. In this document, the Pilgrims pledged themselves to enact and obey "just and equal laws" for the general good of the colony. Their government was to depend upon the will of the people. This was an historic decision and is considered an important step in the history of democracy. John Carver was chosen governor. Miles Standish was chosen its military leader.

The Pilgrims sign the Mayflower Compact.

Life in Plymouth

It was winter when the Pilgrims landed on the New England shore. The weather was cold and more severe than in England. Food was scarce, and the Pilgrims' first winter was one of sickness and terrible suffering. About half of them died, yet they were determined to make Plymouth their home. When the *Mayflower* returned to England in the spring, only the crew was on board. Not one Pilgrim returned to England.

In the spring, friendly Indians showed the colonists how to plant corn. The Pilgrims also raised grains, pumpkins, beans, and peas. God blessed their work, and when they harvested their crops, the Pilgrims gathered to give thanks for the abundant crops. Even the Indians came to the Thanksgiving feast, bringing wild turkeys and deer. Thus, in time, a day of thanksgiving became a custom in America. Thanksgiving Day is a national holiday celebrated on the fourth Thursday in November.

The Puritans

The Puritans were Protestants who wanted to simplify and purify the services of the Church of England. They wanted to do away with everything that made worship beautiful, especially with everything that reminded them of true Catholic practices. For example, they did not like organ music, or the use of the Sign of the Cross, or kneeling. They regarded these practices as evil and thought that any action taken to stamp them out was justified. By destroying these practices, they wanted to make their church more "pure." For this reason they were called "Puritans."

As a result of their stern views and willingness to use violence to enforce their views, many people in England disliked the Puritans quite a bit. Even the king opposed them. He did not want them to interfere with the Church of England. Thus, when they asked the king for a grant of land in America, he gave it to them willingly just to be rid of them.

The Massachusetts Bay Company

In 1627, a grant was made to a group of Puritans organized as the Massachusetts Bay Company. The next year, under the leadership of John Endicott, some fifty Puritan colonists settled at Salem, a previously established settlement. The grant of land that they obtained from the king lay between a point three miles north of the Merrimac River and a point three miles south of the Charles River. This was a strip of land about sixty miles wide. It extended westward, all the way west to the Pacific Ocean. The charter gave the Massachusetts Bay Company the same rights that the London Company had in Jamestown.

The Puritans began to arrive in large numbers in 1630. They came prepared to stay. They brought horses, cows, sheep, pigs, farm implements, and fishing equipment.

The Settlement of Boston

John Winthrop, the governor of the Massachusetts Bay Company, reached Salem in 1630. However, in his desire to establish a settlement of his own, he moved to the present site of Boston. He was accompanied by a large group of Puritans. At first, the settlement was called Tri-mountain, or Tremont, because of the three surrounding hills. However, the name was soon changed to Boston in memory of the Puritans' home in England.

The settlers made their living by farming and fishing. Cod were especially plentiful and, because of this, the point of land that stretches out into Massachusetts Bay was named Cape Cod. This area is still known for its cod, a prevalent fish in the cape. Shipbuilding, too, has flourished since the founding of Massachusetts.

The Puritans and Religious Freedom

Although the Puritans came to America seeking religious freedom, they were completely intolerant of other religions. In fact, there was no such thing as religious freedom in the colony that they founded. They especially disliked Catholics and Quakers. Catholic priests were forbidden to enter the colony. The Puritans flogged and imprisoned any Quakers who came into the colony. Everyone was forced to attend the Puritan church and everyone was required to support the Puritan church, whether or not they belonged to it.

John Winthrop was completely opposed to democracy. He said it was "the meanest and worst of all forms of government." Those who wanted to be tolerant objected to his prejudice and to the practices of the Puritans. As a result, people who desired to get away from the intolerance of the Massachusetts settlements founded Rhode Island and Connecticut.

Spot Check

1. Who were the "Pilgrims"? Why were they called by that name?
2. What document is often considered the foundation of democratic government in America?
3. Who was Miles Standish?
4. What caused some colonists to leave Massachusetts for Rhode Island and Connecticut?

RHODE ISLAND

Roger Williams

Rhode Island owes its beginning to Roger Williams. He was a young preacher who strongly opposed the intolerance of the Massachusetts Puritans. Although he was more accepting of other Christians and did not hesitate to criticize the Puritan leaders, his tolerance did not extend to Catholics. He also claimed that the king had no right to give away land in America. He insisted that the land belonged to the Indians, and that they should be paid for it. His ideas caused him to be banished from Massachusetts. He was ordered to return to England. However, he refused to obey the order. Instead, in 1636, he and his followers secretly went to the region at the head of Narragansett Bay. There he purchased land from the Indians. He called the settlement Providence and invited people who desired political and religious freedom to come to his colony. Catholics, however, were not welcome.

About this same time, Mrs. Anne Hutchinson, another exile from Massachusetts, founded Portsmouth on the island of Aquidneck, southeast of Providence. Later, other dissenting groups founded Newport on the southern part of the island. The settlements founded by Roger Williams and Anne Hutchinson, combined with Newport, grew into the colony of Rhode Island. In 1644, Williams went to England and obtained a charter from the king. The charter

united these settlements and gave the people the right to govern
themselves.

CONNECTICUT

Thomas Hooker

In 1636, the same year that Roger Williams fled from
the Massachusetts colony, Thomas Hooker, a Puritan minister of
Cambridge, Massachusetts, founded a new colony in the valley of the
Connecticut River. Hooker had criticized the Puritan government for
limiting the right to vote to church members. With about one hundred
men, women, and children, he traveled through the wilderness of
western Massachusetts. It took them about two weeks to reach the
Connecticut River. Transporting their household goods on carts or
on the backs of horses and driving their few cows, they traveled to
the site of present-day Hartford. Dissatisfied Puritan groups from

Thomas Hooker and his followers travel through the wilderness.

Massachusetts had already established two other settlements: Windsor and Wethersfield.

In 1638, representatives from Hartford, Windsor, and Wethersfield, met at Hartford. They drew up a plan of government that they called the Fundamental Orders of Connecticut. The Orders, adopted in 1639, were based on the common consent of the people. Among its good points, the Orders did not require a religious test for citizenship. Most significant was that the Orders established government by written law. When disputes arose, the Fundamental Orders were the written law that would provide the answer. The answer did not depend upon the opinions of the members of the lawmaking assembly. The government was organized under a system of written principles and laws. It was organized under a "constitution." This would later become one of the basic ideas of government behind the Constitution of the United States. The Fundamental Orders are considered the first constitution in North America.

In 1662, the king granted Connecticut a charter based on the Fundamental Orders. Due to the tolerant policy of the charter, it served as the constitution for Connecticut until the early part of the nineteenth century.

Maine and New Hampshire

Various groups and companies claimed the northern New England coast. After a while, it became a part of Massachusetts. However, in 1679, New Hampshire became independent of Massachusetts. Dissatisfied Puritans and fishermen, who founded Dover and Portsmouth, settled New Hampshire. Later, the king gave the land to two of his friends: Gorges and Mason. Six years after these settlements were established, they divided the land between them. Mason took the western part and kept the name New Hampshire. Gorges took the eastern part and called it Maine. For protection, both colonies were soon joined to Massachusetts. Later, New Hampshire became a separate colony again, one of the original thirteen colonies. Maine, however, remained a part of Massachusetts until it was admitted to the Union in 1820.

UNION FOR PROTECTION

The Pequot Indian War

The Pequot Indians lived in the land that is now the state of Connecticut. They were a tribe of hunters and deeply resented the coming of the settlers. They became fiercely angry when the settlers moved into their hunting grounds. To defend their land, they killed many settlers. In 1637, the settlers of Massachusetts and Connecticut attacked the tribe and almost wiped them out.

In 1675, King Philip, chief of the Wampanoag Indians, secretly united the tribes of New England and attacked the colonists. The war lasted two years. However, with the united forces of the

King Philip urges the Indians to resist.

New England Confederation, the Indians were defeated. King Philip was killed, and the power of the Indians was broken.

The New England Confederation

In 1643, six years after the first of the Pequot Indians' wars, the colonists of Plymouth, Massachusetts Bay, Connecticut, and New Haven organized the New England Confederation. These colonies united for protection not only against the Indians, but also against the threat of the French on the north and the Dutch on the south. The Confederation was a committee composed of representatives from the four colonies. It had the power "to determine all affairs of war or peace, leagues, aids, charges, and numbers of men for war." In reality, it was a union of colonies which contained the seed of a United States of America.

The Confederation lasted from 1643 to 1684. Had it not been for the Confederation, the Indians might have driven the colonists out of New England. Though it is chiefly important for the role it played in the defeat of the Indians, the Confederation also taught the colonists the advantages of united action.

Spot Check

1. Name the two founders of the colony of Rhode Island.
2. Who was Thomas Hooker?
3. Give two reasons why the Fundamental Orders of Connecticut are important.
4. Which New England state today was not part of the original thirteen colonies?

THE MIDDLE COLONIES

A Wedge Separating the English Colonies

The southern colonies and the New England colonies had been founded and settled by English colonists. Between these two groups of English colonies were colonies established by the Dutch in New

York and New Jersey, and by the Swedes in Delaware. The Dutch and Swedish colonies formed a wedge that separated the southern from the northern English colonies. However, disagreements and quarrels soon arose between the Dutch and the Swedes. Only a few years after it was founded, the Dutch occupied the Swedish colony. The Dutch made it a part of the colony of New Netherlands. Not many years later, the Dutch, in turn, were forced to surrender all of New Netherlands to the English. Eventually, all the colonies along the Atlantic coast from New Hampshire to Georgia became English possessions.

NEW YORK

The English in Control in New York

Although the Dutch were the first to settle New York, the English denied that the Dutch ever had any claim to the territory

New Netherlands surrenders. Stuyvesant had lost his leg in battle in the West Indies.

called New Netherlands. They knew that Holland had done little to support Peter Stuyvesant, the Dutch governor. They knew also that New Amsterdam (present-day New York City) was poorly protected and that Stuyvesant was unable to defend the colony. Thus, when war broke out between England and Holland, the English government sent a fleet to capture New Amsterdam. Stuyvesant was helpless. He was unable to arouse the people to take up arms against the English. As a consequence, in spite of his brave words, "I would rather be carried to my grave," he was forced to surrender without a shot having been fired in defense of his territory. In 1664, all New Netherlands passed from Dutch to English control. The name of the colony was changed to New York in honor of the king's brother, the Duke of York.

However, English control did not destroy the influence of the Dutch. The Dutch remained on their farms. They continued to live as before, retaining many of their Dutch customs. They played an important part in their new homeland. In fact, some of the old Dutch families, such as the Vanderbilts, the Schuylers, and the Roosevelts, have been among America's prominent families. Three of our presidents were descendants of the early Dutch: Martin Van Buren, Theodore Roosevelt, and Franklin Delano Roosevelt.

Blessed Kateri Tekakwitha (1656-1680)

The history of early New York would be not be complete without the name of Kateri Tekakwitha. Since the Mohawk Indians were allies of the Protestant English, they opposed Catholic missionaries preaching to them. The Mohawks killed many missionaries. Yet it was to the Mohawks that the saintly Kateri Tekakwitha belonged. She is called the "Lily of the Mohawks." Jesuit missionaries instructed this lovely Indian girl in the Faith at Fonda, near Auriesville, New York, in 1667. Following her baptism, she spent the rest of her life on a reservation for Christian Indians. She died at the age of twenty-four

The Baptism of Blessed Kateri Tekakwitha

after a life of great sanctity. Pope John Paul II beatified her on June 22, 1980. She is the patroness of ecology and the environment.

New Jersey

Origin of the Colony of New Jersey

The Dutch colony of New Netherlands included what is now New York and New Jersey. When this territory passed into the hands of the English in 1664, the Duke of York kept New York and gave the other section to two of his friends, Lord Berkeley and Sir George Carteret. This grant of land lay between the lower Hudson and Delaware rivers. The new owners called it New Jersey in honor of Carteret. He had been lieutenant governor of the island of Jersey in the English Channel.

Though the colony of New Jersey was thinly settled, its people were of many nationalities and religions. It was, therefore, more tolerant than some of its neighbors. As a result, it attracted many settlers from Europe. Its growth was not rapid, however, until the arrival of English settlers. In 1665, Elizabethtown was settled. One year later, Puritans from New Haven, Connecticut, founded Newark.

The Division of the Colony

In 1674, New Jersey was divided into East Jersey and West Jersey. East Jersey belonged to Carteret and West Jersey went to Berkeley. After some years, the two men sold their holdings to the Quakers. Naturally, these changes caused much confusion. The settlers claimed that they had purchased their land directly from the Indians and therefore owed no duties to the holders. To avoid further trouble, the territory was returned to the English crown in 1702. Meanwhile, it retained its own assembly. However, for a number of years, the governor of New York controlled it. Later, it became a separate colony again and took its place among the original thirteen colonies.

PENNSYLVANIA

The Quakers in Pennsylvania

The Quakers are a religious sect. They call themselves the Society of Friends because they believe that all people are friends. They do not believe that ministers or priests are needed. A meetinghouse and the practice of brotherly love is all that is necessary. They believe that everyone is equal and, as a result, they refuse to address a nobleman as "Sir" or "Lord" and address everyone as "Friend," from the lowest person to the king himself. They refuse to serve in the army or navy because they consider war unlawful.

William Penn's Treaty with the Indians, by Benjamin West

The Quakers' beliefs caused them to be severely persecuted by the English. However, the more they were persecuted, the more they were determined to practice their beliefs. They refused to change their ways. They became stronger and stronger and their numbers grew larger. Among them was William Penn, the son of a distinguished Admiral in the British navy. William used his influence to find a refuge for the Quakers in America.

William Penn

Young William Penn joined the Quakers at the age of 22. From the beginning, he was interested not only in the doctrines of the Society of Friends but also in its future. This displeased his father very much. When William refused to sever his membership with the Quakers, the elder Penn drove his son from home. However, when his father died, he willed all his property to his son. Part of the estate of Admiral Penn was a claim of 16,000 pounds that he had loaned to King Charles II of England.

This inheritance helped William establish a colony for the Quakers in America. Instead of asking the king for the money, Penn requested a grant of land in America. King Charles gladly agreed to this easy way of paying the debt. The grant that Penn received contained more than 40,000 square miles. It was named Pennsylvania, which means Penn's woods. When Penn objected to the name, the king replied that he was naming the land in honor of William's father.

Philadelphia Is Settled

In 1681, three shiploads of colonists, led by William Markham, Penn's cousin, came to Pennsylvania. A year later, Penn himself came with one hundred more settlers, most of whom were Quakers. A site was selected between the Delaware and Schuylkill rivers. On this site, Philadelphia, the "City of Brotherly Love," had its beginning. Its splendid harbor and friendly atmosphere soon made it a brisk trade center for the colonies. It grew and prospered beyond Penn's expectations. It quickly became the largest city in the colonies. Swedes, Welsh, Germans, Irish, and Scots settled in Philadelphia. Catholics and Protestants alike found refuge in the Quaker colony.

The Mason-Dixon Line

Around 1730, trouble arose over the boundary between Maryland and Pennsylvania. Maryland claimed that the Pennsylvania line extended into territory that belonged to the Maryland colony. In 1767, two surveyors, Mason and Dixon, finally set the boundary line. It became known as the Mason-Dixon line. After the War of Independence, it became the dividing line between the free states and the slave states.

DELAWARE

A Colorful History

Delaware lies on the Delaware Peninsula between the Chesapeake and Delaware Bays. Its name comes from Lord de la

Warr, an early governor of Virginia. In 1610, his ships, while on their way to Virginia, were blown off course. They were blown into the bay that the sailors called Delaware.

The Indians destroyed the first settlement in Delaware, which the Dutch made in 1631. In 1638, the Swedes created the first permanent settlement. They called it Fort Christina, in honor of the Swedish queen. The colony was called New Sweden and lasted until 1655. In 1655, it was taken over by Peter Stuyvesant, the governor of New Netherlands. However, he was forced to surrender it to the Duke of York in 1664.

In 1682, it became a part of Pennsylvania. It shared the same government as Pennsylvania until 1776, when it became the independent state of Delaware.

Spot Check

1. What colonies were founded by the Dutch and the Swedes?
2. Who was Peter Stuyvesant?
3. Who was Kateri Tekakwitha?
4. What religious group founded Pennsylvania?
5. How did William Penn obtain the land for Pennsylvania?
6. What does the name "Philadelphia" mean?
7. How did Delaware get its name?

CHAPTER REVIEW

1. Why did the Pilgrims leave Holland and come to America?
2. Where did the Pilgrims land when they arrived in America?
3. What is the significance of the Mayflower Compact?
4. What colonies were founded as a result of religious intolerance in Massachusetts?
5. Who founded Rhode Island?
6. Who founded Connecticut?
7. What was the purpose of the New England Confederation?
8. When and why was the name New Netherland changed to New York?
9. Who is known as the "Lily of the Mohawks"?
10. Who founded Pennsylvania? To what religious group did he belong?
11. Who settled Delaware?

FRANCE AND ENGLAND STRUGGLE FOR A CONTINENT WHILE THE CHURCH STRUGGLES FOR SOULS

The Death of General Wolfe at the Battle of Quebec in 1759, by Benjamin West (1770)

FRENCH AND ENGLISH RIVALRY

The Five Colonial Powers in North America

Five countries shared in the early claims to territory in North America. They were England, France, Holland, Sweden, and Spain. The English settlements extended along the Atlantic seaboard from Maine to the northern boundary of Florida. The French settlements were established in the St. Lawrence Valley, along the shores of the Great Lakes, and down the valleys of the Mississippi and Ohio rivers. The Dutch and the Swedes settled around the mouth of the Hudson River and north of Chesapeake Bay. The Dutch occupied the Swedish settlements and joined them to their own. In 1664, the Dutch settlements were taken over by the English. They were re-named New

York, New Jersey, and Delaware. Florida, which had been colonized by Spain, remained a Spanish possession until the signing of the Treaty of Paris in 1763.

A Century of Wars

For almost a century, France and England were at war with one another in North America. They were also at war in Europe and in India. Each nation was attempting to establish a great colonial empire. Each nation wanted to be a world power.

In 1643, Louis XIV became king of France. For his entire reign, he sought to make France the most powerful country in Europe. To achieve this, he waged war with England, Austria, and Prussia. He tried to establish colonies in Canada, the West Indies, and many other parts of the world. However, his main colonial interest was the development of Canada. King Louis XIV not only spent huge sums of money on the Canadian colony, but also arranged for its protection and security. He appointed a royal governor and a military commander with a special regiment of French troops to guard and defend his interests in the New World.

By the middle of the eighteenth century, rivalry between the French and the English was very bitter. Both countries claimed the territory between the Appalachian Mountains and the Mississippi River. To protect their claims, the English established settlements in these lands. The French opposed the English by building trading posts and forts on the land the English claimed. The French were friendly with the Indians. They traded with the Indians and also tried to convert them. However, the French were at a great disadvantage. They were outnumbered by the English fifteen to one.

The rivalry between these great powers led to war. The war between France and England in Europe was a signal for war between the French and English in America. In fact, it led to three wars: King

William's War, Queen Anne's War, and King George's War. These three wars cost many lives, but settled very little.

King William's War

King William's War lasted from 1689 to 1697. It was not an important war. The French tried to seize the Hudson Valley, but they failed because of the resistance of the Iroquois Indians. Neither side gained or lost territory. The Treaty of Ryswick restored peace.

Queen Anne's War

In 1702, a second war broke out between the French and the English. This war was costly to France. The English seized the famous French settlement of Acadia, later called Nova Scotia. When the war ended, the Treaty of Utrecht gave Nova Scotia, Newfoundland, and the territory around Hudson Bay to England. Thus, France lost much of its territory in the New World.

King George's War

King George's War broke out in 1744. A force of four thousand English colonists under the command of Sir William Pepperrel of Maine attacked the French fort of Louisbourg on the Gulf of the St. Lawrence. After six weeks of bitter fighting, the French were forced to surrender. However, the treaty that was signed four years later returned Louisbourg to the French. Once again, the claims of France and England in America remained unchanged.

THE FRENCH AND INDIAN WAR (1754-1763)

The Beginning of War

The westward movement of the English deeply concerned the French. The English claimed that their charters gave them all the lands between the Atlantic and the Pacific. The French, on the other hand, claimed all the lands drained by the St. Lawrence and

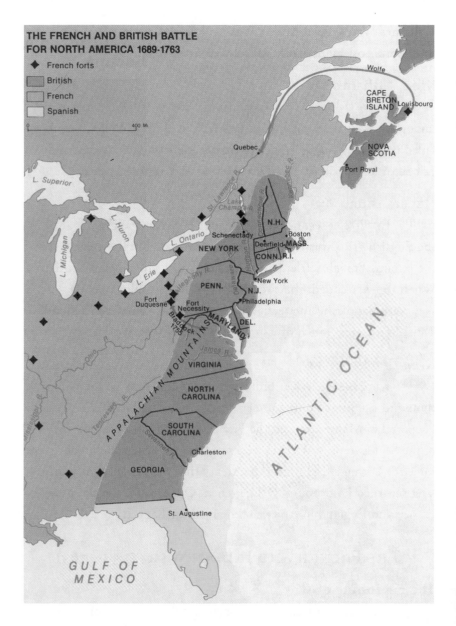

THE FRENCH AND BRITISH BATTLE FOR NORTH AMERICA 1689-1763

◆ French forts

British

French

Spanish

0   400 Mi.

L. Superior

L. Michigan

L. Huron

L. Erie

L. Ontario

Lake Champlain

St. Lawrence R.

Quebec

CAPE BRETON ISLAND   Louisbourg

Wolfe

NOVA SCOTIA

Port Royal

Schenectady

N.H.

Boston

Deerfield   MASS.

CONN.   R.I.

NEW YORK

New York

PENN.

N.J.

Fort Duquesne

Fort Necessity

Philadelphia

Braddock 1755

MARYLAND

DEL.

Allegheny R.

Ohio R.

Tennessee R.

Mississippi R.

James R.

VIRGINIA

NORTH CAROLINA

SOUTH CAROLINA

Charleston

Savannah R.

GEORGIA

St. Augustine

APPALACHIAN MOUNTAINS

ATLANTIC OCEAN

GULF OF MEXICO

the Mississippi Rivers. The French laid claim also to all lands drained by the tributaries of the Mississippi. As the English pioneers moved west, they came into conflict with the French.

When the English began to move into the disputed territory, the French built a chain of forts between the Great Lakes and the Mississippi River. Among the most important French forts were those erected at Niagara Falls, and the present-day sites of Detroit, Vincennes, and Kaskaskia. New Orleans protected the mouth of the Mississippi River, and St. Louis guarded the central part of the Louisiana Territory.

Meanwhile, the English took steps to secure their claims to the Ohio Valley. They organized an Ohio Company and sold tracts of land to English settlers. Governor Dinwiddie of Virginia was determined to protect the interests of the Ohio colonists. He sent a remarkable twenty-one-year-old surveyor to warn the French that the Ohio Valley was English territory and that they were trespassing there. That young surveyor would soon make his mark on American history. His name was George Washington.

George Washington

The journey to the Ohio Valley was difficult and dangerous. It was winter, and most of the trip was made through heavy wilderness. However, Washington and his seven companions delivered Governor Dinwiddie's message to the French in good time. It had little effect. They refused to recognize the English claims. They continued to build Fort Le Boeuf on the Allegheny River in the upper Ohio Valley.

With Governor Dinwiddie's permission, Washington and a small group of men hurried to southwestern Pennsylvania to build a fort at the junction of the Allegheny and Monongahela Rivers. However, the French destroyed the fort before it was finished. In its place, the French erected a new fort. They called it Fort Duquesne in honor of the governor of Canada.

Fort Necessity

Washington then quickly built another fort not far from Fort Duquesne. He called it Fort Necessity. Attacked by superior numbers on July 3, 1754, Washington was forced to surrender. The capture of Fort Necessity was the beginning of the war known as the French and Indian War. In this conflict, the Indians generally allied themselves with the French.

The French and Indian War was the first major war to have its beginning in America. Even though war was not declared, the English government sent General Braddock with an army from England to drive the

French out of the Ohio Valley. Braddock did not understand the war tactics of the Indians. He tried to fight as he would have fought in Europe. As a result, the French and the Indians hiding behind trees found the English easy targets. The English suffered heavy losses. Most of the English officers were killed. Braddock was mortally wounded. The English army would have been wiped out had it not been for Washington and his men. Washington's army hid behind trees just like the French and Indians. They protected the

George Washington

shattered English army. Under Washington's leadership, the surviving men of Braddock's army were gathered together and returned to Virginia.

After Braddock's defeat, the French continued to win victories over the English. Under General Montcalm, the smartest of the French generals, they drove the English from the northern front. They captured Fort William Henry on Lake George and defeated the English forces around Lake Champlain.

English Successes

The French victories did not continue for long, however. William Pitt, the wise prime minister of England, realized the importance of the war in America. He was determined to defeat the French. So he sent fresh troops to America and replaced the commanding officers with abler and younger men.

The French claimed three regions in the New World: the St. Lawrence Valley, guarded by Louisbourg; the Great Lakes region, protected by Fort Niagara; and the Mississippi Valley, which the French had named Louisiana. The gateway to Louisiana was the Ohio Valley. It was strongly guarded by Fort Duquesne. The English planned to attack the approaches to all three of these regions.

An expedition under General Forbes, one of Pitt's new commanders, accompanied by George Washington, made its way through the wilderness and captured Fort Duquesne in 1758. They renamed the fort, Fort Pitt, in honor of the prime minister. The capture of this fort opened the Ohio Valley for English settlement. The settlement of Louisbourg also was captured in 1758. The following year, the English captured Fort Niagara. This made it possible for the English fleet to sail up the St. Lawrence River.

Quebec Is Captured

Quebec was a powerful French fort. The great French Catholic General Montcalm defended it. The French knew that as long as they held Quebec, Canada would remain in their possession. However, English General Wolfe, a young and aggressive leader, decided to attack the city. After many unsuccessful attempts to take the city, Wolfe's scouts discovered an unguarded, narrow trail that led to an open stretch of land north of the French forces. Since the trail was narrow and steep, the French did not expect an army to use it. Under cover of darkness, Wolfe and nearly five thousand men climbed in single file up the narrow path.

When Montcalm awoke the next morning, September 13th of 1759, before him stood the English army. It had taken position between the fort and the city of Quebec on what is known as the "Plains of Abraham." In the bitter battle that followed, both generals, Montcalm and Wolfe, were killed. The French were defeated. This victory at the Battle of Quebec gave the English control of Canada and ended French power in the New World.

The Treaty of Paris of 1763 settled all claims between the two countries. France gave England her Canadian province and all the territory east of the Mississippi River, except the historic city of New Orleans. England gained possession of Florida from Spain, who had helped France in the war. In return for Spain's losses during the war, France gave Spain New Orleans and all of Louisiana west of the Mississippi River.

French Influence in America

Though French power in America was destroyed with the fall of Quebec, French influence remained. Many villages and towns in the St. Lawrence Valley have French names. French is the official language of the Canadian province of Quebec. French geographical names in the Great Lakes country also give evidence of French exploration.

New Orleans, sometimes called the "Queen City of the Gulf," has a strong French influence. Its history goes back more than two centuries. The French founded New Orleans in 1718, and it became the capital of the great Louisiana Territory in 1722. The part of the city known as the "French Quarter" is almost a city in itself.

West of New Orleans is the land of the Acadians (popularly called "Cajuns"). There the descendants of many of the Acadians, who were driven out of Canada by the English at the time of the French and Indian War, now dwell. The Acadians were French Catholics. They were driven out of their homes because they refused to take an oath of allegiance to the English king. This would have been the same as accepting membership in the Church of England. The sufferings and the hardships of these people are vividly told in Longfellow's poem *Evangeline*. He vividly describes the villagers of Grand-Pre leaving their homes and loved ones.

The Struggle of the Church

Since its earliest days, the Church has had to struggle to survive. First it struggled against the Jews, then the Romans, and even in America, the Land of the Free, the Church struggled. While England and France were fighting over land, the Church in America was fighting at times for its very existence. Empires come and go, but Our Lord made a promise to a poor fisherman on the shores of Lake Galilee: His Church would be eternal. While the Church must endure

The Acadians are driven from their homes.

hardship, it never loses sight of its mission: to save souls. Even in the midst of persecution, the Church sends out missionaries. America was just the latest mission field.

Spot Check

1. Which five nations made claims on North America?
2. What are the dates of the French and Indian War?
3. What event marked the beginning of the French and Indian War?
4. What battle decided the outcome of the French and Indian War?

THE CHURCH IN THE ENGLISH COLONIES

Maryland

The first Mass in colonial Maryland was celebrated on St. Clement's Island, March 25, 1634. Jesuits Andrew White and John Altham were the first missionaries to this territory. From the beginning, their work was difficult. They were not accustomed to the food and living conditions that became part of their life. There were no buildings. Also, they knew little of the Indians' language.

The two priests first worked to instruct and convert the Indian chiefs before approaching the other natives. Then, with the help of a good lay brother, Thomas Gervase, the Jesuit priests built a chapel. This became the first Catholic shrine in Maryland. As time went on, the priests learned the language of the Indians. Before the close of 1635, another priest and lay brother joined them. Though their coming brought relief to Father White and his associates, it was short-lived.

Father Andrew White was the founder of the Maryland mission. Although a full account of his remarkable work cannot be given here, we should at least mention something of his life. Father White was born in London in 1579. He was educated at Douay,

France, and was ordained a priest about 1605. In 1607, he entered the Jesuit Novitiate and later became a seminary professor. After this, Father White volunteered for the missions.

For ten years, Father White devoted himself to missionary labors among the settlers and the Indians. Unlike the other English colonies, the relations between the Europeans and Indians were friendly, largely because of Father White. Sadly, the rise of the Puritans in England had ruinous effects on Catholic interests in Maryland. A raiding band of Protestants from Virginia attacked Maryland. Father White and two companions were seized and sent back to England in chains. In London, Father White was tried for treason for being a Catholic priest in England. He was acquitted as he showed that he had been forced to enter the country against his will. Old and physically exhausted by his work, he lived the rest of his life quietly in England.

Father White is sent back to England in chains.

As we have seen, Lord Baltimore set the pattern for religious freedom in our country with his Toleration Act of 1649. He was concerned also about the Indians. He wanted to preserve the Catholic missions among the native peoples. To this end, in 1651, Lord Baltimore set aside 10,000 acres near Calverton Manor as an Indian preserve. He placed it under the direction of the Catholic clergy. However, his dream of a colony where Catholics could live and worship in peace was soon shattered. Anti-Catholic feeling was running high. By 1654, the freedom of religion that Maryland Catholics enjoyed came to an end. The missionaries were driven out and the missions were destroyed.

For a time, all missionary activity stopped. Then, in the late 1660s, it was revived. The Maryland mission reopened. From 1669 to 1690, the Jesuits and Franciscans worked side by side. Following the Revolution of 1688 in England, in which the Catholic King James II was overthrown, toleration of Catholicism in Maryland was stopped again.

Conditions in the Other Colonies

With the exception of Pennsylvania, the other colonies were Protestant. Only a few Catholics, most of whom were Irish, settled in them. Catholics were not allowed in the Dutch settlements on the Hudson, nor were they permitted to settle in the Swedish districts in Delaware. The few Catholics living in New York before the War of Independence were forced to go to Philadelphia to receive the sacraments.

From its beginning, Pennsylvania permitted freedom of worship. Encouraged by this position, many Catholics, unable to settle in Maryland, lived in Pennsylvania. We do not know who these pioneer Catholics and their priests were. However, it is known from several sources that the Mass was said openly in Philadelphia at the end of 1707 or early the next year.

These were the days of widespread Catholic persecution in England. Thus, it was necessary to hide the activity of the Church in English territory. However, the Catholics in Pennsylvania apparently were not concerned with what England thought of public worship in Philadelphia. They continued to worship in spite of England's protests.

The Work of the Spanish Missionaries

Our Lady of Guadalupe

Cortes had conquered Mexico in 1521. In 1524, twelve Franciscans arrived in Mexico and founded missions. In 1526, the Dominicans joined the Franciscans. In 1533, the first Augustinians arrived in Mexico. The Church grew, and the religious houses multiplied. However, the Gospel would not have spread so quickly had it not been for the apparition of Our Lady, the Blessed Mother, at Guadalupe.

On the morning of December 9, 1531, Juan Diego saw a vision of the Blessed Mother on the slopes of Tepeyac hill outside of Mexico City. She asked him to build her a church on the site. When Juan Diego told his bishop about the vision, the bishop asked him to return to the hill and ask the lady for a miraculous sign to prove her claim. Juan returned and relayed the bishop's request. Our Lady told Juan to gather flowers from the hilltop, although it was winter and no flowers bloomed. On the hilltop, he found roses. He gathered them together and the Blessed Mother herself arranged them in his tilma (a blanket-like shawl). When Juan returned and presented the roses to the bishop, the image of Our Lady had miraculously appeared on his tilma.

In 1754, Pope Benedict XIV declared Our Lady of Guadalupe the patroness of New Spain. Pope Pius XII made Our Lady of Guadalupe the Patroness of the Americas in 1946. In 2002, Pope John Paul II canonized Juan Diego. The colors of the image on Juan's tilma are still as rich today as they were almost 500 years ago. The Basilica of Guadalupe, on the outskirts of Mexico City, is the world's most visited Marian shrine. Only the Vatican itself receives more pilgrims.

News of the apparition quickly spread through Mexico. In the seven years from 1532 through 1538, eight million native Mexicans became Catholics. All through Mexico, the missions prospered. The Church built schools and colleges to educate a native clergy who went

The Old and New Basilicas of Our Lady of Guadalupe

out to preach the Faith. Later, the Jesuits, who had been laboring in Florida, moved their missionary activity to the northwestern coast of Mexico. There they worked among the native people. For centuries, the Church in Mexico grew steadily. Schools and colleges multiplied. Eventually the entire country became Catholic. The work started by Cortez had reaped a bountiful harvest.

Spot Check

1. How did the colonies treat Catholics?
2. Where did the Blessed Mother appear to Juan Diego?

The Spanish Missionaries in New Mexico

In 1539, Franciscan priests discovered New Mexico. Among the missionaries to settle in New Mexico was Father Juan de Padilla. Brave Father Padilla would later fall victim to the Indians. After a time, the Franciscans reached the western frontier of Arizona. There they studied the language of the Indians and established a mission. Some time later, they reached Lower California. Sadly, the hostility of the Indians became so bitter that the California missions were abandoned.

Meanwhile, destruction of the missions was widespread. The blood of martyrs truly became the seed of Catholicism in our country.

Father Padilla

The Franciscan, Father Juan de Padilla, was the first martyr in the territory that later became the United States. As early as 1528, Father Padilla came to Mexico. He labored there for the conversion of the Indians living in the border territory. He founded convents, built monasteries, and taught the natives. After working with success among the border tribes, he crossed the Rio Grande and made his way northward. This was the beginning of the end of Father Padilla's missionary work and his life. Along with a few companions, he made his way onto the plains. There the little party met a band of savages who attacked them and killed Father Padilla as he calmly knelt in prayer. The time and place of their martyrdom are not known.

Missions in Florida

Florida was the missionary territory of the Spanish Franciscans. As early as 1521, priests, eager to teach the natives the truths of our holy religion, accompanied Ponce de Leon. For a time, the work of the missionaries thrived, but like all the other early missions, it met with disaster. The treachery of the natives and the inability of the priests to cope with the harsh conditions brought an end to the missions. Sadly, many Indians wanted nothing to do with religion or with the priests who came to teach them.

The most important names in the history of the Florida missions are Pedro Menendez de Aviles and Father Francisco Lopez. The explorer Menendez not only ordered the Indians to be instructed in the Faith, but he himself went out evangelizing them. Father Lopez was the first parish priest in St. Augustine. The work of the Catholic Church went well until Protestant England took over Florida. The English nearly destroyed the Faith in Florida.

Father Margil and the Texas Missions

Missionaries from Mexico City had come to the Texas territory to preach the Gospel early in the sixteenth century. Of the names prominent in the story of Texas, one of the most famous is that of Father Antonio Margil. The life of Father Margil is quite remarkable. It is almost unbelievable, and yet is it quite true. As a sacrifice, he walked everywhere in his bare feet. He carried only his walking stick, his prayer book, and the materials he needed to say Mass. Barefoot, he walked from the jungles of Costa Rica to the east of Texas. Along the way, he founded hundreds of missions. He preached the Gospel to thousands and thousands of natives. The local peoples loved him and revered him as a saint. He is rightfully called the Apostle of New Spain and Texas.

What is most interesting about Father Margil is that he started his missionary work in Texas when he was already sixty years old. From 1716 to 1726 he labored untiringly among the natives there. The work was especially difficult. There was little money to fund the work. Nevertheless, he continued successfully to found missions. He became well known for performing miracles. He died August 6, 1726. He was sixty-eight years old. He had been a Franciscan for fifty-three years and a missionary in North and Central America for forty-three years. In 1836, Pope Gregory XVI declared him Venerable. Despite the numerous miracles that he performed, as of 2010, he had not yet been canonized.

Some idea of the work of the early missionaries may be gained from the report of Father Solis, the official inspector of the Texas missions, on Mission Rosario, Texas. Writing in his diary, February 26, 1768, he noted: "This mission was founded in 1754. Its minister... Father Joseph Escovar labors hard for its welfare, growth and improvement. He treats the Indians with much love, charity, and gentleness.... He makes them work, teaches them to pray, tries to teach them the catechism, and to instruct them in the rudiments of our Holy Faith and in good manners."

Father Kino in the Southwest

The Jesuits were the first missionaries in California. In 1683, Jesuit Father Eusebio Kino accompanied the Spanish Admiral Isidro Atondo y Antillon on his expedition to Baja California. Father Kino laid the groundwork for the Faith in Baja California. Today little remains to tell the story of his daring and courage except the scattered remains of the missions.

Father Kino was then sent to what is today southern Arizona to work among the Pima Indians. He was a very successful missionary. He acquired enormous influence among the Indians. Father Kino is often called the "Apostle to the Pimas." He

The Mission of San Xavier del Bac founded in 1699 by Eusebio Kino

thoroughly explored what is today the southwestern part of the United States. He wrote detailed letters and drew maps, both of which are invaluable sources of information about seventeenth century southwestern United States.

In addition to introducing the Faith to the area, Father Kino introduced cattle ranching into the Southwest. He brought cattle, horses, and sheep into the region. He pioneered the planting of wheat, European cereals, and fruits. Along with Father Margil, Father Kino is the greatest missionary who labored in this country. In 1965, the state of Arizona enshrined Father Kino's statue in the Capitol building in Washington, D.C., as a person worthy of national honor.

Spot Check

1. Who was Fr. Padilla?
2. Who was Fr. Margil?
3. Who was Fr. Kino?

CHAPTER REVIEW

1. Name the five countries that made early claims to territory in North America.
2. Why was the Ohio Valley important to the French?
3. What was the main cause of the French and Indian War? When did it begin and end?
4. What did George Washington do in the French and Indian War?
5. What was the historical significance of the fall of Quebec?
6. Name the two great generals who were killed in the Battle of Quebec.
7. Why did Catholics living in New York before the War of Independence need to go to Philadelphia to receive the sacraments?
8. Identify the following people:
    a. Fr. Margil
    b. Fr. Kino
    c. Fr. Padilla
    d. Juan Diego
9. What was the most important event in the conversion of Mexico?
10. Who are the most prominent names in the history of the Florida missions?

The People of the Colonies

George Washington's Home, Mount Vernon

Life Among the Colonists

Different Nationalities in the Colonies

At the end of the French and Indian War, there were about two million people living in the thirteen English colonies. While most of these people were English or of English descent, more than a quarter of the population consisted of men and women from almost every other country in Europe. Of this group, the Scots and Scots-Irish were the most numerous. They had come from Ireland and Scotland to escape the cruel English laws. They were not afraid of the hardships they would have to endure in the colonies as long as they could escape English rule. They settled along the Atlantic seaboard from New Hampshire to Georgia.

In the middle colonies, many of the settlers were Dutch. Some of them had come directly from Holland. However, most of them were descendants of the original Dutch settlers in New Netherland. There were also Germans among them. Many Germans had come to this country to escape the religious wars that ravaged their mother country. The Pennsylvania Dutch of today are descendants of these German immigrants. ("Dutch" is a corruption of the German word "Deutsch" which means "German.")

Many French Protestants sought refuge in America. They settled mostly in New York, South Carolina, and Georgia. However, some could be found in every colony.

In general, the language of the colonies was English. Their institutions and governments were also English. Yet as time went on, the people, their institutions, and their governments were becoming less English and more American. A distinctly American culture was beginning to form. The hardships and adversity that they suffered together welded them into a single people who respected hard work and self-sufficiency. There was a difference between the people of New England and those of the South, between frontiersmen and the settlers in the middle colonies. However, they were all struggling Americans whose living conditions and working conditions were different. Though they had some religious differences, they were nevertheless all alike in their desire to be free.

Homes and Home Life

The homes of the early colonists were very simple. They varied from crude one-room huts to rough log cabins of different sizes. Many of them had thatched roofs and lacked floors or windows. Usually the settlers themselves built them. It was not until the middle of the eighteenth century that many of the pioneer homes were replaced by more sizeable buildings.

In New England, simple frame houses were built to replace the simple cabins with thatched roofs. At first, these houses were of one story and covered with unpainted boards. Later, they were enlarged to include two stories and painted white.

In the southern colonies, the wealthy planters built huge mansions. Travelers and tourists can still see many of these mansions today. Some examples of Southern mansions include Mount Vernon, the home of George Washington, and Monticello, the home of Thomas Jefferson. Of course, most people lived in homes often no better than cabins.

Thomas Jefferson's home, Monticello

In the middle colonies, the houses were built of wood, brick, or stone. In New York, the Dutch influence was very evident. The spacious manor houses, recalling the early Dutch settlers called "patroons," could be seen everywhere. The homes in the middle colonies were simple, yet neat and comfortable.

The frontiersmen still lived in cabins. Their homes were made of roughly hewn logs with dirt floors and windows made of paper. A better standard of living on the frontier came about very slowly.

Home Furnishings

The kitchen was the main room in the early colonial home. Usually there was a large fireplace at one end of the room. Around the fireplace hung some of the common kitchen utensils. Elsewhere in the room were stools, chairs, and a table. The pioneer family ate, lived, and entertained neighbors in the kitchen. The fireplace provided heat for the home and fire for cooking. Only the wealthy settlers owned iron stoves. In general, the early colonists relied on the fireplace. In the better homes, there was a fireplace in almost every room.

The kitchen was the main room in the early colonial home.

Great care was taken to keep the main fire burning. There were no matches, so kindling a fire every day must have been tiresome. It would be necessary to use a flint and steel or bring live coals from a neighbor, the nearest of whom might live many miles away.

The furnishings of colonial houses were either very elaborate or very simple. It depended upon the wealth or the taste of the owners. Poor people usually made their own furniture. The wealthy were able to import theirs from Europe. However, even today, we recognize genuine beauty in the simplicity of colonial furniture.

In general, candles lighted the homes. Candles were made in the home from tallow produced on the farm. Pine torches were also used. In some of the wealthy homes, whale-oil lamps were used. It was not until after colonial times that gas and coal oil came into use.

Spot Check

1. What two virtues were particularly respected and emphasized in the emerging American culture?
2. What was the main room in most colonial homes? Why?

HOW THE COLONISTS EARNED A LIVING

Principal Occupations

Farming was the chief occupation of the colonists. Fishing, shipbuilding, and manufacturing were next in importance. Farming in colonial days was much more difficult than it is now. The farmer did most of the work by hand. He had no modern machinery and none of the conveniences found on the modern farm. Each farmer made his own furniture as well as his own carts.

The women and the girls worked hard, too. The spinning wheel was as much an essential in every home as were the churn and the candle mold. The home was really a small factory. Furniture, butter, cheese, soap, candles, rugs, cloth, and clothing were made in the colonial home. Preserves, jam, and cider also were made. Meats were salted and smoked. Fruits of all kinds were dried or preserved in large stone crocks. Women and girls cared for the home but also helped in the fields.

Farming in America

Although farming was the main occupation of colonial America, farming differed from region to region. Farming was different in New England than it was in either the southern or middle colonies.

The farms in the New England colonies were small. The soil was very stony and difficult to cultivate. By hard work, the farmers raised corn and vegetables for their own needs; however, there was little left for sale. Fortunately, most of the New England settlers lived near the sea. Since farming was difficult, they devoted much time to fishing. They caught codfish, mackerel, and herring for food and for sale. They shipped fish to Europe, to the West Indies, and to the southern colonies. Fishing not only became a leading industry but also gave to many farmers an added means of income. It helped them to support their families and did much to make up for the poor crops and the lack of extra products to sell.

In the southern colonies, the most important crops were tobacco, rice, and indigo. They also raised grain, potatoes, vegetables, and livestock. However, tobacco was the major cash crop. Virginia became the center of tobacco growing. The soil and climate of Virginia were especially suited for tobacco. The English were the first importers of tobacco. When their needs were met, merchants brought the surplus to markets in northern Europe. This began a trade with Europe that continues to this day. Most of the rice and indigo was grown in the Carolinas. The surplus crops were shipped to Europe. There they were exchanged for clothing, furniture, tools, and other necessities that the colonists could not purchase in America.

The middle colonies were the great producers of foodstuffs. They were sometimes called the "bread colonies." The soil and climate of these colonies were suited to the production of wheat, corn, oats, barley, peas, and beans. Good pastures helped the farmers to produce large quantities of butter and cheese. In time, a great export trade was developed.

> ## Spot Check
> 1. What was the chief occupation of most of the colonists?
> 2. Why was the home a "small factory" in colonial times?
> 3. What was the second largest occupation in colonial New England?
> 4. What non-food crop was vital to colonial Virginia's economy?
> 5. Why were the middle colonies called "the bread colonies"?

Other Occupations and Trades

While farming was the most important of the colonial occupations, there were many other kinds of employment. The forests and streams were filled with fur-bearing animals. Trapping soon became a leading occupation for farmers and trappers. Furs were a leading export and brought significant wealth to the traders.

In New England, the colonists engaged in lumbering, shipbuilding, and commerce. The New England forest produced excellent lumber to build ships. It is no wonder, therefore, that New Englanders became the leading shipbuilders, fishermen, and sailors

The village blacksmith was essential to colonial life.

in the land. They sailed their ships to foreign ports with cargoes of fish, lumber, furs, tobacco, and rice. They developed a whaling industry that paid better than any other kind of fishing. By such trading, the colonists obtained money to buy in Europe the articles they needed in their homes and in their work.

The village workman and the village blacksmith were essential people. They made most of the articles that were ordinarily used on the farm or in the home. Today, almost everything that is offered for sale is manufactured in factories. In colonial days, shoemakers, blacksmiths, weavers, carpenters, tanners, dyers, cabinetmakers, and silversmiths did the work. Each of these tradesmen had his own shop, and each one took pride in the quality of his work.

A Colonial Weaver

The southern colonists shipped their most important crops to England or to English colonies such as Bermuda, Jamaica, and Barbados. Tobacco, sugar, and molasses were the most important crops. Huge fortunes were built up through this trade. The southern colonies soon became quite wealthy.

The people of the middle colonies, like their New England neighbors, were great shipbuilders. Their ships were used to carry the commerce between the New World and the Old. Later, industry developed in the middle colonies. Thus the people had many more opportunities for employment.

Colonial Amusements

The boys and girls of colonial times did not have amusements like we have today. There were no televisions or theaters, no video games and Internet. Yet they enjoyed themselves even though they had to help with the work around the home and farm. For them, there was a time to play and a time to work.

The New Englanders usually spent their leisure hours at home. Their strict Puritan beliefs caused them to frown upon amusements. They were strict observers of the law and had time for only the simplest entertainment, such as checkers, dominoes, and other homemade games. Now and then the neighbors came together for quilting parties, husking bees, spelling matches, or house raisings. They were more concerned about their work than about amusements. However, in spite of their sternness, they remained a friendly people.

In the South, there were four social classes: the slave owners, whites who did not own slaves, the "poor Whites," and the slaves. The wealthy landowners and leading citizens of such towns as Charleston, Savannah, and Williamsburg imitated the aristocracy of England. Most of these wealthy people were slave owners and did

Travel was difficult in colonial days.

not need to work hard for a living. They had time for social activity and amusements: dances, foxhunts, and horseback riding. The grand ballrooms of the plantation mansions were the scenes of some of the most colorful colonial social events.

Life in the middle colonies was midway between the sternness of the North and the frivolity of the South. The fun-loving Dutch settlers were fond of music, dancing, hunting, fishing, horse racing, golf, bowling, and tennis. In the Quaker settlements, there was less merriment, but that was in keeping with Quaker beliefs.

Travel in the Colonies

Travel was difficult in colonial days. There were few good roads. In general, the roads were narrow Indian trails, perhaps widened a bit. At first, the only method of travel was by horseback or by boat along the sea and rivers. Later, when somewhat better roads were built between the most important towns, stagecoaches came into use.

The main colonial roads were the Boston Post Road between Boston and New York, the Albany Post Road between Albany and New York, and a road between New York and Philadelphia. Even though these major roads were an improvement over the common Indian trails, travel was slow and tiresome. The stagecoach often bogged down in the mud. When that happened, the passengers would get out and help push the heavy vehicle back onto solid ground. There were very few bridges. Frequently the stagecoach had to be transported across a river on a ferryboat.

Some idea of the time required for travel can be obtained from the early stage schedules. For example, it took a week to make the journey by coach from New York to Boston. In 1766, a stagecoach made the trip from New York to Philadelphia three times a week. The trip that then took about two days now takes less than two hours by car.

Communications in the Colonies: The Postal Service

Postal service in the colonies was irregular and not satisfactory. Stagecoach and postal rider both carried the mail. The post rider was a mail carrier who rode from place to place. He charged for his service and did not begin his trip until he had enough pieces of mail to make the trip worthwhile. As late as 1760, mail was carried only eight times a year from Philadelphia to places in the southern colonies. It takes less time for mail to be delivered around the world today than it did to deliver mail from New York to Boston in those days.

Mail was not delivered to the home as it is today. Usually the post rider stopped at the inn where he would spread his letters out on the table. The people looking for mail would search through them. If there were letters addressed to towns farther away, anyone going that way would take them with him.

It was not until 1753, when Benjamin Franklin became deputy postmaster general for the colonies, that a more efficient system was created. Newspapers were allowed to be sent through the mail. By 1765, there were newspapers in all but two of the colonies. The paper that had the greatest influence was Benjamin Franklin's *Pennsylvania Gazette*. Franklin started the practice of printing business advertising. Since that day, the newspaper has been a medium not only of news, but of sales as well.

Spot Check

1. Why did colonial New Englanders disapprove of many amusements?
2. Name the four social classes in the South.
3. Name several of the amusements and social activities of the slave owners in the southern colonies.
4. Besides walking, what were the three main methods of transportation in colonial America?

Religion played a central role in colonial life.

RELIGION IN THE COLONIES

Importance of Religion in America

Religion played an important part in the life of the colonial people. In all the colonies, the church was the center of community activity. The minister was the most important person in the community. The churches were used not only as places of worship but also for public meetings.

These meetinghouses were usually poorly constructed. There were no ornaments. The windows were of clear glass or oiled paper. There was no heating. In spite of these discomforts, the people gathered in their meetinghouse Sunday after Sunday to spend the day praying, singing, and listening to long sermons. The men occupied one side of the church and the women, the other.

Some form of Protestantism was the religion of nearly all the colonies. Maryland and Pennsylvania had a sizeable Catholic minority. In New England, the people were Puritans, Pilgrims, or Congregationalists. The strict religious rule of these people made them people of strong discipline and rigid character. So strict and so austere were the Puritans that it was considered a sin to smile in church. In the southern colonies, the Church of England was the leading faith. However, there were numerous Baptists, Presbyterians, and Methodists. In the middle colonies, the majority of people were Quakers or belonged to the Church of England.

Hardships of Catholics

Catholics lived under great difficulties in the colonies. Not only did the Protestants vastly outnumber them, but they were also subjected to very unfair laws. In many colonies, Catholics were taxed to support the Church of England or the church established by the people of the colony. They could not vote or hold public office. Only in Pennsylvania could Catholics own land or engage in business. While the colonists spoke of tolerance, they did not practice it. Sadly, Catholics were suppressed everywhere. They were even suppressed in Maryland after the days of the Catholic Lord Baltimore. In fact, freedom of religion did not exist in most colonies until after the American War of Independence.

The small number of Catholics in the colonies made it easy to suppress them and to forbid them to have churches of their own. In 1760, there were perhaps no more than 25,000 Catholics and only 25 priests in all the colonies. Most Catholics saw a priest only a few times a year. In this situation, the leadership of the laity was a necessity. Laymen conducted baptisms and funerals since there was no priest to perform them. In those areas where there were two or three Catholic families who would meet to worship, there was rarely a priest to say Mass. The Catholics gathered to say the Rosary and sing hymns. The lack of priests, Catholic schools, and catechisms prevented most Catholics from learning very much about their Faith. As a result, the practice of American Catholics came to resemble the practice of the Protestants who surrounded them.

The difficulties of the work of the priests during these colonial days are described in a letter written by the Jesuit priest Joseph Mosley. Written September 1, 1759, the letter reads in part: "Our journeys are very long, our rides constant and extensive. We have many to attend and few to attend 'em. I often ride about 300 miles a week and (every week), I ride 150 or 200, and in our way of living, we ride almost as much by night as by day in all weathers, in heats, colds, rain, frost, and snow."

Education in the Colonies

The people in colonial America realized the value of education. However, the opportunity for schooling varied greatly in the New England, the southern, and the middle colonies.

Education in New England

In New England, education went hand in hand with religion. Frequently, the churches or meetinghouses were used as schools, and the minister was the teacher. There was more opportunity for education in New England than there was in the other colonies. As early as 1647, a law was passed in the colony of Massachusetts requiring each community of fifty or more families to establish and support an elementary school. Though this law was not always observed, it laid the foundation of American public education.

These pioneer schools were quite different from modern schools. The typical schoolhouse was a log or frame one-room building. Sometimes school was kept in the home of a local woman. Such a school was called a dame school. The colonists knew that the place in which school was held was not as important as what the children learned.

The children sat on long, backless benches. Instead of using paper, they used a board or a piece of slate. Charcoal or slate pencils were used in place of regular pencils. The pupils had few subjects to study. Only the three R's, reading, 'riting, and 'rithmetic were taught. The beginners learned to read from the "hornbook," which really was not a book at all. It was a thin, paddle-shaped board on which were printed the alphabet and sentences from the Bible. This odd-shaped board was covered with a sheet of transparent horn to protect the paper from dirt and wear.

The grammar schools were more advanced. There, the pupils made a beginning in the study of Latin and prepared for further education.

Education in the South

There were fewer schools in the southern colonies. Generally, the children of the rich plantation owners were home schooled by tutors or attended private schools. Sometimes they were sent to study in England or France. Thus, the children of the South's upper class had excellent opportunities for education. Sadly, the poor often received no education at all. Their parents were unable to home school them.

Education in the Middle Colonies

Education in the middle colonies was more widespread than in the South. However, it lacked the enthusiasm of New England. It was difficult to promote education in the middle colonies because they did not have any tax-supported schools. The schools were maintained either by the church or by several families who provided a school. Such a school was taught by a minister or a retired soldier. In either case, the teacher was paid a very small salary. In addition to his salary, however, he was given room and board in the homes of his pupils. This arrangement was known as "boarding around."

Catholic Education

The Jesuit Fathers laid the foundation for Catholic education in the colonies soon after arriving in Maryland in 1634. In 1640, the Jesuits established Newton Manor on the west shore of Chesapeake Bay, not far from the Potomac River. In 1682, Jesuits founded the New York Latin School in New York at the request of Governor Thomas Dongan, a Catholic. However, the Protestant Revolt of 1688 in England forced the Jesuits to abandon the school about 1690. In 1742, the Jesuits established Bohemia Manor in the northwestern part of Maryland. Among the notable persons educated there were Charles Carroll, a signer of the Declaration of Independence, and his cousin, John Carroll, the first bishop and archbishop of Baltimore. Other than in Maryland, however, there was little opportunity for a Catholic education.

There were far more Catholic schools in the early wilderness missions than in the English colonies. The Franciscans, Capuchins, Jesuits, and the Ursuline nuns made small beginnings in education in the frontier colonies. The Franciscans founded a school in St. Augustine, Florida, as early as 1606. Later, they worked in Texas, New Mexico, and

Ursuline Convent in New Orleans

California territory. The Jesuits were active in the Northwest Territory during the early part of the eighteenth century. They are credited with having established schools in Detroit and in the Great Lakes region. The French Capuchins established a school in Maine about 1640. The Ursuline Nuns opened Ursuline Academy in New Orleans in 1727.

Colleges

The first college established in the colonies was Harvard College. It was founded in 1636 near Boston to train young men for the ministry. By 1764, six other colleges had been founded. William and Mary was founded in Williamsburg, Virginia, in 1693. Yale was founded at New Haven, Connecticut, in 1701. The University of Pennsylvania was established in Philadelphia in 1740. In 1746, the College of New Jersey, now called Princeton, was founded in Princeton. Kings College, now called Columbia, was founded in New York City in 1754. Lastly, Rhode Island College, now known as Brown University, was founded at Providence in 1764. With the exception of the University of Pennsylvania, Protestant church groups founded these colleges. None of the colleges were Catholic.

Spot Check

1. Give two examples which show that religion was important to colonial people.
2. What were some of the disadvantages established by colonial law, from which Catholics suffered during colonial times?
3. What religious orders started Catholic education in the colonies?
4. What order of nuns started the first girls' school in the colonies?
5. What was the first college established in the colonies?

COLONIAL GOVERNMENT

Beginning of Self-Government

Almost as soon as the colonies were settled, the people sought the right of self-government. They were skeptical that a king two thousand miles away knew what was best for them, or even understood their situation. They wanted a voice in the making of their laws, in the raising of taxes, and in the discharge of the affairs of the colonies. They wanted freedom of religion and freedom to educate their children as they thought best.

The House of Burgesses in Virginia was the first representative assembly in Virginia. However, the seeds of true self-government were planted in the Mayflower Compact, which the Pilgrims signed on board their ship before landing at Plymouth. Using the Old Testament example of a covenant, the settlers agreed among themselves and with God to form a just and Christian society. The Pilgrims agreed that they would make just laws for the general good of the colony. By this act, the signers committed themselves to a political society with a religious character. Americans should never forget that the very first American political document began "In the name of God."

The Mayflower Compact especially influenced local government in New England. The Compact set an example of ordinary citizens taking part in making the laws under which they were to live. Out of this example grew the town meeting form of government in New England.

The charters granted to Connecticut and Rhode Island by King Charles II gave them the right to hold assemblies and to elect their own governors. Nineteen years after the signing of the Mayflower Compact, the residents of Connecticut created a similar document: the Fundamental Orders. This document began with an appeal to God. It declared that the people "associate and conjoin ourselves to be as one Public State or Commonwealth . . . to pursue the liberty and purity of the Gospel of Our Lord Jesus Christ."

William Penn and Lord Baltimore allowed Pennsylvania and Maryland representative assemblies from the beginning. Georgia was allowed to have an assembly about twenty years after it was founded. In fact, by 1763, each of the thirteen colonies had its own legislative assembly. Each assembly had the power to pass laws subject to the approval of the colony's governor and the government in England.

Governors and Legislatures

There were many similarities in the colonial governments. Each colony had a governor, although the method of his selection differed from colony to colony. Most of the legislatures had two branches: an upper and a lower house. The upper house was known as the Council. It was selected in three ways depending on the type of colony. In the charter colonies (Massachusetts, Connecticut, and Rhode Island), the people selected the Council members. In the proprietary colonies (Maryland, Pennsylvania, and Delaware), the proprietors chose the Council members. In the royal colonies, (New Hampshire, New York, New Jersey, Virginia, the two Carolinas, and Georgia), the king selected the Council members.

The people chose the members of the lower house in all the colonies. "People" meant white adult males who owned property. However, the governor had absolute veto power over the acts of the lawmakers. Nevertheless, the colonial assemblies did control grants of money to be spent by the colonial governments. Often, assemblies would grant money to the governor only if he did things the assembly wanted. No colony was allowed to pass laws opposing the laws of England.

Local Government

There were three kinds of local government in the colonies. New England had the township system. In the South, there was the county system. The middle colonies had a system known as the township-county system.

In New England, the people lived mostly in villages, towns, and cities. For that reason, it was not difficult for the people to gather together to discuss matters of common interest. Such meetings were known as town meetings. These town meetings were held at regular intervals. All the voters could attend. At the meeting, the voters could address the members, state their views on government matters, and vote upon any or all questions. Through this form of direct representation, a spirit of liberty and independence developed.

Local government in the southern colonies was known as the county system. The county was the local unit. County officers managed local affairs. Under this plan, meetings were held once a year at the county seat. The king appointed the county officers. The people had nothing to say about the officers. Due to the difficulty of travel and the distance of the plantations, it was not always possible for the people to attend the meetings in person. Therefore, they elected some of their number to represent them at the county meetings. Since they did not

A colonial family builds their home.

have a direct say in the government, there was not the same high interest in local government that there was in New England.

In the middle colonies, there was a combination of the other two systems. This form of government was known as the township-county system. The people played an important part in the government. They controlled township matters at the township meetings, and elected representatives to handle county affairs.

They also elected representatives to go to the colonial legislature to handle the affairs of the particular colony.

These three types of local government are the forms of local government throughout the United States today.

The Spirit of Independence

By the 1760s, each of the thirteen colonies had some sort of self-government. At the same time, the controls and taxes imposed by the English government were beginning to feel heavier, leading Americans began to believe that they could run their affairs better than the government in England. This growing belief would soon become a full-fledged movement for independence.

Spot Check

1. What was politically important about the Mayflower Compact?
2. List the three different ways that members of the upper houses were chosen in colonial assemblies.
3. What limits were placed on the power of colonial assemblies?
4. What power could the colonial assemblies use to limit the power of the royal governor?
5. What were the three types of local government in the colonies?

CHAPTER REVIEW

1. From which country in Europe did the Pennsylvania Dutch come?
2. What were the four most important occupations of the colonists?
3. What was the major cash crop in Virginia?
4. What were the four social classes in the South?
5. Why was travel difficult in colonial days?
6. Who printed the *Pennsylvania Gazette*?
7. What privileges did Catholics enjoy in Pennsylvania that no other colony granted them?
8. What order of nuns established the oldest girls' school in America? Where was it?
9. What was the first college established in the colonies?
10. What was the first representative assembly in Virginia?
11. What were the three kinds of local government in the colonies?

DISPUTES AND QUARRELS WITH ENGLAND

The Boston Tea Party

NEW TENSIONS BETWEEN ENGLAND
AND HER COLONIES

Taxes and More Taxes

After the French soldiers were finally driven from America
in 1763, unrest among the colonists increased. There was constant
quarreling between England and her colonies in America.
King George III and the English Parliament had little sympathy for the
colonists. England was faced with heavy debts because of the war with
France, especially the French and Indian War. England had added vast
new territories in India and America. Thus, England was confronted
with two great problems. First, the war debt had to be paid, and, second,
the British Empire had to be more firmly united. The British taxpayers
were already groaning under the burden of taxes in England. They
believed that financial help should come from the colonies.

The merchants and manufacturers in the English Parliament believed, like most of the Europeans of the time, that colonies should benefit the mother country. However, the colonists believed that colonies should be governed for their own benefit. It was this difference of opinion that was chiefly responsible for the War of Independence.

What the colonists thought did not matter to England. Thus, in the year following the treaty of 1763, King George III and his ministers decided upon a new policy in dealing with the American colonies. Their new policy included three measures. These measures were: a strict enforcement of the Navigation Laws; the direct taxation of the colonies by acts of Parliament; and the quartering of soldiers in the colonies.

Spot Check

1. What did England think was the role of the colonies?
2. Name the three measures that were part of King George III's new policy towards the colonies.

THE NAVIGATION LAWS

Attitude of the Colonists

The Navigation Laws had been passed into law a hundred years earlier, but had not been enforced. By enforcing the Laws, England had two goals. First, England hoped to compel the colonies to share in the payment of her war debts. Second, England wanted to protect her shipping industry from foreign competition. The Navigation Laws that were passed in 1660 and 1663 contained two important provisions. First, all colonial goods were to be carried on English or colonial ships which must pass through English ports and pay a tax. Second, the colonies were prohibited from manufacturing goods that were already being produced in England. This forced the colonists to buy goods from England.

Though these laws had been passed a century earlier, it was not until 1763 that efforts were made to enforce them. Meanwhile, all kinds of abuses had crept in. Customs officials in the colonies actually helped merchants to escape paying port duties. Smuggling was common. In fact, John Hancock of Boston, who became the first governor of the state of Massachusetts, was a noted smuggler. The colonies ignored the requirements of the Navigation Laws. They often traded directly with the Spanish West Indies and with other foreign ports. They manufactured what they wanted despite the Navigation Laws. The colonists did not protest as long as the laws were not strictly enforced.

Meanwhile, in England, Parliament's decision to enforce the Navigation Laws was very popular. It meant better business conditions in England. It meant an increase of manufacturing and increased sales for the English merchants. It meant that all foreign trade would be centered in England. Naturally, the English merchants and manufacturers welcomed this. In addition to these benefits, the English people were pleased because a strict collection of duties might mean lower taxes for them.

A Source of Resentment

However, the colonists felt differently. When the plan to enforce the Navigation Laws became known, it awakened bitter opposition in the colonies. To the colonial merchants, the enforcement could seriously injure their business. To the colonial manufacturer, it meant financial ruin. To the people of the colonies in general, it meant a higher cost of living. No longer able to obtain manufactured items locally, they would need to import them from England. Protest meetings were held in all the important colonial cities. The opposition in commercial New England was strongest. There, Samuel Adams and John Hancock led the fight against the Navigation Laws. They knew the feelings of the people and worked diligently to urge the colonists to resist. In England, Benjamin Franklin acted as an informal ambassador of the American people. He tried to convince the English government that its plan to enforce the Navigation Laws would cause trouble with the colonies. However, King George III had chosen ministers willing to carry out his plan. There was strong support for the plan in Parliament. Thus, in spite of every warning, the king was determined to put his plan into action.

New Methods of Enforcement

England intended to enforce the Navigation Laws in two ways. First, she sent a fleet to patrol the American coast and seize smugglers. However, England's blockading fleet found it impossible to stop smuggling completely. The fleet simply could not watch the one thousand miles of colonial coastline. The colonists, believing the Navigation Laws unfair, determined to ignore them. Angry feelings arose between the colonists and the English coast patrol. At Providence, Rhode Island, a group of colonists became enraged at the heavy-handed manner of the captain of the *Gaspee*, an English boat sent to guard Narragansett Bay. To show their resentment, they boarded the ship at night and burned it. This incident clearly revealed the defiant mood of the colonists. It plainly bore out the truth of Benjamin Franklin's warning to King George.

The Burning of the *Gaspee*

102

The second way to enforce the Navigation Laws was through "Writs of Assistance." These writs were actually blank search warrants that allowed customs officers to enter any house or board any ship to search for smuggled goods. They were not like today's search warrants, for they did not specify the particular place to be searched or what kind of goods the officer expected to find. The use of these unfair warrants naturally aroused sharp resentment in the colonies.

James Otis of Boston, a prosecuting attorney in the king's service, resigned his office to protest the "Writs of Assistance." He held that these warrants broke English law and that Parliament could not make them legal. Otis eloquently urged the colonists to demand their rights. He declared, "every man's house is his castle," and opposed British interference with personal liberty. Commenting on Otis' speech, John Adams said that "then and there, the child Independence was born."

Spot Check

1. What were the two key provisions of the Navigation Laws?
2. What abuses were caused by the lack of the enforcement of the Navigation Laws in the colonies?
3. Why was the enforcement of the Navigation Laws popular in England?
4. Who acted as an informal ambassador of the American people to England?
5. What were the two methods the British government used to enforce the Navigation Laws?
6. What legal reason did James Otis of Boston give for opposing the writs of assistance?

THE STAMP ACT

Taxation without Representation

The second part of King George's policy in dealing with the American Colonies was to have Parliament directly tax the colonies. He wanted the colonies to help pay the expenses of the British Empire. However, the idea of direct taxation was even more hateful to the colonists than the Navigation Laws. The colonial leaders were incensed. They argued that since there were no American representatives in Parliament, Parliament had no authority to tax the colonies. The colonies were willing to pay part of the cost of the war against France, but refused to pay any taxes except those levied by their own legislators.

In general, the English people had no sympathy for the colonists' argument against "taxation without representation." There were many people in England who had no voice in the election of Parliament. Yet Parliament taxed them without representation. In America, too, there were people who supported the king. They believed that his colonial policy did not violate the rights of the colonists as Englishmen. However, leaders of the Whig party in England, William Pitt, Edmund Burke, and Charles Fox, opposed the king's party in Parliament. These men championed the cause of the colonists.

Passage of the Stamp Act

The Stamp Act was England's first attempt at direct taxation. In 1765, the British ministers passed this act to obtain new income for the English government. It required the colonists to place stamps on all legal documents such as deeds, mortgages, and wills. Stamps were required on newspapers, almanacs, and other publications. The stamps were not very expensive. Their cost ranged from one cent to fifty dollars. However, most stamps cost from one cent to twenty-five cents. Agents appointed by the government sold the stamps.

The English government insisted that the Stamp Act would cause little hardship in the American Colonies. However, the colonists looked upon the Act as unjust and unfair. They objected to the Act, not because it was oppressive, but because it was a tax levied on them by a Parliament in which they had no representatives. They declared that a Parliament in England, in which there was not one member from the colonies did not representative them.

Resistance to the Stamp Act

Strong opposition followed. Pamphlets appeared, denouncing the action of King George III and Parliament. In Virginia, Patrick Henry, a young lawyer and a new member of the House of Burgesses, attacked the Stamp Act in a forceful speech in which he set forth the reasons for colonial opposition. In fiery eloquence, he warned the king against tyranny. He said, "Caesar had his Brutus; Charles the First, his Cromwell; and George the Third..." Before he could complete the sentence, some of the members of the House of Burgesses shouted, "Treason! Treason!" (Brutus killed Caesar and Cromwell killed Charles, so Patrick Henry appeared to be hinting that someone should kill King George). Patrick Henry finished by saying, "and George the Third may profit by their examples. If this be treason, make the most of it."

Many other colonial leaders opposed the Stamp Act. Samuel Adams led the protest in Massachusetts. James Otis declared that "taxation without representation is tyranny." Otis published an important pamphlet in which he said that only a parliament composed of representatives from all parts of the British Empire could rightfully regulate trade and levy taxes for imperial purposes. All through the colonies, the agents who sold and distributed the stamps became figures of scorn. There was violent rioting in New York, Pennsylvania, and New England.

The Stamp Act Congress

At the suggestion of James Otis, the Stamp Act Congress was held in New York in October 1765. Twenty-seven representatives from nine of the colonies attended. It drew up a declaration stating that only their own colonial assemblies could levy taxes on

Patrick Henry denounces the actions of King George and Parliament.

the colonists, not Parliament. Protests were sent to the king and Parliament asking for the immediate repeal of the Stamp Act. The Stamp Act Congress marks the first united action of the colonies against England.

When the stamps were placed on sale, the colonists refused to buy them. In some cases, the stamps were seized and destroyed. In New York, a mob burned the governor in effigy and defied the sale of stamps. Many colonial merchants pledged not to buy any more goods from England until Parliament repealed the Stamp Act. The storm of protest that followed was not expected in England, but it was not without its effect on Parliament.

In Parliament, William Pitt urged that the hated law be repealed. Parliament agreed and repealed the Stamp Act in 1766. However, that could not heal the breach that had been made. The Stamp Act succeeded in making the colonists unite to protect their rights. Their success in getting the act repealed only encouraged them further.

News of the repeal was warmly received in America. However, the colonists soon learned that they had not completely won. In the repeal, known as the "Declaration Act," Parliament declared that it had the right to tax the colonies if it wanted to do so. As a result, the agitation against "taxation without representation" continued. Colonial dissatisfaction increased.

Spot Check

1. What was the American colonists' main argument against taxation from the British Parliament?
2. Why did many of the people in England not agree with the colonial argument?
3. Who said, "Taxation without representation is tyranny"?
4. What did James Otis argue about Parliament in his pamphlet against the Stamp Act?
5. What did the Stamp Act Congress do?
6. Why is the Stamp Act Congress important in our history?

THE TOWNSHEND ACTS

A Tax on Imports

The violent opposition of the colonies against the Stamp Act did not teach the English government a lesson. Parliament still believed that it had the authority to tax the colonies. Thus, in 1767, one year after the repeal of the Stamp Act, King George's new prime minister, Charles Townshend, introduced a new plan to tax the colonies. His plan, called the Townshend Acts, easily passed Parliament. These Acts imposed taxes on many of the goods imported by the colonies. This kind of tax on imported goods is called a **tariff**.

The tariff was to be paid when the goods landed in America. The colonists were furious. They refused to import English goods and pay the hated tax. Instead, they bought smuggled goods even though the cost was often greater than that charged for English goods. Once more, the English merchants, manufacturers, and ship owners, unwilling to lose their colonial business, appealed to Parliament. All taxes were repealed except the tax on tea.

The tariff on tea was not high. English tea, plus the import tax, was actually cheaper than any other tea on the market. In fact, it cost less than the same tea bought in England. However, low taxes did not influence the colonists. They were determined not to pay England any taxes, no matter how small. They would pay only taxes that their own legislatures levied. Under such conditions, they refused to buy tea from England. The smuggling of tea from Holland increased at a rapid pace.

Sadly, trouble followed. Two regiments of English soldiers were sent to Boston in 1767 to enforce the Townshend Acts. The very sight of these soldiers further angered the colonists. On the night of March 5, 1770, a mob gathered and the soldiers were booed and pelted with rocks and snowballs. The soldiers answered by firing into the crowd. Several men were killed and several more wounded. This unfortunate incident raised the resentment of the colonists over the shedding of colonial blood to a fever pitch. Many of the colonists called the event the "Boston Massacre."

The Boston Tea Party

Though all other taxes had been repealed, the English government insisted that the tax on tea remain, not for the income it would bring, but to show the colonists that England could tax them if she so desired. Of course, the colonists objected. Everywhere they refused to buy tea. They even forbade tea to be brought in at some American ports. In some cases it was stored in damp warehouses where it was allowed to spoil.

The most serious trouble began in Boston. When three ships loaded with tea entered the Boston harbor, the people of Boston refused to let the ships unload. However, the governor declared that the ships could not leave until their cargo was landed. The enraged colonists, led by Samuel Adams, held a meeting on December 16, 1773, to protest against the landing of the tea. That night, a band of citizens dressed as Indians rushed through the streets of Boston to the waterfront where the ships were moored. They overcame the guards and boarded the ships. They split open and dumped every chest of tea into Boston Harbor. This was the way the people of Boston answered England's tax on them.

Samuel Adams Pointing to the Charter of Massachusetts

The Intolerable Acts of 1774

Not surprisingly, this act of violence astonished the English government. At the request of the king, Parliament quickly passed several acts to punish Boston and Massachusetts for its disloyalty. These laws became known as the "Intolerable Acts." The five decrees were: (1) that the port of Boston be closed to all trade until the town paid for the tea that had been destroyed; (2) that the people be deprived of all voice in their government and placed directly under officers appointed by the king; (3) that new troops be quartered in the colony; (4) that any of the king's officers accused by the colonists be tried in England instead of in the colonies; and (5) that Massachusetts, Connecticut, Virginia, and New York be deprived of their western land claims. All land north and west of the Ohio River was made part of Quebec.

The Quebec Act

The fifth of the Intolerable Acts was the Quebec Act. This Act guaranteed freedom of religion to all French Catholics living in Canada. It also recognized Catholicism as the official religion of that province. Unlike the other Acts that were done to punish Massachusetts, this Act was a just one. Since the vast majority of the people of Quebec were Catholic, the Act was fair. Yet, this Act, combined with the transfer of the north and western lands to Quebec, caused tremendous resentment among the Americans. The transfer of what many considered to be their land to a Catholic country, incensed them. A number of Americans had already begun to settle in these Western lands. The thought of American Protestants living in a Catholic province shocked and appalled them.

Reaction of the Colonists

The Intolerable Acts amounted to direct military control of the colonies. Colonial resentment rose to new heights. Patrick Henry, addressing the Virginia legislature, expressed the feeling of thousands of colonists when he cried out: "Is life so dear, or peace so sweet, as to be purchased at the price of chains and slavery? Forbid it, Almighty God! I know not what course others may take, but, as for me, give me liberty or give me death!"

Spot Check
1. What were the Townshend Acts?
2. How did the colonies react to the Townshend Acts?
3. What was the Boston Massacre?
4. Why did Parliament insist on keeping the tea tax?
5. What was the Boston Tea Party?
6. What were the five decrees of the Intolerable Acts?
7. Who said, "Give me liberty or give me death."?

THE FIRST CONTINENTAL CONGRESS

United Action

A meeting of colonial representatives was held in Philadelphia on September 5, 1774. This was the First Continental Congress. All the colonies except Georgia sent delegates to the meeting. Among the members were the most influential men of the colonies: Samuel and John Adams from Massachusetts, John Jay from New York, and Patrick Henry and George Washington from Virginia. The Congress represented the majority colonial opinion and was very qualified to present the views of the colonies to England.

George Washington

The Congress issued a Declaration of Rights and Grievances. The members demanded the right to levy all taxes and petitioned the king to relieve their wrongs. They further agreed that the colonies would *buy no goods* from England and would *send no goods* to her until the laws they resented had been repealed. Before adjourning, the Congress resolved to meet again in May 1775, to receive the reply of the king. However, the king refused to accept the petition. Parliament refused to repeal the laws against the colonies.

Before the Continental Congress met again, leaders in Massachusetts were asking the towns to collect arms and ammunition, and to see that their militia was well trained. Other colonies followed the example of Massachusetts. On his return from the First Continental Congress, Patrick Henry urged Virginia to prepare for war. Most of the colonists were beginning to think of themselves as Americans rather than as Englishmen. They were beginning to hope for an independent America. The patriots declared that armed conflict was the only course to follow against tyranny. Before the Second Continental Congress met, war had already begun. England drove the colonies to armed resistance in order to gain their independence.

Spot Check

1. When and where was the First Continental Congress held?
2. What did the First Continental Congress demand in the Declaration of Rights and Grievances?

CHAPTER REVIEW

1. What were the Navigation Laws?
2. Why did England decide to enforce the Navigation Laws when they had not been enforced for a hundred years?
3. What effect would enforcement of the Navigation Laws have had on American merchants and manufacturers?
4. What were the "Writs of Assistance"?
5. On what ground did the colonists oppose the Stamp Act?
6. What was most important about the Stamp Act Congress?
7. What were the provisions of the "Intolerable Acts"?
8. When and where was the First Continental Congress held?
9. Who was Samuel Adams?
10. Who said, "Give me liberty or give me death."?

THE AMERICAN WAR OF INDEPENDENCE

The Signing of the Declaration of Independence

THE WAR BEGINS

The Chances of Victory

As soon as war with England became a reality, serious thought was given to its possible outcome. To the casual observer, England seemed to be much stronger than the colonies. England's total population was three times as great. Its army was strong and its navy was the most powerful in the world. Despite its debts, England had financial resources sufficient to carry on a decisive war. On the other hand, the colonies were weak in all of these essentials. They had no standing army, no navy, and little money to pay for the war. In addition, many colonists were loyal to the king and refused to join their fellow colonists against the mother country.

However, there were four factors that gave the colonists an advantage. First, they would be fighting on their own ground while the English were three thousand miles away from home. Next, France had long been England's enemy and therefore might be counted on by the colonies as an ally. Third, the colonies had one of the best generals of the time in George Washington, the commander of the Continental armies. He was a great soldier, a wise statesman, and a good businessman. In contrast, the English generals were poor, unimaginative leaders. Fourth, and most importantly, the colonists had more at stake. They were thinking of saving their homes and families while many of the English soldiers were tired of war and were fighting only as a duty or as an occupation.

Spot Check

1. What three factors seemed to give England the advantage in going to war with the American colonies?
2. What four factors actually gave the American colonists an advantage?

EARLY EVENTS OF THE WAR

The Battle of Lexington

The spirit of rebellion that caused the Boston Tea party spread quickly. All through Massachusetts, men responded to the call to arms made by the Massachusetts Assembly. They were the "minutemen" who had volunteered to fight at a minute's notice. At the time, these men had no thought of independence from England, but they were willing, if need be, to take up arms against the king to defend their property and their rights.

On April 19, 1775, General Gage, the British commander, sent a force of British soldiers to Concord. They were to seize the colonial supplies stored there and to arrest Samuel Adams and John Hancock. By seizing the colonists' ammunition and by arresting their leaders,

Gage hoped to avoid serious trouble with the minutemen. However, the patriots had learned of Gage's plans. During the night, the thundering beat of a galloping horse awakened the colonists. With the sharp cry, "The British are coming!", the rider, Paul Revere, spread the alarm. As a result of Revere's warning, Adams and Hancock escaped and an army of colonial patriots gathered, ready for the coming of the British.

It was dawn when the British reached Lexington. There, on the village green, stood a small army of minutemen. The British commander ordered them to disperse, but they refused. Then, unordered, someone fired a shot. The British fired a volley at the minutemen. In the skirmish, eight minutemen were killed. War had begun.

The Minutemen meet the British on the village green.

At Concord Bridge

The British soldiers marched on to Concord. At Concord, they destroyed whatever supplies the colonists had been unable to remove. Near Concord Bridge, they encountered a group of "embattled farmers," who, as the poet Emerson said, "fired the shot heard 'round the world." A number of redcoats (British soldiers wore red coats, thus the nickname) fell to the ground. This was unexpected, and the British began a return march to Boston. On the way back, a distance of about twenty miles, colonists firing from concealed positions attacked the redcoats on all sides. The retreat became a rout. The British left nearly three hundred casualties to tell the story of the beginning of the American War of Independence. The number of colonists killed or wounded was about one hundred.

The news of American bravery and success at Concord sped from colony to colony. The victory gave the colonists new hope. It was evident that this first success made many ready to resist England.

The Second Continental Congress

When the Second Continental Congress met in Philadelphia on May 10, 1775, war had already begun at Lexington and Concord. John Hancock was elected President of the Congress and George Washington was appointed commander in chief of the colonial army. The Continental Congress had the job of fighting the war and uniting the colonial army. Under the leadership of George Washington, the command was in good hands. He had distinguished himself in the French and Indian War. He knew military problems and he knew the country. His appointment instilled new hope in the colonial army and gave the men new confidence.

The Green Mountain Boys

The same day the Second Continental Congress convened, Ethan Allen and a group of soldiers from Vermont, who called themselves the Green Mountain Boys, surprised and captured Fort Ticonderoga on the southern end of Lake Champlain. The seizure of this English fort gave the colonial army a number of British cannons. These would prove very valuable to George Washington in driving the British from Boston the following year.

Stirred by the news of Lexington and Concord, colonial volunteers poured into Massachusetts. Though untrained, the volunteers soon formed an army of nearly sixteen thousand men to besiege General Gage in Boston. Under Joseph Warren and Colonel Prescott, the colonists took possession of Bunker Hill and Breed's Hill across the bay from Boston. From these hills overlooking Boston, the Americans would be able to bring the British under fire. As a result, the British commander ordered that they be chased off the hills.

The Captured Cannon from Fort Ticonderoga

The Battle of Bunker Hill

On June 17, 1775, the English attempted to drive the colonists from their position. Twice the redcoats charged, and twice the deadly fire of the Americans drove them back. However, the colonists' powder finally gave out, and they were forced to retreat. The English captured the hill, but the price was heavy. Their losses were far greater than those of the colonists. Bunker Hill proved that the Americans would and could fight.

A patriotic American woman burns her crops lest they fall into the hands of the British.

George Washington arrived in Cambridge two weeks after the Battle of Bunker Hill. Although the British had seized the hill, Washington fortified Dorchester Heights overlooking Boston. This forced the English to evacuate the city. On March 17, 1776, General Howe and his troops, accompanied by a thousand citizens who were loyal to England, left on the fleet that lay in the harbor and sailed for Halifax, Nova Scotia. The American army then entered the city. Boston remained free from attack during the rest of the war.

Canada Remains Loyal

The colonists had hoped that the French Canadians would join in the revolt against England. In the fall of 1775, an expedition of New England troops under General Montgomery and Benedict Arnold attempted to invade Canada. The brave but useless expedition failed. Montgomery was killed and Arnold was wounded.

An attempt at peaceful cooperation also failed. In February 1776, Congress sent four distinguished leaders to Quebec to discuss the possibility of Canada's cooperating with the colonists against England. The four men were Benjamin Franklin, Charles Carroll of Carrollton, Samuel Chase, and Father John Carroll, who later became the first Catholic bishop in America. Though the people of Quebec were French and Catholic, England, just two years before, had given them guarantees of religious freedom, a measure of self-government, and new territory. The Canadians were suspicious of the promises of the colonists and their guarantees of freedom of worship. They saw no good reason for revolting against British rule. The Americans returned, unsuccessful.

Spot Check

1. Who were the Minutemen?
2. Who was Paul Revere?
3. What was important about the Battle of Lexington?
4. What did Ethan Allen and the Green Mountain Boys do? Why was this important to the American cause?

MOVES TOWARD INDEPENDENCE

A Fight for Liberty

The events of 1775 and early 1776 caused the colonists to think in terms of independence rather than loyalty to the British king. In August 1775, King George III issued a proclamation calling the Americans "rebels." He called upon all British subjects to aid in defeating them. In September 1775, the British hired twenty thousand German soldiers to put down the colonial rebellion. In October, British warships destroyed Portland, Maine. A thousand people were left homeless as winter approached.

If the colonists had considered reconciling with England, these events changed their minds. In addition, a pamphlet entitled "Common Sense," written by Thomas Paine, argued that it was time for a final separation from England and that Americans must fight for liberty. This pamphlet was widely read. It convinced many colonists that independence must be obtained. Paine showed how inconsistent it was for the colonists to wage war against England and at the same time declare their loyalty. Paine wrote: "I challenge the warmest advocate for reconciliation to show a single advantage that this continent can reap by being connected with Great Britain.... Everything that is right or reasonable pleads for separation. The blood of the slain, the weeping voice of nature cries, 'TIS TIME TO PART!"

The Declaration of Independence

On June 7, 1776, Richard Henry Lee of Virginia offered a resolution in the Continental Congress. His resolution said that "these United Colonies are, and of a right ought to be, free and independent states; that they are absolved from all allegiance to the British Crown, and that all political connection between them and the state of Great Britain is, and ought to be, totally dissolved." John Adams of Massachusetts, a cousin of Samuel Adams, seconded the motion. However, a vote on the resolution was postponed until July 1 to give the delegates time to confer with their home states. Meanwhile, a committee of five, consisting of Thomas Jefferson, Benjamin Franklin, John Adams, Roger Sherman, and Philip Livingston, drew up a Declaration of Independence.

Jefferson wanted John Adams to write the Declaration. However, Adams refused for two reasons. He felt that a Virginian should appear at the head of it and he thought that Jefferson could write it in much better style than he could. Jefferson consented. Thus this immortal document is almost entirely his work. The committee approved it with some minor changes suggested by Adams and Franklin.

Franklin, Adams, and Jefferson draft the Declaration of Independence.

Congress was impatient. Everyone was in a hurry, so the Declaration of Independence was reported in Jefferson's own handwriting, according to Adams. Congress eliminated about a quarter of the statement, including a passage that condemned slavery. On July 4, 1776, the Declaration of Independence was adopted. By this act, the purpose of the war was changed from a fight for the rights of Englishmen to a war for independence. From this time on, the thirteen colonies were part of an independent American nation. It was the birth of the United States of America.

Content and Meaning of the Declaration

The Declaration of Independence is one of the most important documents in all of human history. It is a statement of the American theory of government and an explanation for the war. It expresses the colonists' ideals of government and lists the reasons why they declared their independence. It claims that all men are created equal and that they are entitled to life, liberty, and the pursuit of happiness. It further states that governments are created to secure these rights. Moreover, governments obtain their power from the consent of the governed. It reviews the appeals for justice that the colonists had made to England and how these appeals had been denied.

From the Catholic point of view, the Declaration of Independence contains many good ideas. These include recognizing that the power of government is limited by the higher power of God and by the natural rights God gives to people. The Declaration said that prayer should be included in government. It states that a government cannot lose its authority lightly. Only a long history of abuse from an absolute despot can justify dissolving loyalty to a government. Even so, the document could have more clearly taught that all government ultimately receives its authority from God and is limited by His law.

Today, the Declaration of Independence is preserved, along with other significant documents and papers, in the National Archives Building in Washington, D. C.

Spot Check

1. What did Thomas Paine argue in his widely read pamphlet "Common Sense"?
2. Who wrote most of the Declaration of Independence?
3. How did the Declaration of Independence change the reason the war was being fought?

THE WAR IN THE MIDDLE COLONIES

The English War Plan

Though the British had been driven out of Boston, they were not defeated. They now turned their attention from New England to the middle colonies. They planned to take control of the Hudson River in order to cut New England off from the rest of the colonies. A British army was to proceed from Canada to take control of the upper Hudson. At the same time, General Howe would begin operations at the mouth of the river.

If the English could seize New York City and the Hudson River, they could paralyze the middle colonies with an army of occupation. Once in control of this region, they could prevent the southern colonies from sending food and supplies to New England. In addition, they could keep New England from aiding the other colonies. It was a plan of isolation by which they could defeat each group of colonies in turn and bring the war to a speedy close.

Very aware of the English plan, Washington, against his better judgment, decided to defend New York City. However, at the Battle of Long Island, his poorly equipped army met a disastrous defeat at the hands of the British under General Howe, but Howe neglected to follow up his victory. Instead, he allowed Washington and his entire army to escape up the Hudson.

Defeat and Discouragement

Unable to hold the forts on the Hudson, the colonial army turned south. Washington's purpose now was to protect Philadelphia. The Second Continental Congress was using the city as a colonial capital. Most important of all, Washington realized that he must keep the army together, whether he won any victories or not. With Howe in close pursuit, Washington led his shrinking army through New Jersey and crossed the Delaware River. At Trenton, New Jersey, General Howe left a force of German mercenary soldiers called Hessians. Howe returned to New York. The English general Cornwallis took up winter quarters at Princeton, New Jersey.

Washington had succeeded in avoiding capture and in placing his army in a position to defend Philadelphia. However, the dream of independence seemed shattered. The men in Washington's army were discouraged. Many deserted because they had received no wages for months. Many more went home because their terms of enlistment had expired. Those who remained in the army suffered terribly because of poor equipment and insufficient shelter. Winter was coming and the army was shrinking.

Victory at Trenton

In his darkest hour, Washington made a move that showed why he was the greatest general in North America. He knew that if he went into winter quarters with his men demoralized that the war would be over. The army would simply fade away in the night. He had to revive the fading hopes of his army.

Thus, on Christmas night 1776, he led twenty-five hundred troops across the Delaware River in small boats through floating ice and landed about eight or nine miles north of Trenton. Through a blinding snowstorm, he marched to the British camp. There he captured the entire garrison at midnight in the midst of their holiday celebration. He took about one thousand prisoners, mostly Hessians, and many valuable supplies. This victory had a powerful effect on the British. It convinced them more than anything that had happened before that the war was not over. However, more important was the fact that it restored the American army's morale. The patriot army now knew they could fight professional soldiers, and win.

Victory at Princeton

When General Cornwallis heard of the surprising victory at Trenton, he left Princeton at once to attack Washington. By a stroke of luck, he managed to trap Washington near the Delaware River. He was so sure that he had Washington trapped that he decided to wait until morning to capture "the old fox," as he called him. However, Washington was not to be fooled. He built huge campfires to make the British think that his army was still in camp. Meanwhile, under cover of darkness, he led his army up the riverbank. He slipped around Cornwallis' army and made a surprise attack on the small force left in charge of Princeton. A desperate battle took place. In this victory, the Americans took about five hundred prisoners and great amounts of supplies and ammunition.

By these victories at Trenton and Princeton, Washington recovered New Jersey. He then withdrew to Morristown where he took up winter quarters. His brilliant retreat showed the British that the Americans were not to be taken lightly. By this act, too, new hope was born in the hearts of the Americans.

The Battle of Princeton

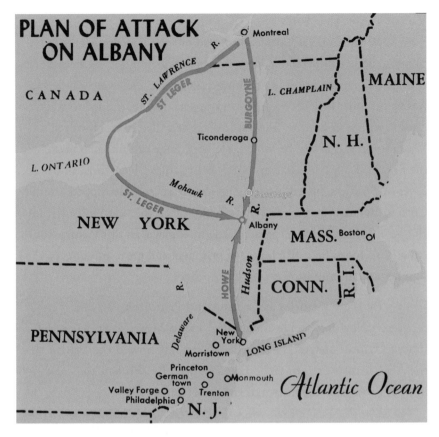

PLAN OF ATTACK ON ALBANY

THE TURNING POINT OF THE WAR

The Plan to Capture Albany

The English had captured New York City, but they did not control the Hudson River. In the spring, after Washington's New Jersey victories, the English were determined to capture Albany. Once this key city was in their possession, they would control the Hudson and could separate New England from the other colonies. To achieve this, a three-pronged attack was planned on Albany. The first prong would come from the north. General Burgoyne was to advance on Albany by way of Lake Champlain and the Hudson. The second prong was from the west. General St. Leger was to march on Albany from Lake Ontario through the Mohawk Valley. The third prong would come from the south. There, General Howe was to send an army up the river from New York City.

British Surrender at Saratoga

The British plans failed completely. St. Leger was defeated and turned back by the settlers of the Mohawk frontier. General Howe, instead of sending an army directly to Albany, set out to capture Philadelphia, the headquarters of the Continental Congress. Though Washington's troops fought desperately at Brandywine and Germantown, they could not stop Howe from taking the city.

However, Howe's victory at Philadelphia was very costly because it prevented him from aiding Burgoyne at Saratoga. Burgoyne, expecting to be joined by St. Leger and Howe, advanced toward Albany. In the rough country north of Albany, colonial sharpshooters harassed Burgoyne's army on all sides. In vain, he asked New York for help. General Howe had taken all the men that could be spared for the march on Philadelphia. There were no men to send to Burgoyne. At Saratoga, the remarkable bravery of Benedict Arnold won the day for the Americans. General Burgoyne was decisively defeated. He surrendered his entire army of six thousand men, with their weapons and supplies, to General Gates on October 17, 1777.

This was by far the greatest victory of the war. For the first time, an entire British army had been forced to surrender. This victory also meant the end of Burgoyne's plan to seize the Hudson Valley. The Battle of Saratoga was beyond doubt the turning point of the War. It is generally considered one of the most important battles in world history.

Spot Check
1. What was the British plan to bring the war to a speedy close?
2. Why was the Battle of Trenton important?
3. What was the threefold British plan to take Albany?
4. Why is the Battle of Saratoga considered the war's turning point?

The French Alliance

The effects of the American victory at Saratoga were felt in Europe. Until this victory, Europeans had not believed that the Americans could win. After this victory, bankers became more willing to make loans to the Continental Congress. The French were now convinced that the time had come for them to avenge themselves upon England. Consequently, a few months after the victory at Saratoga, France made a treaty of alliance with the Americans. France agreed to help the Americans with both men and ships. In return, the colonies agreed that they would not stop fighting until independence had been won. They also agreed to help France protect her islands in the West Indies in case of war between France and England.

The defeat at Saratoga and the danger of a French alliance caused England to make peace offers. In fact, England offered the Americans all they had asked for except independence. However, the war had gone too far. The colonists had promised France that they would fight until independence was achieved. Thus, England's offer of peace and the rights of Englishmen came too late.

The Winter at Valley Forge

Difficulties Confronting the Colonists

Hardships at Valley Forge

After his unsuccessful attempt to drive the British from Philadelphia, George Washington and his army spent the winter of 1777-1778 at Valley Forge. There he and his men spent a winter of almost unbelievable suffering. While the British army lived in comfortable Philadelphia homes, Washington's men, not more than twenty miles away, were freezing and suffering in their rough huts. Their uniforms were in tatters and their shoes were worn thin. About three thousand soldiers had no shoes at all. Their bloody footprints could be seen in the snow. To make matters worse, they did not have enough food and medicine. Sometimes they went whole days without food. Yet the courage and persistence of General Washington fired them with the desire for victory and independence. He convinced them to endure any kind of hardship for the cause of independence.

The winter in Valley Forge was not completely bleak. The news of the French alliance brought the army new hope. With Baron von Steuben, a veteran of Prussian wars, as drillmaster, the army at Valley Forge was so well trained during the long winter that it emerged in the spring as a more effective fighting unit.

Financing the War

The lack of money contributed greatly to the suffering at Valley Forge. The Continental Congress had no power to levy or collect taxes. It had to depend upon contributions from the states or upon loans from individuals or foreign countries. Contributions from the states were very uncertain. Individuals and foreign governments alike feared that the war would fail and their money would be lost. The best the Continental Congress could do was to issue paper money which was practically worthless. It was backed up not by gold or silver but merely by a promise to pay should the war be won.

Fortunately, some individuals had the courage to contribute to the financial support of the war. While Washington was at Trenton, Robert Morris, a wealthy Philadelphia merchant and a member of the financial committee appointed by Congress, went house-to-house meeting with the leading men in Philadelphia. By pledging his own wealth as a guarantee that the loans would be repaid, Morris induced the people of Philadelphia to lend about fifty thousand dollars in gold to the Continental Congress. Lafayette, a young French nobleman, gave freely of his private fortune. Franklin, Washington, and others likewise gave vast sums. After the French alliance, money was less difficult to obtain both at home and abroad. By the close of the war, the colonies had borrowed nearly ten million dollars from France, Spain, and Holland.

The Tories

Not all the colonists agreed with the war against England. Those who favored England were known as loyalists or Tories. They did much to increase the difficulties of the patriots. However, the Tories were not really traitors. They believed that they were right in supporting England. They were as sincere in their loyalty to England as the patriots were in their loyalty to America.

The Tories suffered at the hands of the patriots. Many were forced into exile and lost their property. In the South, the feeling between the two camps was very bitter. When armed Tories were captured, they were treated as traitors rather than prisoners of war. Tories who fought with the English treated captured patriots in the same way. Army officers on both sides tried to restrain their men, but without success. The two sides grew to hate each other and added great bitterness to the war.

Benedict Arnold Betrays America

The most famous officer to betray his country was Benedict Arnold. This was particularly distressing to Washington. Arnold was one of the best and most trusted of his generals. However, Benedict Arnold was angry. He believed that his heroic leadership at the Battle of Saratoga had not been properly rewarded. Sadly, a man who had done much to help America became a traitor. Perhaps his wife, whom he loved and was a Tory, encouraged him to commit this dreadful act.

Arnold was in charge of West Point, where the American military supplies were stored. In return for gold and a commission in the British Army, he agreed to give the British control of West Point. However, his treason was discovered in time to prevent the plan from being carried out. Arnold fled to the British side. During the rest of the war, he fought against the Americans. After the war, he went to England to live. There he was completely ignored. People who knew what he had done had no respect for him.

The Lack of a Navy

At the beginning of the war, the Americans were at a huge disadvantage because of the lack of a navy. Though Congress had authorized privately owned vessels to fight under the American flag, it was not until the French fleet came to aid the colonies that English power was seriously threatened. Meanwhile, however, such daring seamen as John Paul Jones and John Barry made conditions most unfavorable for British vessels.

LEADERS IN THE STRUGGLE FOR FREEDOM

Our European Friends

Much of the success of the war can be attributed to the aid given the colonists by European military leaders. From France, early in the war, came the Marquis de Lafayette. This young nobleman, filled with zeal for the rights of the common people, gave not only his services but also vast sums of money to support the war. With Lafayette came De Kalb, a stern Bavarian who had been serving in the French Army. De Kalb gave his life to the cause of American freedom. From Poland came

Count Pulaski who served ably as a commander in the Colonial Army. He, too, was killed in battle. Another Pole, Thaddeus Kosciusko, was the chief engineer in constructing the fortifications at Saratoga and West Point. The great Prussian leader, Baron von Steuben, served as chief drillmaster of the American Army. John Barry, born in Ireland, served in the navy throughout the war. He is often called the "Father of the American Navy."

Catholic Patriots

Chief among the Catholic American patriots was Charles Carroll of Carrollton. This wealthy Catholic leader represented Maryland at the Second Continental Congress and was a signer of the Declaration of Independence. It was his patriotism and the loyalty of Catholics to the cause of independence that ensured religious freedom for the Church after the war. Other prominent Catholic patriots were John Fitzgerald, Stephen Moylan, Thomas Fitzsimons, and Joseph Orono. John Fitzgerald was secretary and aide-de-camp to George Washington. Stephen Moylan had control of supplies and organized the first army and navy of the United States. Thomas Fitzsimons, of Pennsylvania, gave large sums of money to aid the soldiers. Joseph Orono, a chief of the Penobscot Indians, solicited and obtained the support of the Indian tribes to strengthen the force of the patriots.

Spot Check

1. What two obstacles made it difficult for the Continental Congress to get money to finance the war?
2. Name four people who courageously gave money for the American war effort from their private wealth.
3. Name and briefly identify three European military leaders who helped the Americans in the war.
4. Who was Charles Carroll of Carrollton?

THE WAR IN OTHER PARTS OF THE COLONIES

On the Frontier

When the war began, the colonial frontiersmen in the Northwest (present-day Ohio, Illinois, Indiana, Michigan and Wisconsin) suffered severely from Indian attacks. In fact, the frontiersmen accused the governor of the British territory north of the Ohio River of encouraging Indian attacks. The English were friendly with the Indians, so, they had no trouble in keeping the old French settlements of Kaskaskia, Cahokia, Vincennes, and Detroit.

During the fourth year of the war, a young Virginian, George Rogers Clark, set out to drive the British from the land north of the Ohio. Many of the settlers in that territory were French trappers. At best, their loyalty to England was lukewarm. Thus, when they were told that France had signed a treaty of alliance with the colonies, they gladly took up the American cause. Clark, with a small force of Virginia volunteers, seized Kaskaskia and Vincennes. Within a short time, they succeeded in driving the British out of the land south

George Rogers Clark

of the Great Lakes. As a result of his success, America obtained the Northwest Territory at the end of the war.

Jesuit Father Pierre Gibault, known as the "Patriot Priest of the West," aided George Rogers Clark in his efforts in the Northwest

Territory. Father Gibault strongly supported the War of Independence. He was in Kaskaskia when George Rogers Clark arrived with his men. Father Gibault told Clark that he supported the American cause but that his first concern was for the Catholics in the region. Clark assured him that Catholics would have religious freedom in the new country. Father Gibault's influence made it possible for George Rogers Clark to achieve military victory in the Northwest Territory and secure it for the United States.

In the South

Having failed to conquer the North, the British began efforts to conquer the South. They believed that the southern colonies were full of Tories who would rally to the king. With little difficulty, Savannah and Charleston were captured. Soon Georgia and most of South Carolina were under British control.

To halt the British advance, the local militia under such leaders as Thomas Sumter, Andrew Pickens, and Francis Marion fought a guerrilla war in South Carolina. These men had no regular military equipment, but with bands of men from farms and mountains, they continued to harass the British. At King's Mountain on the border between North and South Carolina, and at Cowpens in the same region, these patriotic bands of guerrilla fighters defeated the English.

General Gates, whom Congress had given command of the Army of the South, was defeated at Camden, South Carolina, by General Cornwallis. At length, General Greene was sent to replace Gates. After Washington, Greene was perhaps the finest of the American generals. Greene's strategy was to lure Cornwallis farther and farther from the coast cities, the English base of supplies. Finally, the two armies met in battle at Guilford Courthouse (present day Greensboro, North Carolina) on March 15, 1781. The battle was one of the most important of the war and a decisive victory for the Americans.

Cornwallis was forced to retreat to Wilmington, North Carolina, on the coast, for supplies.

Not resting on his laurels, Greene then dashed into South Carolina and Georgia. Soon he had recaptured Georgia and the Carolinas. All that the British were able to hold were the three coast towns of Savannah, Charleston, and Wilmington. The British had spent two years fighting in the South. They held little more than the area around these three towns.

THE END OF THE WAR

The Battle of Yorktown

Undaunted, Cornwallis advanced northward into Virginia. There he was opposed by Lafayette, who did everything possible to obstruct the advance of the British. At the same time, the young Frenchman was careful to avoid a pitched battle with Cornwallis' army. Once more, Cornwallis was forced back to the coast. He fortified Yorktown in Virginia and there awaited aid from the British fleet along the coast.

Meanwhile, General Clinton, in command of the British forces in New York, prepared to send reinforcements to Cornwallis. However, Washington, pretending that he was going to attack New York, made a quick overland march to Virginia. There, joining forces with Greene and Lafayette, he besieged Cornwallis and his troops in Yorktown.

The Surrender of General Cornwallis

Cornwallis had hoped that a British fleet would come to his aid in time. A fleet did come, but it was not the British. A French fleet, under Admiral de Grasse, came to guard the entrance to Chesapeake Bay. The French prevented any aid from reaching Cornwallis. Surrounded on land and sea, and with many of his men sick with fever, General Cornwallis at last was forced to give up. He surrendered on October 19, 1781.

The Surrender of the British at Yorktown

The surrender of the British was a real spectacle. The combined French and American armies were drawn up in two lines more than a mile long on both sides of the road. Washington, mounted on his horse, awaited the British garrison. The brilliant uniforms of the French troops and their band of musicians added pomp to the event.

The British came forth with solemn march, their drums beating and their flags furled. Their leader, General O'Hara, rode up to General Washington. O'Hara apologized for the absence of Cornwallis, with the excuse that he was ill. Washington received General O'Hara courteously but refused to receive the sword of surrender at the hands of a subordinate officer. Instead, he indicated Major General Benjamin Lincoln as the officer who would receive Cornwallis' sword.

The Treaty of Paris

Although the war ended on October 19, 1781, peace negotiations were not completed until September 3, 1783. Benjamin

Franklin, John Jay, and John Adams represented the United States in arranging the peace terms. The Continental Congress approved the treaty and it became effective January 14, 1784. Since the treaty was signed at Paris, it is known as the Treaty of Paris.

The treaty had several important provisions. First, Great Britain recognized the independence of the United States of America. Second, the Mississippi River was fixed as the western boundary of the new nation. Third, because Spain had helped America in the war, England returned Florida to Spain. Fourth, the Continental Congress was to recommend that the various states return the property taken from English subjects and loyalists.

Reasons for Victory

Several factors made the American victory possible over what was then one of the greatest powers in the world. First, the distance of the American colonies from England was a major factor in the success of the war. With three thousand miles separating England's army from her main base of supplies, it became more and more difficult to wage the war. Second, it was impossible to blockade all of the ports along a thousand mile coastline. England soon learned that she could not defeat the colonies merely by cutting off their trade. They were able to live on their own products. Third, the colonists had a vast country into which to retreat. Finally, the English were greatly hampered by the lack of familiarity with the territory in which they were fighting.

Spot Check
1. Who was responsible for taking the Northwest Territory from the British? Why was this possible despite the small size of the American force?
2. What did General Cornwallis hope would happen when he fortified his army within Yorktown?

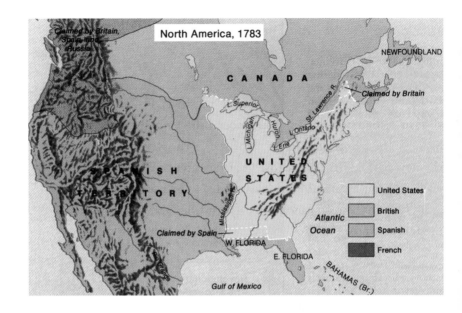

North America, 1783

Claimed by Britain, Spain, and Russia

CANADA

NEWFOUNDLAND

Claimed by Britain

L. Superior

L. Michigan

Huron

L. Ontario

St. Lawrence R.

L. Erie

UNITED STATES

SPANISH TERRITORY

Mississippi R.

Claimed by Spain

W. FLORIDA

E. FLORIDA

Atlantic Ocean

Gulf of Mexico

BAHAMAS (Br.)

United States

British

Spanish

French

CHAPTER REVIEW

1. State the four advantages the colonists had over the English.
2. What is the significance of the Battle of Concord?
3. Who were the Green Mountain Boys?
4. Who is the author of the Declaration of Independence?
5. How did the Declaration of Independence change the purpose of the war?
6. Why did the English wish to obtain control of the Hudson River?
7. Why was the Battle of Trenton important?
8. Why was the Battle of Saratoga the turning point of the war?
9. What did France hope to gain by allying herself with the colonists?
10. How did the colonists finance the War of Independence?
11. Name some of the foreign soldiers who fought for the colonists in the War of Independence.
12. Name some of the prominent Catholic patriots during the War of Independence.
13. Who was George Rogers Clark?
14. List the provisions of the Treaty of Paris, 1783.
15. Give four reasons why America won the war.

ARTICLES OF CONFEDERATION AND CONSTITUTION

Scene at the Signing of the Constitution, **by Howard Chandler Christie**

GOVERNMENT UNDER THE ARTICLES OF CONFEDERATION

The Continental Congress

During the War of Independence, the colonies had been drawn together into a loose union. However, they were still thirteen separate colonies, each with its own government. Although the Continental Congress managed the war from May 1775, until March 1781, it had no legal basis for doing so. Each state, as it preferred, obeyed or disregarded the requests of the Continental Congress. However, the states realized that they must work together if they hoped to win the war. Thus, they gave the Continental Congress significant support.

At first, the states were very concerned about any form of central government. They feared that such a government would interfere with their liberties. They feared a central government would become as tyrannical as the British government had been. Even during the war, they were hesitant about delegating any real authority to a central government. Once the war ended, many colonists felt that there was no longer any need for a central government.

A Legally Established Government

A short time after the Declaration of Independence, the Continental Congress took steps to provide for a legally established government. A committee of thirteen drew up the Articles of Confederation. This document provided for a union to be known as the United States of America. However, it left all real authority in the hands of the states. The central government was to be a national congress with authority to act only as an advisory council. The states, as each wished, might accept or reject its advice. A central government of this type would have no real authority over the states.

Five years passed before the Articles of Confederation were ratified by the states. The main reason for the delay was a dispute over the ownership of western lands. Seven states claimed huge stretches of land beyond the Appalachian Mountains based on their colonial charters. The states without land claims, especially Maryland, feared that these states would become too powerful. These states refused to sign the Articles of Confederation until the western lands became national property. Maryland did not sign until it was assured that all the states with western claims would give these lands to the central government. With Maryland's acceptance, the Articles of Confederation went into effect. Thus, on March 1, 1781, only a few months before the end of the war, the colonies officially became the United States of America.

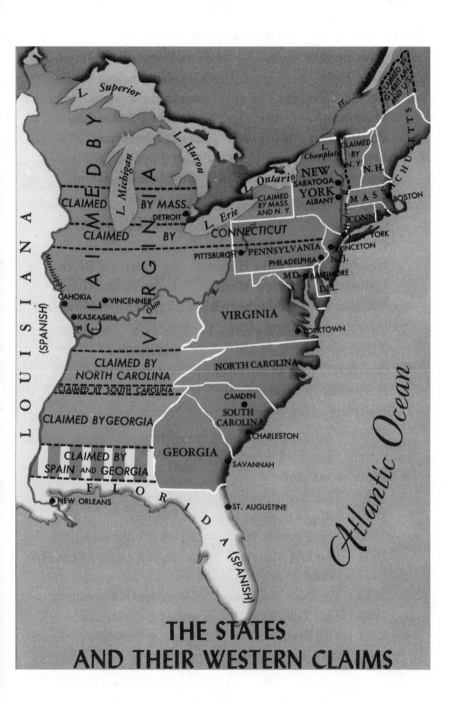

THE STATES
AND THEIR WESTERN CLAIMS

Weaknesses of the Articles of Confederation

The end of the War of Independence soon convinced the thirteen new states that there were basic weaknesses in the Articles of Confederation. Mostly, the Confederation lacked the necessary power to deal with individuals directly and could not effectively function as a central government. The Confederation lacked power in four specific areas. First, it could not raise money by taxation. Second, it did not have the sole power to coin money because each state also retained that right. Third, it could not regulate interstate commerce. Last, it could not call out troops to enforce law and order.

Lack of Financial Power

The Articles of Confederation gave Congress no power to levy taxes or to collect tariff duties on foreign trade. The national government, therefore, had to obtain its revenue by asking the states for contributions. If the states made a donation, that was fine. However, if the states chose not to give money, there was nothing Congress could do about it. The states usually paid only a small part of the amount Congress requested.

The war debt was staggering. During the war, about ten million dollars had been borrowed from foreign countries. Vast sums had been borrowed at home. Certificates of indebtedness had been issued to pay soldier's wages and to buy army supplies. All this required payment, but Congress did not have enough money even to pay its daily expenses. In fact, the interest on the war debt was either unpaid or was paid by borrowing more money. As a result, the United States was rapidly losing her credit and the respect of the other nations of the world.

Continental Currency

At the end of the war, Congress had paid each soldier a bonus of five years wages. However, this payment was made in Continental currency, or paper money. This was practically worthless because

Congress had no gold to back up its value. As a result, a hundred-dollar bill would not buy a dollar's worth of potatoes during the critical period following the war. A worthless object was spoken of as "not being worth a continental," meaning a Continental paper bill.

The soldiers became discouraged. A group of rebellious ex-soldiers stormed the meeting place of Congress in Philadelphia. They demanded that their paper money be redeemed in gold or silver. Though the uprising was suppressed, it was most embarrassing to the government. Nothing was done to punish the offenders. Congress was completely helpless. It had no way of collecting gold with which to redeem its paper money and pay its debts.

To make matters worse, the states printed their own paper money. This added to the confusion that already existed. Foreign nations and many merchants at home refused to accept paper currency in return for products and insisted on payment in gold or silver. Likewise, the money of one state generally could not be used in another state. This hindered commerce between states.

People were desperate because of the scarcity of sound money. Though some states tried to force merchants to accept the paper money, Massachusetts, on the other hand, refused to issue such currency. The results brought havoc to the people of Massachusetts. Many farmers lost their farms because they had no money to pay interest on mortgages. Working people who could not pay their debts were put in prison.

Shays' Rebellion

A group of disgruntled men in western Massachusetts banded together under the leadership of Daniel Shays. Shays had been a captain in the Continental Army. These men began to burn, rob, and plunder in order to obtain food. They even attacked the arsenal at Springfield with the idea of securing arms and ammunition. They

Shays robbed, burned, and plundered.

demanded that paper money be issued and that it be accepted at face value in payment of debts. Though the state militia quickly put down this revolt, it revealed the desperate conditions of the country at large.

The national government was powerless to regulate the currency or to help the states keep order when discontent over the value of paper money caused rioting and disorder. Congress needed the power to coin money and to issue paper money for the whole country. It also needed the power to levy taxes to raise money to pay debts.

Lack of Power to Regulate Commerce

The Articles of Confederation provided no means to regulate commerce. As a result, no regulation for commerce existed either between the United States and foreign nations or between one state and another. Each state governed the trade of its citizens as best suited its own interests. Tariffs often were levied on farm products brought from one state to another.

As a result of all these problems, Europe closed its ports to American shipping. Britain, France, and Spain refused to trade with the United States. The Barbary Pirates seized American ships in the Mediterranean Sea for **tribute**, that is, money for protection. The lack of a centrally controlled tariff system seriously threatened what was left of the American economic structure.

Lack of Military Power

Revolts, disorder, and uprisings emphasized the need for military power. Without the power to call out troops, it was impossible to make citizens obey the law peaceably. Without this power, Congress could not even enforce its own treaties. For instance, Britain claimed that Congress was not enforcing some of the clauses of the treaty of 1783. Therefore, Britain refused to withdraw her troops from certain garrisons on our borders. Spain, too, occupied large parts of territory in the Southwest in complete disregard of the same treaty.

There was trouble between the states, too. These disputes were not only about tariffs and currency. They were also about boundaries and land. No less than eight states quarreled over their boundaries. There was even danger that these disputes might result in war.

The greatest weakness of the Confederation was that it could recommend but it could not command. If it was to continue, it would need the power to command.

The Northwest Territory

Despite its problems in the thirteen states and abroad, the Confederation Congress did perform one valuable service. This was passing the Northwest Ordinance of 1787 that organized the Northwest Territory. This territory included the region from the Ohio River to the Great Lakes, and from New York and Pennsylvania to the Mississippi River. The Ordinance contained

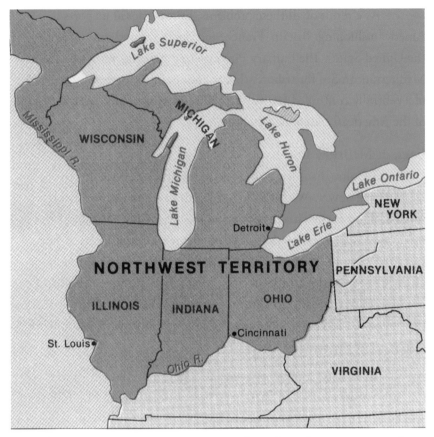

several important provisions. First, not less than three nor more than five states were to be made from this territory. Second, these states were to be admitted to the Union on an equal basis with the original states. Third, religious freedom was guaranteed to all. Fourth, slavery was forbidden in the region. Fifth, free public education was provided. Sixth, trial by jury was guaranteed to the inhabitants. The Ordinance of 1787 is important because it laid the foundation for many of the political doctrines of the American people. Ohio, Indiana, Illinois, Michigan, and Wisconsin were formed from the territory.

Spot Check

1. What was the relationship between the thirteen colonies and the Continental Congress during the War of Independence?
2. Why did it take five years for all the states to ratify the Articles of Confederation?
3. What were four weaknesses of the Articles of Confederation in regard to an effective central government?
4. What was the result of the fact that the Confederation government had no power to regulate commerce?
5. What is considered a major accomplishment of the Confederation government?

THE CONSTITUTIONAL CONVENTION

A Convention to Amend the Articles

Even before the Articles of Confederation were adopted, men like George Washington and Alexander Hamilton realized that the central government that it created was too weak to command respect either at home or abroad. After the Articles had been in effect for five years, most of the nation's leaders had become disturbed over the situation. They came to agree with Washington and Hamilton. Finally, because of a problem with interstate commerce, a convention to amend the Articles of Confederation was called.

In 1785, delegates from Maryland and Virginia met at Alexandria, Virginia, to discuss regulating navigation on the Potomac River. At this conference, someone suggested that all the states send representatives to a meeting the next year to discuss navigation in general. The meeting was held at Annapolis, Maryland. Though all the states had been invited, only five were represented. At the Annapolis meeting, it was proposed to convene again in 1787 in Philadelphia with representatives from every state in order to amend the Articles of Confederation.

Leaders of the Convention: The Founding Fathers

All the states except Rhode Island responded to the Call for the Convention which opened in May 1787. In Independence Hall, Philadelphia, there assembled a group of men remarkable for their character and ability. Of the fifty-five members, most of them were already well known. About three fourths of them had served in Congress. Nearly all of them were active in their own state governments.

Some of the major leaders of the War of Independence were absent. Strong opponents of central government like Samuel Adams, John Hancock, and Patrick Henry were not present. Thomas Jefferson and John Adams were representing America in Europe. Jefferson was in France and Adams was in England. However, other men prominent during the War were present. Virginia sent George Washington, who was unanimously chosen president of the Convention. Also from Virginia was Edmund Randolph, the governor of the state. George Mason was another Virginian. Along with Jefferson and Madison, Mason had written the Virginia Constitution. After Washington, perhaps the most important Virginian was James Madison. Madison was too young to have been a leader in the War; however,

Benjamin Franklin

he probably knew more about government than any other man at the convention. For the work he did at the Convention, Madison is known as the "Father of the Constitution."

Pennsylvania sent Benjamin Franklin among its delegation. For many years, Franklin had served splendidly as America's diplomat in England and France. He was the most democratic of all the representatives. He was now a wise, old man of eighty-one. It was his wisdom and common sense that helped save the Convention from being torn apart by disagreements. With him came Robert Morris, the man who had financed the war. Morris had served as Superintendent of Finance under the Articles of Confederation.

Brilliant young Alexander Hamilton was a representative from New York. He had won Washington's admiration and confidence as his aide in the War. Although Hamilton was a young man, all the members of the Convention recognized his wisdom and intelligence. He became one of the most important leaders in the Convention.

The Changed Purpose

The Convention had been called to amend the Articles of Confederation. However, it soon became obvious that establishing a satisfactory government would require more than a mere revision of the Articles. Therefore, under the influence of such farsighted statesmen as Washington, Hamilton, and Madison, the original purpose of the Convention was changed. Instead of a Convention to amend the Articles of Confederation, it became a convention to write a new constitution.

Spot Check

1. What was the main reason why conventions were called to amend the Articles of Confederation?
2. Name important leaders in the United States that did not attend the convention.
3. Name important leaders from Virginia, Pennsylvania, and New York who did attend and were influential at the Philadelphia convention.
4. What was the changed purpose of the convention?

THE UNITED STATES CONSTITUTION

The beginning of the United States Constitution

Three Branches of Government

The Constitutional Convention divided the new government into three branches: legislative, executive, and judicial. The fathers of the Constitution planned that the legislative branch should make the laws. The executive branch should enforce, or carry out the laws. The judicial branch should settle disputes and try cases involving violation of the law.

The Legislative Branch

In creating the legislative department, three compromises were necessary. First was the question of representation in Congress. The smaller states wanted a Congress in which all the states would have equal representation, regardless of population. The larger states wanted a Congress in which each state would be represented in proportion to its population. After long and heated debate, a compromise was reached. There would be two houses in the Congress: a Senate and a House of Representatives. Each provided a different proportion of representation. In the Senate, the states are equally represented. In the House of Representatives, each state is represented in proportion to its population.

Next came the question of whether slaves should be counted as part of the representative population. The southern states wanted the slaves counted for representation, but not for taxation. The northern states insisted that the slaves must be counted for both purposes or not at all. After bitter debate, a compromise was reached. The delegates agreed that three-fifths of the slaves be counted for both representation and taxation. Thus, if a state had fifteen thousand slaves, they would count as nine thousand inhabitants.

In the third great compromise, the matter of commerce and the slave trade was settled. The industrial states of the North wanted Congress to have power to protect their trade by exacting a tariff from foreign ships entering American ports. However, the agricultural South, which traded largely with Europe, was opposed to the delegation of this power. A compromise was finally reached. Congress was empowered to regulate trade but could not abolish the slave trade before 1808.

In general, Congress was given power to control the currency, the postal system, the Army and Navy, and foreign and interstate commerce. These were the very powers that Congress had needed so much during the critical period from 1781 to 1789. However, beyond these powers, the Congress would have no authority to make law.

The Executive Branch

The executive branch was given the power to enforce the laws Congress passed. The president was made the highest law-enforcing authority in the land. Besides the authority to enforce the laws, the president was given the power to appoint the national officials, to make treaties with the approval of the Senate, and to veto laws that he considered undesirable. He is also the commander in chief of the armed forces. The functions of the executive branch are carried out through department heads, that is, members of the president's Cabinet. Though the Cabinet is not provided for in the Constitution, it has developed through necessity in order to assist the president.

The Judicial Branch

The Constitution created a national judicial branch consisting of a Supreme Court and such lower courts as Congress should create by law. These national courts were given power to try all cases arising under the Constitution. They also had the power to settle disputes between states as well as controversies between a state and the national government. If the Supreme Court decides that any law is contrary to the Constitution, it declares that law unconstitutional.

Checks and Balances

To protect the rights of the people and to prevent any misuse of power in the government, the Constitutional Convention worked out a system of checks and balances. The president was given many vital powers, but at the same time his authority is limited. He is in charge of relations with foreign countries, but all treaties are made with the advice and the consent of the Senate. He is commander in chief of the armed forces, but may not declare war. Congress does that. He makes appointments to various positions in the government. However, the Senate must approve his appointees. He may veto, or refuse to sign acts passed by Congress, but Congress may overrule his veto. To overrule the president's veto, Congress must re-pass the bill in question by a two-thirds vote in each house.

The delegates to the Constitutional Convention kept the control of taxation in the hands of the people. The members gave the House of Representatives the sole right to originate bills for the raising or spending of government money. The two houses of Congress also serve to check each other. Any bill must be passed or approved by a majority vote in each house. The president may, by his veto, force the bill to be re-passed by a two-thirds vote of both houses.

If the Supreme Court decides that any law is contrary to the provisions of the Constitution, it declares that law unconstitutional and void. This serves as a final check on the power of Congress and makes the Constitution the supreme law of the land.

A further check to the power of the national government was the power of the states. The states would guard their power against any attempt by the national government to take it away. The state government would stand between the individual and the national government to protect the liberties of its citizens.

Amending the Constitution

Once the convention had drawn up the Constitution and defined the powers of the government, the issue arose of how changes to the Constitution might be made. The convention provided that the Constitution could be amended by a two-thirds vote of both houses of Congress with ratification by three-fourths of the states. Thus, it was possible, but not easy, to change the Constitution. Since the first ten amendments were added to the Constitution in 1791, there have been only seventeen additional amendments. The Twenty-Seventh Amendment was added in 1992.

Spot Check

1. Name the three branches of government.
2. What was the problem about representation in Congress? What compromise was agreed upon?
3. What was the problem with slaves being counted as part of the representative population? What compromise was reached?
4. What powers were Congress given that the Confederation Congress felt it needed but it did not have?
5. What is the system of "checks and balances"?
6. What power does the House of Representatives alone have? Why?
7. How do the houses of Congress check and balance each other?
8. How does the Supreme Court check the power of Congress?

How the Constitution Was Ratified (Accepted)

Federalists and Anti-Federalists

The work of the Constitutional Convention was completed September 17, 1787. Thirty-nine members of the convention signed the Constitution. It was then submitted to the states for ratification. The Constitution would become effective when nine states had ratified it. The signers of the document left the Convention and journeyed to their home states to work for the ratification of the new plan of national government. The men who had refused to sign the Constitution also went home. However, they returned home to oppose its ratification.

The fight over the ratification of the Constitution lasted almost a year. Meanwhile, the first political parties in America were formed. One party was the Federalists, who favored the Constitution. The other party was the Anti-Federalists, who opposed it. The opposition was so strong that the issue was constantly in doubt.

In Virginia, Patrick Henry fought against the Constitution. However, Washington used his great influence to help James Madison, who was working for its ratification.

Some of the strongest opposition came from New York. Of the three New York delegates to the Convention, Alexander Hamilton was the only one who favored ratification The other two had walked out. However, John Jay helped Hamilton to swing the state in favor of the Constitution. The New York Legislature ratified the Constitution by a slim margin of three votes.

Madison and Hamilton, and occasionally Jay, published a series of articles in a New York newspaper explaining every part of the

Constitution. They argued brilliantly for its adoption. Newspapers in many other states copied these articles. These articles helped a great deal in securing the acceptance of the new plan of government. They were later collected in a book called *The Federalist Papers*. *The Federalist Papers* are still the best authority on the meaning of the Constitution.

The Constitution Is Ratified

By June 21, 1788, nine states had ratified the Constitution. However, Virginia and New York had not yet acted. It was impossible to set up a strong central government without the aid of these two large, powerful states. Two months later, both states had accepted the Constitution. When formal notice reached Congress that the ninth state had ratified, Congress fixed January 1789, as the date for the first presidential election. The first Wednesday in March, March 4, 1789, was set for the meeting of the first Congress under the Constitution. New York City was chosen as the temporary capital. The last two states, Rhode Island and North Carolina, ratified after Washington became president.

Alexander Hamilton

The Importance of the Constitution

The adoption of the Constitution marked an important step forward in the history of government. A written constitution was something new in the eyes of the world. Our Constitution put certain new ideas about government into operation. It put into practice on a large scale a government by the people. It recognized no social classes. It was for all people, high and low, rich and poor.

The Convention did its work very well. The greatness of the Constitution has been shown by its results. Although it is not a perfect document and courts have misinterpreted it over the years, it set forth lofty goals. It has stood the test of time and lasted over two hundred and twenty years. This makes America the world's oldest republic. Americans owe a debt of gratitude to the men who created this nation.

Spot Check

1. What issue created the first political parties in the United States?
2. What were the parties called?
3. What two states were vital to the Constitution's ratification? Why?

CHAPTER REVIEW

1. Why did the states not want to set up a strong central government?
2. What was the chief reason why the states hesitated to sign the Articles of Confederation?
3. What is meant by the "western claims" of the states?
4. What were the fundamental weaknesses of the Articles of Confederation?
5. What conditions caused Shays' Rebellion?
6. What were the provisions of the Northwest Ordinance?
7. Who is known as the "Father of the Constitution"?
8. Name three of the prominent members of the Constitutional Convention.
9. What were the three great compromises in the Constitution?
10. Explain what is meant by "checks and balances" in the Constitution.
11. In what year did the government organized under the Constitution go into effect?
12. What are *The Federalist Papers*?
13. Who wrote *The Federalist Papers*?

THE CHURCH IN EARLY AMERICA

Old St. Joseph's Church in Philadelphia. At the time of its construction, it was the site of the only legal Mass in the English speaking world.

The First Missionaries

Missionaries to our country, like to every other new country, followed closely behind the explorers. In 1493, missionaries followed Columbus to Haiti, Cuba, and Puerto Rico. They also followed Ponce de Leon to Florida and Balboa to the Pacific. They went with De Soto to the Mississippi and Coronado to New Mexico. The first missionaries to North America were Franciscans, Dominicans, and Carmelites. The Jesuits soon followed these brave priests.

The First Parish in the United States

The oldest Catholic parish in the United States is in St. Augustine, Florida. Pedro Menendez founded it in 1565. Though the church is no longer standing, its site is well established by the historical record. It was built near the mouth of the St. John's River in 1566. The Jesuits and the Franciscans worked in the Florida territory from 1566 to 1704. Their holy work was stopped as a result of Governor Moore's invasions from Carolina.

The Work of the Church in the English Colonies

The early missionaries in the New England colonies came from Canada. Among them were Franciscans, Jesuits, Sulpicians, and Capuchins. All these brave men worked mostly among the Indians. Their missions extended from Maine to Maryland. Sadly, over time, English soldiers and Indian uprisings destroyed these missions.

We have learned that Catholics were unwelcome in the Protestant colonies. A law passed by New York in 1700 made it illegal for priests to remain in the colony. The law read: "It was by law enacted that every popish priest caught within the province should be imprisoned for life; and if he escaped and was recaptured, he could be hung."

Of the original thirteen colonies, Pennsylvania can be proud of its policy towards Catholics. Few events occurred there to mar this splendid record. As early as 1686, there was a Catholic chapel in Philadelphia. However, the Faith *really* took root there in 1730. That was the year that Jesuit Father Joseph Greaton became the first permanent missionary in the city. In 1733, the Jesuits founded Old St. Joseph's Roman Catholic Church. It is Philadelphia's oldest Catholic church. (It is still staffed by Jesuits. The church has been in continuous existence since 1733.) Within a few years, numerous Irish and German immigrants arrived. They greatly increased the number of Catholics in Philadelphia.

As we have seen, Maryland was planned as a Catholic colony. This colony became the home to most of the Catholic immigrants to the English colonies. Religious toleration was one of the first laws of Maryland. However, during the Protestant domination, Maryland Catholics did not enjoy freedom. The Jesuits were the first missionaries in Maryland. Besides attending to the religious needs of their scattered flock, they worked to convert the Indians.

Kaskaskia Mission

In 1675, the Jesuit explorer Father Jacques Marquette established the Immaculate Conception Mission known as Kaskaskia. In 1700, Father Grovier moved this mission to Kaskaskia. Kaskaskia was the settlement in the Illinois country near the junction of the Kaskaskia River and the Mississippi. Father Grovier worked there for twenty years to convert and civilize the Indians. Sadly, this holy man was martyred by one of the cruel natives whose sins he had admonished. This village later became the seat of government for the French. In 1763, it was taken over by the English. It remained in their hands until the time of the War of Independence.

After the English took possession of Kaskaskia, the Jesuits were driven out. The college, which the Jesuits had started in 1721, was turned into a fort. However, the work of conversion continued. Father Pierre Gibault of Canada became the missionary. For years he labored in the vast lands from Kaskaskia to Detroit to Vincennes. He became the champion of American independence. We have seen how he worked with George Rogers Clark in the fight between the British and the Americans for the Northwest Territory.

The Church in Louisiana

The beginnings of the Faith in Louisiana date from 1682. In that year, two French Franciscans accompanied La Salle down the Mississippi River to its mouth. They offered the first Masses said in that area. The first church was built in 1717 for the Indian Mission of San Miguel de Linares.

Jean Baptiste Bienville founded New Orleans in 1718. In 1721, the Capuchins built the first chapel there. It was destroyed by a hurricane and later rebuilt on the site of the present cathedral.

The Church in the Southwest

In 1629, the Spanish Franciscans came up from Mexico to begin their mission activities. They were active in New Mexico, Texas, and California where they built churches and schools. In time, the Dominicans, Jesuits, Capuchins, and Augustinians also worked in this same region. However, for the most part, the Church in the Southwest owes its beginnings to the Spanish Franciscans. They sought to convert and civilize the natives. In this, they were successful. However, revolts and suspicions drove them from this huge mission field. The native uprisings were so fierce that by 1800, all traces of the Faith were completely wiped out.

The California Missions

Franciscan Father Junipero Serra founded the first mission in what is now California. He founded it at San Diego in 1769. Father Serra, with a band of well-trained companions, established a number of missions from San Diego to the present-day city of San Francisco. Of these famous California missions, twelve were established after Father Serra's death. The last, San Francisco Solano, was founded in 1823.

Among the missionaries were engineers, doctors, and men versed in almost every skill known at the time. They taught the Indians how to farm and how to build. They introduced livestock and crops of every available kind. The missionaries raised the standard of living of the Indians. Frequently, the missionaries clashed with the military over its treatment of the Indians. The mission buildings were built so well that most still stand today after hundreds of years and in spite of earthquakes and other natural disasters.

PLACE	MISSION
CARMEL	SAN CARLOS
JOLON	SAN ANTONIO DE PADUA
LOMPOC	LA PURISIMA CONCEPCION
NILES	SAN JOSE
OCEANSIDE	SAN LUIS REY
SAN DIEGO	SAN DIEGO
SAN FERNANDO	SAN FERNANDO REY
SAN FRANCISCO	SAN FRANCISCO DE ASIS
SAN GABRIEL	SAN GABRIEL, ARCANGEL
SAN JUAN BAUTISTA	SAN JUAN BAUTISTA
SAN JUAN CAPISTRANO	SAN JUAN CAPISTRANO
SAN LUIS OBISPO	SAN LUIS OBISPO
SAN MIGUEL	SAN MIGUEL, ARCANGEL
SAN RAFAEL	SAN RAFAEL, ARCANGEL
SANTA BARBARA	SANTA BARBARA
SANTA CLARA	SANTA CLARA DE ASIS
SANTA CRUZ	SANTA CRUZ
SOLEDAD	SOLEDAD
SOLVANG	SANTA INEZ
SONOMA	SAN FRANCISCO SOLANO
VENTURA	SAN BUENAVENTURA

THE CALIFORNIA MISSIONS

Father Serra was blessed with incredible energy. He walked almost everywhere. Nevertheless, he was able to baptize and confirm some 6,000 Indians. He also translated a catechism into one of the Indian languages. He wrote numerous letters and kept a diary. He died in 1784 at the Mission of San Carlos, where he is buried. In 1988, Pope John Paul II beatified him.

Father Serra was not only a very holy priest, but also was one of the pioneers who guided the settlement of California. His work was essential in creating a place where people could work and live. In 1931, the state of California honored Father Serra's contribution to the history of California. They put his statue in the Statuary Hall in the Capitol Building in Washington, D. C.

Father Serra's work was carried on in the face of ever-increasing opposition. Finally, in 1833, the Mexican government, which opposed the Church, seized the missions and their endowments. The Franciscan priests and brothers were forced to leave and the missions closed. The Indians became impoverished and drifted away from the Catholic Faith.

Bishop John Carroll

The end of the War of Independence brought new hope to the Church in America. In 1784, Father John Carroll was appointed "Superior of the Missions in the thirteen United States of North America." As head of this vast mission territory, Father Carroll took up residence in Baltimore. There he immediately sought to unify the work of his priests and people. He organized schools, promoted higher education, and constantly urged toleration for all religions.

Bishop John Carroll

During the debates preceding the adoption of the Constitution, Father Carroll went to Philadelphia. He pleaded before the convention delegates for the rights of his fellow Catholics. His words had much to do with the adoption of Article VI of the

Constitution. This Article abolishes all religious tests for any public office.

In 1789, Pope Pius VI appointed Father Carroll bishop of Baltimore. Pope Pius gave him charge of all Catholic interests in the United States. At that time, there were about twenty-five thousand Catholics in this country. Almost all of them lived either in Maryland or Pennsylvania.

Bishop Carroll was a great American. He loved his country almost as much as he loved the Church. Born in Upper Marlboro, Maryland, on January 8, 1735, Carroll played a significant part in the history of religious freedom for Catholics. He was educated at Bohemia, the first Jesuit school in Maryland. He finished his studies for the priesthood in Europe. When he returned to America, he carried on his missionary life in Maryland and Virginia. Both Catholics and Protestants loved him. This great first bishop of the United States died in Baltimore on December 3, 1815.

Commenting on his funeral, one Baltimore paper wrote: "We have never witnessed a funeral procession where so many eminent… standing among us followed the train of mourners. Distinctions of rank, of wealth, of religious opinion were laid aside in the great testimony of respect to the memory of the man."

CHAPTER REVIEW
1. What is the oldest parish in the United States?
2. How was Pennsylvania the most religiously tolerant colony?
3. Describe the missionary work of Father Junipero Serra.
4. In addition to spiritual benefits, what other benefits did the missionaries bring to the Indians of California and the Southwest?
5. What did Father Carroll do for religious freedom in the United States?
6. Why was John Carroll a great first bishop of the United States?

STRUGGLES AND TRIUMPHS OF THE NEW NATION

Washington's Inauguration

A NEW NATION

Washington as the First President

While Americans differed in their views of the Constitution and the merits of constitutional government, they did agree on the man who should put this form of government into operation. It is not surprising that George Washington, who had led the American armies to victory, should be chosen to lead the American people in freedom and peace. "Long live George Washington, President of the United States," cried the huge crowd on the day of his inauguration as our first president.

March 4, 1789, had been set for the opening of the first Congress. However, because of poor roads and bad winter weather, it was April before enough congressmen could reach New York City to make a session of Congress legal. When the electors from each state met to vote for president and vice president, each of the electors gave one of his two votes to Washington. Thus, he was elected president. As second choice, John Adams of Massachusetts received the highest number of electoral votes. Thus, he was chosen vice president.

On April 16, 1789, George Washington began his long journey to New York City. It took seven days to travel from Mount Vernon to New York. However, the difficult trip was not without its comfort and cheer. All along the route, applause and well-wishers greeted Washington. Though he was hesitant to leave Mount Vernon, he knew before he reached New York that he had the confidence of the people. He knew that he was respected, admired, and loved.

The Day of Inauguration

On April 30, 1789, George Washington appeared on the balcony of Federal Hall on Wall Street in New York City. There he solemnly took the oath of office. It was a day of rejoicing. Bells rang, cannons boomed, bands played music, and the people in the streets cried out, "Long live George Washington, President of the United States."

Washington deserved the confidence that the people had in him. During the dark period of the war, he had held the struggling American forces together by the strength of his personality. He led his troops in prayer on a daily basis. After the war, he had retired to private life. However, even as a private citizen, he had devoted himself to the interests of the new nation. His influence had been far-reaching in framing the Constitution and in securing its adoption. He had a calm and dignified manner that inspired confidence. However, his calmness was not the calmness of inactivity. Rather it was the calmness of self-restraint. He was noted especially for the soundness of his judgment and for his high sense of honor and public duty.

Washington Leaving Mount Vernon for his Inauguration

The First Cabinet

The new president surrounded himself with four very able advisers to assist him. These men formed the first Cabinet. There was a Secretary of State, a Secretary of the Treasury, a Secretary of War, and an Attorney General. The Secretary of State managed our relations with foreign nations as head of the State Department. The Secretary of the Treasury handled the monetary affairs of the government. The Secretary of War was in charge of the Army and the Navy. Finally, the Attorney General was the legal adviser to the president and the other executive officers.

Thomas Jefferson was chosen to be the first Secretary of State. Jefferson, the author of the Declaration of Independence, was well suited for the post because of his experience as an ambassador to France. Alexander Hamilton became the first Secretary of the Treasury. This was also a wise choice. Hamilton was a brilliant young lawyer and financier. General Henry Knox of Massachusetts was chosen Secretary of War. Knox had been one of Washington's best officers during the war and was very reliable. For Attorney General, Washington chose Edmund Randolph. Randolph was a very good lawyer from Virginia. He had also given the keynote speech at the Constitutional Convention.

Washington began the custom of using these executives as an advisory council. They were called the president's Cabinet. As the nation grew and the duties of the Cabinet increased, it was necessary to add new officers and new departments. As of 2010, there are fifteen members of the Cabinet.

Representatives in Foreign Lands

President Washington appointed representatives to look after the interests of the United States in other countries. All American representatives of this type are under the authority of the Secretary of State. There are two classes of such foreign representatives.

The first class acts as political representatives for our country. They are called ambassadors or ministers, depending on the importance of the country to which they are sent. Ambassadors are sent to the more important nations. Only one ambassador or minister is sent to each country.

The other class of representatives looks after our trade relations with other countries. They are called consuls. Consuls also look after the interests of Americans visiting or living in foreign countries. There may be several consuls sent to a country. It depends on how important that country is to our trade interests.

During the War of Independence and the early years of our history, such men as Franklin, Jefferson, Jay, Adams, and Monroe represented our country abroad. Much of the success of the new nation was the result of their skillful diplomacy.

National Courts

The Constitution provided for a Supreme Court and such additional courts as Congress should from time to time establish. To carry out this provision of the Constitution, the first Congress established a system of federal district courts. It declared that the Supreme Court should consist of one Chief Justice and five associate judges. Today there are nine Supreme Court judges.

Washington appointed John Jay as the first Chief Justice of the Supreme Court. Under Jay and one of his successors, John Marshall, the power of the national government was greatly strengthened. While Marshall was Chief Justice, the Supreme Court assumed powers that it has exercised ever since. It decided whether laws passed by the Congress were constitutional or not. It set aside state laws in conflict with the Constitution. The Supreme Court also reviewed the decisions appealed from lower federal courts and from state supreme courts. By upholding the doctrine of implied powers, the Supreme Court gave the national government expansive powers not specifically mentioned in the Constitution.

John Marshall

The Bill of Rights

During the fight for ratification of the Constitution, some of the states were won over by the promise that the Constitution would be amended to protect the rights of the people. One vital task of the first Congress was to make the promised amendments. Congress framed and recommended to the states a number of amendments intended to protect the rights of the people. Ten of these were ratified by the states. They became part of the Constitution during the first year of the new government.

These first ten amendments are known as the Bill of Rights. They guarantee freedom of religion, speech, and the press. They include the right to bear arms. They protect against unreasonable searches of one's home by the police. They guarantee jury trial and they protect people from being forced to testify against themselves. They prohibit cruel or unusual punishments. The Ninth Amendment also recognizes that people have rights beyond the ones mentioned in the Constitution that the national government must respect. Finally, the Tenth Amendment declares that the states and the people retain the powers not specifically given to the national government or prohibited to the states.

Spot Check

1. Who united the nation behind the new national government?
2. Who was the first vice president of the United States?
3. Where did George Washington's Inauguration take place?
4. Who was the first Chief Justice of the United States?
5. Why did many people want a list of rights attached to the Constitution?
6. Give some examples of rights guaranteed by the Bill of Rights.

NATIONAL FINANCIAL POLICY

The Financial Problem

The new nation faced a serious financial crisis. The need for money was so great that one of the very first acts Congress took was to pass a tariff bill that placed a low duty on imports. However, it fell to Alexander Hamilton, the first Secretary of the Treasury, to solve the financial problem that the new nation had inherited from the government under the Articles of Confederation. The problem was threefold. First, there was not enough money to meet current government expenses. Second, the nation was heavily in debt. Third, national credit had fallen into disrepute.

Hamilton's Plan

Alexander Hamilton proposed that the national debt be paid in full. He said that the only credit worth having was credit based on the fact that the United States paid all its debts in full. He proposed that the national government take over the unpaid state debts. Hamilton said the federal government would redeem the Continental paper money at face value. The total national debt, including money borrowed at home and abroad, the unpaid war debts, and the Continental paper money, was about seventy-five million dollars.

To pay the debt and to place the United States on a sound financial basis, Hamilton proposed four measures. First, he planned to borrow money from the American people by a sale of government bonds. People were willing to lend money to the government now that Congress had the power to collect taxes. Second, he proposed that Congress levy tax on all distilled liquor and wine produced in the United States. His third measure called for the establishment of a national bank. The bank would serve as a depository for government money, help in the sale of government bonds, and issue sound paper money. The fourth proposition was that a government mint be established to print money.

Paying off the National Debt

Hamilton's plan to include the unpaid state war debts in the total national debt met with strong opposition. The opponents of a strong national government argued that Congress did not have the authority to assume this burden. Some of the states opposed the plan.

Led by Virginia, these states opposed the plan because they had already paid off some of their debts.

At this time, Congress was considering the issue of a permanent site for the capital. When George Washington was inaugurated, New York City was the temporary capital. In 1790, the capital was moved south to Philadelphia. However, this did not completely satisfy the southern states. Virginia and her southern sisters wanted the national capital moved farther south. In order to get his plan to pay the debts through the Congress, Hamilton made a deal with the southern states. In return for their support, Hamilton would persuade the representatives of the northern states to agree to move the nation's capital south. The selection of Washington, D.C. as the site for the capitol was the result.

The Whisky Rebellion

Congress passed the tax on distilled liquors proposed by Hamilton. Such a tax on goods made and used in a country is called an "excise tax." The tax brought unpleasant results. Along the frontier, from Pennsylvania southward, this tax was violently resented by the backwoods farmers. They had found the transportation of grain over the mountains too expensive. Therefore, they distilled their grain into whisky, which was easier to transport and to sell. When government officials tried to enforce the tax in western Pennsylvania, organized bands of frontiersmen resisted them. These embittered farmers refused to pay the tax and even tarred and feathered the tax collectors.

Finally, at the urging of Hamilton, President Washington sent an army to put down the Whisky Rebellion, as it was called. As Washington hoped, the feeling of the farmers cooled. When the troops reached western Pennsylvania, the rebellion fell apart. However, its leaders were arrested. As a result of this action, people spoke in a new tone of respect about the authority of the national government. However, Hamilton and his followers had lost popularity in the West.

The National Bank

In 1791, Hamilton influenced Congress to establish the first national bank. It was known as the Bank of the United States. It was located in Philadelphia where a year later, the first United States mint was built. Immediately, the bank began to issue paper money with the credit of the United States government behind it. As confidence in the national government increased, the money was accepted at face value. It replaced the old money issued by state banks. The mint issued gold and silver coins in denominations based on the decimal system. These coins replaced the pounds and shillings of the English system.

Emergence of Political Parties

The founding of the bank divided political leaders into two distinct camps. One camp was led by Hamilton. His followers were known as Federalists, who favored a broad interpretation of the Constitution. They favored a strong federal government that was insulated from the changing opinions of the American people, and they felt this would be a protection against the danger of "mob rule." The defended the national bank. The Federalists argued that the Constitution gave Congress the right to make all laws "which shall be necessary and proper for carrying into execution" the powers of Congress named in the Constitution. They also insisted that the national government had implied powers in addition to those specifically granted by the Constitution.

The other camp was the Anti-Federalists. Thomas Jefferson led them. They opposed Alexander Hamilton. They insisted that Congress only had those powers that were specifically named in the Constitution. They believed the national government should not be given any power not specifically given to it by the Constitution. They did not believe in "implied powers." Since they believed in placing a strict, literal interpretation on the Constitution, they became known as "strict constructionists." They were also concerned that the federal government would become too strong and would take away the powers of the states. The Anti-Federalists later called themselves the Democratic-Republicans. The present day Democratic party traces its beginning to this party.

Thomas Jefferson in 1791

The passage of Hamilton's financial measures caused great bitterness between the two parties. Hamilton's supporters said that Jefferson and his followers were trying to destroy the national government by giving it to the "mob." Jefferson's supporters accused Hamilton's faction of trying to make the United States a monarchy run by the rich.

Spot Check

1. What was the three-fold money problem that the new national government had?
2. How did Hamilton succeed in overcoming the southern opposition of the southern states to his debt payment plan?
3. How did Democratic-Republicans and Federalists differ on their interpretations of the Constitution?

FOREIGN RELATIONS

Citizen Genet Comes to America

In 1789, France had a terrible Revolution, not a War of Independence like in the United States. The revolutionaries attacked the Church and the society in France. Once they had murdered their king and many of the nobles, they began a systematic attack on the Church. France became a land of martyrs.

The French revolutionaries expected America to support them. The French had helped the U.S. in our War of Independence. Thus, they believed that America would assist them. To obtain aid, the new French government sent an agent named Genet to the United States. However, Genet, when he arrived, did not present himself to the president as was proper for every foreign minister. Instead, he landed in the South where there was greater sympathy for the Revolution. He obtained a number of ships to go out as privateers to attack English commerce. He also planned with some Westerners to seize Spanish Florida.

When Genet finally arrived in Philadelphia and presented himself to Washington, the president refused to accept him. He ordered Genet out of the country. France, not wishing to anger the United States, dismissed Genet. They sent another minister to ask for help from America.

Washington's Proclamation of Neutrality

Washington realized that the United States must not become involved in a war in Europe. Many people thought that because of our treaty of alliance with France, made during the War of Independence, we were required to lend them aid. To settle the matter, Washington issued a proclamation of neutrality. He declared that the United States intended to take a neutral stand in all disputes among foreign nations.

The French government was unhappy and disappointed that America refused to aid them. Some in America criticized Washington for his position. However, the Proclamation of Neutrality became one of the foundations of America's relations with the rest of the world. It was probably best for the safety of the new United States.

English Soldiers in the Northwest

Since the end of the War of Independence, the presence of English soldiers in the Northwest Territory troubled the United States. By the treaty of Paris of 1783, Congress had pledged to recommend that the states restore the confiscated property of Englishmen and Tories. By the same treaty, the English government had agreed to remove all its soldiers from United States land. Sadly, neither government had kept its pledge. The Americans had failed to restore Tory property. British fur traders in the Northwest Territory had persuaded their government to use the Americans' failure as an excuse to leave English troops along our western borders. Also, American pioneers in that region accused the British of encouraging Indian attacks. These pioneers wanted the national government to intervene on their behalf.

The English Interfere with U.S. Trade

In addition to the presence of English soldiers in the Northwest, England was also interfering in America's commercial trade. England was in a war for her life with revolutionary France. England was seizing America's ships bound for France and confiscating any cargoes that could be used in the war. England also had a grievance against the United States. Under the influence of Citizen Genet, American privateers had seized British ships.

Another issue involved England taking men from American ships for the British Navy. When the English boarded a ship, they would often claim that a sailor was English and take him away. Thus, American sailors were forced to serve on English warships. This English policy would soon lead to war.

Moreover, American ships were forbidden to trade with the English colonies of the West Indies. England's laws demanded that all trade to and from her possessions be carried out on English ships. American merchants were furious. They protested that they were losing a rich trade. They wanted a commercial treaty giving them the right to trade with the West Indies as well as protecting their cargoes and crews from seizure.

The Jay Treaty

The troubles in the Northwest and the trading problem needed to be fixed. President Washington sent John Jay to England to see if he could settle these matters. Jay returned with a treaty. First, it provided that England would withdraw her soldiers if the U.S. paid for or returned the property seized during the war. Second, an unbiased judge would settle damages to American merchants from British seizures and to the British for losses from American privateers.

Though American merchants did not completely like the treaty, it was the best that could be concluded. Washington felt that the United States must either accept the treaty, unsatisfactory though it was, or risk war with England. He used his influence for its ratification. In spite of some protests, the treaty was accepted. As a result, British soldiers were removed from the western border of the U.S.

The Pinckney Treaty with Spain

The removal of British soldiers did not free our western settlers from all foreign interference. The vast holdings of Spain were another potential threat to peace. The possession of Louisiana and of Florida, which at that time extended to the Mississippi River, gave Spain ownership of both banks of the Mississippi River. As a result, Spain controlled the mouth of this great river. This prevented American settlers in Tennessee and Kentucky from shipping their surplus crops to

John Jay

the East by way of the Mississippi. Likewise, it prevented merchants in the East from using the river to reach the Westerners.

These difficulties with Spain were settled by treaty on October 27, 1795. Thomas Pinckney negotiated this treaty; thus, it bears his name. The treaty gave the western settlers the right to ship their goods down the Mississippi. They received the right to deposit their products at New Orleans free of duty while awaiting shipment. This treaty settled the boundary between our country and Spanish Florida at the thirty-first parallel of latitude.

The XYZ Affair

Despite the desire of many Americans that he continue, George Washington retired after two terms as president. His vice president, John Adams, was elected the new president. When John Adams became president, French anger towards the United States had reached the boiling point. The Jay Treaty with Great Britain incensed the French because they felt it was pro-British. The treaty allowed the English to use more soldiers and sailors in Europe against the French dictator, Napoleon. Thus, the French refused to receive our minister,

President John Adams

Charles Cotesworth Pinckney. Moreover, they recalled their minister back home to France. This action aroused great anger in our country.

At the suggestion of Talleyrand, France's minister of foreign affairs, John Marshall and Elbridge Gerry were sent to France. They hoped to negotiate peace and to try to iron out the quarrel. However, Talleyrand himself did not meet the delegation. Instead, he sent three Frenchmen to represent the government. These French agents said that war could be avoided only by paying huge sums of money to certain French officials and loaning money to the French government. To this disgraceful proposal, the Americans' answer was an emphatic "NO!" Pinckney replied, "No, no, not a sixpence." The cry, "Millions for defense, but not one cent for tribute!" was sounded throughout America.

When this affair was reported to Congress, President Adams used the letters X, Y, and Z instead of the names of the French agents. For this reason, the talks in France became known as "the XYZ Affair."

Spot Check
1. Give three reasons why England interfered with American commerce on the high seas.
2. Who became president after George Washington?
3. Why was France angry at America for the Jay Treaty with England?
4. What was "the XYZ Affair"?

Undeclared Naval War with France

In April 1798, Congress created a Department of the Navy. The Navy placed a squadron of ships under the command of Captain John Barry. The Navy was ordered to capture French ships that interfered with our merchant vessels. Fighting began in the neighborhood of the West Indies. President Adams called George Washington from retirement and appointed him commander in chief of the Army to prepare for possible war. Though there were no battles on land, fighting at sea lasted for about a year and a half. During that time, about eighty-five armed French ships were seized while the French took only one American ship.

Neither country officially declared war. The French ruler, Napoleon, had enough trouble in Europe without fighting a war with America. France, therefore, assured our minister to Holland that a representative from the United States would be received with the respect demanded by President Adams. A commission was sent to France. A treaty satisfactory to both nations was made on September 30, 1800. This treaty released the United States from the conditions of the alliance of 1778.

John Barry, Father of the American Navy

PARTY RIVALRY

Opposition to President John Adams

While Washington was president, his reputation and personal qualities won him the love and respect of the people. While he encountered a great deal of opposition, his opponents rarely attacked his character. They aimed most of their criticisms at his official acts.

With President John Adams, it was a different story. He was deeply devoted to the service of his country. However, he lacked tact and patience. Although a brilliant man, he was not personally likeable. As a result, he was very unpopular. He soon found himself the target of merciless personal abuse. Adams was a Federalist, and the Democratic-Republicans, especially those living in the South, did not approve of the aggressive measures that he and Congress had taken toward the French. There was considerable sympathy for France in the southern states, especially in Virginia and the Carolinas. These friends of France strongly denounced President Adams and the leaders of the Federalist Party in speeches, newspaper articles, and books. One of the leading opponents of Adams was Thomas Jefferson, the vice president. Encouraged by his example, many French aliens in America loudly condemned Congress and the president in very abusive language.

Unpopular Federalist Laws

To protect the president and members of the Congress against such verbal attacks, the Federalists persuaded Congress to pass three laws in quick succession. Congress passed the Naturalization Act, the Alien Law, and the Sedition Act. The Naturalization Act of 1798 made fourteen years the period of residence required for an alien to become a citizen of the United States. [Immigrants tended to join the Democratic-Republican Party rather than the Federalist Party.] The Alien Law authorized the president to order foreigners, who might be considered dangerous to the peace and safety of the United States, out of the country. The Sedition Act imposed heavy fines and long prison terms for those who defamed by speech, writing, or action, the president or the members of Congress.

Bitter criticism followed the passage of these laws. The Democratic-Republicans accused Congress of depriving them of their constitutional rights of free speech and a free press. Some of them even accused President Adams of trying to establish a dictatorial government. However, it is clear that this was not Adams' intention. In fact, the offensive laws had been passed against the advice of both Adams and Hamilton.

The Kentucky and Virginia Resolutions

To protest the Naturalization, Alien, and Sedition laws, the legislatures of Kentucky (which became a state in 1792) and of Virginia passed resolutions declaring these laws contrary to the letter and spirit of the Constitution. They pronounced them **null and void**, that is, they are not recognized as having any legal effect within their borders. Jefferson wrote the Kentucky Resolutions and Madison wrote the Virginia Resolutions. These resolutions were sent to the other state legislatures for their approval and support. All the replies opposed the resolutions.

The situation was dangerous. The Kentucky and Virginia state legislatures had openly defied the authority of the national government. It was the first application of the **states' rights doctrine**. This doctrine holds that each state has sovereign rights that could be exercised in case of need. President Adams handled the matter with prudent restraint. He fully realized that any attempt to force Kentucky or Virginia to accept the offensive laws might destroy the Union. Therefore, he did not enforce the three laws in either of these states.

The Kentucky and Virginia Resolutions had far-reaching political effects. They became part of the platform of Jefferson's party, the Democratic-Republicans. Jefferson and Madison had declared, "In a democracy, the government belongs to the people." On that principle rested the hopes of many citizens.

Spot Check
1. Why was John Adams unpopular?
2. Why did Congress pass the Naturalization Act, the Alien Law, and the Sedition Act?
3. What were the Kentucky and Virginia Resolutions?

The Election of 1800: Adams, Jefferson, and Burr

In 1800, another presidential election was held. Naturally, John Adams hoped to be re-elected. However, as a result of his unpopularity, the majority of the presidential electors chosen in 1800 were Democratic-

Republicans. They had resolved not to make the mistake of electing a president and a vice president of opposing parties as had happened when Adams was elected president and Jefferson, vice president. Therefore, before the electoral votes were cast, they held a caucus, or private party meeting. At the caucus, they all agreed to vote for Thomas Jefferson and Aaron Burr. They expected to elect Jefferson president and Burr vice president.

However, at the election, something unexpected happened. When the electoral votes were counted, Congress found that Jefferson and Burr had received exactly the same number of votes. They were tied for the highest place. Adams was third in the list of candidates.

The Constitution provided that, if the electors failed to elect a president, the names of the three persons receiving the greatest number of votes should be placed before the House of Representatives. The members of the House, voting by states, with each state casting one vote, were to elect one of the three for president.

The three names, Jefferson, Burr, and Adams, were submitted to the House of Representatives. There, a bitter fight over the election of the president developed. After thirty-five ballots, the matter still stood at a deadlock. It was clear that the choice would need to be either Jefferson or Burr. It was Alexander Hamilton's advice that broke the deadlock and led to Jefferson's election. Hamilton gave his frank opinion of both candidates. Although he had profound philosophical disagreements with Jefferson, he believed that Jefferson was a good and honorable man. However, he did not think that he could trust Burr. He denounced Burr as wholly unfit for the presidency. The result was that Jefferson became president and Burr, vice president. Burr would never forget what Hamilton had said. It would eventually cost Hamilton his life.

The Twelfth Amendment

To make sure that a tie vote would not occur again, the Twelfth Amendment was added to the Constitution. It provided that each elector should name in one ballot the person voted for as president and in another distinct ballot the person voted for as vice president. The Twelfth Amendment was adopted in 1804. Since that time each elector has cast one ballot for president and a separate ballot for vice president.

Jefferson Takes Office

In 1801, the United States had a new president and a new capital. Thomas Jefferson was the first president to take office in Washington, D.C. Despite his aristocratic background, Jefferson was democratic in speech and manner. He opposed the formality of both Washington and Adams. He emphasized that the government should consider the interests of the farmers and the common people. He promoted religious freedom, free public schools, freedom of speech, and the abolition of slavery. He

Thomas Jefferson, at the Time of his Election as President

believed, too, that the citizens possessed the ability to govern the nation wisely.

On March 4, 1801, Jefferson walked to the Capitol to take the oath of office. He wanted no pomp or pageantry. He wanted the people to know that the United States was their country. He wanted them to know that it would be governed by them and for them. He always claimed to be no more than a representative of the people. He soon became a great favorite of all the people.

Early in Jefferson's presidency, the objectionable laws passed by the Federalists were repealed. In keeping with his belief in governmental economy, the army was cut down to just over three thousand men. The navy was reduced to seven ships.

Although Jefferson was a poor speaker, he was a great writer and a brilliant man. He had great influence on those around him. Perhaps no president more completely controlled the actions of Congress. His self-confidence and forceful personality won him popularity in the South and respect in the North. Jefferson was the leader of a party that stood for a strict interpretation of the Constitution and for a limited national government. In addition, he showed that when given an opportunity to make a deal doubling the size of America, he was willing to do so.

The Death of Alexander Hamilton

Perhaps it need not have been, but Hamilton's opposition to Burr cost him his life. Burr challenged Hamilton to a duel with pistols. On July 11, 1804, Hamilton was shot and mortally wounded. The Federalists lost their brilliant and highly effective leader. The Federalists had no one who could fill Hamilton's shoes and their influence steadily declined.

Spot Check
1. What was the constitutional difficulty that occurred in the election of 1800?
2. Whose influence broke the deadlock in the House of Representatives and allowed Jefferson to become president?
3. Why was the Twelfth Amendment added to the Constitution?
4. Who was the first president to take office in Washington, D.C.?

The Death of Alexander Hamilton

CHAPTER REVIEW

1. When and where was George Washington inaugurated as the first president of the United States?
2. Name the four members of Washington's Cabinet.
3. What is the Bill of Rights?
4. Name at least five of the important rights guaranteed in the Bill of Rights.
5. What were Hamilton's proposals for placing the United States on a sound financial basis?
6. What was the Whiskey Rebellion?
7. What were the political principles or beliefs of Hamilton and Jefferson?
8. What were the Kentucky and Virginia Resolutions?
9. Explain the election difficulties of 1800. How does the Twelfth Amendment to the Constitution prevent such difficulties from happening again?
10. Who was the first president to take office in Washington, D.C.?

THE SETTLEMENT OF THE WEST

Lewis and Clark Descending the Columbia River to the Pacific Ocean

THE FRONTIER BEYOND THE APPALACHIANS

Kentucky and Tennessee

In 1775, the great border scout, Daniel Boone, cut a wagon trail from Cumberland Gap to Boonesboro in Kentucky. Boone loved the dangers of frontier life. He had trapped and hunted in Kentucky as early as 1767 and was well acquainted with that vast wilderness.

At the close of the war, settlers began to arrive in Kentucky in large numbers. Despite constant warfare with the Indians, the settlements became so numerous that the restless Daniel Boone moved on to Missouri for "elbow room." Kentucky became our fifteenth state in 1792.

In Tennessee, John Sevier and James Robertson were pushing the frontier back toward the great Mississippi River. After much fighting, peace treaties were made with the Indians in the lands drained by the Tennessee and Cumberland rivers. Many immigrants from Virginia and the Carolinas began to settle there. Tennessee became a state in 1796.

Alabama and Mississippi

While Kentucky and Tennessee were crying for statehood, pioneers from Georgia and South Carolina were migrating to the lands now known as Alabama and Mississippi. These determined settlers fought their way across the country against defiant Cherokee, Chickasaw, and Creek Indians. They established homes in the new country. They settled down to make lumbering and farming their main jobs. Mississippi became a state in 1817. Alabama was admitted to the Union two years later.

The pioneers of these lands shipped most of their products to the East by means of the Mississippi River and the Gulf of Mexico. This had been made possible by the treaty with Spain during Washington's presidency.

THE NORTHWEST TERRITORY

The Ordinance of 1787

The Northwest Ordinance was to the people north of the Ohio River what the Constitution was to the original thirteen states. The generous provisions of this enactment induced many Easterners to make their homes in the Northwest Territory: the lands bordered by the Ohio River and the Mississippi River. The fertile land with its abundance of forests lent itself naturally to trapping, lumbering, and farming. The new settlers were delighted with the region. They sent word back to their friends in the East about their good fortune. Shortly after 1800, great numbers of Easterners, chiefly from New England, came to this territory.

Eventually, five states were carved out of this territory: Ohio, Indiana, Illinois, Michigan, and Wisconsin. The Northwest Ordinance stated that when a territory reached sixty thousand inhabitants, it could apply for statehood. The bill also said that when new states were admitted, they should come in as equals of the original states.

These territories grew quickly. The growth was due in large part to the fact that the ordinance encouraged education, prohibited slavery, and granted complete political and religious freedom to the inhabitants. Catholics eagerly moved to these states in order to enjoy religious freedom.

The Native Americans of the Northwest

Though the Northwest Ordinance opened the door to the Northwest Territory, several years passed before settlers in large numbers entered the region. The Native Americans of the Northwest Territory were very hostile. They resented being robbed of their lands by the coming of the white men. Shortly after the Jay Treaty was made during Washington's presidency, General Anthony Wayne, who fought in the War of Independence, led an expedition to drive the Indians out of the Northwest. Wayne, whose daring won him the nickname "Mad Anthony," defeated the Indians. He made them sign a treaty giving American pioneers the right to advance into the West.

However, rather than attempting to convert and civilize the Indians as the Catholic French and Spanish did, Protestant Americans viewed the Indians as a nuisance. Over time, the Native peoples were pushed farther and farther west. Resentful of this, the Indian leaders urged their people to disregard the treaties they had made with the United States and to refuse to give up their lands.

Chief Tecumseh

The strongest attempt to stop the advance of the pioneers into the Northwest Territory was made by Tecumseh, chief of the Shawnees. He went from tribe to tribe, urging the Indians to unite and defend themselves against the invasion of the white settlers. He went as far south as Florida. He gained the support of most of the tribes of the Northwest. He was even joined by some of the Southern tribes.

In the fall of 1811, General William Henry Harrison, the governor of Indiana Territory, defeated Tecumseh's forces at Tippecanoe River. The fight was known as the Battle of Tippecanoe.

After the battle, rifles made in England and other pieces of English equipment,were found on the battlefield. This aroused the suspicions of the Westerners. They were convinced that the English fur traders had caused the Indian uprising and had supported Tecumseh. Although their suspicions were not justified, anger towards England intensified. However, it was true that the English traders had encouraged the Indians not to sign away their lands

Chief Tecumseh

by treaties with the United States. The English knew that the fur trade of the Northwest would disappear if the settlers drove out the Indians.

Spot Check

1. Name the five states that came from the Northwest Territory.
2. What political provisions of the Northwest Ordinance made the Territory attractive to settlers?
3. Who was General Anthony Wayne?
4. Who was Chief Tecumseh?
5. Who were the opposing leaders in the Battle of Tippecanoe? What was the result of the battle?

THE LOUISIANA PURCHASE

The Land West of the Mississippi

Until 1803, the United States extended only as far west as the Mississippi River. West of the Mississippi lay a great land stretching all the way to the Rocky Mountains. This vast region was known as Louisiana.

Spain owned this wide expanse of land. In 1762, near the end of the French and Indian War, France had given Spain all of this territory. Spain had received the port of New Orleans. To prevent any trouble, President Washington made a treaty with Spain permitting the Westerners, on payment of a small tax, to ship goods down the river to New Orleans. However, in 1802, the Spanish suddenly forbade the Americans to use the port of New Orleans. This caused great anxiety. The frontiersmen feared that they would not be able to ship their surplus goods to the markets of the East or of Europe.

Napoleon Regains Louisiana

About the same time, news came that Napoleon, the French ruler, had conquered Spain and forced her to give Louisiana back to France. The transfer scared the Americans. They had heard of Napoleon's military successes in Europe. They knew that he wanted to make France a great world power and build up a huge French empire in America. The people feared the power of France. When Jefferson heard the news, he said that America would need to wed itself to the British navy. Americans wondered what would happen to the frontier settlements if France closed the port of New Orleans.

All of this happened during the second year of Thomas Jefferson's presidency. Jefferson knew that Napoleon would probably refuse to renew the right of the Western settlers to use the Mississippi and to land at New Orleans. To prevent France from closing the Mississippi to western trade, the president tried to buy a piece of land at the mouth of the river. In 1803, Jefferson sent James Monroe to France to help Livingston, our ambassador to France, to buy New Orleans from Napoleon.

The Deal of the Century

James Monroe arrived in France ready to buy the port of New Orleans. Imagine his surprise when he learned that Napoleon wanted to sell all of Louisiana! France had been at war with England for ten years. Although there was a temporary peace, Napoleon was making plans for his next campaign. He desperately needed money to continue the war. Also, a revolt in the French West Indies had dimmed his hopes of a vast colonial empire. Moreover, when war resumed, the English navy might seize New Orleans anyway. Thus, Napoleon decided to sell the entire territory. Therefore, when Monroe and Livingston approached him with the idea of buying New Orleans, Napoleon offered to sell all of Louisiana, the territory between the Mississippi River and the Rocky Mountains, for about fifteen million dollars.

Though the Monroe and Livingston had no authority to purchase so large a territory, both men realized the value of Louisiana to the United States. Knowing that Napoleon might change his mind if there were any delay, they quickly accepted the offer at once without consulting the President Jefferson. (Contact with America took several

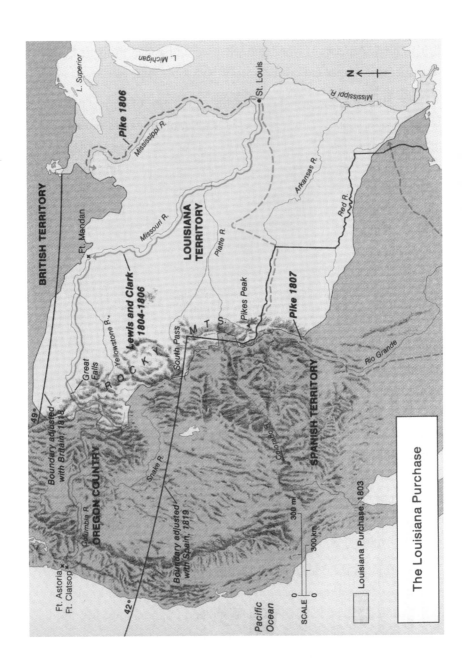

The Louisiana Purchase

BRITISH TERRITORY

L. Superior

L. Michigan

Pike 1806

Mississippi R.

St. Louis

N

Missouri R.

Ft. Mandan

Lewis and Clark
1804-1806

Yellowstone R.

Great
Falls

R O C K Y   M T S.

South Pass

LOUISIANA
TERRITORY

Platte R.

Arkansas R.

Mississippi R.

Red R.

Pikes Peak

Pike 1807

Boundary adjusted
with Britain 1818

49°

OREGON COUNTRY

Columbia R.

Snake R.

Colorado R.

Rio Grande

SPANISH TERRITORY

Boundary adjusted
with Spain, 1819

42°

Ft. Astoria
Ft. Clatsop

Pacific
Ocean

SCALE

0   300 mi
0   300 km

Louisiana Purchase, 1803

192

weeks at this time.) Livingston and Monroe signed the treaty on May 2, 1803.

When Jefferson received the news of the purchase, he was faced with a problem. The party that had elected him president believed in a strict construction of the Constitution. He had always insisted that the national government had only the powers specifically given it by the Constitution. There was no mention in the Constitution about the right to purchase foreign territory. Consequently, he was not sure whether the Senate would ratify the treaty. He finally justified the purchase under the Constitution's treaty-making and war-powers clauses. Though some members attacked the purchase, in the end, the Senate ratified the treaty. It was too good a bargain to miss. The House of Representatives voted to issue bonds to pay for it.

Importance of the Purchase

Through this purchase, the United States almost doubled its size. It gave the U.S. some of the finest farmland in the world. It gave complete control of the Mississippi River. No longer were the farmers and tradesmen disturbed about a waterway to world markets. They knew that the port of New Orleans and the fur-trading post of St. Louis belonged to the United States. They knew that this vast area would remain within the Union.

Until the Louisiana Purchase, the Mississippi had served as a barrier to the westward expansion of our nation. Through this purchase, the young republic was extended over a huge new region. The vastness of the Louisiana territory, as well as its rich resources, would in time provide homes and work to millions of American families. Minerals, waterpower, forests, grazing lands, and fertile plains were all part of the new area's God-given natural riches. Fifteen states, in whole or in part, were eventually developed from this great new tract the United States had obtained through the Grace of God.

The Lewis and Clark Expedition

Americans knew little of the newly purchased land. It had not been explored. Few people had any idea of its real value. In 1804, President Jefferson sent an expedition to explore the Louisiana Territory. He selected two young army officers to head the expedition. The two men were Captain William Clark, the youngest brother of George Rogers Clark, and Captain Meriwether Lewis, who for several years had been Jefferson's private secretary. Both men were from Virginia. Captain Lewis was in charge of the mission. Upon their appointment, the two men selected a force of frontiersmen, scouts, and soldiers. These were men who knew how to withstand the hardships of exploration.

With their party of hand-picked men, Lewis and Clark left St. Louis. They made their way up the Missouri River to the present site of Bismarck, North Dakota. There, among the friendly Mandan Indians, they spent the winter of 1804-1805. When the explorers resumed their journey in the spring, an Indian woman, known as Sacagawea, or "Bird Woman," accompanied them. This unusual woman was of great service to the white men. She secured Indian guides for them along the way. She was able to direct the explorers through the mountain passes to the upper part of the Snake River and on to the source of the Columbia River. Weary, tired, and sick, the expedition paddled on until it reached the Pacific Ocean. It was a great achievement.

Results of the Expedition

After spending more than two years exploring, Lewis and Clark returned to St. Louis. The journey there and back covered more than eight thousand miles. On that long, hard journey, they had traced the Missouri River to its source. They had crossed the great western highlands. They had discovered the source of the Columbia River and had sailed down that river to the Pacific Ocean. Most importantly, they had kept a careful record of their observations and discoveries. The party had explored the northwestern boundary of the Louisiana Territory. A New England sea captain, Robert Gray, had discovered the Columbia River more than a dozen years before the Lewis and Clark expedition. However, the work of Lewis and Clark gave the United States her best claim to the territory known as Oregon.

Pike's Explorations

While Lewis and Clark were exploring the northern part of Louisiana and the region northwest of the Rockies, a party led by General Zebulon Pike explored the southern part of the Louisiana Territory. Crossing the present state of Kansas and making his way into Colorado, Pike's party continued as far west as Santa Fe, New Mexico. As a result of his explorations, Pike's Peak in Colorado was named in his honor. The work of Lewis and Clark, along with that of General Pike, gave Americans a better idea of the character of the vast Louisiana Territory.

Spot Check

1. What name was given to the vast area between the Mississippi River and the Rocky Mountains?
2. What was Jefferson's difficulty, at first, with the treaty to purchase Louisiana?
3. Give three reasons why the Louisiana Purchase was extremely important to the future of the United States.
4. Who did Jefferson choose to explore the Louisiana Territory?
5. What area of the Louisiana Purchase did Zebulon Pike explore?

THE FLORIDAS

East and West Florida

The Florida territory was divided into two parts, East and West Florida. East Florida consisted of most of the present state of Florida. West Florida consisted of a narrow strip of land along the Gulf of Mexico. It was part of the present states of Alabama and Mississippi. At the time, East Florida belonged to Spain. However, the ownership of West Florida was in dispute. Spain insisted that West Florida was not a part of Louisiana. Therefore, it was not included in the Louisiana Purchase.

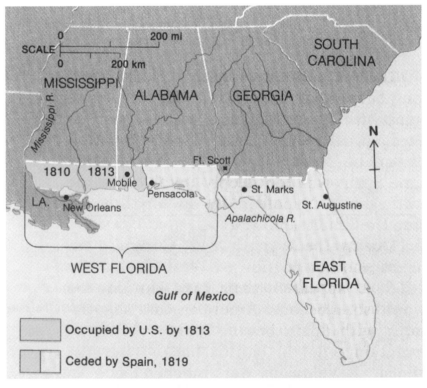

Map showing East and West Florida

The Florida Treaty

In 1818, General Andrew Jackson invaded East Florida with an American army. His goal was to stop Indian raids on settlements in Georgia and Alabama. Spain, knowing that she could not defeat the United States in a war, agreed to sell East Florida and the disputed territory of West Florida. By the Treaty of 1819, the United States gained possession of both the Floridas. Moreover, Spain gave up all her rights to the territory east of the Mississippi River.

Andrew Jackson in 1819

The Florida treaty gave the United States control of the northern shore of the Gulf of Mexico. It gave the people of the South a new feeling of security. Never again would the farmers and the merchants in that area be in danger of being cut off from their markets by foreign countries. It gave them new assurances of regular trade and a ready outlet for their goods and produce.

TRANSPORTATION INTO THE WEST

The National Road

Today our country is linked together by the greatest highway system in the world. It is the envy of other nations. However, this was not always the case. The early roads were very poor. For the most part, they were trails cut through the wilderness, connecting the East with the frontier.

President Jefferson wanted to unite the East with the West by means of good roads. At the same time, Eastern merchants, eager to get as much of the Western trade as possible, demanded a way to transport the goods. The Western settlers also wanted good roads. Those who had settled away from the navigable rivers were especially desirous of good roads. The farmers throughout the West realized that easier communication with the East would give them more and better markets for their products.

The Work Begins

Jefferson's party, which controlled Congress, had always believed that the powers of the national government were strictly limited. Since there was no provision in the Constitution for road building, it was unclear if Congress had the power to do this. At first, Congress did not care to set aside national funds for that purpose. However, after much discussion, Congress finally voted to fund the National Road. Construction began.

The National Road was the first road in our nation built with funds from the national government. The road followed the

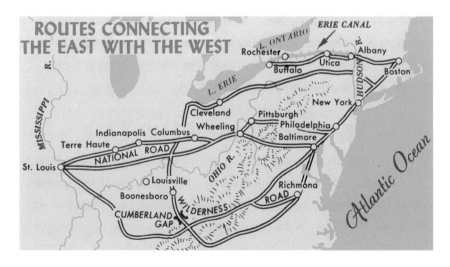

ROUTES CONNECTING THE EAST WITH THE WEST

trail from western Maryland to Wheeling, West Virginia. From there, the road went west through Columbus, Ohio, and then on to Indianapolis, Indiana. Though Congress voted funds to continue the construction of the road after the War of 1812, the project was never entirely completed. In time, however, the road was built to central Illinois, where it connected with St. Louis. Today, the national highway is known as U.S. 40.

The great National Road, sometimes called the Cumberland Road, made travel to the West much easier and safer. Lodges or inns were built along the way where travelers could find food and shelter. Many towns sprang up along the road. A large number of people in Ohio settled in a zone extending a few miles north and south of the National Road.

The Steamboat

Robert Fulton of New York invented the first commercially successful steamboat in America. Using the steam engine improved by James Watt, Fulton saw the possibility of developing the steamboat. Robert Livingston, the American minister to France, gave him support and encouragement. Fulton finally succeeded in building a steamboat that he called the *Clermont*.

In 1807, the *Clermont* was launched in the Hudson River. It proved that steamboat navigation was practical. On its first trip on the river, the *Clermont*, or "Fulton's Folly" as scoffers called it, traveled from New York to Albany, a distance of 150 miles, in thirty-two hours. It made the return trip in thirty hours, which was an average of nearly 5 miles per hour both ways. As the strange craft chugged up the Hudson, belching smoke and live cinders from its tall smokestack, it frightened the people along the banks of the river. It was like a sea monster snorting and churning the water. Its two side-wheels splashed and creaked as it went along. With the current

The *Clermont* Making a Landing at Cornwall on the Hudson in 1810

and against the current, it overtook and passed the sailing ships on the river.

The experiment was a great triumph for Fulton. It started him on the road to success. It was a great step forward in navigation. It marked the beginning of steamboat transportation in America.

A Great Benefit to the West

Steamboats played a great role in the development of the West. They had a huge advantage over sailing ships because they did not need to wait for favorable winds. They could attack the river currents and could travel with greater speed and safety than the flatboats and rafts. Settlers were quick to notice the advantages of steamboat transportation over other methods.

Easterners who had feared to go west because of the poor methods of transportation, now eagerly journeyed on the western rivers. Trade between the outlying settlements and the important river towns increased dramatically because of the steamboat. Western expansion went forward. The frontier territory rapidly changed into a regular part of the United States. Travel became one of the main forms of vacation in our nation. In fact, there was far more traveling west of the Appalachian Mountains by steamboat than by land. Travel on the Mississippi was especially attractive.

The Erie Canal

The rapid expansion of the West aroused the interest of the eastern merchants. They wanted a share in the increasing western trade but found it difficult to solve the problem of transportation. The roads were inadequate to handle the increased traffic, and the toll rates were too high to make trading with the West profitable. To make matters worse, the high cost of transportation kept the West from sending its goods eastward. Most of the trade to and from the West never reached the eastern seaboard. It either passed by way of the Mississippi through New Orleans in the South or by way of the St. Lawrence River through the Canadian cities in the North. Water travel was so much cheaper and easier than overland transportation that most of the trade followed the rivers.

When De Witt Clinton became governor of New York, he suggested the development of a waterway between the Hudson River and Lake Erie. He offered such powerful arguments in favor of a canal between these two points that the state voted funds for its construction.

Work on the Erie Canal began in 1817. Eight years later, in 1825, the canal was opened to traffic. "Clinton's Ditch," as the people called the canal, was three hundred sixty-three miles long and forty feet wide. The canal follows the Mohawk Valley, one of the original gateways to the West. The canal connects the Great Lakes with the Atlantic Ocean. As a symbol of the joining of these two bodies of water, Governor Clinton, at the celebration opening the waterway poured a keg of Lake Erie water into the harbor of New York.

The Erie Canal was an immediate success. It not only became the most important route to the West, but it also helped to develop the territory all along the way. The cost of transportation between the East and the West was cut in half. The travel time dropped from twenty days to eight days. Western farmers began to send their goods directly to New York City. The Erie Canal became the main trade route from the West. As a result, thousands of Eastern farmers now moved to the more fertile lands of the West.

Spot Check

1. What country owned East Florida and claimed West Florida?
2. What was the constitutional difficulty about the building of roads?
3. How was the National Road "a first"?
4. Who invented the first successful steamboat? What was its name?
5. Why did steamboats play such a big part in developing the West?
6. What important bodies of water did the Erie Canal connect?

CHAPTER REVIEW

1. Who was Daniel Boone?
2. From which states, for the most part, did the early settlers of Kentucky and Tennessee come?
3. When was the Northwest Ordinance passed?
4. Name the five states that came from the Northwest Territory.
5. Who was Tecumseh and what did he try to do?
6. Why did the United States want to buy New Orleans from France?
7. Why was France willing to sell Louisiana to the United States?
8. Why was President Jefferson faced with a difficult problem as a result of the Louisiana Purchase?
9. What was the purpose of the Lewis and Clark Expedition?
10. Of what help to the Lewis and Clark Expedition was Sacagawea?
11. How far west did the National Road extend when construction finally stopped?
12. What advantages did steamboats have over earlier means of transportation?
13. What was Governor Clinton's purpose in building the Erie Canal?
14. Which two bodies of water did the canal connect?

OUR NATION AND CHURCH AT THE BEGINNING OF THE NINETEENTH CENTURY

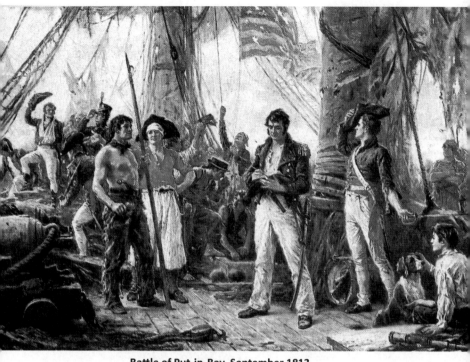

Battle of Put-in-Bay, September 1813

WAR WITH THE BARBARY STATES

Putting an End to Piracy

Pirate attacks on merchant ships in the Mediterranean Sea had been common for many years. For years, the Barbary States of Tripoli, Algiers, Tunis, and Morocco, located on the north coast of Africa, raided European and American merchant ships. To protect their ships from pirates, European nations paid high **tribute**, or money for protection, to these Barbary criminals. Before Jefferson became president, the U.S. government had paid huge sums of protection money to these pirate thugs. Every few years, the greedy pirates increased their demands. More and more, America became unwilling to pay the money.

When Tripoli demanded an increase in tribute from our country. Jefferson knew his duty as president was to defend America. He answered the demand by creating a Mediterranean fleet to protect U.S. shipping interests. As a result, Tripoli declared war on the United States. In 1804, Jefferson sent American ships to blockade Tripoli. A small group of brave marines landed and managed to seize the fort of Derna. This daring attack and the continuing blockade were so successful that the pirates asked for peace. The Barbary States stopped their attacks, not only upon our shipping, but also upon the commerce of the European countries. This victory made the Mediterranean Sea lanes safe and won for us the respect of the other nations of the world.

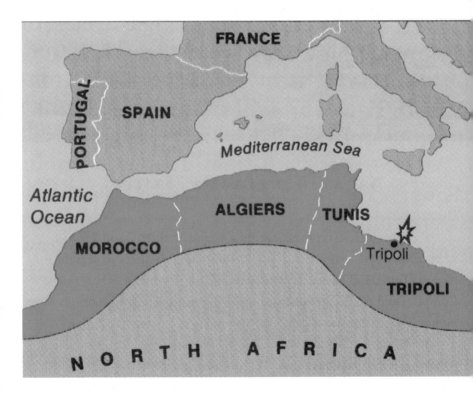

Drifting toward War with England

Interference with American Trade

The long war between England and France had been of great financial benefit to our country. Besides forcing Napoleon to sell Louisiana, the war had created a large demand for American goods. While the European nations were fighting, they were not able to produce enough supplies for themselves. Thus, the United States built up a thriving export trade. New England, in particular, with its commercial and shipbuilding industries, became very wealthy.

On the other hand, during the Napoleonic wars, both England and France interfered with American commerce. In their efforts to defeat each other, they seized American cargoes, captured American ships, and denied to American commerce the freedom of the seas. Both countries issued decrees against American shipping. England forbade neutral ships to trade with French ports. France retaliated by forbidding neutral ships to trade with England. Both countries claimed the right to seize American ships to enforce their orders. England even stationed warships off the coast of the United States to prevent American ships from trading with France. These warships actually seized American ships sailing for France. After the crushing defeat of the French fleet by the English at the Battle of Trafalgar, the French were unable to interfere much more.

Since England had the strongest navy, America had most of its problems with her. England felt perfectly justified in taking these measures. It was locked in a deadly war with Napoleon who had conquered most of Europe and plunged the world into two decades of war. England believed that it was fighting not only for its own survival but also for the survival of the United States. All that stood between America and Napoleon was the British Navy. They could not allow anyone to trade with Napoleon.

Not being able to trade with Europe caused American merchants to lose a great deal of money. However, it did not stop those merchants from sending ships to Europe. The profits were so great that they were willing to risk the loss of a ship rather than give up trade with Europe. However, they did demand that President Jefferson do something to protect their ships.

The Embargo Act

Though Jefferson protested strongly and often, both England and France ignored him. When he found that his protests carried no weight, he persuaded Congress to pass the Embargo Act. This act forbade American vessels to set sail for any foreign port and closed our harbors to English and French ships. Jefferson hoped to bring both nations to terms by depriving them of American goods and thereby avoid war.

However, the embargo had the opposite effect. It did more harm to the American merchants than it did to the French and English. The only American merchants who prospered during the embargo were those who violated the law and defied the authority of our government. The president was helpless. The navy was too small to enforce the embargo. There were not enough vessels to patrol the entire coast.

The people of New England did not want the embargo at all and were the most resistant to it. They suffered the most under it. Merchants endured tremendous losses in business income. Laborers were without work. Thousands of seamen were idle. The shipbuilding yards were closed down. The farmers were almost ruined. Meanwhile, the effect of the embargo on England and France was slight compared with its effect on America. The embargo almost destroyed New England's commerce. The people of New England resented Jefferson and his party for years.

At the end of Jefferson's term in office, Congress repealed the Embargo Act, Congress replaced it with the Nonintercourse Act. This act forbade trade with England and France only. However, the situation did not really change since most of U.S. foreign trade was with these two nations. Once out of port, American ships went and traded where they pleased. The new act did not prevent ships from sailing for France and England.

American Seamen are Impressed

During the war with France, England had trouble finding enough sailors to man her warships. The sailors in the English navy were poorly paid, poorly fed, and, often, poorly treated. Conditions on American ships were much better. The wages were higher, there was plenty of food, and the treatment of the men was better. All this was an attraction for English sailors. As a result, many deserted their ships to work on American ships.

The British were in a serious situation. Without their navy, England would be invaded by Napoleon. The British realized that their ships were alarmingly undermanned, so they resorted to forcing men into their navy. This was something that the British had always done, but in their desperation, they took it to a new level. Besides seizing old sailors whom they found in English ports, they went aboard American vessels. They boarded American ships on the high seas to take off sailors who were British by birth. This practice was called impressment. Often, native-born Americans were seized and forced to serve in the English navy.

England went so far as to assume the right to search an American warship. The *Leopard*, a British ship, hailed the American warship, the *Chesapeake*, off the Atlantic coast. When the American commander refused to permit a search, the *Leopard* attacked the *Chesapeake* and forced her to yield. Four men were taken off the ship.

The *Leopard* attacks the *Chesapeake*.

Three of them were Americans. The American people demanded action. They wanted American ships protected and England punished. Jefferson realized that he had little to gain and much to lose by going to war. Instead, he ordered all British ships out of American waters.

Madison and the "War Hawks"

In 1809, James Madison became the fourth president of the United States. The situation he faced was just as bad as it had been under Jefferson. Although President Madison did all he could to keep the United States out of war, the "War Hawks," as the leaders of the war party were called, loudly demanded war against England. They blamed the English for the Indian uprisings and massacres that had occurred in the West. They criticized the poor state to which the army and navy had fallen during Jefferson's term. They were angry because the United States had no Navy and no adequately trained young officers. In all, the country had about a dozen good ships. Most of the officers were veterans of the War of Independence.

The South and the West were clamoring for war because they wanted to avenge the insults given to our country. However, New England did not want a war. The shipping trade built up by New England was paying good money. Hence, New Englanders opposed a war. They did not want their European trade destroyed. They did much to prevent the declaration of war, but to no avail.

News of the Battle of Tippecanoe and the charges that the English fur traders had provided the Indians with weapons and supplies aroused the Westerners' demand for war with England. In Congress, two young men, Henry Clay of Kentucky and John C. Calhoun of

John C. Calhoun   Henry Clay

South Carolina voiced the demand of the South and West for war with England so forcefully that they were nicknamed the "War Hawks" by their opponents. They also won a large following in Congress.

Spot Check

1. How were the Napoleonic Wars beneficial to the United States?
2. How were the same wars harmful to the United States?
3. Why did Jefferson persuade Congress to pass the Embargo Act?
4. Why did the Embargo Act not work?
5. Why did England press American seamen into its navy?
6. Who were the "War Hawks"? Whose sentiments did they represent?

THE WAR OF 1812

The Second War with England

The influence of the "War Hawks" and their followers was so strong that Madison could no longer delay war. Despite a weak army and a poor navy, the president sent a message to Congress asking for a declaration of war. On June 18, 1812, war was declared on England.

Feelings ran high against war, both in this country and in England. The New England merchants did not want war. They were reaping the benefits of a prosperous trade with the countries abroad. After war was declared, they actually refused to support it. There was even talk of seceding from the Union. England did not want war with the United States. She was in the middle of a desperate struggle with France. She needed trade with our country to meet the rising costs of war. In fact, two days before Congress declared war on England, the English decided to repeal their offensive navigation orders. Sadly, there was no way to send the news quickly to the United States. If modern communications had been available in 1812, there likely would have been no war.

The Invasion of Canada

England was too occupied in her desperate war with Napoleon to send a large army to America. Also, the United States knew its tiny navy was no match for England's navy, then the largest and finest in the world. Thus, the United States decided to invade Canada. Members of the "War Party" in Congress believed that the Canadians would welcome the invasion as an opportunity for them to gain independence. However, Americans again misjudged the feelings of the people of Canada. Many Canadians were loyalists who had sought refuge in Canada during the American War of Independence. The Canadians did not want independence. They were satisfied with English rule.

From the beginning, the Canadian invasion was a failure. The American generals argued among themselves and did not cooperate. The New England states and New York refused to let their militias leave their own borders. The invasion was finally abandoned. Our western frontier remained in the hands of England until American naval victories forced them to leave the region. After the failure to invade Canada, the American land forces made no more attempts to wage an offensive campaign. For the rest of the war, they took a defensive position.

American Sea Victories

England had the largest and the best navy in the world. "Britannia rule the waves" was her proud boast. The American fleet was small and poor. Realizing that it would be foolish to meet the British navy in pitched battle, the United States sent its ships out in ones and twos. In the face of the odds, it was the only safe strategy to use. Whenever the American ships saw a large English squadron, the American ships hoisted full sail and escaped. When only two or three English ships appeared, they fought. Additionally,

President Madison had commissioned hundreds of merchant ships as privateers. This meant that private American ships were authorized by the government to attack English shipping. This was a great help to our navy. The privateers inflicted heavy losses on British merchants by seizing their ships and cargoes.

The most famous American ship of the War of 1812 was the USS *Constitution*. It won three important major battles and several minor ones. In fact, it was never defeated in battle. Though made of wood, as were all ships of the period, it was affectionately nicknamed "Old Ironsides," after a battle in which cannon balls bounced off its hull, as though they were made of iron. Today the *Constitution*, or "Old Ironsides," is a national monument permanently anchored in Boston harbor. It rests there in proud witness to the humble but gallant beginnings of the United States Navy.

USS *Constitution* fighting the British warship *Guerriere*.

American Lake Victories

The ocean was not the only scene of great naval battles. Other battles were fought on the Great Lakes and on Lake Champlain. The most important of these battles was a naval victory on Lake Erie. Under the command of Oliver Hazard Perry, a young man with remarkable naval skill, the American ships drove the British from Lake Erie and removed the danger of a British invasion of the Northwest.

Perry's victory was a remarkable feat. Perry and his men had hurriedly built the American fleet. He named his flagship *The Lawrence* in honor of the brave commander of the *Chesapeake*, who had lost his life in an ill-fated battle with the British. The blue banner fluttering from the masthead of his ship bore Lawrence's last words, "Don't give up the ship." These valiant words have become the motto of the United States Navy. With courage that matched the words of his banner, Perry forced the surrender of the entire British fleet.

However, the Battle of Lake Erie was not the end of the lake battles. The British still controlled Lake Champlain. From there they had threatened New York since the beginning of the war. Under the command of Captain Thomas MacDonough, the American fleet engaged the English near Plattsburgh and defeated them. The Battle of Plattsburgh, also known as the Battle of Lake Champlain, cleared the lake of enemy ships. It forced the British to retreat to Canada.

Captain Thomas MacDonough

The English Attack Our Coast

Although our Navy had done a brilliant job and won some small victories, England still controlled the seas. During the early part of the war, she was too busy fighting for her life against Napoleon to give much attention to the war against the United States. However, the defeat of Napoleon in the spring of 1814 allowed England to throw her full strength against the United States.

England sent a fleet carrying an English army to Chesapeake Bay. The soldiers landed and marched toward Washington. They easily defeated the poorly trained American forces that opposed them. Alarmed by the news of the British advance, President Madison and his wife, together with the government officials, abandoned Washington to avoid capture. They took what valuables they could as they fled. The English army set fire to the Capitol and the White House. Both buildings were burned and priceless records were destroyed.

After burning Washington, the English marched on Baltimore. However, this time the going was not so easy. Baltimore offered such a strong resistance that the British gave up their attack. During the bombardment of Fort McHenry, which guarded the city, a young American, Francis Scott Key, was detained on a British ship off the

"...the flag was still there."

coast. The firing on the American fort lasted all night. At dawn, the

214

first streaks of light showed that the American flag was still flying over the fort. Francis Scott Key felt such great joy at seeing his country's flag waving after that terrible siege that he wrote "The Star-Spangled Banner." In 1931, it became our national anthem.

The Battle of New Orleans

After the siege of Fort McHenry, General Pakenham led a British army against New Orleans. It was the largest and finest British army assembled in America during the War of 1812. It was composed of veteran soldiers who had fought in the Napoleonic wars.

General Andrew Jackson of Tennessee was in charge of the defense of New Orleans. He had quickly gathered an army of about four thousand frontiersmen from Kentucky and Tennessee. With great skill, he threw up strong defenses and awaited the British attack. From the banks of the river to the swamps beyond, he built defenses of cotton bales and cypress logs. Behind these, in the first firing line, he placed his best riflemen. Their deadly fire drove the British back and completely routed them. In the defeat, the British dead and wounded were more than two thousand men, including their general, who was killed. The American casualties were only about seventy men. The Battle of New Orleans was the greatest American land victory during the war. It made Andrew Jackson a national hero.

The night before the Battle of New Orleans, the wives, mothers, and sisters of Jackson's men had gathered in the Ursuline convent chapel in the city to pray before the statue of Our Lady of Prompt Succor. Afraid that the city would be invaded and the soldiers killed, the women prayed throughout the night. The next day, Jackson decisively defeated a British force much larger than his own force. The Mother Superior of the convent made a vow that if the Americans won, a Mass of Thanksgiving would be said every year thereafter. This Mass is still said today. It has been said every year since 1815. The Convent chapel with the statue still exists and is a shrine to Our Lady of Prompt Succor. Following the battle, the Vatican decreed Our Lady of Prompt Succor to be the patroness of the City of New Orleans and the state of Louisiana.

The End of the War

The victory at New Orleans had a sad note. The battle was fought two weeks after peace between the warring nations had been made. On Christmas Eve, 1814, a treaty of peace had been signed by representatives of the United States and Great Britain at Ghent in Belgium. However, news of the treaty did not reach the United States until February. Some days later, the United States Senate ratified the treaty. Peace between the two countries was re-established.

The Treaty of Ghent provided for the return of all land taken by either nation during the war. The settlement of the northeastern boundary between Canada and the United States was referred to a commission. The issue of impressment was set aside without mention. A close relationship between countries destined to be great allies began.

Spot Check

1. Why was New England opposed to the War of 1812?
2. Why did the United States decide to invade Canada at the beginning of the War of 1812?
3. Why was the invasion of Canada a failure?
4. Why is the ship, USS *Constitution*, remembered in history?
5. Who was Oliver Hazard Perry?
6. What is the motto of the United States Navy? What is its origin?
7. What change in Europe allowed England to send a large force to invade the United States?
8. What is the national anthem of the United States? What is its origin?

THE RESULTS OF THE WAR OF 1812

Respect for the Young Republic

In terms of what the War of 1812 had been about, the war had really settled nothing. The impressment of seamen had been the major point of dispute, but it was not even mentioned in the treaty. The war cost the United States in both money and lost life. Yet, many Americans felt as though national pride had been established. The United States had stood up to the English and shown that it was truly independent.

The gallant stand of our country against England earned the respect of all of Europe. The victories of the small but growing United States Navy over the British fleet, and Jackson's miraculous victory at New Orleans, gained us the respect of Europe. More than anything else, victory gave the United States a true place among the nations of the world. It convinced them that our country would fight to protect her freedom and her claims, even against the most powerful nation on earth.

Though many had objected to the War of 1812, after the war, the nation came together. Many Americans began to think more in terms of the nation and worked for the national interests. The ten years following the war were marked by the lack of political strife. For the first and only time in American history, there was only one major national party. Also, there was little disagreement over the proper conduct of the government. This was in marked contrast to the period before and during the war. New Englanders had been known for their lack of national spirit. They were more interested in the government protecting American shipping than they were in the good of the Union. New England merchants actually blamed the government for their losses during the war and demanded that the war be stopped.

The Federalists had not only opposed the war when the president issued the call to arms, they also had refused to help. Feeling was so strong that the Federalist Party called a convention at Hartford, Connecticut, to protest the continuation of the war. The convention met in Hartford on December 15, 1814. The delegates declared that the war was ruinous. They demanded that the government make peace. They even advocated secession from the Union. However, this meeting was the death knell of the Federalist Party. Peace was declared before the Hartford Convention presented their resolutions to Congress. The Federalists were accused of being unpatriotic. They never attained national power again. In fact, the convention never reconvened.

The Hartford Convention had raised the idea of secession. A question remained: did the states have the right to leave the Union? The answer was fifty years away. Sadly, almost half a million Americans would die before there was an answer.

The "Era of Good Feeling"

In the election of 1816, many people who had supported the Federalists joined with the Democratic-Republicans. They elected James Monroe as the fifth President of the United States by a large majority.

Monroe's election was the climax of a long career as a public servant. In his teens, he had left college to answer Washington's call to arms in the War of Independence. From that time on, he was devoted to the service of his country. He served Virginia, his native state, as legislator and as governor. He served the national government as a member of Congress, as a foreign diplomat, and as secretary of state. He was known for his good judgment. His good judgment served him well as president. He surrounded himself with Cabinet members of unusual ability.

As president, James Monroe kept the country free from political strife. He became one of history's most popular leaders. His administration of two terms (1817-1825) is usually referred to as the "era of good feeling." This was because of the general prosperity in the land and the absence of rival political parties.

The Monroe Doctrine

After the War of 1812, the United States adopted an important policy known as the Monroe Doctrine. In his annual message to Congress, President Monroe clearly stated that the United States did not want any European nation to increase its territory in America. This meant North, Central, and South America. This warning was issued because it was known that Russia had plans for America's western coast. Also, France was thinking of taking over Texas, which at that time was a part of Mexico. There were also reliable rumors that some of the nations of Europe were thinking about helping Spain re-establish its rule over its former Latin American colonies. These colonies had declared their independence from Spain.

James Monroe at the end of his Presidency

To clarify the position of the United States, President Monroe outlined America's policy in what became known as the Monroe Doctrine. This policy was set forth in three critical points. First, the American continents were no longer open to added colonization by European nations. Second, the United States would consider an attempt to interfere with the political affairs of the republics in the Americas as an unfriendly act. Last, the United States would not interfere with European affairs or with European colonies that already existed in the Western Hemisphere.

As a result of the Monroe Doctrine, the United States has frequently been called upon to settle disputes between European nations and Central or South American countries. This doctrine has shielded many countries of the Western Hemisphere from European intrusion.

Spot Check

1. Why did the War of 1812 result in a new European respect for the United States?
2. Why were the years of James Madison's presidency known as the "Era of Good Feeling"?
3. List James Monroe's qualifications for being president.
4. Why did President Monroe issue the Monroe Doctrine?
5. Give the three provisions of the Monroe Doctrine.

THE EXPANSION OF THE CHURCH

Baltimore Becomes an Archdiocese

As the new nation grew, so did the Church. In 1789, the year that Washington became president, Father John Carroll was appointed Bishop of Baltimore. It was not long before the tiny "mustard seed" that was the diocese of Baltimore had grown beyond the care and management of Bishop Carroll. Therefore, in 1808, Pope Pius VII (1800-1823) made Baltimore the first metropolitan See in the United States. The pope made Bishop Carroll an archbishop.

The year 1808 saw the creation of four new dioceses in the United States. New York, Philadelphia, Boston, and Bardstown all became dioceses. Bardstown, Kentucky, was the first diocese created in the new states west of the Appalachian Mountains.

After the Louisiana Purchase, the diocese of New Orleans also became part of the province of Baltimore. The diocese of New Orleans had been established in 1793. In the following years, other dioceses were created to meet the advance of the Faith in the various areas of our country. At the time these new dioceses were formed, our country was a huge mission field. Even the bishops were called upon to perform missionary service. Wherever missionaries were located, they were doing pioneer work. The lack of priests and the steady influx of immigrants increased the missionaries' burdens.

Colleges and Academies

With the growth of the Church after the War of Independence, there was an awakened interest in education. Nuns established several schools for girls at this time. While the bishops were as concerned about education for girls as boys, they had a special concern with the education of Catholic boys. They needed priests to administer the sacraments and carry on the work of the missions.

From the beginning, Bishop Carroll was involved in education. As early as 1786, he proposed the founding of a Catholic institution for educating and preparing young men for the priesthood. To meet these needs, Georgetown College was established in 1789, in what is now Washington, D. C. It was the first Catholic college in the United States. It became the center of Jesuit education. It remains one of the major Catholic universities in the country.

In 1799, St. Mary's College in Baltimore was established in connection with the seminary there. The Sulpicians pioneered in this work. The college served the people of Maryland until it closed in 1852.

In 1818, the Jesuits took over St. Louis Latin Academy in St. Louis, Missouri. This school later became St. Louis University. It is the oldest university west of the Mississippi River.

Georgetown University

Meanwhile, new centers of Catholic education were developed in the East and beyond the Alleghenies. The seed planted by Bishop Carroll soon bore fruit in New York, Pennsylvania, Virginia, Kentucky, and Missouri. Though all of the schools did not survive, they served their purpose in each locality.

Seminaries

Lack of priests has always been a great handicap to the work of the Church in our country. The clergy and bishops were well aware of the need for more priests if the Kingdom of God was to grow in this missionary territory. At first, they relied on help from Europe. However, later they began to promote an American clergy.

During this early period, four seminaries were established. Remarkably, they all still exist today. Two are located in Maryland: St. Mary's in Baltimore and Mount St. Mary's in Emmitsburg. Another St. Mary's was founded in Missouri. It later became known as Kenrick Seminary in St. Louis. The fourth is the Athenaeum, which later became known as Mount St. Mary's Seminary of the West. It is located in Cincinnati, Ohio.

St. Mary's in Baltimore was founded in 1791. Four Sulpician Fathers from France and five students who had accompanied them made up the faculty and the enrollment of this mother seminary in the United States. The Sulpicians also founded Mount St. Mary's in Emmitsburg. They founded it in 1808. It was established as a seminary but later was changed into a college. It was open to both clerical and lay students. St. Mary's in St. Louis was founded by the saintly Felix de Andreis. St. Mary's accommodated both laity and seminarians. Bishop Fenwick established the Athenaeum in Cincinnati in May of 1829. This seminary served the needs of Ohio, Illinois, Michigan, Kentucky, and Tennessee.

Father Demetrius Gallitzin (1770-1840)

One of the most fascinating stories of the Catholic Church in early America is that of Father Demetrius Augustine Gallitzin. Demetrius was born on December 22, 1770, at The Hague in the Netherlands. His father was Prince Dmitri Gallitzin, a member of one of the wealthiest and most famous families of Imperial Russia. His mother was Countess Amalie, the daughter of a Prussian Field Marshal. Demetrius was baptized in the Russian Orthodox Church. However, his father did not practice his faith and his mother was a fallen-away Roman Catholic. Thus, Demetrius grew up in a family that cared little about religion.

In 1786, his mother returned to the Catholic Church, and Demetrius joined her. Even though his father was not a practicing Russian Orthodox Christian, he and his relatives were not pleased with his son's choice of religion. This would eventually have grave consequences for Demetrius.

The custom of the time was for young aristocrats to travel abroad to further their education. Therefore, his parents sent

Demetrius to America. In October 1792, he arrived in Baltimore with a letter of introduction to many of the leading men of America, including Bishop John Carroll. Apparently his meeting with Bishop Carroll awakened a calling in the young man. To the great dismay of his father, he decided to enter the priesthood. Moreover, he was willing to give up his inheritance in order to become a priest. Fr. Gallitzin was ordained in 1795. He had the distinction of being the first man to receive all the degrees of Holy Orders while in the United States. Other men had received the earlier parts in another country.

Father Gallitzin was first assigned to missionary activities in Baltimore. However, later his ministry extended from Maryland to southern Pennsylvania and northern Virginia. It was during this period that Father Gallitzin had the idea of establishing Catholic settlements. With the permission of Bishop Carroll, he purchased large tracts of land in what is now Cambria County, Pennsylvania. He named the village Loretto. With his own money, he built gristmills and other means of production for the community. He also built a church that he named in honor of St. Michael the Archangel. He provided parcels of land to settlers for little or no cost to them. Thus many Catholics were attracted to Loretto, Pennsylvania.

In 1802, Fr. Gallitzin became a naturalized citizen of the United States. After his father's death in 1808, the government of Russia prevented him from claiming his rightful inheritance because he was a Catholic priest. He was, for all practical purposes, bankrupt. In 1827, to remedy Father Gallitzin's situation, Bishop Carroll approved a public appeal for funds to pay off the generous priest's debts.

In 1827, Father Gallitzin was made vicar-general of Western Pennsylvania. Though he was also offered the Sees of Cincinnati and

The interior of St. Michael's Basilica in Loretto, Pennsylvania

Detroit, he refused. He felt he could do more good where he was. Throughout his life, Loretto was a flourishing mission and a growing Catholic population center. He remained in Loretto until his death in 1840. He was buried by St. Michael's church, which he had founded.

In 1899, the one-hundredth anniversary of the founding of the Loretto mission, Charles Schwab the steel magnate funded the construction of a large stone church in Loretto. Fr. Gallitzin's remains were moved to a beautiful tomb in the church that was named St. Michael the Archangel in honor of the first church he had built. On September 9, 1996, Pope John Paul II declared the church to be a basilica. On June 6, 2005, the Holy See announced that Fr.

Gallitzin had been named a Servant of God, the first step in the canonization process.

St. Elizabeth Ann Seton (1774-1821)

Elizabeth Ann Seton founded the second religious community for women in this country: The Sisters of Charity of St. Joseph. She was born Elizabeth Bayley in New York in 1774. Her family were wealthy Protestants. In 1794, she married William Seton who was from a wealthy Protestant family. They had five children. Sadly, William lost his fortune and his health. The family went to Italy in the hopes that the climate would cure his illness. Sadly, it did not. He died in 1803 in Italy. However, while living with a Catholic family in Italy, Elizabeth became attracted to the Faith. In 1805, after her return to the United States, she became a Catholic.

Elizabeth's conversion caused her Protestant family and friends to abandon her. It left her in financial difficulties. In 1808, at the invitation of a priest, Elizabeth Ann Seton and three other women opened a Catholic school for girls in Baltimore. As the women wished to devote themselves more completely to God, they formed a religious community. Since Elizabeth was superior of the religious community of women, she came to be known as Mother Seton. In 1812, the community came to be known as the Sisters of Charity. The order spread rapidly. The sisters established orphanages and hospitals. However, they gained their renown for their devotion to the growing Catholic school system in the United States. Mother Seton died in 1821. At the time, her community numbered some twenty groups spread across the United States. Pope Paul VI canonized her in 1975. She is the first native-born American citizen to be canonized. She is a patron saint of Catholic schools, especially in the United States. There are several Catholic churches, schools, and even one home study school named in her honor.

St. Rose Duchesne (1769-1852)

St. Rose Phillippine Duchesne was born in Grenoble, France. She had been a Visitation nun, but after the French Revolution suppressed the Order, she joined Mother Madeleine Sophie Barat's Society of the Sacred Heart. In 1818, Rose came to New Orleans to work in the American missions. She founded her main mission at St. Charles, Missouri (the site of her shrine). Six additional missions followed which included schools and orphanages. She had a special concern for Native Americans. She devoted much of her work to their care and education. At the age of 72, she began a school for Indians, who soon came to call her "the woman who prays always." She had great courage in frontier conditions and was single-minded in her dream of serving Native Americans. During her lifetime, Pope Leo XII made note of her accomplishments and blessed her work. Pope John Paul II canonized her in 1988.

St. Mother Theodore Guérin (1798-1856)

Anne-Thérèse Guérin was born in France in 1798. At the time of her birth, the French Revolution was trying to destroy the Catholic Church in France. The government was closing schools and churches. Consequently, her mother home schooled Anne-Thérèse. At the age of ten, she felt called to a vocation. She wanted to enter a religious community when she was fifteen, but could not because she had to care for her sister and her sick mother. In 1823, she was finally able to join the Sisters of Providence. In 1825, after two years of training, she took her final vows and took the name Sister St. Theodore. She spent her next years teaching and caring for the sick and the poor.

In 1839, the Bishop of Vincennes, Indiana, sent a priest to France to find a religious order that could come to his diocese to teach and to assist with the poor. The bishop knew how valuable such an order could be. He had worked with St. Elizabeth Ann Seton and her Sisters of Charity. In October 1840, Sister Theodore and five other nuns arrived in Vincennes. As head of the new mission, she would be called "Mother."

Mother Theodore and her sisters immediately began their missionary activities. From 1840 to 1855, she and her nuns opened several parish schools in Indiana. In 1841, they established a boarding school for girls. This school later became St. Mary-of-the-Woods College. She also established two orphanages in Vincennes. Pope Benedict XVI canonized her in 2006.

Spot Check

1. Name the first Catholic college in the U.S. When was it started?
2. Name the oldest university west of the Mississippi River. When was it founded?
3. Who was Demetrius Gallitzin? What distinguished him from other priests in the United States?
4. Give two reasons why Elizabeth Ann Seton is remembered.
5. Who was Rose Philippine Duchesne?
6. Who was St. Mother Theodore Guérin?

CHAPTER REVIEW

1. Give the names of the Barbary States.
2. Why did the United States pay a tribute to the Barbary pirates?
3. How did the Napoleonic wars affect our commerce?
4. How did the Embargo Act differ from the Nonintercourse Act?
5. What were the chief causes of the War of 1812?
6. Why were New Englanders opposed to the War of 1812?
7. What is another name for the United States ship USS *Constitution*?
8. Who was Oliver Hazard Perry?
9. What effect did opposition to the war have?
10. When did Father Carroll become bishop of Baltimore?
11. Name the first five dioceses in the United States.
12. Name three women involved in the early teaching sisterhoods.

THE AGE OF ANDREW JACKSON

Battle of New Orleans. General Andrew Jackson stands on the parapet of his makeshift defenses as his troops repulse the attacking British. Following the War of 1812, Andrew Jackson was the most popular man in America.

THE RISE OF THE COMMON MAN

Sectional Rivalry

As we have seen, geography played an important part in the attitude of the people toward political questions. During the decade 1820 to 1830, strong sectional differences arose among the East, the South, and the West. The East was industrial in its outlook. It favored a protective tariff, a strong banking system, cheap labor, government road building, and a better market for its products. The South opposed a protective tariff because it was harmful to its

229

people. The South wanted the expansion of slavery, cheap western lands, and cheap manufactured goods. The West was agricultural. It wanted cheap land, cheap goods, and good transportation. It opposed the National Bank. It favored state banks because it felt that the National Bank put too much power into the hands of the East.

The Right to Vote is Extended

Up to this time, not all white male citizens had the right to vote. A number of states required both property and religious qualifications of voters and office holders. The "common man" could neither vote nor hold office.

However, west of the Appalachian Mountains, it was a different story. As each new state in the West was organized, the right to vote was given to every free male citizen as soon as he became twenty-one. News of these privileges aroused the class of non-property-owners in the East. They demanded a voice in the government. Under this pressure, religious and property qualifications were slowly removed. By 1828, only five of the original states had such qualifications for voting or holding office. It was a victory for the common people. The "common man" was given an equal footing with his fellow citizens.

At the same time that voting rights were being extended, a change was taking place in the way that presidential electors were chosen. The Constitution gives each state legislature the right to determine the method of choosing electors. At first, the legislatures themselves chose the electors. However, by 1828, in all but two states, the electors were chosen by popular vote.

The Election of 1824

The presidential election of 1824 created new alignments. It was as much a contest between political parties as a conflict between geographical sections. It involved the East, the South, and the West.

New England supported the unpopular but efficient statesman, John Quincy Adams of Massachusetts, son of the second president. The South gave its support to William H. Crawford of Georgia. The West had two candidates. Henry Clay, the brilliant orator and famed speaker of the House, was the favorite of Kentucky. General Andrew Jackson, "Old Hickory," was the proud choice of Tennessee. He was perhaps the most popular man in the country because he was the hero of the Battle of New Orleans.

John Quincy Adams

Election Thrown into the House

When the electoral votes were counted, Jackson had received the highest number. Adams, Crawford, and Clay ranked second, third, and fourth. However, no candidate had received a majority. Therefore, in accordance with the Constitution, the election went into the House of Representatives. There, the candidates who had received the three highest totals were put to a vote. Clay, as the fourth candidate was out of the race. However, he was Speaker of the House and had much influence over the other members. He gave his support to Adams. As a result of his influence, Adams was elected the sixth president of the United States.

Jackson and his supporters were very bitter at the outcome of the election. This resentment was heightened when Adams made Clay his Secretary of State. Jackson and his followers accused Adams and Clay of corrupt politics. They maintained that Jackson, who had received the highest number of both electoral and popular votes, was entitled to the House election. The accusations hurled against Adams and Clay seemed to be without foundation. Nevertheless, Jackson's supporters in Congress were strong enough to kill almost all legislation that the Adams administration proposed.

Jackson left Washington to return to Tennessee. He stopped at every city along the way to accuse Adams and his followers of disregarding the will of the people. He accused the whole system of being undemocratic and unjust. For the next four years, Jackson encouraged his supporters to campaign for him. The campaign was so successful that, four years later, Jackson was swept into office as the defender of democracy. The Democratic Party was formed around the personality of Andrew Jackson.

Spot Check

1. Who received the most votes in the election of 1824?
2. Was he elected president?
3. Why did John Quincy Adams win in the House of Representatives?
4. What did Adams do that made Jackson resentful of him?

ANDREW JACKSON AS PRESIDENT

The Election of 1828

Andrew Jackson was the first president to come from humble beginnings. The previous six men had all been from wealthy and "aristocratic" families. Jackson had been born to a poor family. His father had died before he was born and his mother died when he was a young boy. His was the story of a man who had "pulled himself up by his own bootstraps." He had risen from the lowest ranks of the common people. He had neither wealth nor family name behind him. The common people in this election had turned their government over to a bold frontiersman. He was the first self-made man to be president. Jackson had become famous as an Indian fighter. His great victory at New Orleans during the War of 1812 had made him a national hero. He was the idol of the West and the hope of the Eastern working man.

Andrew Jackson in 1833. Despite being the president, he chose to pose in his uniform.

The new president was a tall, lean Scots-Irishman. Though a battle-scarred frontiersman, he was dignified and striking in appearance. His white hair enhanced this dignity. A man of strong likes and dislikes, he was either passionately hated or intensely loved. His abrupt tongue and quick temper at times created bitter enemies. However, his warm sincerity and his love of the common people won the admiration of the masses.

Jackson stood out in sharp contrast to the men who had preceded him as president. All six past presidents had been reared and educated in Virginia or Massachusetts. These men represented culture and refinement of manners. Not so with Jackson. When he was inaugurated, the rough dress and crude manners of the "common folk" shocked the members of Washington society. Even Jefferson had commented before his death that he knew of no one less suited for the job of president than Andrew Jackson. Farmers and frontier people came to the White House to see "their" president take the oath of office. They upset punch bowls and stood with muddy boots on damask-covered chairs. Dignified Federalists were horrified at what they saw and heard. As they witnessed the inauguration, they were convinced that the government had been turned over to an uncouth mob. They viewed Jackson as a very dangerous man.

The Spoils System

After Jackson took office, he rewarded the most enthusiastic of his party workers with federal offices. To do this, he removed a large number of competent men and gave their jobs to men who had supported his election. During the first year, about eight hundred fifty men, or about one-tenth of the total number of office holders, were removed. During his two terms, about one-fifth of the offices changed hands.

This practice is known as the Spoils System. The name comes from the saying, "To the victors belong the spoils." The Spoils System did not originate with Jackson, though it has come to be connected with his name. It had been practiced in local and state politics for a long time. It was applied to national offices when Jefferson became president. Other presidents had appointed men that they trusted to support them. However, Jackson went much further than they had. He did not replace only a few high level people but many people at every level. He also fired people rather than waiting for vacancies in order to make room for his own supporters.

While Jackson never intended to injure America, the Spoils System harmed the public welfare. From Jackson's time until the Civil Service reform, more than fifty years later, every president accepted it as the basis for appointment to government office. Able and experienced workers would be replaced with inexperienced and often unqualified political supporters.

Spot Check
1. Why was Jackson already famous when he ran for president?
2. What was the Spoils system?
3. Why was the Spoils system detrimental to the public welfare?

JACKSON'S WESTERN POLICIES

The Removal of the Indians

Jackson was as harsh as he was firm in some of his policies. In support for the Westerners who wanted the frontier free of Indians, he resolved to remove all the Indians east of the Mississippi to a territory west of the Great River. (Remember "the West" at this time consisted of the lands between the Appalachians and the Mississippi River.) Naturally, the Indians objected. They had been granted the right to stay on the land by treaties with the United States government. They had a legal right to their lands.

When federal troops were sent to remove them, the Indians appealed in 1832 to the Supreme Court. The Court ruled that the treaties between the Indians and the government were valid. The Indians had a right to their eastern lands. However, Jackson refused to follow the Court's decision. He continued his policy of removal. By the end of his administration, only the Seminoles in Florida remained east of the Mississippi. Jackson's refusal to respect the decision of the Supreme Court was bitterly criticized by his political opponents. However, on the frontier, his Indian policy was very popular. In a sad moment in American history, government soldiers rounded up the Indians and forcibly moved them. There was little concern for the Indians' health or survival.

Some sixty thousand Indians were moved beyond the Mississippi. Of that number, perhaps some fifteen thousand Indian men, women, and children died in the forced journey west. The Catholic Church protested this intolerable treatment. The Church had been working to convert these Indians and defended their right to remain on their lands. Sadly, the Church was ignored.

This painting, from the Woolaroc Museum in Oklahoma, shows an idealized portrayal of the Indians forced march westward. The journey was known as the "Trail of Tears." In this painting, the Indians are shown with warm blankets and sturdy horses. The true picture is one of misery and death. The artist is attempting to show the dignity of the Native Americans as they endure the march.

Internal Improvements

There was an obvious need for better roads in the West. However, Jackson believed that road building and similar internal improvements were the function of the states and not of the national government. Yet, on this matter there was a sharp difference of opinion within Jackson's own party. Many members of Congress disagreed with this point of view. Time and again, Congress tried to pass bills authorizing the spending of national funds for internal improvements, but Jackson kept vetoing them.

Jackson vetoed all general bills for such internal improvements. He was victorious over the opposition group in his party. The practice of leaving the work of internal improvement in the hands of the states became an established policy of the Democrats. It remained so for many years.

Public Lands

When Jackson became president, he was faced with the demands of Westerners that the price of public lands be reduced. He sympathized with the Westerners but the people in the East opposed the policy. The East not only opposed the lowering of the price of the land but also proposed that its sale be limited.

The land dispute caused one of the greatest debates in American history. Senator Robert Hayne of South Carolina defended the position of the West. He denounced the East for selfish sectionalism. Hayne argued that the United States was merely a league of independent states. Moreover, if one section insisted on national legislation that harmed another section, the states that were harmed had the right to declare such legislation void.

Senator Daniel Webster of Massachusetts replied to Hayne in what is considered one of the finest speeches ever delivered in the U.S. Congress. First, Webster defended the East against the charge of being selfish. Then he denied that the Union is merely a compact of states. He strongly maintained that the Union was not of states but of people. He spoke of "the people's government, made for the people, made by the people, and answerable to the people." He said that the states had no right to annul laws passed by the national government, and that only the Supreme Court had that power.

The Eastern proposal to restrict land sales did not pass. The price of land was not lowered. The question of the western lands was not settled until after Jackson left office.

Spot Check
1. How many Indians were forcibly removed by Jackson's policy?
2. What did Westerners want Jackson to do about public lands?

JACKSON AND NULLIFICATION

The Tariff of Abominations

A short time before Jackson was elected to his first term as president, the industrialists in Congress demanded a higher tariff on imported manufactured goods.

The industrialists wanted to protect the goods manufactured in the United States from competition from Europe. The Southerners were very opposed to this tariff, but they realized that they were not strong enough alone to defeat the votes of the North. Hence, they joined with the farmers of the West and added duties on raw materials to the proposed tariff on manufactured goods. In this way, by including duties on the raw materials that manufacturers had to buy, the South and the West hoped that enough Northerners

Daniel Webster

and Easterners would vote against the tariff bill to defeat it. The bill passed anyway. The scheme of the South and the West had failed. However, the measure was hateful not only to the South; it was wholly unsatisfactory to everyone. Since it was such a bad and hated piece of legislation, it became known as the "Tariff of Abominations."

When Jackson became president, the controversy over the tariff was at its height. The people in the South were confident that Jackson would support their opposition to the tariff. They invited Jackson to be their guest at Thomas Jefferson's birthday dinner. In the after-dinner speeches, the general theme was protest to the tariff. These speeches stressed the idea that a state had the right to declare national laws null and void. Moreover, a state would be justified in seceding from the Union if Congress refused to change a law that violated the state's rights.

When the toastmaster presented the President of the United States, Jackson made this toast: "Our Federal Union: it must and shall be preserved." The president's toast made it unmistakably clear that the Union stood above the tariff. No state, whatever their grievance, would be allowed to nullify national laws or to secede from the Union.

John Calhoun, the senator from South Carolina, rose from his seat to respond. Facing the president, he offered a toast of his own: "The Union: next to our liberty, the most dear." For the South, the freedom of the states to act as they desired was more basic than the Union.

South Carolina Passes the Nullification Act

In the summer of 1832, Congress enacted a new tariff. Although this new law lowered the rates a little on many things, it was still high. Opposition grew bitter throughout the South. In the middle of the controversy, South Carolina called a convention. On the advice of John Calhoun, the convention passed the Nullification Act. This act declared that after February 1, 1833, the tariff law of the United States would be null and void in South Carolina. The convention also declared that any attempt of Congress to enforce the tariff law in South Carolina would be "a just cause for the secession of the state from the Union." The history of the Virginia and Kentucky Resolutions of 1798, and the Hartford Convention of 1814, seemed to be repeating itself.

The South Carolina Nullification Act created a national crisis. If a tariff law is to be effective, it must operate in all parts of a nation. If there is any place where it is not enforced, the whole system breaks down because foreign goods will be sent to that place. Charleston, South Carolina, was a major harbor. The revenue collectors in South Carolina resigned, leaving no one to collect the tax. Knowing this, European merchants prepared to ship goods to Charleston.

Prompt Action by Jackson

Jackson acted without delay. He immediately issued a proclamation declaring that no state had the power to annul a law of the United States. He warned South Carolina that secession was treason. He declared that the power of one state to annul a law of the United States was incompatible with the existence of the Union. He also said that such an act was expressly contradicted by the Constitution and inconsistent with every principle on which it was founded.

In addition to the proclamation, Jackson appointed new revenue collectors. He warned South Carolina that, if necessary, he would use the Army to enforce the tariff. At his request, Congress passed a bill authorizing the president to use the forces of the United States to maintain order. Jackson then ordered the Army and Navy to be prepared for action the minute South Carolina tried to put nullification into effect. South Carolina was equally determined. She began collecting arms. She organized her militia in preparation for defense in case the matter led to war.

The Compromise

Meanwhile, Henry Clay and others were able to put through Congress a compromise tariff act that met the objections of South Carolina and was acceptable to the North. It was a great triumph for Clay. His effort at peacemaking was successful. South Carolina repealed the Nullification Act. The president canceled his orders to the army and navy.

Armed conflict had been averted. However, the basic issue of whether a state could refuse to accept the authority of the national government had not been settled. It had only been postponed. The time for the answer was drawing closer. The time for the rending of America was drawing closer.

Spot Check

1. Why was the Tariff of 1828 called the "Tariff of Abominations"?
2. Who protested the tariff in the name of the South?
3. What was Nullification?
4. What did South Carolina threaten if Congress did not respect its Nullification Act?
5. How did Jackson respond to South Carolina's nullification?

THE NATIONAL BANK CONTROVERSY

Jackson's War on the Bank

Andrew Jackson hated the National Bank. He believed with the common people that the "wealthy bankers" were a money monopoly that operated for profit without regard for the people's interest. Despite the fact that the National Bank was well-managed and was rendering a great service to the government, Jackson wanted to destroy it. During his first term, he promptly vetoed the bill that Congress passed to extend the bank's charter.

The friends of the National Bank were unable to muster enough votes in Congress to override the president's veto. Naturally, they tried to prevent Jackson's re-election in 1832. In spite of their efforts, Jackson was re-elected. Martin Van Buren, an experienced politician and statesman from New York, was made vice president. The contrast was striking. Van Buren was as gentle and polished as Jackson was fiery and rough.

"Pet Banks"

His re-election was a great personal victory for Jackson. It convinced him that he had the support of the people in his war against the National Bank. Thus, he ordered the Secretary of the Treasury to withdraw all the United States funds from the National Bank and to deposit them in various state banks. Hostile newspapers called the president's action another application of the "spoils system." They said that the banks to which government money had been transferred were Jackson's "pet banks."

Nicholas Biddle, the president of the National Bank

The management of these "pet banks" was not always good. Some were far less stable than the National Bank. Many of them followed unsound banking policies. They loaned money too freely. This encouraged wild speculation in huge land purchases and in shares in new railroads to the West. Many people invested not only all their own money but also everything they could borrow. These speculators agreed to pay high interest rates on loans, and state banks willingly gave them all they requested. Some banks even loaned money from their reserve funds.

The state banks issued paper money, although it was not backed up by gold and silver reserves in the bank. Speculators made money by this practice. They used the paper money to buy large tracts of land. Then they sold the land at a good profit to western settlers. To prevent this wild speculation and to protect the national government from worthless paper money, just before the close of his term, Jackson issued a "specie circular." This act forbade the United

States Treasury to accept, in return for land, anything other than gold, silver, or notes backed by gold or silver. President Jackson had accomplished what he had set out to do. For better or for worse, he had placed control of the nation's money into the hands of the common people.

Spot Check

1. Why did Jackson hate the National Bank?
2. Why were state banks called "pet banks" by Jackson's opponents?

MARTIN VAN BUREN AS PRESIDENT

The Panic of 1837

Jackson was eager to have his trusted advisor, Martin Van Buren, succeed him as president. The Democratic Party carried out his wishes. They elected Martin Van Buren president in 1836.

Shortly after Van Buren assumed office, in 1837 a financial panic swept the country. Although Van Buren was not personally responsible for the panic, he was blamed for it. When business fails and people suffer, the party in power usually is blamed. However, in this case, the blame was justified.

President Martin Van Buren

Although several factors caused these hard times, chief among them was Jackson's unsound financial policy. Another factor was a very poor crop. Consequently, food had become very expensive. A third factor was that European creditors were demanding the money which American merchants owed them.

A financial panic followed. When people asked for the money that they had deposited with the state banks, the banks, because of their poor lending policies, did not have it. When the banks tried to call in their loans, the borrowers did not have the money to pay the banks. Many of the banks that had made loans to speculators were forced to close. Depositors made runs on the banks and withdrew such large amounts that even sound banks were forced to close their doors.

The bank closures, in turn, affected employers. With no money to pay their employees, they were forced to shut down their factories and shops. Everything was at a standstill. With no money in circulation, people could not pay their rent or their food bills.

The Whig Victory

During Jackson's presidency, his opponents formed a new political party called the Whig party. The party derived its name from the English Whigs. This was the name of the opponents of the king of England used during the American War of Independence. The new Whig party was opposed to "King Andrew," as they called Andrew Jackson.

The panic during Van Buren's presidency added many followers to the ranks of the Whigs. Though the causes of the panic were complicated, the fear of more hard times in the future was associated with the candidacy of Van Buren. When he ran for re-election, he was opposed by the Whig, William Henry Harrison. Harrison was a Westerner and the hero of the Battle of Tippecanoe.

In order to win the votes of the South, the Whigs supported John Tyler of Virginia for vice president.

Tippecanoe and Tyler Too

The campaign in this election was hysterical, noisy, and completely lacking in reason. There was no Whig party platform. The Whigs merely agreed on a slogan, "Down with Van Buren!" Their favorite song was "Tippecanoe and Tyler Too." In the end, the Whig campaign was successful. Harrison was elected president, and John Tyler, vice president.

"Tippecanoe and Tyler Too."

However, Harrison's term as president was short. He died within a month after taking office. John Tyler became president, the first vice president to succeed to the presidency. It was a bitter promotion. Disowned by the Democrats and in disagreement with the policy of the Whigs, Tyler actually became a man without a party.

Tyler was constantly at odds with Congress. As a result, only three actions were passed during his term in office. One was the acceptance of a treaty with England that permanently established the boundary of Maine. Since Daniel Webster, the Secretary of State, and Lord Ashburton, England's representative, drew up this treaty, it is known as the Webster-Ashburton Treaty. The second measure was to raise the tariff. This destroyed Clay's compromise measure passed a decade earlier. Lastly, Tyler paved the way for Texas to become a state.

Spot Check

1. Who succeeded Jackson as president in 1836?
2. What were the three factors that led to the Panic of 1837?
3. Who was the first vice president to become president because the president died in office?

CHAPTER REVIEW

1. What were some of the difficulties that arose between the South, the East, and the West during the decade 1820 to 1830?
2. What sort of restrictions had been placed on voting and office holding by the original states?
3. How did John Quincy Adams win the presidential election in 1824 when Andrew Jackson had received the highest number of votes?
4. Why was the spoils system harmful to the best interest of the country?
5. What was Jackson's policy toward Native Americans?
6. What was the Nullification Act?
7. How did Jackson meet the crisis caused by the Nullification Act?
8. How were the difficulties rising out of the Nullification Act finally settled?
9. What were "pet banks"?
10. Who was president after Andrew Jackson?
11. What was the significance of the phrase "Tippecanoe and Tyler Too"?
12. How did John Tyler become president?

OUR NATION PUSHES WEST

Pioneers on the Oregon Trail, by Bierstadt

THE STORY OF TEXAS

A Land of Hope and Promise

In 1821, two years before the Monroe Doctrine was declared, Mexico gained its independence from Spain. At the time, Mexico was much larger than it is now. It included not only what is today called Mexico, but also the land now occupied by Texas, New Mexico, Arizona, California, Nevada, and Utah. It included parts of Wyoming, Colorado, Kansas, and Oklahoma. This great expanse of land, which stretched from the Rio Grande to the United States border, was only partly explored. Outside of Texas and California, it was thinly populated. The people living there were some Indian tribes and some men raising cattle.

247

This was a land of hope and promise. American pioneers were interested in the fertile land across the border because it was cheap. It offered great prospects to new settlers. The new Mexican government in the 1820s encouraged settlers from the United States to move into Texas by giving them large tracts of land. In return, settlers pledged to support the Mexican government. Many cotton growers, ranchers, and small farmers took advantage of the offers made by Mexico.

American Settlers

One of the first Americans to realize the value of the land in Texas was Moses Austin of Connecticut. In 1821, he received permission from the Spanish government to settle a colony of three hundred families in Texas. Unfortunately, he died before he could carry out his plans. The work fell to his able son, Stephen F. Austin, whose name is famous in Texas history.

Others were attracted to Texas. Frontiersmen from Tennessee, Kentucky, and near-by states came to establish homes in this fertile region. Southern plantation owners arrived there with their slaves, as the land was good for growing cotton. Pioneer farmers arrived from every part of the Union. By the middle of Jackson's first term, there were about twenty thousand Americans living in Texas.

Stephen Austin

The customs and backgrounds of the American settlers were very different from those of the people of Mexico. The two peoples did not speak the same language. They did not practice the same religion. Their ideas of government were different. The settlers from the United States were mostly Protestants and Anglo-Saxon in origin. The people of Mexico were Catholic. Their language and ancestry were Spanish.

At first, the Mexican government welcomed Americans. However, as the numbers of American settlers began to grow, the official attitude changed. The Mexicans became alarmed. They were afraid they might lose control of the territory. Eventually, Mexico passed laws forbidding any more immigration from the United States. They made Texas a part of the Mexican state of Coahuila.

The Texas Revolt

The Americans in Texas soon became dissatisfied with the Mexican government. They mistrusted Santa Anna, Mexico's president. They wanted their own government. When Santa Anna began to abolish the rights of the Mexican states, the settlers were more determined than ever to be free from Mexican rule. In 1835, the Americans set up a government of their own. They chose Sam Houston commander in chief of their forces.

Santa Anna, with an army of more than four thousand men, moved into Texas in March of 1836 to restore Mexican control. He laid siege to the Alamo, an old mission in San Antonio used as a

The Alamo

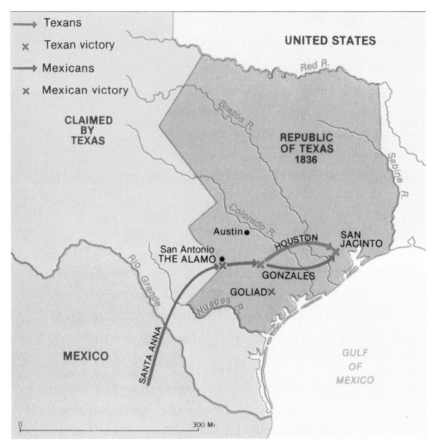

Texans
x Texan victory
Mexicans
x Mexican victory

UNITED STATES

Red R.

Brazos R.

CLAIMED
BY
TEXAS

REPUBLIC
OF TEXAS
1836

Sabine R.

Colorado R.

Austin

HOUSTON

SAN
JACINTO

San Antonio
THE ALAMO

Rio Grande

GONZALES

GOLIAD

Nueces R.

MEXICO

SANTA ANNA

GULF
OF
MEXICO

0   300 Mi

Texas wins its independence from Mexico, 1835-1836.

fort by the Texans. The small force of about two hundred Americans made an heroic stand. After a siege of thirteen days, Santa Anna took the Alamo by storm. All of the Alamo's defenders were killed. However, their death provided inspiration that drove the Texans on to final victory.

Santa Anna, excited by his "victory," continued his advance. He took more places and drove the Texans back toward the American border. Meanwhile, Sam Houston managed to gather a small well-organized army together. However, he was forced to order his men to retreat before Santa Anna's larger army. Then, with about eight hundred men, Houston surprised Santa Anna, in command of a force of twelve to fifteen hundred men at the San Jacinto River. The Texans rushed upon the enemy with the shout "Remember the Alamo!" In the battle, almost all the Mexicans were killed or captured. Santa Anna was taken prisoner. Sam Houston lost fewer than thirty men.

Santa Anna agreed to withdraw his troops to territory west of the Rio Grande. Then, the people of Texas set up a government patterned after that of the United States. They elected Sam Houston president. They proclaimed their state an independent republic. They called themselves the Lone Star Republic. Although Mexico refused to acknowledge their independence, the United States recognized the new republic.

Texas Joins the Union

For several years, Texas struggled along as an independent republic. For the entire time, the Texans wanted to become a part of the United States. However, there were two reasons why the United States was reluctant to admit Texas to the Union. First, Texas was a slave state. The Northern States opposed admitting a state that would give the slaveholders more influence in Congress. Second, the government was concerned that allowing Texas to join the Union would lead to war with Mexico.

The question of Texas statehood was one of the main issues in the presidential election of 1844. The Democrats and their candidate, James K. Polk of Tennessee, came out strongly for Texas statehood. They also favored the annexation of Oregon. Thus they pleased both the North and the South. The Whigs nominated their great western leader, Henry Clay. Not wishing to offend the North, Clay took no stand on the Texas issue. In 1844, Polk was elected.

President Tyler was himself a keen supporter of Texas statehood. He interpreted Polk's election to mean that the nation wanted Texas to join the Union. Thus, before Polk took office, Congress passed a joint resolution calling for the admission of Texas. President Polk quickly approved it. On December 29, 1845, Texas became the twenty-eighth state.

Spot Check

1. How did Mexico encourage Americans to move into Texas in the 1820s?
2. Who was one of the first Americans to realize the value of Texas?
3. Who was commander of the Texas forces that revolted against the Mexican government?
4. What event inspired the Texans to go on to final victory?
5. Why was the United States reluctant to let Texas join the Union?

THE OREGON TERRITORY

Disputed Claims

When we hear the name "Oregon" today, we naturally think of the state of Oregon. However, until about the middle of the nineteenth century, "Oregon" referred to a much larger region. The name applied to all the land extending from the northern boundary of Spanish territory (the present northern boundary of California), to the southern boundary of Alaska.

Both the United States and England claimed the Oregon territory. The U.S. claim was based on three facts. The first was the discovery and exploration of the Columbia River by Robert Gray, a Boston sea captain, in 1792. The second was the explorations of Lewis and Clark. The third was the establishment by John Jacob Astor in 1811 of a fur trading post called Astoria at the mouth of the Columbia River. The English also based their claim upon discovery, exploration, and settlement.

THE OREGON COUNTRY

54°40'

Pacific

Ocean

ALASKA

OREGON

COLUMBIA RIVER

COUNTRY

49°

LOUISIANA

TERRITORY

SPANISH   TERRITORY

AMERICAN

BRITISH

In an act of great mutual respect, each country recognized the claim of the other. Therefore, during James Monroe's presidency, the United States and England made an agreement. The agreement allowed the citizens of both nations to settle in the Oregon territory. This deal remained in effect until ownership of the territory was finally established.

The Oregon Treaty

The settlers themselves became a major factor in the settlement of claims in Oregon. While England stood by, Americans in large numbers made their way into this mutually-owned territory.

The pioneers traveled by way of the historic Oregon Trail. They moved along this trail in covered wagons, through wilderness, across plains, and over mountains. Men, women, and children suffered hardship and danger to settle in this great, free territory. The starting point of the Oregon Trail was Independence, Missouri, where the groups gathered before they began the long trek that led to Oregon.

As the American settlers became more numerous, they expressed a growing desire that all of the Oregon territory be added to the United States. In the campaign to elect Polk president, the northern Democrats used as their battle cry the slogan "Fifty-four forty or fight." "Fifty-four forty" referred to the southern boundary of Alaska. It meant that the United States was laying claim to all of Oregon. The slogan became popular and helped Polk win the election.

Great Britain believed that her claims on Oregon were just. She refused to yield to America's demands for all of the Oregon territory. A treaty settled the issue in 1846. The Oregon Treaty fixed 49 degrees as the northern boundary of U.S. claims. The treaty added the present states of Washington, Oregon, Idaho, and parts of Montana and Wyoming to the territory of the United States. It also secured a foothold for the United States on the Pacific coast.

The Father of Oregon

The great hero of Oregon's pioneer period is a Catholic: John McLoughlin. McLoughlin was born in Quebec, Canada, in 1784. In 1824, he travelled with the Hudson Bay Company to the Columbia River area in the Oregon territory. The river today is the border between the states of Washington and Oregon. For twenty-two years, McLoughlin was in charge of the Company in that area. Though a shrewd businessman, McLoughlin was known for his justice and generosity. He treated everyone fairly whether they were British,

American, or Native American. In fact, his wife was part Native American.

Despite being British and working for a British company, John McLoughlin was on very good terms with the American settlers who came in increasing numbers into Oregon. In 1841, a wagon train full of American settlers arrived at his outpost. Despite the orders of his company, he provided them with aid. Over the years, he continued to help Americans in Oregon. His aid to American settlers caused him to come into disagreement with the Hudson Bay Company. As a result, he resigned in 1846. He settled in Oregon City, which he had founded.

In 1842, John McLoughlin became a Catholic. In 1846, Pope Gregory XVI awarded him the Knighthood of St. Gregory for the work that he had done for the Church. In 1851, he became an American citizen. Sadly, his last years were difficult. Some Protestant missionaries prevented him from claiming his own land after the treaty. He lost the land and his fortune. He died in poverty. Five years after his death, the Oregon legislature restored his lands to his heirs. In 1953, his statue was placed in the National Statuary Hall in the Capitol in Washington, D.C. to represent Oregon. Four years later, on the 100th anniversary of his death, the state of Oregon officially declared him to be the "The Father of Oregon."

Spot Check
1. Who jointly claimed the Oregon Territory?
2. Who is the "Father of Oregon"?

THE SOUTHWEST

The Mexican-American War (1846-1848)

The war between the United States and Mexico broke out within a year after Texas became a state. In a sense, both nations were responsible for the war. The issue was about the border. Texas claimed that her southern and western boundary line was the Rio Grande. Mexico claimed all territory south of the Nueces River. When the Mexican government refused to receive the minister sent by President Polk to discuss the question of boundaries, Polk ordered General Zachary Taylor to occupy the territory in dispute. The Mexicans sent an army into the territory. The two armies clashed. Each claimed the other was invading its territory. The war that had been predicted by the opponents of Texas statehood began in May 1846.

The war with Mexico involved three campaigns. General Taylor defeated the Mexicans in two great battles and occupied most of northern Mexico. Colonel John Fremont, with the help of a naval

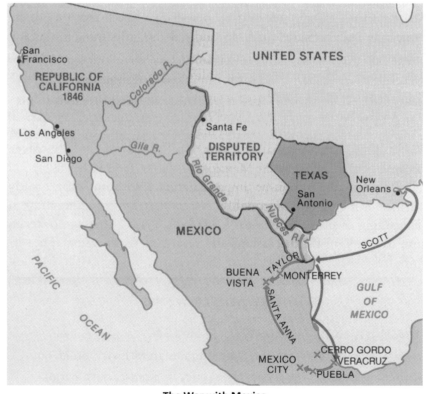

The War with Mexico

squadron commanded by Commodore Stockton, took California. General Winfield Scott went to Mexico by water and landed at Veracruz. His troops made their way across Mexico and captured Mexico City, the capital. The capture of the capital basically ended the war.

The Peace Treaty

A treaty of peace was signed at Guadalupe-Hidalgo in February 1848, officially ending the war. The United States agreed to withdraw all its troops from Mexico. Mexico would sell the United States all the lands north of the Gila River and the Rio Grande. The United States agreed to pay Mexico fifteen million dollars for the land. The U.S. agreed to pay all claims of American citizens against Mexico.

Five years later, in 1853, the United States purchased a narrow strip of land along the southern borders of New Mexico and Arizona for ten million dollars. This purchase was made so that the United States could build a southern railroad through that territory. It settled the boundary between the two countries. James Gadsden, the American minister to Mexico, arranged to buy the land. Thus, the region came to be known as the Gadsden Purchase.

The Mormons in Utah

While the war with Mexico was still going on, a band of settlers was making its way to the barren region around the Great Salt Lake. These people belonged to a religious sect known as the Mormons. They were followers of Joseph Smith, the founder.

Some of the Mormons' beliefs and customs were so different from those of most American communities that they were persecuted wherever they went. Among other things, they practiced polygamy. (Polygamy is having more than one wife at one time.) This was the main cause of their trouble since polygamy was illegal in all of the states. From New York, the Mormons migrated to Ohio, and from Ohio to Missouri. When they were forced out of Missouri, they crossed into Illinois. There, a mob killed Joseph Smith.

Under a new leader, Brigham Young, the Mormons decided to settle in the West, beyond the borders of the United States. In 1847, thousands of Mormons traveled west to the desert region of Utah. At the time, Utah belonged to Mexico. The Mormons settled on the shores of the Great Salt Lake, Utah.

In a few years, the Mormon settlers changed this dry, barren region into a fertile land. They dug irrigation ditches that brought the water down from the mountains to irrigate their flat but fertile fields. Although the Mormon settlements grew and prospered, almost fifty years passed before Utah was admitted to the Union. Congress refused to admit Utah until the Mormons gave up the practice of polygamy. Utah became a state in 1896.

"The Forty-Niners"

In 1848, at the close of the Mexican War, gold was discovered in California. When the news of this discovery reached across the country, thousands of people rushed to California. By 1849, the gold rush was on at top speed. All over the country you could hear the cry, "Gold! Gold in California!"

Fortune hunters came by land and by sea. Men raced madly across the country to California in covered wagons, on horseback, and on foot with their few belongings loaded upon the backs of mules. Those coming by sea sailed around Cape Horn at the tip of South America and disembarked at San Francisco. The adventurers who took part in the California gold rush of 1849 have since been known as "the forty-niners."

The discovery of gold caused an incredible change in California. It went from being an almost unknown region into a great, booming center of activity. Between 1848 and 1849, California's population swelled from a few thousand to nearly a hundred thousand. San Francisco grew from a few shacks into a thriving port.

Not all the "gold seekers" struck it rich. Some returned home. Others remained to make their homes in California. Farmers found that the land was fertile and good for raising fruits and vegetables. They planted orchards, engaged in gardening, or turned to general farming. California grew so fast that it was admitted to the Union in 1850, only two years after the discovery of gold.

Spot Check

1. What was the immediate cause of the Mexican-American War?
2. What American general occupied most of northern Mexico?
3. What American general captured Mexico City?
4. What was the name of the followers of Joseph Smith?
5. What practice of Smith's followers caused them to be persecuted?
6. What nickname was given to those who came to California looking for gold?

THE SPREAD OF THE CATHOLIC FAITH IN THE NEW STATES

Texas

Long before Americans settled in Texas, Spanish missionaries from New Mexico had visited western Texas. Missionaries from Mexico City had come to the Texas territory. They came to preach the Gospel and establish the Church. Many had traveled from St. Augustine in Florida, west to the Texas territory.

Oregon

Missionaries had blazed the trail to the Oregon territory long before the great influx of covered wagons. In 1837, at the request of some of the early Canadians, the bishop of Quebec sent Father Blanchet and Father Demers into this land. Later, the Flathead Indians of the Rocky Mountains asked the bishop of St. Louis for priests. In 1840, Father de Smet, the famous Jesuit missionary of the Northwest, began his work among the Indians.

Father Peter de Smet was born in Belgium in 1801. In 1821, he came to Maryland where he began his training to become a Jesuit priest. He later moved to Missouri where he was ordained in 1827. His great ambition was to convert the native peoples. He studied Indian customs for many years. In 1838, he began his missionary work among the Sioux Indians, explaining to them the doctrines of the Catholic Faith. In the meantime, he met several other tribes and established friendly relations with them. In 1840, when the Flatheads asked the bishop of St. Louis for a priest, Father de Smet was sent. He journeyed to Westport, now Kansas City. There, several months later, he celebrated Mass before a crowd of Flathead warriors.

Father de Smet's missionary journeys carried him all the way to the Northwest. There he met the two great missionaries from Canada: Father Blanchet and Father Demers. Together these three brave priests laid plans for the growth of the Church in the Northwest. Father de Smet returned to Europe several times to ask for money and for more priests. In the days when ocean travel was long and hard, he traveled to Europe nineteen times on behalf of the Indians. Meanwhile, Fathers Blanchet and Demers continued their work. Later

Fr. de Smet

both men were named bishops for the area in which they operated as missionaries. Blanchet was appointed the first Archbishop of the Northwest and became known as the "Apostle of Oregon." Father Demers was made bishop of Vancouver Island.

Father de Smet labored in the West for over a quarter of a century. From 1840 until his death in 1873, he spent most of his time with the Indians. He taught them the truths of the Catholic religion. He tried to help them improve the quality of their lives. He, more than anyone else, helped to keep peace between the Indians and the Whites. The United States government recognized his influence with the Indians. He constantly interceded on behalf of the Indians with the U. S. government. Through his influence, the bloody Sioux War in Oregon was stopped, and a peace treaty was drawn up in 1868 that brought to an end the long Sioux rebellion. His work, together with that of many other missionaries, helped to strengthen the claim that the United States had on the Oregon territory.

Everywhere missionaries went, they established schools. In 1843, St. Joseph's College was opened in the Oregon territory. A short time later, the Sisters of Notre Dame de Namur opened a girls' school. This was the beginning of schools to be opened in Washington and Idaho within the next two decades.

California

During the period that the United States was gaining control over California, there was little Church activity. The missions had been closed by the Mexican government or destroyed by Indian uprisings. Only one Catholic school, a seminary, had been established, Santa Inez at Santa Barbara in 1844. It was not until Bishop Joseph Alemany came to California after his consecration in 1850 that the Catholic Faith took root again in that region.

Spot Check

1. Why did Father Peter de Smet go to the Flathead Indians?
2. Why could Father de Smet be called the "Apostle of the Rockies"?

ANTI-CATHOLIC MOVEMENTS IN AMERICA

Reasons for Anti-Catholic Feelings

During the first half of the nineteenth century, the Church came under growing attacks from anti-Catholic groups. Many American Protestants believed that a person could not be both a good American and a good Catholic. The American tradition of individualism and democracy made many Americans distrustful of strong religious authority. The growing feeling of nationalism made some Americans wary of any non-American influence, like a pope in Europe. Sadly, the American belief in fair play and justice was outweighed by fear and ignorance.

The Native American Movement

As a result of immigration, the number of Catholics in the United States increased dramatically during the early part of the nineteenth century. In fact, so many Catholics came to this country that by 1850, Catholicism was one of this nation's largest religions. Many of these immigrants came from Ireland. From 1845 to 1850, Ireland suffered a terrible famine. The growing number of Catholic immigrants stirred up the resentment of some American Protestants.

In the 1840s, a new organization was formed to deal with the Catholic "problem" caused by the heavy immigration. The members of this organization called themselves the Native American Party. However, they were more commonly known as "Know-Nothings." The name came from the fact that whenever they were questioned about their organization, they would respond, "I know nothing."

Members of this secret organization promised never to vote for any foreign-born or Catholic candidate.

During the 1830s, the feeling against Catholics in the United States grew. Books and newspapers were printed that inflamed the passions of the mob against Catholics and the Irish. Bishops and priests were slandered. The Faith was misrepresented and ridiculed. The verbal attacks then escalated. Acts of violence were committed against Catholics and their property.

Riots and Church Burnings

One of the first serious incidents of violence occurred in 1834 in Charleston, Massachusetts, just outside of Boston. Spurred on by reports that a young woman had been seized and forced into a convent against her will, an angry mob attacked the convent. The Ursuline convent, which also served as a Catholic school, was burned to the ground by the mob. Police and firefighters looked on, unmoving. The next day, another mob assembled with the intention of going after the Catholic churches. When armed Catholics surrounded their cathedral to protect it, the mob decided not to act.

Another incident occurred in Philadelphia in 1844. Following a talk on the "evil plots" Catholics were concocting to destroy the Union, an angry mob began to assemble. Some Catholics were pushed into an argument with the mob and before long, a riot was under way. The National Guard was called out and the riot subsided temporarily. The next day, the Know Nothings paraded through the streets blaming the Catholics for the riot. The crowd grew more angry and began to set fire to houses. The militia again dispersed the crowd. However, by evening, the troops were withdrawn. Under cover of darkness, the mob came out again. It set fire to two Catholic churches as well as a number of homes where Irish families lived. At one of the churches, firemen stood by and allowed the adjoining church library and seminary to be devoured by the flames. However, they threw water on neighboring houses that were owned by Protestants. The mob next attacked a Catholic school where again the firefighters made no effort to extinguish the blaze. Fearing for the safety of his fellow Catholics, Bishop Kenrick suspended services and closed all the churches in Philadelphia on Sunday, May 12, 1844.

Following their "success" in Philadelphia, the Know Nothings planned to have a meeting in New York City the following year. The bishop of New York City was John Hughes. He urged the mayor not to allow the meeting for fear of violence. However, Bishop Hughes also made plans to protect Church property. The mayor forbade the meeting. Civil order was maintained. It was Bishop Hughes' fearless attitude that prevented the meeting from being held. Bishop Hughes fought the Know-Nothings with all his power. His great love of the people and his self-sacrificing patriotism at last obtained for him the support of fair-minded Americans. Through

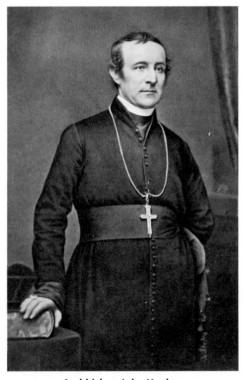

Archbishop John Hughes

the work of men like Bishop Hughes, the power of anti-Catholic bigotry was temporarily broken.

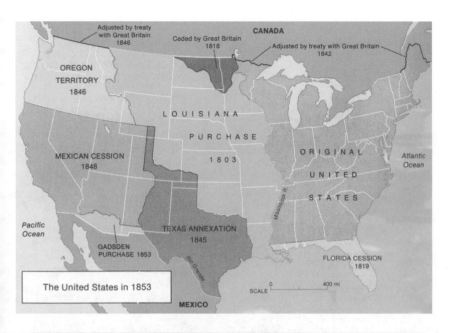

The United States in 1853

CHAPTER REVIEW

1. What was the Battle of the Alamo?
2. Who was president of Mexico at the time of the Texas revolt?
3. Who became the first president of the "Lone Star Republic"?
4. What objections were raised against Texas joining the Union?
5. On what three factors did America base the claim to the Oregon country?
6. What was the meaning of the slogan "Fifty-four forty or fight"?
7. When did the Mexican-American War begin? How did it basically end?
8. What were the provisions of the treaty ending the war with Mexico?
9. Why was California able to become a state so quickly?
10. Who is the "Father of Oregon"?
11. Who is the "Apostle of Oregon"?
12. What priest worked untiringly for the Native Americans in the Rocky Mountain region?
13. Give two reasons why American Protestants distrusted Catholics.
14. Where and when did the most serious anti-Catholic riot occur?
15. What is the "Native American Movement"?

SLAVERY DIVIDES THE NATION

A fugitive slave family rides for the freedom of the North. Note the mother turns fearfully and glances South, perhaps as she hears oncoming hoofbeats.

GROWING TENSIONS BETWEEN NORTH AND SOUTH

Two Ways of Life

During the first half of the nineteenth century, two ways of life existed in the United States. Distinct sectional changes had come to exist. They divided the country into the North and the South. These changes took the people north of the Potomac River in one direction and those south of the river in another direction. The South was agricultural while the North had become industrial. The Northerners were against slavery while the Southerners were for slavery. This issue caused stress and tension between the two groups. It finally divided the nation.

Slavery is almost as old as human history. St. Augustine said that slavery was a result of man's fall. In ancient Egypt, slaves were used to build the great pyramids and temples. Slavery was also practiced in ancient Persia, India, and China. The Greeks and Romans also kept slaves. When the Roman Empire converted to Catholicism, laws were passed which said that married slaves could not be separated. Also, children of slaves could not be separated from their parents when very young. During the Middle Ages, as the Church became stronger, she was mostly able to put an end to slavery in Europe.

When the Spaniards came to the New World, some of the Spaniards tried to make slaves of the natives under their control. However, it did not work out very well. Catholic missionaries objected to this practice. The Spanish monarchy forbade the practice of Indian slavery. Sadly, African slavery remained legal for a longer period. Slave traders brought shiploads of Africans to the Spanish colonies. Thus, slavery had its beginning in the New World.

Dutch traders brought African slaves to Virginia in 1619. After 1619, both Dutch and English traders, from time to time, brought slaves to the colonies. As the shipping industry developed in New England, enterprising merchants saw the possibility of profits in slave trade. Laden with rum, New England ships began to trade their cargoes for slaves in African ports. There was little work connected with these transactions other than the exchange of cargoes. Enemy tribes brought captive Africans to the shore to be sold to Europeans and Americans for casks of rum. Later these merchants found a ready market in our country for their slave cargoes.

The Industrial North

There was very little slavery in the North. The climate, the crops, and the size of the farms made slavery impractical. Over time, the development of factories made the North industrial, and there was less and less need for slaves. In fact, during the first half of the nineteenth century, manufacturing became the leading industry in the North. Manufacturing requires a great many workers in a small area. Thus, the cities of the North grew in population.

Samuel Slater started one of the first factories in the North. During Washington's first term as president, Slater built a cloth factory at Pawtucket, Rhode Island. The factory began to make a good profit. Very quickly, other factories developed in the North. When the Embargo Act, and later the War of 1812, created a demand for American-made goods, it was necessary to develop manufacturing on a large scale. After the War of 1812, the growth of factories was further stimulated by the protective tariff that kept imported manufactured goods more expensive than those made in America.

Beginning with Slater's Pawtucket factory, manufacturing plants had grown up throughout the North. By 1850, the region was an industrial beehive. In 1839, Charles Goodyear discovered the process for vulcanizing rubber. Elias Howe, a Cambridge mechanic, invented the sewing machine in 1845. In addition, more than nine thousand miles of railroad tracks had been laid in the United States to furnish factories with a quicker and more efficient means of securing raw materials. All these factors added to the growing manufacturing power of the North.

Factories sprang up everywhere. Sleepy little villages located near waterfalls or on navigable rivers became busy, bustling mill towns. With its abundance of water power, supply of coal, and its many excellent harbors, the North was perfectly suited to the growth and development of factories. Thousands of European immigrants provided the factories with a constant supply of cheap labor. This was actually cheaper and easier for the factory owners than buying

A New England Factory

slaves. They paid the workers a few dollars a week and let them see to their own housing and maintenance. Children were often employed at even lower wages. Hence, there was no need for black slaves in the industrial North. Slavery became less and less important.

Sadly, the working and living conditions for the immigrants in the North were a kind of "industrial slavery." The workers were paid very low wages. Women and children worked in jobs unsuitable for their gender and age. The Church did what it could to address these issues during this period but it lacked a strong voice. Only when the Church became more influential in the later half of the nineteenth century could it begin to address the injustices that the immigrants faced. The South would argue that the black slaves were better cared for than the white workers in the North's factories.

"King Cotton"

While new machines were making black labor unnecessary in the North, cotton became the leading crop in the South. In 1793, Eli Whitney had invented the cotton gin. It completely transformed agriculture in the South. Previously, raising cotton was too expensive to be done on a large scale. The cotton gin made growing cotton a very profitable business. Southern farmers began to grow it in large quantities. The gin was such an improvement over hand methods that it took many more workers in the fields to keep the machines busy. Growing, picking, and cleaning cotton were types of unskilled labor that untrained slaves could do easily. In fact, even women and children could help. This of course meant an increase in labor, slave labor.

The demand for cotton goods steadily grew. Clothing made from cotton was cheap compared to the cost of silk, wool, or linen. The new spinning and weaving machines used in the Northern and New England factories caused a tremendous demand for cotton. The climate of the South made it perfect for growing cotton. In sizing up the situation, one Southern senator declared, "Cotton is King!"

The invention of the cotton gin had more to do with making cotton "king" than anything else. The cotton gin and the weaving machine ensured that the South would remain agricultural and the North would remain industrial. It also meant that slavery would be very profitable in the South but completely unnecessary in the North.

Spot Check

1. How were the North and South different in the way each area made a living?
2. Who brought African slaves to Virginia?
3. What was often traded for slaves in Africa?
4. Name the inventor and the machine that made cotton "king" in the South.

SLAVERY: THE MORAL DEBATE

A World Movement against Slavery

By the end of the eighteenth century, most western nations were outlawing slavery. However, there were few countries in the world where slavery was as widespread or financially practical as in the American South. During colonial days, all of the Southern colonies passed laws forbidding further importation of slaves. However, England vetoed all these laws! England did not want to give up her rich slave trade. Leaders in England raised protests against the African slave trade at the time of the Declaration of Independence. However, these protests fell on deaf ears. In 1807, England finally forbade trade in slaves. The following year, the United States prohibited further importation of African slaves.

The abolition of the slave trade itself was, therefore, relatively easy. However, it is one thing to abolish the slave trade, it is another thing to abolish slavery itself. Abolishing slavery was not easy, just as improving working and living conditions for the northern worker was not easy. It was reasonably easy to abolish slavery in England and in the North where it was not needed for economic prosperity. However, it was a different matter in those areas where slavery seemed to be necessary for the economy. Also, in the south, a slave was considered an investment. Moreover, freeing large numbers of slaves also meant the creation of the serious problem of what to do with those who would be freed. It took England fifty years to rid the British West Indies of slavery. England finally outlawed slavery in the British West Indies in 1833. The government paid the slave owners almost a hundred million dollars to compensate them for their lost "property."

By 1850, slavery had been abolished in the colonies of the European nations in the Western hemisphere. However, in the

United States, the problem was not so easily solved. The North and the South had an equal voice in government so neither side could simply impose its political will on the other. Many of the leading men of the South had opposed slavery. Among them were Washington, Jefferson, Henry, and Madison. However, like many others, they were unable to solve the problem.

The Abolitionists

Many in the North and the South had long recognized slavery as an evil. Neither Washington nor Jefferson, both slave owners, liked slavery. They hoped it would be abolished. In the early nineteenth century, individuals and groups began a movement for the abolition of slavery in the United States. The people behind this movement were called abolitionists.

One of the leading abolitionists was William Lloyd Garrison. He began publishing a newspaper against slavery. His paper was called *The Liberator* because he wanted to free the slaves. In his zeal for reform, he demanded that all slaves be freed immediately and with no conditions. He was so radical in his beliefs that he was willing to see the Union dissolve if only slavery were abolished.

Most people in the North did not agree with the radical abolitionists like Garrison. When he spoke in Boston, his idea of instant and unconditional emancipation angered the crowd which later attacked him. Mostly, the abolitionists just increased the tension between the North and the South. They kept the North's attention focused on slavery. They angered the Southerners by criticizing a system that the South believed was necessary for its prosperity.

The flames were further fanned in 1852. That year, Harriet Beecher Stowe's novel, *Uncle Tom's Cabin*, appeared. The book emphasized the worst evils of slavery. This novel had a definite influence on the abolitionists' cause. People in the North accepted it as a true picture of the South. People in the South were furious at its depiction of slavery.

The Nat Turner Insurrection

For a slave-owning society, its greatest fear is a slave uprising. A short time after the first copy of *The Liberator* appeared, the South was deeply shocked by a slave uprising in Virginia. Nat Turner, a black preacher, led a group of Virginia slaves in a revolt against their masters. The rebelling slaves massacred fifty-five white people. The South was terrified. The people blamed Garrison for the uprising and demanded that *The Liberator* be suppressed. The slaves had probably not been influenced much by Garrison. However, Nat Turner's rebellion increased the gap between the Southerners and the abolitionists.

The South Claims a Double Standard

Many in the South did not consider slavery wrong. These Southerners actually looked upon slavery as good for both Blacks and Whites. They were convinced that they were providing the slaves with a better life than they would have had in Africa. The Southerners pointed out that if the slaves were freed, there would be no one to look after their welfare. They argued that the slaves on the plantation had a happier life than the poorly paid factory laborers in the North. They also believed that

Harriet Beecher Stowe

freedom for the slaves would be a danger to white society, especially after the Turner Insurrection. They believed that slavery was the only way Blacks and Whites could live together in America. As time passed, the bitter attacks of northern writers made the South more determined than ever to defend slavery. The South demanded that the people of the states involved settle the question.

The South was also angry about the claimed moral superiority of the North. Southerners pointed to the miserable working conditions in factories and mines of the North. They decried child labor, long working hours, and dangerous working conditions. People in the South were angry that *Uncle Tom's Cabin* should criticize them when workers in the North were sometimes subjected to worse treatment than many slaves in the South. It seemed to the Southerners that there was a double standard in the North. They ignored their own problems but took every chance to focus on the problems of the South.

The Churches and Slavery

The matter of slavery divided churches just as it did the nation. The issue was so divisive that some Protestant churches split into northern and southern branches of the same denomination. Catholics also had to address the problem of slavery. In 1839, Pope Gregory XVI had condemned the African slave trade. However, as with many political issues in American history, America's Catholic bishops did not take any official position on the abolition of slavery. They also did not take a stand on the expansion of slavery in the territories in the West. Individual Catholics tended to support or oppose it depending upon where they lived. Catholics in the North opposed slavery. However, no Catholics were leaders in the abolitionist movement. Catholics in the South tended to support slavery.

Spot Check

1. Give the name of a leading abolitionist and of his paper.
2. Name the author and title of the book that most influenced northern attitudes toward slavery.
3. Who led an uprising of slaves in Virginia?
4. Which pope condemned the African slave trade?

SLAVERY SHAPES POLITICS

The Missouri Compromise

From the time of the Missouri Compromise to the Civil War, slavery was the main political issue. As the years passed, the differences between the North and South grew in intensity. It became increasingly evident that peace between the two sides was farther and farther away. On many occasions, attempts at compromise were made, but without lasting success. Even the "Great Peacemaker," Henry Clay, found it more and more difficult for the two sides to resolve their differences.

There was no sign of real trouble until 1820 when Missouri sought to be admitted to the Union. At that time, there were an equal number of slave and free states in the Union (eleven free states and eleven slave states). The North had a large majority in the House where representation was by population. However, in the Senate, there were two senators from each state, so the South had equal representation. The South was afraid that if the North obtained a majority in the Senate there would be trouble. Hence, it was important which side Missouri would join.

While debates on the status of Missouri were raging in Congress, Maine applied for statehood as a free state. This offered a solution to the political differences between the North and the South. An agreement was reached, which became known as the

Missouri Compromise. According to the agreement, Maine was admitted as a free state and Missouri as a slave state. Thus, a balance of votes was maintained in the Senate between the North and the South. The Missouri Compromise also provided that no more slave states be established in the Louisiana Territory north of the line 36 degree latitude mark. This was the southern boundary of Missouri.

The Compromise of 1850

It seemed that the Missouri Compromise might settle the slavery question. However, a new problem arose when California asked to be admitted to the Union. To admit California as a free state would destroy the balance of power.

The veteran statesman Henry Clay proposed a compromise, which had five parts. First, California would be admitted as a free state. Second, the slave markets would be closed in the District of Columbia. Third, the states to be formed from the territories of New Mexico and Utah would decide for themselves whether they should become slave or free. Fourth, fugitive slaves would be returned to their owners. Fifth, Texas would give up some of its land for ten million dollars so it could pay its debts.

This compromise gave both sides some things they wanted. The North gained the abolition of the slave trade in the District of Columbia and saw California admitted as a free state. The South gained a new fugitive slave law, which provided that federal officers return runaway slaves to their masters.

The Underground Railroad

The new fugitive slave law actually hurt the South more than it realized at the time. The purpose of the Missouri Compromise was to address the problem of slaves who had escaped to the North. However, it forced officials of free states to aid slave catchers if there were runaway slaves in their area. Also, free Blacks in the North

THE MISSOURI COMPROMISE — 1820

UNORGANIZED

TERRITORY

MICHIGAN TERRITORY

ILL. IND. OHIO
MO. KY. VA.
ARKANSAS TERRITORY TENN. N.C.
LA. MISS. ALA. GA. S.C.
FLA.

N.Y. PA. MD. DEL.
VT. N.H. MASS.

FREE
SLAVE

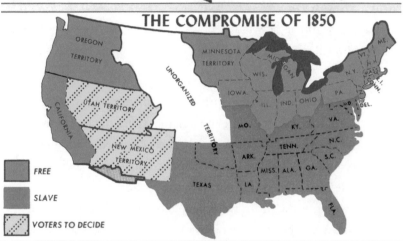

THE COMPROMISE OF 1850

OREGON TERRITORY
MINNESOTA TERRITORY
UNORGANIZED TERRITORY
CALIFORNIA
UTAH TERRITORY
NEW MEXICO TERRITORY
WIS.
IOWA
ILL. IND. OHIO
MO. KY. VA.
ARK. TENN. N.C.
TEXAS MISS. ALA. GA. S.C.
LA.
FLA.

N.Y. PA. MD. DEL.
VT. N.H. MASS. CONN.

FREE
SLAVE
VOTERS TO DECIDE

THE KANSAS-NEBRASKA ACT — 1854

WASHINGTON TERRITORY
OREGON TERRITORY
NEBRASKA TERRITORY
MINNESOTA TERRITORY
CALIFORNIA
UTAH TERRITORY
KANSAS TERRITORY
NEW MEXICO TERRITORY
UN-ORGANIZED TERRITORY
WIS.
IOWA
ILL. IND. OHIO
MO. KY. VA.
ARK. TENN. N.C.
TEXAS MISS. ALA. GA. S.C.
LA.
FLA.

N.Y. PA. MD. DEL.
VT. N.H. MASS. CONN.

FREE
SLAVE
VOTERS TO DECIDE

could be made slaves, despite the fact that they had been freed or never were slaves. The new law basically caused Northerners who would have been content to ignore the slavery problem now to need to deal with it in their own hometowns. Slavery was no longer just a "Southern" problem; it was now a national problem.

The fugitive slave law also led to an increase in the activity of the Underground Railroad. The Underground Railroad was not actually a railroad, but a system whereby thousands of slaves escaped to Canada. It had been started early in the nineteenth century. However, it was at its peak from 1850 to 1860, following the enactment of the new law. In fact, it was the existence of the Underground Railroad that caused the fugitive slave law to be passed.

Instead of cooperating with federal officers, many Northerners helped the fugitive slaves escape to Canada. There they were free from the law and their owners. Some Northerners opposed the federal officers because they believed that the police power was a state right. Therefore, federal officers did not have the authority to arrest runaway slaves. However, most anti-slavery people believed that slavery was wrong. They were not going to obey a law that was so clearly unjust. These were the people in the North who formed the "underground railroad."

The Underground Railroad worked this way. From the border of the slave states to Canada, definite routes for escape were marked out. All along the way there were "stations" where the fleeing slaves could stop. Usually these stations were the homes of abolitionists. At the "stations," the runaways would be given food and a place to hide during the day. At night they would continue, with the help of another abolitionist, to another station, where they would stay until the next night. Often, free Negroes of the North belonged to the Underground Railroad. They also helped the fugitive slaves to make their way to Canada. Frequently, people who were not members of the Underground Railroad helped runaways because they did not like the fugitive slave law.

The Kansas-Nebraska Act

Between 1850 and 1854, the fight over the slavery issue slowed a bit. Then, in 1854, the whole issue flared up once again. In that year, Stephen A. Douglas, a Democratic senator from Illinois, was able to convince the Congress to pass the law known as the Kansas-Nebraska Act. This law provided that the settlers of the Kansas and Nebraska territories could decide for themselves whether their respective territories should be slave or free.

The Kansas and Nebraska territories were north of the Missouri Compromise line. They were to have the choice of becoming slave or free. Though this proposal was contrary to the intent of the Missouri Compromise, Douglas was able to enact his bill. The law provoked great anger in the North and among the members of Congress. Douglas had expected that Northerners would settle in Nebraska and Southerners in Kansas. However, he had seriously misjudged the situation. He had failed to recognize the resolve of the abolitionists, who were determined to exclude slavery from both states. The abolitionists were certain that Nebraska would become a free state. Thus, they focused their attention on Kansas.

As soon as the Douglas bill was passed, many settlers from both the North and the South rushed to Kansas. Each group came for their own purpose. Those from the North came with the idea of excluding slavery. Those from the South came for the purpose of introducing slavery. Aware of the Northerners' antislavery intentions, groups of pro-slavery settlers poured into Kansas from Missouri. Whichever group could produce the most votes would determine the issue.

Kansas soon became a battleground between pro-slave and anti-slave settlers. There were actually large, intense battles between them. The newspapers spoke of the territory as "Bleeding Kansas." It was a preview of the larger war to come. In the end, the anti-slave settlers outnumbered the pro-slavery settlers. Kansas was admitted to the Union as a free state in 1861.

The Dred Scott Decision

In 1857, the Supreme Court decided the *Dred Scott* case. Dred Scott was a black slave. His owner had taken him from Missouri into Illinois and then into the territory that is now Minnesota. Later, he was brought back to Missouri. Dred Scott sued for his freedom on the ground that he had been in free territory. The Supreme Court decided that a slave had no right to sue. Scott's case was dismissed.

The Supreme Court further decided that living in a free territory did not make a slave free. The Court went on to say that a slaveholder could take his property anywhere in the Union. It also declared the Missouri Compromise unconstitutional. The Southerners were overjoyed. The decision, in effect, made the whole country slave territory. The Northerners were enraged. They saw the *Dred Scott* decision as a perversion of justice. They were more aroused against slavery than ever before.

Spot Check

1. What was the Missouri Compromise of 1820?
2. Who worked out the Compromise of 1850?
3. What was the key provision of the Kansas-Nebraska Act?
4. Why did Dred Scott believe he could sue for his freedom?
5. Why was the South overjoyed by the Dred Scott decision?

John Brown's Raid on Harper's Ferry

John Brown was an extreme abolitionist who had been active in the struggle to make Kansas a free state. He had been the leader of several bloody raids on pro-slavery settlements. He had murdered a number of his opponents.

At the close of the Kansas struggle, John Brown went east to carry out his long-held plan to free the slaves by force. On October 16, 1859, with a band of twenty-one followers, he seized the United States arsenal at Harper's Ferry, Virginia. He called upon the slaves to take up arms and free themselves by their own efforts. However, the general uprising on which he had counted did not take place. Instead, some of the state militia and a force of United States marines hurried to the scene. In the skirmish that followed, Brown was captured and two of his sons were killed. Brown was tried for murder and treason and was hanged. Though this uprising was stamped out, Brown's act greatly

John Brown After his Trial

frightened the people of the South. They feared that more men like Brown would continue making trouble and trying to incite slaves to violence.

New Political Parties are Formed

Until 1854, there were two major national political parties. The Democratic Party was the successor to the Democratic-Republican Party of Jefferson. It had been given its identity by Jackson and Van Buren. They had built it up as "the party of the common man." The other major party was the Whigs. The Whigs had elected Zachary Taylor president in 1848. However, after that, they suffered growing stress in their party over slavery.

The passage of the Kansas-Nebraska Act of 1854 caused splits in both parties. Whigs and Democrats in the North opposed the extension of slavery. They formed the Free Soil Party. Pro-slavery Whigs joined the pro-slavery Southerners in the Democratic Party. The Democratic Party became the major pro-slavery party. Since all the Whigs had now left the Whig Party and joined either the Free Soil Party or the Democrats, the Whig party ceased to exist.

The change in the political landscape caused some northern and western leaders to form another new national party. This party would have two goals. It would support the Union and work for the gradual elimination of slavery. In July 1854, the leaders of this new party met at Jackson, Michigan. They called themselves the Republican Party.

The Lincoln-Douglas Debates

In 1858, four years after Stephen A. Douglas had sponsored the Kansas-Nebraska Bill, he was opposed for re-election to the Senate by Abraham Lincoln. Lincoln was the candidate of the new Republican Party. At the time, Lincoln was not well-known.

Both Lincoln and Douglas were eager to gain political influence. Both desired to preserve the Union. However, they differed greatly on the question of slavery. Douglas believed that the issue should be decided by the citizens of each state as provided in the

The Lincoln-Douglas Debates

Kansas-Nebraska Act. He called his position "squatter sovereignty." Lincoln, on the other hand, considered slavery morally wrong. Therefore, he believed it should be prohibited in all new territories. He was convinced that slavery would soon die out if it were excluded from the territories.

During the campaign, Lincoln and Douglas debated each other in several Illinois cities. At one of these debates, Lincoln asked Douglas to declare himself either for "squatter sovereignty" or for unlimited extension of slavery as proclaimed by the *Dred Scott* decision. Douglas, true to his belief, answered in favor of "squatter sovereignty." This answer helped him be elected to the Senate from Illinois. However, it greatly angered the people of the south. They believed that the *Dred Scott* decision made slavery legal everywhere and individual states could not make it illegal.

The Lincoln-Douglas debates attracted national attention. The text of the debates was printed in all the newspapers. People all over the nation read and studied what the two men said.

Two years later, in 1860, both Lincoln and Douglas were nominated for the presidency. When Douglas was nominated, the southern Democrats refused to support him. They withdrew from the party convention and nominated John C. Breckinridge of Kentucky as their candidate. In the election of 1860, because the Democrats split their vote, Abraham Lincoln became the sixteenth President of the United States.

Spot Check

1. What the new political party formed to preserve the Union and work for the gradual elimination of slavery?
2. What solution to the slavery question did Douglas favor in his debates with Lincoln?
3. What solution to the slavery question did Lincoln favor in his debates with Douglas?
4. Why was it possible for Lincoln to win the election of 1860?

CHAPTER REVIEW

1. Why was slavery more prominent in the South than in the North?
2. What was the significance of the invention of the cotton gin?
3. Name some of the colonial leaders who opposed slavery.
4. How had slavery been eliminated in the British West Indies?
5. What were some of the southern arguments in defense of slavery?
6. Who were the Abolitionists?
7. Who was Harriet Beecher Stowe?
8. Why did Missouri's request for admission to the Union raise the slavery issue in Congress?
9. How did the Compromise of 1850 seek to satisfy both the North and the South?
10. What was the effect of the passage of the Kansas-Nebraska Act?
11. What were the provisions of the *Dred Scott* decision by the Supreme Court?
12. What were the goals of the Republican Party?
13. Who was John Brown?
14. Who was the first Republican to be elected president?

THE CIVIL WAR

General Sherman, General Grant, President Lincoln, and Admiral Porter aboard the *River Queen* on March 27 & March 28, 1865

THE SOUTHERN STATES LEAVE THE UNION

The Confederate States of America

The election of 1860 was over. Abraham Lincoln, the candidate of the Republican Party, had been elected president. South Carolina had threatened to secede from the Union if Lincoln were elected. South Carolina opposed the Republican position to abolish slavery. On December 20, 1860, a month after the election, delegates from around the state met at Charleston. They cast the fateful vote to secede from the Union. Alabama, Florida, Georgia, Louisiana, Mississippi, and Texas soon joined South Carolina. On February 4, 1861, one month before Lincoln's inauguration, delegates from the

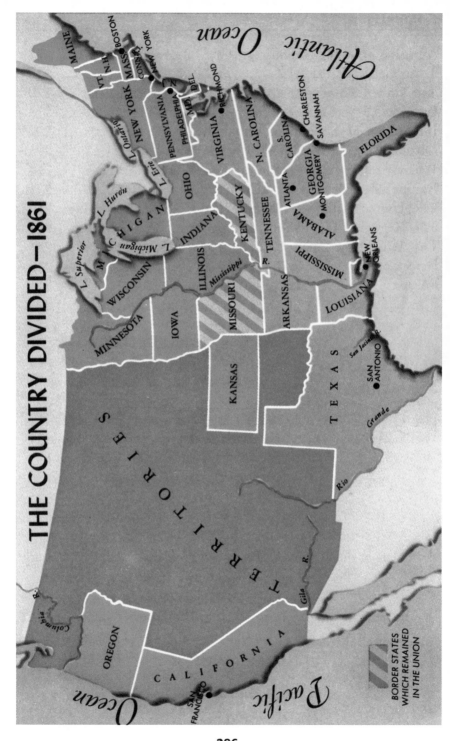

THE COUNTRY DIVIDED—1861

Atlantic Ocean

Pacific Ocean

MAINE
VT. N.H.
MASS. BOSTON
CONN. NEW YORK
N.J.
L. Ontario
NEW YORK
PENNSYLVANIA
PHILADELPHIA
MD. DEL.
RICHMOND
VIRGINIA
L. Erie
OHIO
N. CAROLINA
S. CAROLINA
CHARLESTON
SAVANNAH
FLORIDA
L. Huron
MICHIGAN
L. Michigan
KENTUCKY
TENNESSEE
ATLANTA
GEORGIA
MONTGOMERY
ALABAMA
L. Superior
INDIANA
R. Tennessee
MISSISSIPPI
NEW ORLEANS
WISCONSIN
ILLINOIS
Mississippi
MISSOURI
ARKANSAS
LOUISIANA
MINNESOTA
IOWA
KANSAS
San Jacinto R.
SAN ANTONIO
T E X A S
Rio Grande
T E R R I T O R I E S
Gila R.
R.
Columbia R.
OREGON
C A L I F O R N I A
SAN FRANCISCO

BORDER STATES
WHICH REMAINED
IN THE UNION

286

seceding states held a congress at Montgomery, Alabama. There they organized the Confederate States of America.

The Confederate constitution was modeled after the Constitution of the United States. However, it made three significant changes. First, it protected the rights of the individual states. Second, it specifically protected slavery. Third, it prohibited all tariffs.

Jefferson Davis of Mississippi was elected president of the Confederacy. Alexander H. Stephens of Georgia was elected vice president. They took office on February 18, 1861, at Montgomery, Alabama, the new capital. However, in May 1861, the capital was moved to Richmond, Virginia.

Jefferson Davis was a graduate of West Point. He had served with distinction in both military and civilian life. He had fought in the Mexican War and had served as a senator from Mississippi. For four years, he had served as Secretary of War under President Franklin Pierce.

The Inauguration of Lincoln

On March 4, 1861, the day of President Lincoln's inauguration, an anxious crowd waited to hear what he would say. He offered words of friendship to the states that had seceded. He said slavery would be protected where it already existed. He said the United States government was going to defend its forts in the South, but, he said, "there will be no invasion, no using of force against or among the people anywhere." Nevertheless, Lincoln forcefully set forth the North's principle of a perpetual union. In a solemn voice, he said: "...I hold that ... the union of these States is perpetual.... I therefore consider that...the Union is unbroken.... I shall take care, as the Constitution itself expressly enjoins upon me, that the laws of the Union shall be faithfully executed in all the states." He warned, "In your hands, my dissatisfied fellow

countrymen, and not in mine, is the momentous issue of civil war...
You have no oath registered in Heaven to destroy the government,
while I shall have the most solemn one to 'preserve, protect, and
defend' it."

Spot Check

1. Which was the first state to secede from the Union?
2. In what three ways did the Confederate Constitution differ from the U. S. Constitution?
3. Who was elected president of the Confederacy?

THE WAR BEGINS

Fort Sumter

The Civil War began at Fort Sumter on an island in the
harbor of Charleston, South Carolina. Major Anderson and a small
force of Union soldiers were stationed at the fort. South Carolina

Fort Sumter is fired upon.

insisted that Union troops be withdrawn. Since they did not want to attack the fort, South Carolina refused to allow any supplies into the fort. South Carolina hoped to starve the soldiers out without a fight.

By April, Anderson's food was nearly gone. If the fort were not restocked, he would need to surrender – or starve. Lincoln refused to allow the troops to be withdrawn. He ordered supplies to be sent to the men inside the fort, regardless of the outcome. When the Union tried to re-supply Fort Sumter, General Beauregard, the Confederate commander in Charleston, demanded Anderson immediately surrender. However, Anderson refused to give up. Early in the morning of April 12, 1861, Beauregard began firing on the fort. The war, which many in both the North and the South had hoped to avoid, had finally begun. Two days later, exhausted and nearly starved, Anderson and his men surrendered and left the fort.

The Call to Arms

The day after the surrender of Fort Sumter, President Lincoln issued a call for seventy-five thousand volunteers. The response was immediate. Fired with a desire to preserve the Union, tens of thousands of men answered the call to arms. President Jefferson Davis of the Confederacy also issued a call to arms. The response was equally enthusiastic. Southerners from all ranks of life volunteered.

Eight states lay between the Union and the Confederate states that had seceded. These were the so-called "border states." In these states, opinion was divided. Though all eight were slave states, they were not yet willing to leave the Union. However, as soon as Lincoln issued his call to arms, North Carolina, Virginia, Tennessee, and Arkansas joined the Confederacy.

Now the question was: what would happen to the other four states: Maryland, Delaware, Kentucky, and Missouri? By a combination of tact and force, Lincoln succeeded in keeping them in the Union. Nevertheless, thousands of men from these states joined the Confederate Army.

On the other hand, there were many who supported the Union in the border states of the Confederacy. Large numbers of these joined the Union forces. Many mountaineers from Tennessee and North Carolina gave their support to the North. Furthermore, the western section of Virginia broke away from the eastern part. It later entered the Union as the state of West Virginia in 1863.

Resources of the Union and the Confederacy

A comparison of the Union and the Confederacy shows that the Union had many advantages. It surpassed the Confederacy in number of people, in money, in factories, in supplies, and in railroads to transport soldiers and supplies. There were twenty-three states on the Union side when the war began, twenty-five before it was over. The population of the Union was about twenty-two million.

The Confederacy was at a disadvantage. There were only eleven states in the Confederacy. Its population was about nine million, of whom more than a third were slaves. The South was almost completely agricultural. It had few factories and very poor railroads. Almost ninety percent of the South's manufacturing power was in Richmond, its northernmost city. Under these handicaps, it was difficult to fight a war. However, the Confederacy had excellent generals so its armies were in good hands.

The Confederacy's greatest asset was probably General Robert E. Lee, who was the best general in North America at the time. Lincoln had offered command of the Union forces to General Lee. However, Lee was from Virginia. He felt he could not take up arms against his home state. He fought for the Confederacy.

Comparison of the Union and the Confederacy

CONFEDERATE STATES	**UNION STATES**
Alabama North Carolina	California Maine New York
Arkansas South Carolina	Connecticut Maryland Ohio
Florida Tennessee	Delaware Massachusetts Oregon
Georgia Texas	Illinois Michigan Pennsylvania
Louisiana	Indiana Minnesota Rhode Island
Mississippi Virginia	Iowa Missouri Vermont
	Kansas New Hampshire Wisconsin
	Kentucky New Jersey Nevada (1864)
	West Virginia (1863)

POPULATION — 71% / 29%
IRON PRODUCTION — 96% / 4%
FACTORIES — 85% / 15%
RAILROAD MILEAGE — 72% / 28%
MONEY — 81% / 19%
FARM ACREAGE — 65% / 35%

UNION STATES   CONFEDERATE STATES

Southerners thought that Europe would welcome a divided nation. If the Union and the Confederacy were not one nation, Europe would be able to carry on trade with the Confederacy unhampered by the Union's tariff. England was the world's greatest textile manufacturer and it bought most of its cotton from the Confederacy. Due to their relationship with England, the Confederacy thought that they would be able to import the manufactured goods and munitions that they needed to fight the war. They hoped for an alliance with England or France similar to the French alliance during the War of Independence. However, these hopes were never realized.

War Strategy of the Two Sides

When the Confederate guns roared out at Fort Sumter, the war between the Union and the Confederacy had begun. Each side believed that its cause was just. The Confederacy was defending the right of the states to secede and to make its own decisions. The North was fighting to preserve the Union. To be victorious, each side had its own strategy. The Confederacy needed to hold back the invading Union armies until the Northerners became so tired of war that they gave up. The Union would need to defeat the Confederate armies, destroy its government, and conquer its territory.

Despite the weakness of the Confederacy in terms of men and material, their defeat was by no means certain. The Confederacy did not need to "win" the war. They only needed a draw. They did not need to invade and conquer the Union, while the Union needed to invade and conquer the South. The South was also fighting on its home ground. They knew the land better than the Northern armies. Fighting at home, they could count on the support of the local people. The Union could not. The Southern soldiers were also fighting to defend their homes. This would make them

Robert E. Lee

fight harder. The fact that there were few railroads in the South was actually an advantage to the Confederacy. The Union armies either needed to find food in the South, or bring the food with them, or ship it by rail to the South. The lack of roads in the South was also an advantage. It is difficult to move troops over bad roads. Thus, a good army commander, like Robert E. Lee, was able to turn what appeared to be weaknesses into strengths. Throughout history, it has always been easier to defend against an invasion than to invade a country. The British had not been able to conquer the colonies ninety years before. The Confederacy felt certain that they could fight a defensive war until the Union would become tired of the loss of men and money, and would give up.

The Confederacy did have a limited offensive strategy. Given the opportunity, they would race northward and capture Washington, D.C. They would attack up through Maryland and into central Pennsylvania. The goal was to divide the North in two. The Confederacy would try this twice during the war. Both times, it would fail.

The task for the Union to achieve victory was actually much more difficult. It required the invasion and conquering of the South. The South was a large area. There were not many large towns. As long as the South could keep its armies in the field, it could exist.

To defeat the Confederacy, the Union developed a three-part strategy. First, it would cut the South off from European trade. By means of a blockade, it hoped to prevent ships from entering or leaving Southern ports. Accordingly, President Lincoln declared a blockade of the Southern coasts on April 19, 1861. Second, the Union would prevent the Confederacy from fighting as a unit. To accomplish this, the Union hoped to seize the Mississippi River ports and the important railroad centers of the South. This would divide parts of the South from one another. Third, the Union would attempt to capture Richmond, Virginia, the capital of the Confederacy. This would destroy the seat of government of the Confederacy.

The Union Blockade: The Key to Victory and Defeat

The blockade was the key to victory and defeat for both sides. The Union blockade plan was sound but risky. First, historically, blockades of the United States had failed because there was so much coastline. The British blockade during the War of Independence had failed for that reason. Second, if the blockade did work, it meant that English shipping would be kept out of Southern ports. England was a major trading partner with the South. The Confederacy hoped that the Union's naval blockade would so frustrate Britain and France that they would eventually actively help the Confederacy. Had England become an ally of the Confederacy, the Union would almost certainly have had to stop the war. England was by far the greatest military and economic power in the world. They had the world's largest and finest navy. Had the Union gone to war against England, the capital of the United States today may very well be Richmond, Virginia.

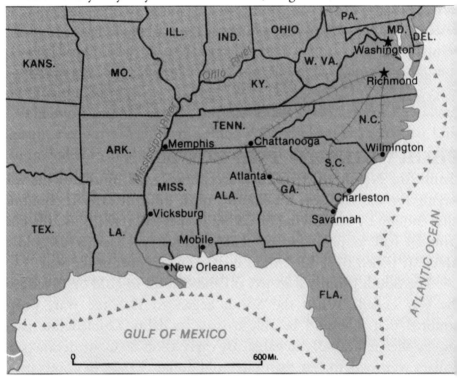

The Union Blockade

The Battle of Bull Run

When the war began, the Union had such a huge advantage in men, industry, and sea power, that they expected the war to be over quickly. In fact, volunteers were enlisted for only three months. Many Northerners believed that the Confederacy would be crushed at once. Everywhere men were impatient to strike and bring the war to a speedy end. Soon the people began to clamor for results. Lincoln yielded to the constant demand for action. He responded to the popular cry, "On to Richmond!" With thirty thousand ill-organized and poorly trained soldiers, Union General McDowell crossed the Potomac River and advanced toward Richmond, the Confederate capital.

The Union army under McDowell and the Confederate army under General Beauregard met on the banks of Bull Run. This was a little stream about thirty miles southwest of Washington, D.C. It was not a question of which army was better trained, but rather of how long these two inexperienced armies could last. At first, it seemed that the Union soldiers would win. However, toward evening of the day of battle, General Joseph E. Johnston brought reinforcements to Beauregard's exhausted troops. By sundown, the Union had lost the battle. McDowell's men were badly beaten and demoralized. They fled in confusion back to safety in Washington.

It was during this battle that General Thomas Jackson won the nickname "Stonewall." In the heat of battle, a fellow Confederate officer rallied his men to new courage by crying: "Look at Jackson! There he stands like a stone wall!" Ever since, that fearless Confederate has been known as Stonewall Jackson.

The rout of the Union forces at Bull Run was more than a stinging defeat. It taught the Union a valuable lesson. It showed that the South could not be defeated in a short time. It proved that victory could not be achieved by a hasty, ill-planned attack. It had a sobering effect upon everyone. As a result, Lincoln issued a call for more volunteers. He was determined that the Union's great advantage in numbers must be used to overwhelm the Confederacy. Lincoln placed General George McClellan, who had been largely responsible for West Virginia's joining the Union, in charge of the Northern armies. McClellan immediately reorganized his forces and set up a program of intensified training. Time would show that McClellan was a great organizer and trainer. Unfortunately, he was not much of a fighter.

The *Merrimac* Attempts to Break the Blockade

After about one year of war, the Confederacy developed a new kind of ship to break the blockade. It was a wooden vessel that had been covered with iron plates. For that reason, it was called an "ironclad." The USS *Merrimac* had been taken over by the Confederates at the beginning of the war. The Union's wooden ships had no chance against the attacks of this ironclad vessel. It sank a number of Union ships. Most importantly, it threatened to destroy the entire Union blockade.

On March 8, 1862, the *Merrimac* had entered Hampton Roads, Virginia. The goal was to break the blockade of Richmond and Norfolk, Virginia's two largest cities. The *Merrimac* destroyed two Union ships and was ready to destroy a third which had run aground when darkness fell. Unable to fight in the dark, the *Merrimac* withdrew. The *Merrimac* officers planned to return the following day to finish off the third Union ship and any others that crossed her path.

The *Monitor* and the *Merrimac* meet in battle.

However, during the night a curious-looking warship came to the rescue of the Union vessels. It was the *Monitor*, an ironclad ship invented by John Ericsson. The *Monitor* carried only two guns. However, the guns were set in a clever revolving iron turret. Therefore they could be fired in any direction. Also, only the turret was above the water, so there was little for the enemy to shoot at.

At daybreak, the two ironclad vessels met in battle. They fought for about three hours. Though each was damaged, neither could claim victory. After three hours, the *Merrimac* withdrew. The withdrawal of the *Merrimac* ended the Confederacy's chances of breaking the blockade. The ships never met again in battle. For the rest of the war, the Union controlled the sea. The blockade remained in place.

The Emancipation Proclamation

In September 1862, President Lincoln announced that if by January 1, 1863, the Confederate States had not returned to the Union, all slaves in states then at war with the United States would be declared free. It was a warning to the South. However, the South did not heed the warning. So, on January 1, 1863, an official document was issued. It was called the Emancipation Proclamation. However, the Emancipation Proclamation did not end slavery in the United States. It granted freedom *only* to those slaves in the areas controlled by the Confederacy. Although Lincoln personally believed slavery was wrong, he outlawed slavery only in those areas controlled by the Confederacy.

The Proclamation had a two-fold purpose. First, it increased public support for the war in the Union states. People were more motivated to support the war when it was seen as a moral crusade to end the evil of slavery as well as to preserve the Union. Also, the Proclamation was probably the single greatest reason that Britain and France did not enter into alliance with the Confederacy. Popular opinion in those two countries was overwhelmingly against slavery. It outweighed any economic profit Britain and France might have gained from helping the Confederacy.

Spot Check
1. What did the Battle of Bull Run teach the North?
2. What was unusual about the battle between the Monitor and the Merrimac?
3. Why did Lincoln issue the Emancipation Proclamation?

New Orleans and Vicksburg

To defeat the Confederacy, the Union needed to blockade the South, divide the South, and capture two great Confederate centers: Chattanooga in Tennessee and Richmond in Virginia. The blockade was successful. To divide the South, the Union set out to take control of the Mississippi River. Lincoln gave this task to General Ulysses S. Grant who was put in charge of the Union forces.

First, Grant captured the forts along the Cumberland and Tennessee rivers. Then he continued to push south. In April 1862, his army routed the Confederate forces at Shiloh in southwestern Tennessee. This was one of the bloodiest battles of the war. Meanwhile, Commodore David Farragut's naval forces took possession of New Orleans in Louisiana.

On July 4, 1863, General Grant, aided by General William T. Sherman, captured Vicksburg in Tennessee. This was the key city on the Mississippi. Union forces now had control of the entire Mississippi River except the 125-mile strip between Vicksburg and Port Hudson. Five days after the fall of Vicksburg, Port Hudson surrendered to the Union without a struggle. This meant control of the entire Mississippi. The Confederacy was cut in two. As a result, Arkansas, Louisiana, and Texas were left helpless. They could no longer send aid to the states east of the river.

In November, General Grant captured Chattanooga, an important railroad center. This forced General Braxton Bragg's entire army to retreat. All Tennessee was now in the hands of the Union. The power of the Confederacy west of the Allegheny Mountains was broken.

The Peninsular Campaign

About the time Grant's army was engaged in battle at Shiloh, the Easterners were clamoring for another advance on Richmond. Forced by public demand and by repeated orders from both the president and the War Department, the fretful, overcautious General McClellan began what is known as the Peninsular Campaign. Instead of advancing directly against Richmond, General McClellan transported his entire army of more than a hundred thousand men down the Potomac River and Chesapeake Bay to the peninsula between the York and James Rivers in southeastern Virginia.

Though at times McClellan came within striking distance, he did not attack Richmond. He was obsessed with the idea that Lee's army outnumbered his. Therefore, he petitioned Lincoln to send him more troops. No troops were sent. While McClellan waited, Generals Lee and Joseph E. Johnston, aided by Jeb Stuart, a daring Confederate cavalry leader, attacked McClellan and defeated him.

As a result of his failure to take Richmond, McClellan was removed by Lincoln. General John Pope was then put in command. However, he was defeated by General Lee. At this point, much to the relief of his men, McClellan was restored to command.

Encouraged by his victories over McClellan and Pope, General Lee advanced into Maryland. He was able to threaten Washington, D.C., the national capital. Lee and McClellan's forces clashed at Antietam in Maryland. There, both armies suffered terrible casualties. More men were killed in one 24-hour period than on any other day in American history. It was said that Antietam Creek turned red with the blood of soldiers. Since the Southern army had fewer men to replace those who fell, Lee was forced to retreat back to Virginia.

The Antietam victory was important to the Union. It temporarily halted Lee's advance northward. It was after this victory that Lincoln issued the Emancipation Proclamation. The victory, together with the Proclamation, renewed northern support for the war. The war now became almost a "holy" war against slavery. Also, the Antietam victory and the Proclamation had a powerful effect in Europe. The victory made the British and the French realize the Confederacy could lose the war. The Proclamation made them realize that the Union now had the moral high ground in world opinion.

However, the slow-moving McClellan failed to pursue Lee after Antietam and to follow up his advantage. Had he done so, he might have been able to destroy Lee's army. Instead, he let Lee escape. As a result of this failure, Lincoln again relieved him of command. Lincoln replaced him with General Ambrose Burnside.

Burnside was as hasty as McClellan was slow. Hence, without delay, he moved toward Richmond. However, at Fredericksburg, Lee inflicted a crushing defeat on Burnside. Again, Lincoln, trying to find someone who would be a match for Lee, removed Burnside. He appointed General Joseph Hooker to command the Union army.

Lee did not wait for Hooker to advance against Richmond. Instead, Lee took the initiative and marched north to meet him. They fought at Chancellorsville during the first week of May 1863. There, Lee inflicted upon the Union Army its worst defeat. However, this great success was not without a great loss. At Chancellorsville, Stonewall Jackson's own men accidentally shot him in the dark, mistaking him for a Union officer. He died a few days after being shot.

The Second Invasion

Following the victory at Chancellorsville, an opportunity presented itself to Robert E. Lee. He could again attack into the North. Although the Confederacy had planned to fight a defensive war, there were three good reasons to go on the offensive. First, an attack on the North would threaten Philadelphia, Boston, and Washington. It might draw off troops in the West that were threatening Vicksburg. (It was the end of May 1863. Vicksburg was still under siege and had not yet fallen. It would not fall until July 4.) Second, Virginia had been almost destroyed by all the fighting that had been going on there. It was said that if a crow flew across the Shenandoah Valley, he needed to take food with him. The people in Virginia were starving. They needed a break from the war. Lee's troops were starving. If they attacked the North, they could live off the bounty of the Northern farms. Even if the invasion was not successful, they hoped to bring wagonloads of food back with them. (This is exactly what did happen.) Finally, the Confederacy had planned to fight until the Union got tired of the war. There was a growing peace movement in the Union. There was even a peace candidate running for president in the North in the 1864 election. An attack into the North would "bring the war home." Thus, Lee decided to take the risk. He decided that he would strike a blow that would end the war.

Spot Check

1. Why was Vicksburg an important city?
2. What was the Peninsular Campaign?
3. Why was Antietam an important Union victory?

The Battle of Gettysburg

In June 1863, General Lee took his army of 75,000 men across the Potomac and marched north into Pennsylvania. On July 1, the Union soldiers, under General George Meade, met Lee's forces at the little town of Gettysburg in southern Pennsylvania. For three days, the two armies were locked in battle. About fifty thousand men were casualties in this battle. It was the bloodiest battle ever fought in North America.

The Southern soldiers fought courageously. As usual, they were outnumbered. However, they trusted that the quality of the men and the brilliance of Lee would make up for that. The crucial moment came on the third day of battle when General Pickett and a force of Confederates tried a desperate charge to break through the Union lines. The cannons and rifles of the Union army were too much. Pickett's charge was smashed and the Confederate advance was halted.

Pickett's Charge

In a pouring rain on the evening of July 4, 1863, Lee began his retreat into Virginia. He and the remaining soldiers were completely exhausted from the terrible struggle. Their minds were wearied by the disappointment of failure. The Confederacy had suffered a serious defeat. "It was all my fault," Lee said in a moment of bitter recollection.

Although this battle was the turning point in the war, at the time neither side knew this. The war would continue for almost two more years. The Confederacy suffered a terrible loss, but Southerners did not think the war was lost. The immediate reaction in the South was that the battle was a setback, not a disaster. Lee had kept the Union army out of Virginia during the summer of 1863. He had also returned to Virginia with enough food for his army to live on for months. In the North, Meade was criticized for not destroying Lee's army when he had the chance.

The Gettysburg Address

Today Gettysburg is an American memorial. Huge monuments and historic markers tell the sad story of that bloody battle. Part of the battlefield was made into a national cemetery. It was dedicated November 19, 1863, with a suitable ceremony. It was on that occasion that President Lincoln delivered his immortal Gettysburg Address. In the simplicity that belonged only to Lincoln, the president began his speech with these immortal words: "Fourscore and seven years ago, our fathers brought forth on this continent a new nation, conceived in liberty, and dedicated to the proposition that all men are created equal." The speech lasted less than three minutes. He concluded with a promise to his listeners "that this nation, under God, shall have a new

Abraham Lincoln

birth of freedom; and that government of the people, by the people, for the people, shall not perish from the earth."

Spot Check
1. Did the South think the war was lost after the Battle of Gettysburg? Why or why not?
2. What was Pickett's Charge?

THE WAR COMES TO A CLOSE

Lincoln is Re-elected

For a time, it looked as if Lincoln would not be re-elected president in 1864. The war was three and a half years old, and anti-war feeling was running high. The Democratic Party's presidential platform called for the immediate end of the war. However, their candidate, General McClellan, did not support the Democratic platform. In the months immediately preceding the election, the tide of the war turned in favor of the Union. It seemed that victory and the end of the war was in sight. Thus, Lincoln was easily re-elected.

Grant and Sherman

Lincoln still sought a general who was able to stand up to Lee. Early in 1864, Ulysses S. Grant was made commander of the Union armies. Immediately, he met with General Sherman, and together they drew up plans that they hoped would end the war. Grant took charge of the army on the Potomac. Sherman was given command of the armies in the West. Sherman was to march from Chattanooga, Tennessee, to Savannah, Georgia, thus splitting the Confederacy a second time. Grant was to march on Richmond, Virginia from the north. The two armies were to crush the enemy and destroy everything in their path.

Grant's Campaign against Richmond

In the spring of 1864, Grant began his advance on Richmond. He was determined to force Lee to surrender. Though Lee's army was small, Lee was still a match for the best the Union could bring up against him. As Grant approached the Confederate capital, Lee hurried out to attack him. He met the Union forces before they could get through an area called Wilderness. This was a forest of scrub oak in central Virginia north of Richmond. In the tangle of trees and undergrowth, Grant could not use his superior numbers to his advantage. Again, Lee had out-generalled his opponent. In the battles that followed in May, Grant lost heavily. However, unlike the men who had gone before him, Grant had a dogged determination. He simply refused to be beaten. When criticized for the slaughter of his men in the Wilderness, he replied that he was going to fight it out on this line of attack if it took all summer. He fought steadily on. Grant lost about 18,000 men to Lee's 11,000 despite outnumbering Lee almost two to one. Grant lost a smaller percentage of his army than Lee did. Moreover, he could get reinforcements while Lee could not.

Grant soon realized that he could not defeat Lee in the Wilderness. Thus, Grant withdrew from the forest. However, unlike his predecessors who had retreated or failed to continue after Lee, Grant continued to attack. He swung around and marched his army southwest toward Richmond. During the fall and winter of 1864-65, Grant took up a position outside Richmond. There, he besieged Lee and his army in the Confederate capital.

Sherman's March to the Sea
While Grant was preparing to take Richmond, Sherman started on his march from southern Tennessee to the Atlantic coast. His first objective was Atlanta, an important railroad and manufacturing city. Sherman captured Atlanta in September 1864. This victory helped Lincoln's re-election. Sherman's army continued its march through Georgia. Sherman's army destroyed everything in its path. It left death and starvation in its wake. From Atlanta, Sherman went on to Savannah almost without opposition. He entered the city on December 20. From Savannah, he turned northward, advancing through South Carolina and North Carolina in order to join Grant in the vicinity of Richmond.

Surrender of the Confederacy
After several attempts to defend his position, Lee was forced to withdraw his army from Richmond. He hoped to join up with Confederate forces farther west and south. However, this proved impossible. His position seemed hopeless. Seeing no chance of escape, Lee prepared to surrender. On April 9, 1865, Lee met Grant

near Appomattox Court House in Virginia to arrange terms of peace between the Union and the Confederacy. The war was finally over.

Emerging victorious, Grant was extremely generous to the South. He demanded merely that the Confederate troops lay down their arms. When Lee told him that his men had little to eat, Grant ordered the Union soldiers to share their rations with their Southern brothers. In addition, at Lee's request, the Southerners were allowed to keep their horses and mules for the spring plowing. The officers were permitted to keep their swords.

The news of Grant's victory was received with great rejoicing in the North. Celebrations were held everywhere. The South, too, was relieved that the war was finally over. After four years of continuous fighting, the soldiers and the civilians were exhausted.

Lee Surrenders to Grant

Everyone in the South had suffered terribly. The people had been reduced to poverty.

The Cost of the War

The war cost over five billion dollars. That does not include the cost of the farms, factories, and homes destroyed by invading armies. Greater still was the cost in human lives to both the Union and the Confederacy. About six hundred twenty-five thousand soldiers lost their lives. Almost half of all the men and women who have died in America's wars died in the Civil War. Think, too, of the tears, the pain, the mourning, and the fruitless waiting for fathers, brothers, and sons to return—none of which can ever be measured. The Civil War was, indeed, an American tragedy.

Lincoln's Assassination

On April 14, only five days after Lee's surrender, President Lincoln was shot. The president had gone to see a play at Ford's Theater in Washington, D. C. During the third act if the play, John Wilkes Booth, an actor, thinking Lincoln a tyrant bent on destroying the South, shot the president. President Lincoln died the next morning.

The death of Lincoln deprived the nation of its leader at a time when his sympathy and understanding were needed most. A great task lay before the country: to bind up the nation's wounds. That task was barely begun. Now the man that many hoped could carry out that job "with malice toward none" and "charity for all" was gone.

Results of the War

The Civil War had three important results. First, it preserved the Union. Second, it led to the abolishment of slavery which was concluded later by the Thirteenth Amendment. Third, it determined that a state could not secede from the Union. This question had remained unanswered since the time the Constitution was first ratified. At different times, states in both the North and the South had threatened to leave the Union. Whatever the original intent of the Framers of the Constitution was, after the war, it was clear that the states did not have this right. From this moment on, the power of the states would decrease, while the power of the Federal government would increase.

Spot Check

1. What was Sherman's March to the Sea?
2. When and where did the Civil War end?
3. When and where was Lincoln assassinated?
4. What were the results of the Civil War?

CHAPTER REVIEW

1. When and where did the Civil War begin?
2. In what three ways did the Confederate Constitution differ from the U. S. Constitution?
3. How did West Virginia become a state?
4. Compare the resources of the North and the South.
5. What was probably the South's greatest resource?
6. How did the South believe it could win the war?
7. What was the North's plan to win the war?
8. Why are the following battles important:
   a. Bull Run
   b. Antietam
   c. Chancellorsville
   d. Vicksburg
9. Which ship won the battle between the *Monitor* and the *Merrimac*? Why?
10. Why did Lee attack into Pennsylvania?
11. Why did the South not think the war was over after the Battle of Gettysburg?
12. Why did Lincoln issue the Emancipation Proclamation?
13. What was Sherman's March to the Sea?
14. When and where did the war end?
15. What were the results of the war?

THE CHURCH AND THE NATION
DURING TROUBLED TIMES

This ruined Southern mansion symbolized the ruin of the South after the Civil War.

THE PROBLEM OF RECONSTRUCTION

The Work of Rebuilding

War always leaves the problem of reconstruction, that is, the task of rebuilding the society after the terrible damage of war. The Civil War was no exception. When the war was over, the thousands of men from the disbanded armies needed to find jobs. Property destroyed by the war needed to be replaced. Business and industry tried to return to a peacetime basis. Those who financed the war on each side wanted to be paid. Money was needed to take care of the wounded and the crippled; the widows and the orphans needed homes and food.

In the North, the problem of reconstruction was different from that in the South. The manpower of the North had not been exhausted by the war. The factories and farms had continued to operate. In the North, there was general prosperity. The soldier who returned and found his job gone, went to the West. There he could purchase government land and establish a new home. The widows, orphans, and cripples made dependent by the war were supported by a system of government pensions.

The South After the Civil War

Almost the entire war had been fought in the South. The war left the South in a tragic condition. Destruction, bankruptcy, desolation, and poverty stalked the land like a child's worse nightmare. Where once there was wealth and prosperity, ruin and blight had taken over. Beyond all the material devastation was the terrible suffering of the people when the wounded and crippled troops returned home. For many, there was no home to which to return. For other families, no one ever did return. The heavy hearts and the sorrow of so many broken homes added still more to the tragedy that had struck the South.

The war completely destroyed the plantation system in the South. Agriculture and trade were paralyzed. Money was worthless. The Confederate government no longer existed. There were no pensions in the South to care for those who had been disabled by the war. The federal government decided that the Confederate states lost their rights as states because of rebellion. They would need to be readmitted to statehood. How would the North receive them?

Lincoln's Reconstruction Plan

Lincoln had no thought of punishing the Southern states or their leaders after the war. He wanted the Southern states to resume their place in the Union. He realized that there could be no reunion if the South were subjected to a brutal occupation. However, the radical Republicans thought otherwise. They wanted vengeance.

They wanted both the Southern states and their leaders punished. To avert all this, Lincoln called a meeting of his Cabinet and proposed a plan of reconstruction. He told them of the dangers of revenge. He said, "I hope there will be no persecution, no bloody work after the war is over...[no] hanging or killing those men, even the worst of them....Enough lives have been sacrificed."

Johnson Takes Over

Two days after this Cabinet meeting, President Lincoln was killed. Had he lived, his desire to make peace, his patience, and his political savvy might have helped "to bind up the nation's wounds." The work of reconstruction now fell to less capable leadership. Andrew Johnson, his vice president, became president.

Johnson tried to carry out Lincoln's plans of reconstruction. He issued a proclamation that pardoned all those who had rebelled against the United States. The only exception were the prominent leaders of the Confederacy. He called upon the states that had seceded to elect officers and organize governments that would repeal the declarations of secession, repudiate the Confederate war debt, and ratify the Thirteenth Amendment. This amendment was adopted on December 6, 1865. It abolished slavery. Though senators and representatives were elected in the Southern

Andrew Johnson

states, Congress refused to seat them. The Radical Republicans, who controlled Congress, believed that the authority to re-admit the South into the Union belonged to Congress and not to the president. They resented what seemed to them Johnson's infringement on their power. They were unwilling to recognize the reconstruction that the state governments set up at the president's direction.

Southern state governments attempted to deal with the problems of reconstruction as best they could. The North, however, rejected some of these attempts. "Black codes," which had been passed by the new Southern governments, added fuel to the fire. These laws gave the former slaves fewer rights than those enjoyed by Whites. It assigned Blacks who were homeless to guardians. In many cases, the guardians were their former masters. Congress believed these codes were an attempt to keep Blacks enslaved.

As a result of these differences, a bitter quarrel developed between President Johnson and Congress. Resentment grew, and Congress even voted to impeach him. He escaped removal from office by only one vote. However, his power was gone. With more than two-thirds of Congress hostile to him, even his veto was powerless.

Congressional Reconstruction Plans

Determined to draw up its own plans for the South, Congress began by voting in the Fourteenth Amendment and submitting it to the states for ratification. This amendment had four goals. One, it granted Blacks the rights of citizenship. Two, it provided that the representation in Congress of any state which denied Blacks the right to vote would be reduced. Three, it disqualified as officeholders the leaders of the Confederacy. Four, it forbade payment of the Confederate war debt or reimbursement for loss of slaves.

Tennessee promptly approved the amendment. Their representatives were admitted to Congress. However, the other

Southern states refused to ratify the amendment. As a result, Congress passed the Reconstruction Act of 1867. This rather harsh Act had four provisions. First, the ten states that had not ratified the Fourteenth Amendment would be divided into five military districts. Each district was placed under a military commander. Second, the commanders were to register all voters, both Black and White. However, those who had held prominent positions in the Confederacy or who had fought against the Union, were denied the right to vote or hold office. Third, the new state constitutions were to give Blacks the right to vote. These new constitutions were to be approved by the voters of the state and by the Congress of the United States. Fourth, the states were to ratify the Fourteenth Amendment.

As the states met these requirements, they were permitted to resume their place in the Union. Within two years, seven of the seceding states had been formally re-admitted to the Union. The other states remained under military rule for almost three years longer.

Spot Check

1. What was the Reconstruction Act of 1867?
2. How was reconstruction different in the North than in the South?
3. What was Lincoln's Reconstruction Plan?
4. What was the Radical Republican attitude toward reconstruction?
5. What was the Thirteenth Amendment?
6. What were the goals of the Fourteenth amendment?

GOVERNMENT IN THE SOUTH

Carpetbaggers and Scalawags

Most of the natural leaders in the South had supported the Confederacy. Therefore, they were not permitted to run for office in the new state governments. This led to shameful corruption and inefficiency. The two classes of politicians who capitalized on the situation were the carpetbaggers and the scalawags. The carpetbaggers were Northerners who rushed into the South to obtain political positions and steal public funds. They were called carpetbaggers because they carried all their possessions in carpetbags: traveling bags made of carpet. The scalawags were Southerners who qualified for public office by swearing that they had not fought against the United States. They were determined to gain political power and were, for the most part, dishonest. The carpetbaggers and scalawags offset all the efforts of honest statesmen to fix the problems in the South. Sadly, corruption and dishonesty thrived all over the South.

The Birth of the Ku Klux Klan

The resentment in the South to northern reconstruction grew intense. To counteract the corrupt rule of the carpetbaggers and scalawags, a number of secret societies were formed. Most important among these was the Ku Klux Klan. To prevent the Blacks from

Members of the Ku Klux Klan terrorize a family.

voting, the Klan promoted a "reign of terror." Dressed in flowing white sheets, members of the Klan paraded the roads and village streets at night. They often visited the homes of black families. In ghostly shrieks, they warned the Blacks not to vote or to leave the community. At times, violence was used.

To end this criminal activity, Congress passed the Force Act and the Ku Klux Klan Act in 1870 and 1871. These Acts empowered the president to use martial law where the rights of Blacks were endangered. Naturally, the South resented such action. At length, public opinion compelled Congress to restore to prominent Southerners the right to take part in government affairs.

Home Rule

With their political rights restored, the Southerners took steps to establish "home rule" in the South. This meant government by the old white leadership of the South. They passed laws fixing voting qualifications that prevented most Blacks from voting. Some of these laws were declared unconstitutional under the Fifteenth Amendment to the Constitution. However, others, such as the law requiring that a voter be able to read, were allowed. In fact, there were similar practices in some Northern states designed to keep former slaves from voting.

It was not until 1877, twelve years after the war, that the last of the federal troops were withdrawn from the South. This closed the tragic era of the carpetbaggers and the scalawags. It restored government by white Southerners to the South. These governments brought greater order and stability. However, they also brought the end of attempts to create equality of Blacks.

Between 1865 and 1870, the Reconstruction Congress was successful in adding the Thirteenth, Fourteenth, and Fifteenth Amendments to the Constitution. These amendments outlawed slavery and racial discrimination. However, once the "home rule" governments were restored in the South, the spirit and intent of these Amendments lost all practical effect. They would not come to be fully realized in the South until the latter half of the 20th century.

Spot Check

1. What did the Thirteenth, Fourteenth, and Fifteenth Amendments do?
2. Why did Congress pass the Reconstruction Act of 1867?
3. Who were the Carpetbaggers? Who were the Scalawags?
4. What was the name of the secret society that terrorized Blacks?
5. What did "home rule" mean for Blacks in the South?

THE CHURCH IN TROUBLED TIMES

The Missions in the West and Southwest

In 1850, the Holy See appointed a Vicar Apostolic to govern Catholics in the area of New Mexico. At that time, this included Arizona, Colorado, and parts of Utah, and Nevada. The Vicar was a Frenchman: the famous Jean Baptiste Lamy. In 1927, Willa Cather immortalized him in her wonderful novel, *Death Comes for the Archbishop*. He took incredible journeys throughout the land. These journeys became legendary. Lamy came to be considered the ideal example of a missionary on the frontier.

In July 1853, Lamy became the first bishop of Santa Fe, the oldest city in the New Mexico territory. Over the next few years, he traveled to Europe to seek help for his struggling diocese. The lack of priests and religious to staff his churches and schools was great. However, by 1875, the situation had improved so much that Santa Fe was made an archdiocese and Bishop Lamy its first archbishop. He had changed a dying diocese into a thriving one. Most of the Catholics spoke Spanish. In addition, Lamy claimed three thousand English-speaking Catholics for the archdiocese. He also had twelve thousand Catholic Pueblo Indians in his archdiocese.

In 1885, American Franciscans came into the area that now includes the states of Arizona, New Mexico, and Texas. The wonderful work of this order had begun many years earlier but the anti-Catholic government in Mexico had destroyed it. They established missions among the Navajos, the Papagos, the Apaches, and the Pueblos of New Mexico. Of all these tribes, the Pueblos remained most steadfast in the Faith. Later, permanent pastors cared for these missions.

The St. Francis Cathedral in Santa Fe was built from 1869 to 1887 by Bishop Lamy. The statue on the right is of Bishop Lamy.

The area comprising the present states of North and South Dakota, Nebraska, Kansas, Colorado, Wyoming, and eastern Montana was known at that time as the Vicariate of Kansas. It was under the authority of Bishop Miege. The bishop administered it from his headquarters at Leavenworth in Kansas.

French Benedictines were active in the "Indian Territory" starting in 1875. This later became part of Oklahoma. The diocese of Oklahoma was established in 1905. Pope Paul VI later split it into two dioceses, one for the eastern part and one for the western part of the state.

Missions in the North

In Minnesota and the Dakotas, the Sioux had known Catholic missionaries from the days of the first French missionaries from the time of Father de Smet. Therefore, there were many native Catholics among them. In 1874, the Benedictines, under the direction of Abbot (later Bishop) Martin Marty of St. Meinrad's Abbey, began their work among the Indians. The Sioux, in both Minnesota and the Dakotas, warmly received them.

MISSIONS TO THE BLACKS

Difficulties of the Work

From the beginning, the Church cared for the Blacks in this country. During the period of their slavery, the Church provided religious services as well as education for them. Most of the Catholic Blacks were located in those southern states originally settled in part by Catholics. As time went on, the work of the Church became more difficult. Protestants passed laws to prevent baptism and missionary activity among Blacks. In spite of all the efforts to deny the Church the right to work among these people, laymen and missionaries alike dared to bring the Faith to them. Members of the hierarchy actively championed the cause of Blacks for good treatment. Among the most prominent was the bishop of Charleston, John England. In the face of every kind of opposition, he provided for the care of their souls.

As early as 1829, a community of Black sisters was founded. This little community was called the Oblate Sisters of Providence. Two years later, the Holy See recognized it as a religious community. Some years later, Henriette Delille founded a second Sisterhood for Black women. These Sisters came to be known as the Sisters of the Holy Family. They adopted the rule of St. Augustine.

The Period after Emancipation

The Church had great difficulty in her work for Blacks before emancipation. After they were freed, new emphasis was placed on promoting their conversion. Both the Second and the Third Plenary Councils of Baltimore pleaded for continued work among Blacks. The Third Plenary Council appealed in particular for Black vocations. The Council urged seminaries to work diligently to promote such vocations.

While the abolishment of the evil of slavery was a great good, the freedom that the slaves received after the Civil War had a very bad effect upon their Catholic Faith. The slaves, once freed, tended to fall away from Catholic practice. There were no Black parishes to take over the religious influence of their Catholic masters. Sadly, thousands of Black Catholics fell away from the Faith. Then came the era of Protestantism. New organizations for Blacks were set up. Protestant missions began to claim many of the fallen away Catholics. The Protestants had many advantages over the Catholics. They could educate missionaries at a much faster rate than the Church could with the long years of study required for the priesthood. The Baptists and Methodists drew many into their pews. They appointed Black preachers with little or no education to organize their own people. The result was amazing. Thousands and thousands of Blacks became Baptists or Methodists.

A Black Protestant preacher visits a Black family.

Religious Communities Help

Up to 1870, mainly individual priests conducted the Catholic mission work among Blacks. There was little activity by religious orders. However, in 1871, a group of priests was organized for the purpose of working among the Blacks in the United States. These were the Josephite Fathers. They were sent from England by their founder, Father Vaughan, who later became a cardinal in England. These priests took charge of St. Xavier Church in Baltimore, which had a large black membership.

God blessed the Josephites in their work. Their success encouraged others to follow their example. In 1872, the Holy Ghost Fathers sent several priests from their motherhouse in Europe to America. In 1874, the Benedictines came to Charleston from France and Italy. In 1905, the Society of the Divine Word sent the first missionaries from their mission center in Illinois to the state of Mississippi. Later, Franciscans, Capuchins, Passionists, Jesuits, Benedictines, and Vincentians all followed.

The work of the missionaries was greatly aided by an ever-growing number of sisterhoods and brotherhoods that worked in the South. Perhaps the most important among the sisterhoods are the Sisters of the Blessed Sacrament. This order was founded in 1891 by Mother Katharine Drexel. Mother Drexel devoted her wealth and energy to the Indian and Black missions. The Sisterhood became a strong religious influence in the South. During her long life, Mother Drexel founded sixty-three schools. The most famous school she

Mother Katharine Drexel

founded is Xavier University. It was established in New Orleans in 1925 and dedicated in 1932. It was the first Catholic university in the United States for Blacks. Mother Drexel died in 1955. She has since been recognized for her holiness. Pope John Paul II declared her a saint in October 2000.

Mother Drexel, like every missionary, knew the importance of a Catholic education. Recognizing the good influence of the Catholic school, the southern bishops invited religious orders both here and abroad to help them. The response was very encouraging. Throughout the South, many elementary schools and high schools were established. Also, convents, monasteries, and seminaries were provided for black Catholics.

Spot Check

1. Which bishop helped the Faith flourish once again in New Mexico?
2. What new difficulties arose for Catholic missions to Blacks after emancipation from slavery?
3. What was the first group of male religious formed to work among Blacks?
4. Who founded the Sisters of the Blessed Sacrament?
5. Why is Xavier University in New Orleans particularly significant?

CHURCH LEADERSHIP

The middle of the nineteenth century was a period of increased activity in the Church in America. Despite war, hard times, and a bigoted opposition, the Church grew and prospered. Several new dioceses were created. The Church was blessed with a long list of distinguished, scholarly bishops. However, of all the great men to be bishops and cardinals in America, so far only one has earned that greatest of distinctions, the title Saint. That man is St. John Nepomucene Neumann. He was the Bishop of Philadelphia.

Bishop John Neumann

John Neumann was born in Bohemia (today the Czech Republic) in central Europe in 1811. However, he came to America before his ordination to the priesthood. In 1836, Bishop Dubois of New York ordained him a priest. For four years, he worked as a missionary among German-speaking Catholics in western New York. Then he became a member of the Redemptorist Order.

In 1852, Neumann was consecrated the fourth bishop of Philadelphia. He built many churches and schools. When he became bishop, Philadelphia had two Catholic schools. When he died, the city had one hundred Catholic schools!

A learned theologian, Bishop Neumann was a distinguished member of the First Plenary Council of Baltimore. He was one of the American bishops invited to Rome by Pope Pius IX for the definition of the doctrine of the Immaculate Conception. He wrote a catechism that was widely used in the United States before the introduction of the Baltimore Catechism.

Bishop Neumann was deeply devoted to the Blessed Sacrament. He was the first bishop in the United States to establish the Forty Hours' Devotion. This devotion is the solemn exposition of the Blessed Sacrament for forty hours in honor of the forty hours Jesus is believed to have lain in the tomb. Bishop Neumann died in 1860. Almost immediately after his burial in St. Peter's Church, Philadelphia, his tomb became a place of pilgrimage. Pope Paul VI canonized him in 1977. He was the first male citizen of the United States so honored.

Bishop John Neumann

The Councils of Baltimore

There are two kinds of councils that bishops hold. The first kind is called a provincial council. A provincial council deals with matters of church discipline and church rules. It does not deal with matters of Faith. The second kind of council is called a plenary or a national council. It cannot be called without the authority of the pope. It is presided over by an Apostolic Delegate, who is the pope's representative at the council. All the bishops of the country must appear at such a council, which deals with matters of discipline as well as matters of Faith.

The First Provincial Council

While the Church was facing the problems of obtaining priests and teachers, the bigotry and prejudice of Protestants made the job more difficult. However, God blessed the Church with fearless, determined leaders. When Archbishop Carroll died in 1815, Bishop John England of Charleston became the leader of America's Catholics. Under his leadership, the First Provincial Council in the United States was called. It was held in Baltimore in 1829, and laid the groundwork for the struggling Church in the United States. In all, six provincial councils were held in Baltimore between 1829 and 1849. Important rules for the welfare of the Church in our country were discussed and enacted.

The bishops who met at the First Provincial Council were concerned with the Church and especially with the need for Catholic schools. They were particularly concerned about the textbooks that would be used in the schools. They were afraid that the books would contain material that was false and harmful to the Faith. Thus, they ruled that all textbooks were to be free from everything harmful to the Faith. Moreover, to insure that the books were free of religious errors, they were to bear the approval of the bishop.

The First Plenary Council

The First Plenary Council met in Baltimore in 1852. Six archbishops and twenty-six bishops attended. Archbishop Kenrick of Baltimore presided as Apostolic Delegate. The assembled bishops approved the acts of all the previous Baltimore councils. They adopted various rules for parish and diocesan governments. The Council recommended building parish schools. Finally, it warned against lay interference in Church affairs. Lay interference was becoming a problem in the United States. Protestants had always interfered in the running of their churches. They had the right to choose their pastors as well as fire them. Catholics in the United States were beginning to think that they had that "right" as well.

The Second Plenary Council

The Second Plenary Council of Baltimore was held in 1866. Seven archbishops, thirty-nine bishops, two abbots, and more than one hundred twenty priests attended. The Civil War had just ended in 1865. The members of the Council knew they needed to rebuild the shattered educational system in the United States, especially in the South. Among its decrees, the Council passed a resolution asking priests to dedicate as much time as they could to the service of the Blacks. The Council also recommended that a Catholic university be built in the United States.

The Third Plenary Council

Archbishop James Gibbons presided over the Third Plenary Council held in Baltimore in 1884. This Council stressed the education of the clergy, the creation of parish schools, and the founding of a Catholic University of America. The Council discouraged marriages of Catholics to non-Catholics. It decreed that there should be six holy days of obligation in a year. The Council also appointed a commission to prepare a catechism for use in the schools. This resulted in the famous Baltimore Catechism.

This Council was a major step toward removing the mission status of the Church in America. It prepared the Church in the United States for the move from being a missionary land to a country ready to provide for its own support. Over the next century, the United States would become the largest financial supporter of the Catholic Church.

Under the influence of this Council, Catholic education was organized in the United States. The national system of parish schools had its beginnings here. The Council also decided to go ahead with plans for the Catholic University of America in Washington, D.C. The stone for the first building of the university was laid in 1888.

Spot Check

1. What statistic shows the energy and zeal of John Neumann as bishop of Philadelphia?
2. What is a plenary council?
3. When and where were three plenary councils held for the United States in the nineteenth century?

CHAPTER REVIEW

1. Describe conditions in the South after the Civil War.
2. What was "Reconstruction"?
3. What was Lincoln's plan of reconstruction?
4. How was reconstruction different in the North than in the South?
5. How did Lincoln's plan differ from the plan put through by Congress?
6. What was the chief cause of friction between President Johnson and Congress?
7. Who were carpetbaggers and scalawags? What was their effect on reconstruction in the South?
8. What was the Thirteenth Amendment?
9. What were the goals of the Fourteenth Amendment?
10. What is meant by "home rule" in the South after the Civil War?
11. What effect did emancipation have on the religious life of Blacks?
12. Who was Bishop John Neumann? Why is he important? Why is he unique?
13. Name four accomplishments of the Third Plenary Council of Baltimore.

New Inventions Transform the Nation

The steam locomotive *Tom Thumb* races a horse.

The Age of the Railroad

The First Railroads

In the early 1800s, people could travel on land only as fast as they could ride on a horse or in a stagecoach. Travel by water was also very slow. Ships and boats could go only as fast as the wind was blowing or people were rowing. The development of the railroad changed all that.

The first railroad in this country, the Baltimore and Ohio Railroad, was built in 1830 in Baltimore, Maryland. From that time until 1850, development of the railroads was slow. The number of railroad track miles increased to about ten thousand. No railroad extended beyond the Appalachians. However, by 1861, there were more than thirty thousand miles of railroad. These railroads extended from the cities of the East to the Mississippi River. There was a network of railroads joining the Northwest with the Northeast. Some parts of the Southwest and Southeast were joined. There were few connections between the North and the South.

The railroads of the early days were very different from today's modern railroad. Many of the tracks were no more than twenty or thirty miles long. They varied in width from three-and-a-half to six feet. As a result, the cars of one railroad could not run on the tracks of another. In appearance and comfort, too, the railroad cars differed from modern railroad cars. The passenger cars were merely stagecoaches chained together and equipped with wheels that could run on tracks or "rails." The freight cars were nothing more than rough platforms on wheels.

As the railroads expanded, improvements were made. The earliest trains had no sleeping accommodations. Smoky, smelly kerosene lamps or candles provided light for the cars. Wood or coal stoves heated them. The constant changing from one railroad to another, the bumping over rough roadbeds, and the soot and cinders made travel very uncomfortable. Yet railroad travel was far superior in speed and convenience to any other method of land travel.

Improvements in Rail Travel

In the late 1850s, George Pullman built the first successful train sleeping car. This greatly added to the comfort of rail travel. Though his first car was not as luxurious as the sleeping cars on modern trains, it did have an upper and lower bed. During the day the upper bed was pushed against the wall and the lower bed became a seat. About the same time, George Westinghouse invented the air brake. This increased the comfort and the safety of rail travel. Before the air brake was invented, the brakes on each car were applied separately. With the invention of the air brake, all the brakes were set at once by compressed air. This made it possible to stop the train more quickly. In 1867, the railroad introduced a dining car. It was then possible to sleep and eat on the train. Train travel was becoming very comfortable indeed.

Another important innovation to the railroad was the addition of the refrigerator car. This made it possible to ship perishable food from one end of the country to the other. Air-conditioning and heating also was added to the train cars. This made travel even more comfortable as the traveler rode in cool comfort on hot days and in warmth on cold days.

The Expansion of the Railroads

The settling of the West had much to do with the growth of railroads in the United States. The Mormons, the "forty-niners," and the followers of the Oregon Trail had settled in the far-western regions as citizens of the United States. By 1860, nearly seven hundred thousand people were living in the Western states. These people were eager to be connected with the East. The railroad was the only way this could be done. Far-sighted Americans realized that this would be one country only if it were united physically as well as politically. A transcontinental railroad, a railroad that connected one coast with the other, was becoming an obvious need.

In 1862, Congress began the work to connect the West with the East. It granted two railroad companies, the Union Pacific and the Central Pacific, with land and money for each mile of railroad that they built. The Union Pacific began work at Omaha, Nebraska, and worked westward. The Central Pacific moved eastward from Sacramento, California.

Many problems in the building of this transcontinental railroad were overcome as the result of ample government funds. However, there were other troubles that confronted the builders.

The problems themselves demonstrated the need that existed for a railroad. Supplies needed by the workmen of the Union Pacific had to be hauled by wagon or sent up the Missouri River in boats. Everything used by the Central Pacific that was manufactured in the East had to be shipped around Cape Horn at the southern tip of South America to Sacramento in California. Besides the hardships caused by mountains, rivers, and uncharted territory, the builders were always in danger of being attacked by Indians.

In 1869, four years after the end of the Civil War, the work was completed. The two crews met at Promontory Point near Ogden, Utah. There, with fitting ceremonies, a golden spike was driven into the ties connecting the rails of the two companies. The first transcontinental railroad system, stretching for more than three thousand miles, united the East and the West.

The Completion of the First Trans-Continental Railroad

The completion of this railroad was an extremely important moment. Prior to this time, the East and West coasts were linked by a thirteen-thousand-mile ocean voyage. The vast spaces of the West could not be utilized as long as travel and communication was so difficult. It was the completion of the railroad that truly made the United States a continental power.

In spite of the difficulty to build the transcontinental railroad, other companies became interested in building transcontinental rail lines. Within twenty years, there were four main lines connecting the East with the Pacific coast. In addition, many spur lines connected regions to the north and south. Railroad building continued steadily for the next one hundred years. It was the main form of transportation until the 1950s. It was only with the development of the automobile and the interstate highway system that the railroad diminished in importance as a means of passenger travel, although it continues to be essential for the transportation of goods and products.

Spot Check

1. What made travel on a nineteenth century railroad uncomfortable by twenty-first century standards?
2. What caused people to see a need for a transcontinental railroad?
3. How did Congress address the need for a transcontinental railroad in 1862?
4. When and where was the first transcontinental railroad finished?

NEW METHODS OF COMMUNICATION

The Telegraph

While the railroad was making it possible for people to travel faster, new forms of communication were making it possible for people to communicate with each other faster. The most notable development during this period was the invention of the telegraph. Samuel Morse invented the telegraph. Morse had worked out a way to translate electrical signals into words. Connecting and disconnecting an electric current created these signals. Wires transmitted the signals. In 1844, after years of experimenting, he sent the first historic message by wire from Washington, D. C. to Baltimore. The brief message read, "What hath God wrought!"

At first, people made fun of the telegraph. However, they slowly began to see its potential as a means of rapid communication. By 1861, communication was established as far west as St. Louis. By 1862, telegraph wires extended as far west as the Pacific. Thus, step-by-step, telegraph stations united the entire country.

The telegraph became an important part of American communication. Daily newspapers began to carry news from distant points of the country almost as soon as it happened. Railroads found the telegraph a great help. They used it to report the movements of trains, to establish schedules, and to improve safety. The value of the telegraph for personal messages and for business, was quickly recognized.

Transoceanic Cables

Once transcontinental communication was established, people began to think about communicating across the oceans. Even at the time of his invention, Morse had expressed the belief that some day telegraphic communication would be established between Europe and America. For communication across the Atlantic, wires could not be strung from pole to pole as they had been on land. Instead, they had to be bound together in waterproof material. The cable thus formed had to be laid on the bottom of the ocean.

The man mainly responsible for laying the first Atlantic cable was Cyrus W. Field. He was a New York businessman. The United States and England aided Field with ships. Due to the distance and the depth of the ocean, it was a huge undertaking. However, after several unsuccessful attempts, the two ships carrying portions of the cable met in mid-ocean. The two parts of the cable were spliced together. Then one ship sailed for Ireland, and the other set out for Newfoundland. The cable was on large spools at the stern of each vessel. As the vessels moved away from each other, the cable sank to the bottom of the ocean. The ships reached their destinations, and the transoceanic cable was laid. It connected Ireland with Newfoundland. A shorter cable was laid to connect Newfoundland with the mainland of North America.

On August 16, 1858, Queen Victoria in England sent a telegraph of congratulations to President James Buchanan. The two countries were united through a new bond of communication. Sadly, the very next month, the cable was destroyed. Someone applied too much voltage while trying to send messages faster. However, Field did not lose faith in the project. He continued his efforts. Finally, a year after the end of the Civil War, he succeeded. More than twenty-five years after Morse invented the telegraph, permanent telegraphic service between Europe and America was established. The success of the Atlantic cable led to the laying of other cables.

The Telephone

After the invention of the telegraph by which messages could be sent by wire, scientists became interested in creating an instrument by which the human voice could be transmitted by wire. This invention is the telephone. The inventor of the telephone was Alexander Graham Bell. Bell was born in Edinburgh, Scotland, in 1847. He was educated at the universities of Edinburgh and London. In 1870, his family moved to Canada. Alexander later moved to Massachusetts. He became a voice and speech teacher at Boston University. He had the very noble goal of teaching the deaf to speak and to read lips. It was this work that gave him the idea of trying to find a way to send the human voice over an electric wire. He worked tirelessly on his idea. He set up a lab in his home. There, with his faithful assistant, Thomas Watson, they worked to solve the problem. Finally, in 1876, he succeeded in making his invention work. However, like many inventors, he was at first the subject of scorn and jokes.

Finally, though, came the chance for recognition. He obtained permission to exhibit the phone at the Philadelphia Centennial Exposition in 1876. The Exposition was held to celebrate progress in America since the signing of the Declaration of Independence. At first, the phone attracted little attention. Then one day, the Emperor of Brazil stopped to talk to Bell about teaching the deaf. During their conversation, Bell told him about his invention. The emperor was curious. He held the receiver to his ear while Bell spoke into the transmitter from the other side of the building. When he heard Bell's voice, the emperor was shocked. He exclaimed: "It talks!" From that moment on, the importance of the telephone was acknowledged.

Alexander Graham Bell

Bell and his phone became world famous. News of the invention was published in America and around the world. It was a year before the first phones were installed in Boston. However, after that, the requests for phones poured in faster than they could be filled. Today the telephone links the world. Along with the computer and the television, it is one of the three most important communication methods in the modern world.

Spot Check
1. Who invented the telegraph and when?
2. Give one example of how the telegraph changed communication.
3. Who was the force behind laying the first transatlantic cable?

The Pony Express

For years, the stagecoach provided the only overland mail service to the West. Then, in 1860, the Pony Express was organized. The eastern starting point for the Pony Express was St. Joseph, Missouri. This was where the railroad ended at that time. The western end of the Pony Express was Sacramento, California. Daring young men on swift horses raced across the country, night and day, through all kinds of weather, carrying mail between these two cities. At the same time a rider left St. Joseph heading west, another rider would leave Sacramento, heading east. Each rider rode about seventy miles a day. They changed horses every ten or fifteen miles. Eighty riders were always on the move. Forty were galloping west. Forty were galloping east. In this way, mail reached the terminals within about nine days. This was an incredible achievement. Consider the summer's heat, the winter's cold, the rough country they rode through, and the dangers of the frontier from animals and Indians. Once the transcontinental telegraph was finished, the Pony Express was discontinued. Though this service lasted only about nineteen months, the Pony Express is one of the great accomplishments in American and world history.

Thomas Edison: The Home Schooled Genius

Thomas Alva Edison is generally considered the greatest inventor of all time. His inventions have had an untold impact on all of humanity. His electric light, phonograph, motion picture machine, and microphone are known universally. These, and the hundreds of other useful items he invented, have enhanced the quality of life around the world.

Edison was born on February 11, 1847, in Milan, Ohio. As a young boy, he showed signs of an inquisitive mind. In fact, in school he asked so many questions that the teacher thought that he was not very bright. After several months, the teacher recommended that his mother take him out of school. His mother home schooled him with great success. He loved to read and try out the things that he read about. When he was nine years old, his parents moved to a town where there was a

Thomas Edison and the Phonograph

public library. He was determined to read every book in it. He did not read all the books. His interest turned to chemistry and he began to focus on that. When he was twelve, he took a job working on a train to earn money for his growing laboratory. Three years later, he took a job as a telegraph operator. He spent his money on books and equipment for his lab.

When Edison was twenty-two, he became a professional inventor. Over the next sixty years, he produced over a thousand patented inventions. These were a result of his amazing energy and determination. At one time, he had as many as fifty inventions in various stages of development. He sometimes would forget to eat or sleep. His interest in his work drove him until he achieved the result he sought.

One of Edison's greatest strengths was his limitless patience. It is said that he and his assistants made as many as ten thousand experiments before they perfected the battery. He was also a good businessman. He never invented anything unless there was a need for it.

CHANGES IN AMERICAN LIFE

The Industrial Age

Before machines were invented, everything had to be made by hand. There were no factories, no huge industrial plants. In many instances, the home was the factory. It was there that many of the necessities of life were made. In this little home factory, family members helped. The slogan was: "Many hands make light work." Then came industrial inventions. Spinning and weaving machines were invented for making clothes. The Industrial Age was born.

The Industrial Revolution

The widespread use of machines in industry began in England. It was not until 1793, when Samuel Slater built his spinning mill in Rhode Island, that it reached America. Soon the inventive genius of Americans sparked the movement. Americans designed machine after machine. Americans invented the cotton gin, the sewing machine, and the reaper. This sped up production in the factory and on the farm.

Crowded factories took the place of "home factories." Large farms took the place of home plots. Factory production increased to such an extent that there was a tremendous need for labor. Employment possibilities encouraged tens of thousands of immigrants to come to this "land of plenty." Agricultural production also picked up. The drudgery of farm life began to disappear. The changes created by mechanical inventions have been called the "Industrial Revolution." They completely altered the life of America and the whole Western world.

THE NEW SOUTH

Agricultural Changes

The Civil War and the emancipation of Blacks changed farming practices in the South. Without workers to care for them, many plantations became areas of weeds and waste, instead of fields of cotton. The war and the heavy taxes of the reconstruction period impoverished the planters. They did not have enough money to hire either white laborers or their former slaves. While some freed slaves remained with their former owners, many did not want to return to work for their former masters. They preferred to rent a little patch of ground or to buy it on the installment plan and thereby enjoy their freedom. Many plantations, therefore, were broken up into small farms and sold or rented to Blacks or to white farmers in exchange for a share of their crops. In this way, small farms came into existence in the South.

The reduction of great plantations into small farms was not the only change in Southern agriculture. The Southern farmers came to realize that a one-crop system of farming was poor business. Thus, they began diversified farming. Cotton remained the chief crop, and rice, tobacco, and indigo were the leading staples. However, the South began to raise oranges, peaches, grapefruit, and other fruits and vegetables. With the improvement in railroad transportation and the eventual introduction of refrigerator cars, the growing of fruits and vegetables proved very profitable. Thus, the agricultural system of the South was gradually changed.

A Great Scientist

An outstanding figure in these changes in the South was George Washington Carver. Born a slave, he became an agricultural scientist of international fame. Early in life, he decided that he must do something to help other Blacks. In spite of many hardships brought on by poverty and racial discrimination, he worked his way through school. He finally graduated from college with a brilliant academic record. Then for forty-seven years, he worked on the staff of Tuskegee Institute. (Booker T. Washington had founded Tuskegee in 1881 as a school to train black teachers.) Carver lectured before the humblest farmers and before Congressional committees in

George Washington Carver

order to improve southern farming. Through his efforts, the people of the South learned to grow a variety of crops that would help replenish the nutrients in the soil. These included vegetables, peanuts, and sweet potatoes. He developed nearly three hundred products from the peanut. From peanuts, he made instant "coffee," soap, and ink. The sweet potato he used in the making of shoestrings, flour, candy, and more than a hundred other useful products.

Changes in Industry and Commerce

Before the Civil War, little had been done to develop industry in the South. However, with the breakup of the plantation system, many of the leaders and laborers gave up on agriculture. They went to the cities and devoted themselves to industry and commerce. Textile industries developed. The rich natural resources of the South were tapped. Coal and iron mines developed. Great sulphur beds in Louisiana and Texas were opened. Then came the exploration and development of the vast oil fields in Texas, Louisiana, Kansas, and Oklahoma. The extensive forests in the South were commercialized, and lumbering became an important business.

The building of the railroads helped the development of industry. The railroads destroyed during the war were rebuilt, and many new lines constructed. This enabled the South to become a great industrial section. The railroad helped the South to concentrate on business between the states, especially in the North and East. The South paid less attention to foreign markets. This strengthened the Union and helped to improve the economy of much of the South.

Social Changes

Naturally, when the plantations disappeared, plantation social life ended as well. The plantation owners had lost not only their main source of income but also their wealth. Hence, everything associated with this wealthy social life also ended.

The breakup of the plantation system benefited those who had held no slaves. As long as the best land was in the hands of plantation owners, the poor white farmers with small farms could not get ahead. The story changed when the plantations broke up. The poorer Whites began to buy portions of plantations. These small farms often became successful. Other poor Whites found employment in one of the new industries in the cities. Schools were provided for their children. Their standard of living became comparable to that of the small Western farmer and the industrial worker in the East.

Under the changed conditions, Blacks found life very difficult. Emancipation had given them freedom, but it had also given them the responsibility of taking care of themselves. As slaves, they had been supplied with food, clothing, and shelter in return for their work for their masters. Now, forced to obtain these things for themselves, the free Blacks faced serious problems.

Faced with these problems, the Blacks chose one of four paths. Some of them worked as hired laborers for their former masters. Very often, food, clothing, and shelter, exactly what they had received as slaves, were all that the impoverished Southerners could afford to pay them. Other Blacks became sharecroppers. These are tenants who pay the landlord a share of the crops as rent. A few, with the aid of generous masters, bought little plots of land and became independent farmers. Many sought employment in the towns and cities of the South and in the industrial centers of the North.

Through the work of generous contributors in both the North and the South, schools for Blacks were gradually established. Then came leaders from the ranks of the Blacks themselves. Among them was Booker T. Washington, who helped bring educational opportunities to his fellow Blacks. The public schools were open to Blacks. However, for many decades the educational opportunities offered to them in many parts of the country were inferior to those provided for white children.

Spot Check

1. What system of farming was destroyed by the changes in the South after the Civil War?
2. What replaced one-crop farming in the South?
3. Who was an internationally famous agricultural scientist from the South?
4. Why did the breakup of the plantation system help poor Whites?
5. List the four ways Blacks tried to make a living after emancipation from slavery.

The Development of the West

Westward Ho!

After the Civil War, when so many in the South had lost their homes and their jobs, the West seemed like a new chance to start fresh. Many in the North saw the untapped potential of the West. They were tired of the crowded Northern cities. The West meant freedom and opportunity. It was the new frontier. The Westward Expansion that had been slowed by the Civil War now went forward with blazing speed.

The vast region east of the Rocky Mountains and west of the Mississippi River that stretched from the northern boundary of this country to the southern, remained unsettled by white men. However, people did live there. The Indians jealously guarded this land of the buffalo. They resented every advance of the white man. They were quick to defend their hunting grounds.

The white man came into this huge area from the south and from the east. First came hunters and trappers. Then miners established isolated outposts. Cowboys and ranchmen moved across the grassy plains, and cattle replaced the buffalo. Then the farmer seized these plains of the cowboy and rancher. This great area became the "bread basket" of America. Meanwhile, the Indians, after being defeated, were placed on reservations. This was land the government reserved for them.

Within fifty years, this extensive stretch of plain and plateau was settled, organized into states, and admitted to the Union. Indeed, in 1912, the forty-eighth state, Arizona, was added to the Union. Three groups were largely responsible for the development of the West: miners, ranchers, and farmers.

Mining

The discovery of gold in California in 1848 lured thousands of immigrants to that land. It was the first mining rush to the Far

Albert Bierstadt's *Among the Sierra Nevada Mountains.* People were drawn to the West not only for its natural beauty but also for its natural resources.

West. Ten years later, another rush took place when gold and silver were discovered in what is now Nevada. Veteran prospectors from California and immigrants from the East joined in the rush. Virginia City, Nevada, the site of the Comstock Lode, the largest silver mine in the world, had a population of about ten thousand. Carson City, Nevada, also became a roaring mining town.

At about the same time these rich discoveries were made in Nevada, prospectors found gold in the area of Pike's Peak, Colorado. Again, this was a magnet that drew thousands of eager men across the plains to the Rocky Mountain country. Covered wagons, packhorse trains, and laden mules rushed a hundred thousand new prospectors to Colorado. Some found wealth. Most did not. They returned home discouraged. In the twenty-five years following the Colorado gold rush, similar rushes took men into Idaho, Montana, Wyoming, Utah,

New Mexico, and Arizona. Deadwood City, in the Black Hills of South Dakota, was the site of another famous gold rush in 1874.

The prospectors in these rushes were often disappointed in their search for gold. However, though they failed to find gold, they often found other valuable minerals. The Western United States was rich in deposits of copper, lead, zinc, coal, oil, and iron.

During these years of "strikes" and "rushes," the Rocky Mountain region was dotted with mining towns. They were rough communities that were generally marked by lawlessness. Along the single street of these towns, saloons, gambling houses, and dance halls flourished. Cheating gamblers and outlaws preyed upon the honest and hard working citizens. Robberies and murders were frequent.

Over time, law and order was gradually imposed. Lawmen like Wyatt Earp began to bring some order to these wild towns. Men began to send for their wives and children. Gradually, the mining camps became settled, law-abiding communities.

Mining is still one of the main industries of the West. The Rocky Mountain States, rich in natural resources, derive much of their income from mining.

The Cattle Kingdom

After the Civil War, the grasslands east of the Rocky Mountains became the "cattle kingdom." Here, adventurers had found half-wild cattle grazing on the plains, particularly on the plains of western Texas. These cattle were a hardy breed. They had descended from European stock brought over by the early Spanish settlers in Mexico. In winter and summer, they fed on the open range with no shelter to protect them from winter weather.

The open grass-covered plains stretched from the Rio Grande on the south to the Canadian border on the north. Since the plains were government-owned, they were free pasture. This induced enterprising men to invest in thousands of cattle and employ cowboys to care for their herds. There were no fences in the cattle kingdom. For this reason, the cattle were branded so that there could be no mistake about their ownership. Most of the herds wintered in Texas. In the spring they were driven northward, sometimes as far north as Montana and the Dakotas. Grown fat and sleek from grazing on the Great Plains they had crossed, the cattle were driven to the nearest railroad station. Then they were shipped to the packinghouses in Chicago and Kansas City.

A threat to this free-range cattle raising developed during the 1880s. Many sheep ranchers settled in the West. Sheep raising and cattle raising could not exist on the same range because the sheep ate the grass so short that there was no pasture left for the cattle. The sheep eat the grass at the roots. After sheep are done eating a pasture, all that remains is dirt. Cows eat the grass higher up so it can keep

In this painting by Charles Marion Russell, cowboys are shown roping cattle.

growing. Fighting developed between the sheepherders and the cattlemen. Many men were killed.

At length, free-range ranching came to an end. Privately owned ranches developed. The open range had become overstocked and overgrazed. Inspection for disease was more difficult on the open range. The purity of select breeds could not be protected. In the 1880s, severely hot summers and cold winters took their toll of cattle on the open range. All these problems could be better handled on a privately owned ranch. Today, private ranches hold an important place in the cattle raising areas. From them comes the beef that is an important item on America's dinner menu. Beef makes up a great part of our domestic and foreign trade.

Spot Check

1. Where was a famous gold rush in Colorado?
2. Why were cattle branded?

Farming

While miners and cattlemen were coming into the West, the farmers were also advancing their frontier westward. Once looked upon as the Great American Desert, the West had come to be regarded as a land of unlimited opportunity. Pioneers hastened with hopeful hearts to settle on farms in this land of promise. Three factors helped to develop the Great Plains: the Homestead Act of 1862; the building of railroads west of the Mississippi; and inventions that helped to solve the problems of farming in that fertile country.

The Homestead Act granted one hundred sixty acres of free land west of the Mississippi to the head of a family or a person over the age of twenty-one. The homesteader must be a citizen of the United States or one who had filed his intention to become a citizen. The homesteader had to reside on the property for five years and show his good faith by working the land. He could obtain outright ownership after six months of residence by paying $1.25 an acre for the land. The homesteader could count periods of military service as part of his residence requirement.

The westward trek of settlers was greatly encouraged by the railroads. They advertised the attractions of the West and offered to sell parts of the vast tracts of land that the government had granted them at very low prices. Lured by the attractive advertising, thousands of immigrants from Northern Europe joined the wagons going west.

From 1860 to 1880, two and a half million people were added to the population of Minnesota, Iowa, and Missouri. During the same period, the population of Kansas increased nine fold. By 1890, there were more than a million people in Nebraska. Colorado had a population of more than four hundred thousand. North Dakota had almost half that number. In fact, so great was the influx that by the end of 1890, all the land west of the Mississippi except Utah, Oklahoma, New Mexico, and Arizona had been organized as states and admitted to the Union.

Farming in the West Differed from Farming in the East

In some respects, farming in the West differed from farming in the East. For example, pioneers who had settled in Tennessee and Kentucky were forced to clear away trees and rocks before they could plow the ground. The pioneers of the Great Plains were faced with a shortage of lumber and stones. They were obliged to build sod houses or dugouts as homes. In the West, as in the East, the small farm was the usual unit of cultivation. However, side by side with these were large tracts of land owned by eastern or foreign companies and cultivated by hired laborers, many of whom came from the Far East.

Rainfall was so slight in many western areas that the farmers needed to use irrigation. Wells were drilled and ditches dug to convert vast stretches of sand and sagebrush into fertile fields. In 1902, the federal government undertook to aid Western irrigation projects. Federal funds were provided for the construction of dams and water canals. Through the combined forces of the farmers, private companies, and the government, millions of acres of Western land are now irrigated.

The invention of farm machinery influenced the development of the West. The McCormick reaper was as important in grain farming as the steam engine was in transportation. Other machines followed. Threshing machines, mowers, rakes, corn planters, potato planters, and cream separators are only some of the long list of additional laborsaving machines that were invented.

In the history of the world, no nation has provided the number of inventions and the number of labor-saving devices as has the United States. Freedom and liberty for American people has given men and women time to use their natural abilities to invent labor-saving devices for all mankind. This is what makes our nation great.

Fishing and Lumbering

Besides mining, cattle raising, and farming, two other industries were of great importance in the West. These were fishing and lumbering. Fishing had been carried on extensively along the West coast, particularly in the Seattle, Washington, area. Salmon and halibut were the chief money fish. Boats from Seattle and other ports would go out for weeks at a time to fish the northern Pacific. Once they had a full cargo they would return to port where canneries and processing plants were located.

Lumbering became a thriving industry in the Rocky Mountain and Pacific coast states. The majestic firs of the Sierra

Nevada and Coast Ranges, the great pines of Oregon, and the giant redwoods of California made the West one of the richest lumbering sections in the world. The federal government owned most of the timberland in the West. Trained forest rangers began to protect the forests from fires and perform many other important duties in connection with these forests.

Spot Check

1. What three factors sped the development of farming in the West?
2. What announcement is considered the end of the American frontier?
3. What were two differences between farming in the West and in the East?
4. In what areas of the West were lumbering and fishing important?

The Plight of the Native American

The story of white America's treatment of Native Americans is a tragic one filled with resentment and grief. The problem lies in the great differences between the two cultures. The basic problem was that the Indians were nomads. They moved from place to place. As with every nomadic culture, they valued only those things that they could take with them from place to place. Thus horses and cattle are the most valuable possessions for the nomad. He rides the horses and raises the cattle for his food. For a nomad, no one owns the land, yet all can use it. Indians never had a concept of private ownership of land. They could not own something that they could not take with them.

The white culture was just the opposite. For Whites, ownership of land was of utmost importance. Whites lived on the land. They were not nomads. The land was the source of their income. Whether they had a farm or a factory, they needed land! Even cattle ranchers raised the cattle on their land. The desire for land on the part of the Whites and the nomadic lifestyle of the Indian made conflict almost inevitable.

The westward march of the white man gradually but steadily forced the Indian to retreat. War after war followed between the Indians and Whites. Treaty after treaty was signed which were supposed to protect the Indians. However, the white men kept moving forward and ignored the treaties. The Indians naturally resented the loss of their hunting grounds and homes. They kept rising in rebellion against the white settlers.

In 1830, President Jackson had sealed the fate of the Indians east of the Mississippi. At that time, he set aside as an Indian reservation land in what is now Oklahoma, "the land of the red people." All the tribes from the southern states, the so-called "Five Civilized Tribes," were moved to this territory.

The westward march of the white settlers could not be stopped. With mining invading the Rocky Mountain area, with the cattle kingdom occupying the Great Plains, and with the farming frontier ever advancing, the Indians were pushed back onto new reservations. The national government gave each tribe a specific tract of land.

However, the Indians were not left alone even on their reservations. In the 1870s, gold was discovered in the Black Hills, a Sioux Indian reservation. Despite a treaty protecting the land, miners began to pour into the area. Government troops drove the Indians from their hunting grounds.

Aroused by these acts, the Sioux Indians, under the leadership of Chief Sitting Bull, made a valiant effort to defend their land. In the murderous war that followed, the lives of hundreds of Indians and Whites were lost. At length, the government compromised with the Sioux. They allowed the Sioux to keep their reservation in the Dakota Territory in exchange for their hunting grounds in the Black Hills. They promised to give

Government troops drive the Indians from their hunting grounds.

the Sioux annual payments in food, money, and the maintenance of schools.

It was not until 1924 that all Indians born in this country were made citizens of the United States. Today, Native Americans are better treated.

Spot Check

1. What activities of the white men caused the Indians west of the Mississippi River to be pushed into reservations?
2. What compromise ended the war with the Sioux Indians under Chief Sitting Bull?
3. Why was conflict between the Whites and the Native Americans probably inevitable?

Business and Labor

The Consolidation of Business

Before the disappearance of the frontier, almost all businesses were small businesses. Individuals, families, or small groups owned the business. Hundreds of little independent companies owned mines, oil wells, cloth mills, iron and steel mills, and factories that made farm machinery. The output of these businesses was small. The business of each organization was largely local. Then a new form of business ownership entered the American scene. Several separate businesses combined into one large company called a corporation. Little mills joined together to form huge industrial plants. Scores of small oil companies and farm equipment factories consolidated.

There were five causes that lead to the consolidation of business and to large-scale production. The first cause was improved transportation and communication. This opened up new markets beyond the local area and made it easier to sell and distribute manufactured goods. The second cause was the ability to pool resources and production to meet the demands of the increased markets. The third cause was the construction of new, large, and expensive machinery. This machinery enabled increasingly large quantities of goods to be made inexpensively. However, the machinery was so expensive that only larger businesses could afford to buy it. The fourth cause was an abundance of laborers. These workers were mostly immigrants from southern and eastern Europe. They provided a cheap labor supply. The final cause was new and increased sources of raw materials and electric power.

As a result of these influences, business consolidation took place rapidly. By the beginning of the twentieth century, corporations carried on nearly three fourths of the country's business and industry. The great oil, steel, railroad, and shipping companies came into existence. The men who owned these huge corporations became extremely rich and famous. Cornelius Vanderbilt, John D. Rockefeller, and Andrew Carnegie became household names.

"Big business" made low-cost production possible. It reduced wasteful competition and gave the buyers the benefit of better prices. It also caused the collapse of many small businesses that could not compete with these giants.

The Organization of Labor

The rise of industry and the development of "big business" were key factors in the growth of labor unions. As employment groups became larger, it became more and more difficult for the individual worker to make himself heard. However, through an organized union, the workers were in a stronger position to bargain for better salaries, benefits, and working conditions.

There are basically two kinds of labor unions: craft unions and industrial unions. Craft unions are organized along craft lines. For example, all the carpenters in a community would join a carpenters' union. The bricklayers, the masons, the musicians, and others join their respective unions. The industrial unions take in all the workers in an industry, whatever their special trade within that industry. Representative of the craft unions was the American Federation of Labor, the AFL. The Congress of Industrial Organizations, the CIO, represented the industrial unions.

One of the leaders of the early organized labor movement was Samuel Gompers, an immigrant from England. He founded the American Federation of Labor in 1886 and for years was its guiding spirit. By 1904, the AFL became the nation's leading union. The union faced much hostility from business owners, but the dignified Gompers earned the respect of his opponents. He was the AFL's president from 1886 until 1924. Though he had many official and social dealings with important politicians, bankers, and business leaders, he never forgot the people for whom he spoke.

For a number of years, there was sharp competition between the AFL and the CIO over the right to organize and represent the workers of various industries. However, in 1955, the two organizations approved a plan for uniting in a single organization. At the time the two organizations united, the AFL-CIO, as it came to be known, had 15 million members.

Spot Check

1. What was the name of a new form of business ownership that came to dominate business by the end of the nineteenth century?
2. Name three famous businessmen of the nineteenth century.
3. What were three advantages to "big business"?
4. What was a great disadvantage of the growth of big business?
5. Why did the growth of labor unions rise with the growth of big business?
6. Who is considered the first great labor leader in the United States?

CHAPTER REVIEW

1. What was the "Industrial Revolution"?
2. What caused the breakup of the plantation system in the South?
3. What were some of George Washington Carver's contributions?
4. Describe the industrial development of the South.
5. What three groups were mostly responsible for developing the West?
6. What was a gold rush?
7. What three factors helped to develop the Great Plains?
8. List the major industries of the West.
9. What made conflict between Whites and Native Americans probably inevitable?
10. What was the significance of the transcontinental railroad?
11. When and where was the first transcontinental railroad finished?
12. Who is history's greatest inventor?
13. Who was Samuel Gompers?
14. What is a "corporation"?
15. Who was Booker T. Washington?
16. Who was George Washington Carver?

POLITICAL REFORMS IN THE 19ᵀᴴ AND 20ᵀᴴ CENTURIES

In this painting, by George Caleb Bingham, a politician speaks to the voters.

CIVIL SERVICE REFORM

The Need for Reform

The Civil War was followed by a long series of government and political scandals. Public money was misused. The great industrial and financial expansion that took place encouraged gambling and speculation. This meant that people put money into a risky business venture in the hope of a quick profit. In their desire for wealth and power, some men in high places traded their honor for gold and silver.

During this period, dishonest men controlled the political process in many city and state governments. These men made all the appointments to city and state offices. They became well-known figures. Of these unsavory fellows, William M. Tweed of New York City was the most notorious. He and his associates, the "Tweed Ring," took for their own use millions of dollars that were to be used for city improvement projects. Tweed was arrested and convicted of fraud in 1873. Other political bosses used public money for their own purposes. Bribery was widespread. Both the Democrats and the Republicans shared in these dishonest practices.

Dishonesty of every sort crept into the national government, particularly while Grant was president. A number of Congressmen accepted railroad stocks and bonds in exchange for their votes favoring land grant concessions to railroad companies. The Secretary of War was found guilty of receiving bribes from dealers in war supplies. The postmaster general overpaid certain favored postal employees. Investigation disclosed that revenue officers had accepted bribes from the makers of alcohol to cancel certain taxes. During this period, the spoils system was at its height. Men were appointed to government positions, not on the basis of ability, but on the basis of the number of votes they could control for the party in power. Bribes were even paid to those who had the power to make appointments.

The Election of 1876

President Grant's administration had been so corrupt that there was widespread demand for reform. As a result, both the Republicans and the Democrats nominated men who stood for honesty and reform. The Republican candidate was Rutherford B. Hayes of Ohio. The Democratic candidate was Samuel Tilden of New York. The 1876 election between the two was very close. Late in the evening on Election Day, it seemed that Tilden had won. However, twenty electoral votes were in dispute.

To settle the dispute, Congress appointed an electoral commission of fifteen members. The commission was made up of five senators, five representatives, and five justices of the Supreme Court. In all, there were eight Republicans and seven Democrats. The eight Republicans voted to count the twenty disputed votes for Hayes. Thus Hayes was elected president. This "vote by party" did little to inspire public trust in politicians.

President Hayes tried to end the spoils system in the federal government. He favored a merit system in which jobs would go to those applicants scoring highest on tests. However, he was not completely successful. He could not convince the Congress to act on such a reform of government. Nevertheless, there were many positions that the president was able to fill by appointment. In making these appointments, he held to his belief that choice should be based on ability and not upon political influence.

The Assassination of Garfield

James A. Garfield, another Republican, succeeded Hayes as president. He believed strongly in the pattern set by Hayes. However, he had hardly been elected before he was besieged by thousands of office seekers. These people were convinced that their membership in the Republican Party should give them political preference. One such person sought appointment as American consul to Paris,

James A. Garfield

France. When he failed to receive the appointment, this half-crazed man assassinated the new president just four months after he had taken office. Garfield's untimely death awakened the whole nation to the evils of the spoils system. The public demanded reform. The newspapers and churches took up the campaign. Both Democrats and Republicans ordered that action be taken.

The Pendleton Civil Service Act

To establish the badly needed reform, Congress passed the Pendleton Civil Service Act of 1883. This Act provided that appointments to government service be made from a list of applicants who take tests to determine their fitness for office. It also created the Civil Service Commission. The Commission administers the tests. Civil Service is sometimes called the "merit system." This is because an applicant's rank on the list depends upon his rating on the test. No one appointed under the terms of this act can be removed from office except for neglect of duty or for improper conduct in office.

Since the enactment of this first Civil Service Act, civil service reform has been extended to cover more and more branches of government. It has spread to state and local governments. In 1940, on the recommendation of President Franklin D. Roosevelt, the Ramspeck Civil Service Act was passed. This Act extended the merit system to include all members of society, not just white men. It allowed the president to add a large number of government employees to the civil service classified list.

Spot Check
1. How did political parties often control voters and their own organizations at this time?
2. How was the electoral vote dispute in the 1876 presidential election resolved?
3. What event increased public demand for an end to the spoils system?

Election Reforms

The Secret Ballot

Until 1890, there was no secrecy on Election Day. The voter received his ballot from party workers and cast it into a ballot box in full view of everyone at the polling place. The ballots of the various parties were of different colors and sizes. Consequently anyone could tell how a man voted. If the voter had sold his vote to a political boss, there was someone there to see if he voted as promised. Honest men were often threatened and forced to vote as the boss directed. This lack of secrecy strengthened party control and made the boss a virtual dictator.

Around 1890, the voting process changed in several states. In order to rid themselves of corruption in elections, these states adopted the secret method of voting that had been used successfully in Australia. Under this system, the voter receives his ballot on Election Day from the election officials at the polls. He then goes into a booth where he marks his ballot in secret. Neither the color nor the size of the ballot reveals how the vote has been cast. No one can frighten the voter into voting against his will.

Adoption of the secret ballot was a great step toward reforming American elections that had become corrupt. By 1900, this change had spread to all parts of our country. Today, many communities have further lessened the dangers of fraud by installing voting machines. Voting is also done by using computers in many places. Although there is likely still some voter fraud in American elections, they are probably the most honest elections in the world.

The Direct Primary

The secret ballot did not completely break the power of the political bosses. They were still able to control the party conventions in local, state, and national elections. This meant that the individual voter had little say in choosing candidates for office. He could only vote at the general election between the candidates put up by the party bosses. The Governor of Wisconsin, Robert M. LaFollette, was a leading opponent of the political machines. He favored the direct primary as a means of giving the individual voter more voice in choosing the party's candidates.

Under the direct primary system, any member of the party may run for nomination. To decide which party member will be the party's candidate, the party holds an election. Every member of the party is allowed to vote for the person he wants to run for office. Thus, the party's nominees for office are chosen by popular vote. They are not chosen by a convention of a few professional political bosses.

However, even the direct primary did not solve all problems. Party bosses were still able to "freeze out" candidates they did not like. Sometimes only "serious" candidates would be invited to debates and party functions. Those deemed not "serious" simply did not receive an invitation. Also, if the people's nominee was someone that the party leaders did not like, that candidate stood little chance of winning the general election. His political party's machine would refuse to give him full support.

The direct primary was quickly accepted by many states. Today, this system is used by almost every state in the Union for nominating its officials. In 1910, Oregon expanded the idea. That year, Oregon held a "presidential preferential primary." Under this plan, the voters chose their preferred presidential candidates. Their presidential electors were "pledged" or "instructed" to vote for a given candidate in the national conventions. Other states also began to use the Oregon plan. Now all states use this method to nominate their choices for president.

Initiative, Referendum, and Recall

The changes in the method of nominating candidates for office were not the only reforms to emerge at this time. There were three other changes intended to increase the individual voter's influence in government. These were the initiative, the referendum, and the recall.

The initiative gives the voter the power to initiate, or propose, laws. The voter needs to obtain the signatures of a certain number of voters favoring the proposed law. Any voter may then demand that such a proposed law be voted upon either by the state legislature or by the people at the polls. In either case, if the proposed bill receives a majority vote, it becomes a law.

Under the referendum, voters have the right to vote upon certain laws enacted by the state legislature. (Usually this applies to new taxes, but can apply to any law). As with the initiative, the voter needs to obtain the signatures of a required percentage of legal voters (usually from five to ten per cent). The voters sign a petition that disapproves a law passed by the legislature. The law in question is then submitted to a vote of all the people for acceptance or repeal. If at the polls the majority of the people disapprove of the law, the law must be repealed.

The recall strengthens the control of voters over elected officials. It provides that if the required number of signatures to a petition (usually twenty-five per cent of the legal voters) is secured, an official may be forced to stand for a new election at any time during his term. If at this special election a majority of the votes are in favor of the official, he retains his office. If they are not, he is recalled, or removed.

Popular Election of Senators

In their fight for greater self-government, many citizens wanted the direct control of the election of U.S. senators. According to the Constitution, the two senators from each state were to be chosen by the state legislature. The people elected the Congressman in the U.S. House of Representatives. Some people supported the direct election of senators because they believed that all power must come from the people. Others supported it in an attempt to limit the power of machine politics in senate elections. One by one, the states began to allow the people to indicate in the primary elections their choice of candidates for the United States Senate. The states also required the members of the state legislatures to pledge to vote for the men chosen by the people. As a result, by 1910, most of the states had direct election of senators. Finally, the United States Senate gave way to popular demand. Congress passed the Seventeenth Amendment, which took effect in 1913. This amendment provides for the direct election of senators by the people. Today, all members of the U.S. Senate are elected by popular vote.

Women Gain the Right to Vote

The push for increased democracy and equality that characterized this period also extended to women. About the middle of the nineteenth century, women began to seek equality with men in political affairs. In fact, in 1848, a "Declaration of Sentiments" was drawn up at a Woman's Rights Convention in Seneca Falls, New York. Shortly after the Civil War, Susan B. Anthony, a teacher and a reformer, proposed that the Constitution be amended to grant for women the right to vote, also called women's suffrage. This proposal was met with jeers and hostility. However, in 1869, Wyoming granted the right to vote to women. The way was opened for passage of the Nineteenth Amendment. By 1896, Colorado, Utah, and Idaho had joined Wyoming in the suffrage movement. By 1914, eleven states had granted women the right to vote. Finally, in 1920, the Nineteenth Amendment was adopted. It granted women everywhere in the United States the right to vote in all elections. They had achieved political equality with men.

Women's suffrage is a great victory for democracy in our country's history. Within four years after the amendment went into effect, Texas and Wyoming elected women governors. Several years later, Miss Frances Perkins served as Secretary of Labor in President Roosevelt's cabinet. In 1948, Margaret Smith of Maine was elected to the United States Senate. Today, many women serve at all levels of State and Federal government.

Spot Check

1. What was voting like before the secret ballot?
2. Where did the secret ballot idea come from?
3. When did states begin to adopt the secret ballot?
4. What is a direct primary?
5. What problem was the direct primary designed to correct?
6. What are "the initiative," "the referendum," and "the recall"?
7. Which state first granted women the right to vote? When?
8. How did the woman's right to vote become law in all federal and state elections?

Conservation of Natural Resources

President Theodore Roosevelt was very fond of the outdoors and was an avid hunter. He knew the value and the importance of preserving and protecting America's natural resources. Consequently, early in his second term of office, he recommended to Congress a program of conservation and reclamation. Roosevelt's program had four well-defined aims. First, preserve the forests. Second, reclaim useless lands. Third, develop the inland waterways. Fourth, care for the water sites and mineral lands.

Roosevelt's plan won a ready acceptance. In 1902, Congress passed the Reclamation Act. It provided for irrigation projects in the desert of the West. These areas would become suitable for farming. Then the president set aside about one-hundred-fifty-million acres as national forests. Next, he organized the Bureau of Forestry, now called the Forest Service. The Forest Service works to prevent forest fires thus saving valuable timber from destruction. No other president ever worked so hard to conserve our nation's natural resources.

Theodore Roosevelt

IMMIGRATION

Immigration From Europe

Immigrants from Europe contributed to the growth of America from our very first days. The War of Independence and the War of 1812 both suspended immigration to our shores. However, at the conclusion of each war, immigration was resumed on a larger scale. At the end of the War of 1812, a steady stream of immigrants came from England, Ireland, Germany, Holland, and Denmark. By 1840, they had pushed the line of settlement as far west as the Mississippi River.

After the Civil War, a new stream of immigrants from other parts of Europe came to America. They were Italians, Greeks, Russians, Poles, Czechs, Hungarians, and

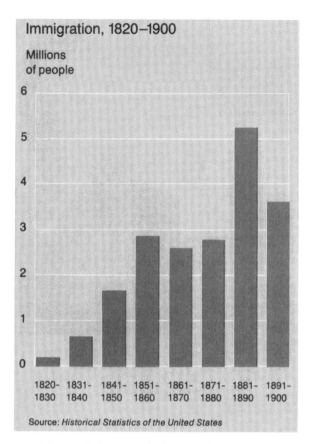

Immigration, 1820–1900

Millions of people

Source: *Historical Statistics of the United States*

Scandinavians. Many of them settled in the large industrial cities. These included such cities as New York City, Pittsburgh, and Chicago. In these places, the problem of employment was quickly solved. Though most workers were unskilled laborers, the factories, construction work, mining, and the mills kept them busy. Others from agricultural areas in Europe settled in the farming areas of this country. Minnesota, Wisconsin, and the Dakotas became the homes of many.

Immigration From Asia

Immigrants also came from Asia and the Far East. Many of these were recruited from China to work with the crews building railroads. However, their employment soon aroused the hostility of the white workers, and riots against the Chinese occurred. Labor leaders appealed to the government to halt their importation. The states on the Pacific coast, particularly California, passed laws discouraging the employment of Chinese. However, since the national government alone had the power to pass such laws, the states could not enforce this type of law.

Urged by residents on the Pacific coast, the federal government in 1882 suspended Chinese immigration for a ten-year period. In 1924, Congress passed laws that permanently stopped Chinese immigration. However, in 1943, this law was repealed. A new law was passed. It allowed a number of Chinese a year to enter the United States. It made all Chinese living in the United States eligible for American citizenship.

At the close of the nineteenth century, large numbers of Japanese began to immigrate to the United States. Most found work on the West coast and later established homes there. By 1900, many of these Japanese immigrants owned large tracts of fertile land in California and other Pacific states. The success of the Japanese farmers caused considerable enmity among their white neighbors. The state governments soon passed laws that prohibited the Japanese from owning land. The states also excluded them from white schools. In 1924, Congress passed the Immigration Act. Japanese immigrants were permanently barred from the United States.

The Immigration Act of 1924 began of a policy of limiting immigration to this country. It established a percentage quota of people of a given nationality who could enter the United States. In the second half of the twentieth century, Congress lifted some bans and limits on immigration.

Problems of Finance

The Tariff

The tariff had been a real problem between the North and the South. It had been one of the causes of the Civil War. The North wanted the tariff to protect the newly developing industries in the North. They thought it would be better for the country in the long run to have a strong industrial base. The South opposed the tariff on the basis that it was injurious to the South and was unconstitutional.

After the Civil War, the tariff was a source of friction between the Republicans and the Democrats. Republicans favored the tariff. This was because Republicans originally gained most of their support from the business interests of the North and East. The tariff protected these interests from foreign competition. Democrats opposed the tariff. Their support came from the South and the West. The South and West did not like the tariff because it generally meant they paid higher prices for goods. They could have purchased imported manufactured goods more cheaply from Europe than from the North or East if the tariff had not been imposed on such goods.

During the fifty years between the outbreak of the Civil War and the election of Woodrow Wilson, the Republicans were always in power. It was not until Wilson became president that the Democrats were able to pass their long-hoped-for reduced tariff measures. Congress passed the Underwood-Simmons Tariff in 1913 during President Wilson's first term. It sharply reduced the tariff. However, it did not abandon all of its protective features. It was the first real tariff reform since the Civil War.

The Income Tax

The Sixteenth Amendment provides for the levying of taxes on income. It was added to the Constitution in 1913. By this amendment, the government received the power to tax the incomes of the citizens. Congress had attempted to impose an income tax in 1894. However, in 1895 the Supreme Court had ruled that such a tax was unconstitutional. After that, it was necessary to pass an amendment to allow this kind of tax. President Taft proposed the Sixteenth Amendment in 1909. The required number of states ratified it in 1913.

Since its inception, the method and the amount of income tax have undergone many changes. When first passed, the tax rate was only about 1% of income. The tax continued to grow until a tax of over 50% on certain high incomes was passed. Today, income tax is the source of most of the revenue for the federal government. It is the most significant tax on most Americans.

The Money Problem

During the latter part of the nineteenth century, money became a serious problem in our country. Most of the money was in New York City and the banking centers of the East. However, there was little money in the rest of the country. The farmers and planters in the West and South were heavily in debt but were unable to obtain money to pay their debts. Farmers needed more money at certain times of the year. Farmers needed money in the spring when seed, fertilizer, and equipment must be purchased, and in the fall when they must pay for harvesting. If the amount of money can be temporarily increased during the times of greatest need, bank loans can be made at reasonable rates.

To address the money shortage and other financial problems, the bankers proposed a large central bank that would be under *their* control. However, President Wilson advocated a central bank under *government* control. After bitter debate, Congress passed the Federal Reserve Act in 1913. The law divided the country into twelve districts or regions. It created a Federal reserve bank in each region.

The Federal Reserve was to regulate the distribution of money. Thus it was made possible to ease many financial difficulties, such as a shortage of currency. Some believe the Federal Reserve has given the country better services and easier credit than it had ever received before. Nevertheless, the creation of this Board was controversial. It put great economic power in the hands of a semi-governmental organization.

Spot Check

1. Why did tariffs tend to be high from the time of the Civil War to the Wilson Administration?
2. Why did Congress need to pass the Sixteenth Amendment in order to tax the incomes of the citizens?
3. How important is the income tax to the federal government?

CHAPTER REVIEW

1. What was the "Tweed Ring"?
2. Of what was it an example?
3. How did Rutherford B. Hayes come to be elected president in 1876?
4. How did his election make the average person react?
5. How did James Garfield die?
6. What was voting like before the secret ballot?
7. Where did the secret ballot idea come from?
8. What is a direct primary?
9. What are "the initiative," "the referendum," and "the recall"? Why are they important to democratic government?
10. Who was Susan B. Anthony?
11. Which was the first state to grant women the right to vote and when?
12. Which amendment gave women the right to vote in all federal and state elections?
13. How did Democrats and Republicans differ on the idea of a tariff? Why did they hold their positions?
14. Which amendment created the national income tax?
15. Name two results of the Federal Reserve Act of 1913.

BUSINESS AND SOCIAL REFORMS IN THE 19TH AND 20TH CENTURY

The Strike, by Robert Koehler

REGULATION OF BUSINESS AND INDUSTRY

The Interstate Commerce Act

In the late 1860s, the Western farmers began to complain about unfair rates charged by the railroads. In most areas, there was only one railroad and it was the only way to transport goods. The farmers had no choice but to pay whatever was demanded. Through an organization called the Grangers, the farmers aired their complaints against the unfair rates. They urged the government to pass laws regulating the railroads.

In response to the request for government regulation of railroads, Congress passed the Interstate Commerce Act in 1887. This marked the beginning of federal control of railroads. The act had several provisions. First, all charges had to be just and reasonable. Second, special rates or rebates for some but not all customers were forbidden. Third, similar distances, types of freight, and connecting lines were treated alike in calculating rates. Fourth, it was forbidden to charge more for a short haul than for a long one. Fifth, all rates had to be made public. Railroads were required, upon request, to submit their schedules, shipping documents, and accounting ledgers for government inspection.

The Interstate Commerce Act was passed just one hundred years after the framing of the Constitution. It was the first step taken by the national government toward the regulation of American business. Previously, such a regulation would have been left to the states. The states would take action if any were taken. However, the railroads crossed into every state. Thus, it is difficult to understand how interstate commerce is *not* within the authority of the national government. Since 1887, a number of other laws have been passed that strengthen the Interstate Commerce Act. Almost all commerce is now regulated by the national government.

The Sherman Antitrust Law

The public desire to regulate "big business" was not confined to the railroads. "Big business" and large corporations had done good things for America. They had made better and greater production possible. However, along with these benefits were practices considered harmful to the public good. Trusts, or super corporations, and monopolies were born. These often made it impossible for fair competition to exist.

A trust is a combination of firms in the same industry. When a trust becomes so strong that it controls the supply and the price of a particular product or service, it is called a monopoly. For example, a trust among companies making paper products might include practically all the paper mills in the country. If this were true, the trust could charge what prices it pleased. It could eliminate competitors and refuse to sell to all rival companies. Under such conditions, it could set prices as high as it chose.

The often callous manner in which the trusts handled competitors and increased the prices of their products aroused the anger of the public. Complaints came pouring in to the president. Publicity of all sorts exposed the methods of the trusts. In reply, some states passed laws against monopolies. However, these laws were often ineffective because the monopolies crossed over many states. Finally, President Harrison responded to the public pressure. He proposed that Congress take a stand against monopolies.

The result was the Sherman Antitrust Act of 1890. This act declared as illegal any "contract, combination, . . . or conspiracy" that had as its purpose "the restraint of trade." However, the terms "contract," "combination," "conspiracy," and "restraint" could be interpreted in different ways. Clever attorneys were able to interpret the terms to suit their clients: the monopolies. As a result, the Act had little effect on the practices of the trusts.

The Trusts Are Prosecuted

By the time that Theodore Roosevelt became president in 1901, the Sherman Antitrust Act was virtually forgotten. However, Roosevelt was a reformer. He believed that there should be no privileged classes in a democracy. He believed that the government should make its control over trusts more effective. As a result, a series of lawsuits were brought against a number of firms accused of breaking the Sherman Antitrust Act. One trust after the other was prosecuted by the government. So vigorous was Roosevelt's prosecution of the trusts that he became known as the "trust buster."

William Howard Taft succeeded Roosevelt as president. He continued to prosecute the trusts. In fact, he prosecuted almost twice as many lawsuits under the Sherman Antitrust Act as Theodore Roosevelt had.

Woodrow Wilson, Taft's successor, also supported the government cases against business trusts. Wilson faced many pressing tasks during his first term in office. However, Wilson considered the abolition of monopolies to be his top priority. He believed that business should be put on a competitive basis. He believed that everything possible should be done to stamp out unfair business practices. Under Wilson's influence, the Clayton Antitrust Act was passed in 1914. This act clarified the Sherman Antitrust Act by defining in detail what unfair business practices were.

President Theodore Roosevelt

To strengthen the Clayton Act even more, the Wilson Administration created the Federal Trade Commission (FTC). The FTC is composed of five experts. The FTC has the power to investigate "big business" and expose unfair business practices.

Labor Legislation

Large factories and mass production caused working conditions in some factories to become unsafe. These factories needed improvement. Labor groups were quick to present their complaints to their employers. However, the response of the employers did not come quickly enough. As a result, the workers turned to state governments and then to the federal government for support.

During this period, the federal government passed many laws that improved working conditions in America. Laws regulating child labor were passed. Laws were passed that established the maximum number of hours an employee could be required to work in a day or a week. Congress also passed laws regulating sanitation facilities, proper lighting and ventilation, and other health safeguards. Safety programs, health insurance, and even unemployment compensation were also put in place.

The Pure Food and Drug Act

During his second term, Theodore Roosevelt made public some of the bad practices in the food and drug industry. These included adding impure ingredients to foods and using harmful drugs in medicines. To correct these evils, President Roosevelt urged national regulation through the passage of a pure food and drug law. In 1906, the bill was passed. This was the Pure Food and Drug Act. It provided, among other reforms, for the truthful labeling of all foods and drugs. Another law passed in 1906 was the Meat Inspection Act. It required that packing houses be inspected by the government. Meat must be approved by a federal inspector before being shipped from one state to another.

Spot Check
1. What was the Interstate Commerce Act?
2. What was the Sherman Anti-Trust Act?
3. What is a "trust"?
4. What is a "monopoly"?
5. Why was the Pure Food and Drug Act passed?

The Church and Labor

Catholics in the Labor Movement

In this era of social and business reform, the role of the Church was crucial. In fact, Catholics and the Catholic Church played a leading role in the reform movement. In our country the need for social reform grew as the country grew more wealthy. The country was in danger of becoming a nation of extremes: the very rich and the very poor. Most Catholics in the second half of the nineteenth century were workers in the factories. They were in the ranks of the poor. Long hours, meager wages, little security, unhealthy and dangerous working conditions, and the lack of leisure time convinced many in the Church that something needed to be done for workers. Since most American Catholic workers were poor, most priests and bishops supported the labor movement.

One of the leaders in the movement for social reform was Archbishop Martin Spalding of Baltimore (1810-1872). He championed the cause of better social and working conditions. He helped to establish the Society of St. Vincent de Paul in America. He also worked to convert the Blacks in his diocese. He had both zeal for his faith and an interest in the welfare of his country.

Another leader of this time was the Archbishop of St. Paul, John Ireland (1838-1918). He had a great understanding of the conditions of the workingman. He was able to convince many to consider their cause. He defended the right of the worker to organize. He also stressed the need that they be paid a living wage. His interests were not only focused on labor. He emphasized the right of the Church to provide for the religious and moral training of her children. With others of the American hierarchy, the Archbishop assumed the heavy burden of *double taxation for the sake of religious schools*. For Catholics not only pay taxes to support public schools, but in the face of many financial hardships, support Catholic schools as well.

Cardinal Gibbons and The Knights of Labor

The greatest friend that American labor had in the Catholic Church was Cardinal James Gibbons (1834-1921), the Archbishop of Baltimore. Under his leadership new emphasis was given to the rights of workers. In 1887, Cardinal Gibbons met with Pope Leo XIII on behalf of the Knights of Labor.

James Cardinal Gibbons

The Knights of Labor was organized in 1869. It was a semi-secret organization set up to advance the interests of all laborers. The Knights sought to help workers who were skilled and unskilled, immigrant and native-born, men and women, Blacks and Whites.

A number of Church leaders opposed the Knights because of its secrecy. The Knights believed secrecy was necessary so that employers would not harass or fire a worker for being in the union. However, secret rituals were a common feature of many anti-Catholic societies. Cardinal Taschereau, the Archbishop of Quebec, had forbidden Catholics in Canada from joining it. In fact he said they were excommunicated if they did. The fact that its head, Terrence V. Powderly, was a Catholic only made things worse.

Cardinal Gibbons realized that the matter needed to be addressed. Therefore, he looked into the charges against the Knights. Meanwhile, Cardinal Taschereau advised Pope Leo XIII to consider barring Catholics from joining the Knights. In 1887, Cardinal Gibbons went to Rome and spoke to Pope Leo. He defended the Knights' right to organize. He said that the Knights were the answer to oppression. As a result of his defense, the Holy Father decided that it was not necessary to prohibit membership in the Knights as long as they had no secret rituals. Many scholars believe that Gibbons' defense of the Knights paved the way for Pope Leo XIII's encyclical: *Rerum Novarum: On the Condition of the Working Classes.*

Pope Leo XIII

Rerum Novarum

Pope Leo XIII (1878-1903) was the first pope to write an encyclical (teaching letter) on modern social issues. In 1891, Leo issued the first of these encyclicals to have a wide influence, even beyond the Church. In *Rerum Novarum: On the Condition of the Working Classes*, Leo XIII wrote of the moral principles of justice and charity. These principals should regulate the relationship between capital (managers and investors) and labor (workers). He said the laborer is entitled to a living wage. A living wage is a salary that would allow a workingman and his family to live decently. Leo also wrote that the worker had the right to organize unions to secure better wages and to improve working conditions.

Most bishops in the United States fully supported the ideas in *Rerum Novarum*. However, many years passed before its teachings were widely accepted in the United States. In 1891, the right to unionize and bargain for wages still seemed to many to be dangerous ideas. However, starting in 1919, the American bishops began to promote *Rerum Novarum* more strongly. They issued several pastoral letters that helped advance its teachings. Finally, in the first half of the twentieth century, Congress enacted laws with many ideas similar to those in *Rerum Novarum*.

Cardinal Gibbons: the most respected and useful citizen

From a childhood during the days of Andrew Jackson until after World War I, James Gibbons saw America grow. He observed first hand the great increase in the Catholic population. As a churchman, he believed that a good Catholic was likely to be a good American. He also firmly believed the Constitution was favorable to the Faith.

Under Cardinal Gibbons' leadership, the Third Plenary Council of Baltimore was held in 1884. The one hundredth anniversary of the appointment of the first bishop, John Carroll, was celebrated in 1889. Also that year, the Catholic University of America was opened in Washington, D. C. As the leading churchman in America, Gibbons also resolved disputes between Catholics of different nationalities, between bishops, and between American bishops and Rome.

Andrew Carnegie, President William Howard Taft, and Cardinal Gibbons

In addition to being a leader in the Church, Cardinal Gibbons was also a best-selling author. His book, *The Faith of Our Fathers*, is a simply written explanation of Catholic doctrine and practice. It helped to bring thousands of converts into the Church. His writings and actions did much to convince Protestant Americans that they had nothing to fear from the Catholic Church.

Cardinal Gibbons' influence extended even outside of the Church. Every president, from Rutherford B. Hayes to Woodrow Wilson, looked to him for counsel and advice. Some of them were his close friends. In 1917, former President Theodore Roosevelt said to Cardinal Gibbons: "Taking your life as a whole, I think you now... the most respected, and venerated, and useful citizen of our country."

Spot Check

1. Who was Archbishop Martin Spaulding?
2. What were the Knights of Labor?
3. How did Cardinal Gibbons help the Knights?
4. What are some of the ideas contained in *Rerum Novarum*?
5. What is the name of Cardinal Gibbons' best selling book?

The Social Work of the Church

Helping others is an important part of practicing the Catholic Faith. From the time of the Apostles, the Church has been concerned not only with the spiritual, but also the physical welfare of all people. The history of the Church is filled with many great examples of men and women who have expressed their love of God and of neighbor by serving those in need. The history of the Church in America during this period is no different.

In its social work, the Church has always tried to help the poor, the disabled, immigrants, the homeless, the sick, and the neglected of God's flock. There is some type of Catholic agency to care for them all. Also, as part of its social work, the Church has always worked to spread the Gospel in some way. Since the end of the nineteenth century, various Catholic organizations have been established to care for people in need.

One of the best-known Catholic social service groups is the Society of St. Vincent de Paul. A Frenchman, Frederic Ozanam, founded the Society. He and a group of his friends began the society in Paris in 1833. The Society was started in America in Saint Louis in 1845. By the latter part of the nineteenth century, it had grown into a major Catholic service organization. It is still very active today. The Society consists of parish units of men and women who visit poor and distressed families in their own parish. When physical aid is necessary, families are given material relief like food, clothing, and shelter. When spiritual help is needed, the case is always referred to the pastor. Inspired by their patron, whose life was a model of Christian charity, Vincentians imitate the works of St. Vincent de Paul. They become living examples of the charity of Christ.

We have already learned about Katherine Drexel and her work among the Blacks and the Indians. Despite her work and that of many religious orders in these missions, it was felt that a national association was needed. This society would be able to coordinate the Church's activities among Indians and Blacks more efficiently. In 1874, the Bureau of Catholic Indian Missions was established. Later, the Bureau began to help Blacks. It is now part of the Black and Indian Mission Office.

In 1882, Fr. Michael McGivney founded the Knights of Columbus. It was originally started to help working men pool their resources to help each other and their families. However, it soon became involved in helping others in need. Today the Knights support a wide range of activities. They are very active in promoting vocations and pro-life activities. They were instrumental in having the phrase "under God" added to the pledge of allegiance in the 1950s. They continue to assist the poor and the needy.

The Society for the Propagation of the Faith was organized in this country in 1897. It is under the direction of the Holy See. It has two main functions. First, it is the Church's main means of increasing awareness of her worldwide missions. Second, it generates financial support for the missions. The work of the Society is so vital that each diocese has a director, whose duty is to collect funds for the foreign missions and to educate the faithful in the value of this work.

In 1905, the Catholic Church Extension Society was organized. It supports the Church in areas with few Catholics. In these areas, the work of the Church cannot continue without outright charity. The headquarters is located in Chicago.

As our country grew, so did the need for charity. At the turn of the century it became clear that charity must be better organized if it were to meet the demands of modern society. In 1910, Cardinal Gibbons created the National Conference of Catholic Charities. Today it is known as Catholic Charities, U.S.A. It has grown to be the major service organization of the Church in the United States. It serves a network of more than 1,700 agencies and institutions. It provides consultation, planning, assistance, and evaluation. Diocesan member agencies provide shelter, food, counseling, services to teens, parents, and the elderly, and many other services.

Spot Check

1. Who founded the Knights of Columbus?
2. Who started the National Conference of Catholic Charities?

CHAPTER REVIEW

1. Who began to complain about the unfair rates charged by the railroads? When?
2. What organization aired grievances against the railroads?
3. What was significant about the Interstate Commerce Act beyond its regulation of the railroads?
4. What is a trust?
5. How were trusts considered harmful to the good of all?
6. Why were state laws enacted against trusts usually ineffective?
7. What was the key provision of the Sherman Antitrust Act? When was it enacted?
8. Which president is especially know as the "trust buster"?
9. On what labor issues did Congress pass laws at this time?
10. Name and briefly explain the two laws passed in 1906 to regulate the food and drug industries.
11. Why did the bishops in America tend to support labor in the nineteenth century?
12. Describe Cardinal Gibbons' intervention on behalf of labor.
13. What encyclical set the Catholic pattern for social reform?
14. Name some of Cardinal Gibbons' contributions to the Church.
15. Why should the Church be concerned with social problems?

AMERICAN POWER AND INFLUENCE GROWS ABROAD

Ships from the U.S. Navy Parade on the Hudson River in 1899

EXPANSION TO 1853

The Basis for Power

Our early presidents laid the foundation for America's current power and influence. "The Americas for Americans" was the idea behind the foreign policies of Washington, Adams, Jefferson, and Monroe. It was on this basis that the Monroe Doctrine was issued.

During President Monroe's term in office (1817-1825), the Holy Alliance (Austria, Russia, and Prussia) was determined to check the spread of revolutions in South America. The Alliance had also considered helping Spain to regain the colonies she had lost in South America. In 1823, President Monroe declared that any attempt by a foreign power to colonize the Western Hemisphere would be considered an unfriendly act. This "hands-off policy" insured that the United States would remain the strongest power in the hemisphere.

In 1823, the original area of the United States had already been quite extended. The first land to be added beyond the borders created by the treaty that ended the War of Independence was the Louisiana Purchase. This land was obtained from France in 1803. After this purchase, a small area north of the Louisiana territory was gained by treaty with England in 1818. One year later, in 1819, Spain sold Florida to us.

More land was not added until 1845. In 1845, the republic of Texas joined the Union. The next year, 1846, the Oregon Territory became part of the United States through a treaty with Great Britain. A large part of the Far West was taken from Mexico during the Mexican War, which ended in 1848. Finally, the Gadsden Purchase of 1853 extended the borders of Arizona and New Mexico southward.

TERRITORY IN THE NORTH

The Purchase of Alaska

Before the Civil War, the United States owned no land beyond its continental borders. In 1867, Russia offered to sell the United States the peninsula of Alaska because their fur trade there had declined. Secretary of State William H. Seward agreed to the deal. The price agreed upon was $7,200,000. This was less than two cents per acre. The territory covered 586,400 square miles. Extensive areas of the land are tundra, or level Arctic grasslands on which large herds of caribou and musk oxen graze.

At first, the government was severely criticized for buying what was considered a barren Arctic wasteland. Some critics referred to it as a "frozen wilderness." Others called it "Seward's Icebox." However, the land soon proved to be worth many times its purchase price.

Shortly before 1900, gold was discovered in the Klondike region of the Yukon River basin in near-by Canada. With the frenzied eagerness characteristic of the "forty-niners," men rushed to the gold fields. Other gold fields were discovered along the Yukon and the coast of Alaska. New towns sprang up as if by magic.

When gold was discovered in Alaska, both Canada and the United States wanted to claim the gold regions. However, the two countries agreed to settle the dispute by arbitration. A joint commission from England, Canada, and the United States met in 1903. It fixed the border between Alaska and Canada. Over the next fifty years, the population of Alaska continued to grow. Finally, in 1959, Alaska joined the Union. Alaska was our 49th state.

The Development of Alaska

The wealth of Alaska is derived from a number of sources. In addition to the gold, other minerals found there include copper,

Seward (holding pen) invites the Russian envoy (touching the globe) to sign the contract to sell Alaska to the United States.

silver, lead, tin, gypsum, platinum, coal, and tungsten. Most recently, it has become one of the nation's world's top producers of natural gas and petroleum. Billions of barrels of oil have been discovered there. The oil industry has made Alaska and her citizens wealthy. Fishing is also an important industry. The Bering Sea and North Pacific bordering Alaska have been one of the most productive fishing areas in the entire world.

In 1891, a few reindeer were imported from Siberia to provide food and hides for the people of Alaska. The breeding of reindeer proved very profitable in the early twentieth century. The Pribilof Islands in the Bering Sea are the refuge of more than two million fur seals each year. For many years, the fur trade from these animals was a very valuable industry. Today, however, the fur trade is strictly controlled.

An Outpost of Defense

Before the Second World War, Alaska was generally considered to be isolated in the far North. During World War II, the Japanese threatened to invade Alaska. In fact, Japan actually occupied two islands. In order to connect Alaska to the lower forty-eight states, the Alaska Highway was hastily built through Northern Canada and Alaska. This 1,422-mile road through mountains, swamps, and rivers was built in only eight months in 1942. This road remains the only land route linking the lower forty-eight states with Alaska.

After World War II, there was a period called the Cold War. (We will study more about it in a later chapter). It was a time when America and the Soviet Union were not fighting actual battles but actual warfare could break out at any time. Alaska became an important outpost for watching the actions of the Soviets in Northern Asia. Only the Bering Strait, which is just fifty-three miles wide, separates Russian Siberia from Alaska. Also, the Aleutian

Islands, which are part of the Alaskan territory, form a chain that reaches almost to the shores of Asia.

ISLANDS IN THE PACIFIC

The Hawaiian Islands

As early as 1798, New England merchant ships on their way to the Far East had stopped in Hawaiian harbors. Through the years, a profitable trade developed. American missionaries began to work among the Hawaiians. Though the missionaries were not Catholic, they converted many to the Christian faith. Also, a number of Americans moved to Hawaii. By 1893, the number and power of Americans had grown so large that they successfully led a revolt against Hawaii's queen, Liliuokalani. The Americans feared she wanted to reduce their power in her government.

After the revolt against Hawaii's queen, the Americans petitioned the United States to annex Hawaii. President Harrison favored the idea. Thus, a treaty was drawn up. However, before the treaty was signed, Grover A. Cleveland was elected president. President Cleveland was suspicious about the validity of the revolt, so he sent

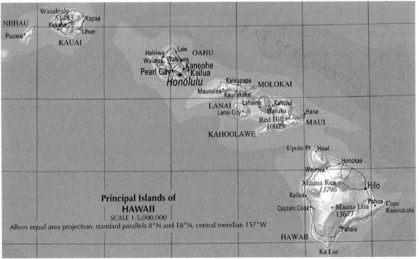

Principal Islands of
HAWAII
SCALE 1:5,000,000
Albers equal area projection, standard parallels 8°N and 18°N, central meridian 157°W

a minister to Hawaii to investigate. He learned that Americans in Hawaii had deposed the queen and requested annexation. As a result, Cleveland dropped the idea of annexation.

In 1897, William McKinley became president. The Hawaiians again urged the United States to annex the islands. McKinley liked this idea. He drew up a new treaty and Hawaii in 1898 was annexed. Two years later, Hawaii was organized as a territory and given a degree of self-government. Over the next sixty years, Hawaii made many requests for statehood. Finally, in 1959, Hawaii was admitted into the Union. She became the fiftieth state.

William McKinley

There are eight major islands in the Hawaii Island chain. The islands are generally considered some of the most beautiful places in the world. The islands of Maui and Oahu attract tourists from all over the world. In addition to tourism, they are also a source of food products, particularly pineapples. During World War II, Hawaii formed an important outpost of American defense.

Spot Check

1. Why was Alaska called "Seward's Icebox"?
2. What natural resources does Alaska supply?
3. Why was Alaska important during the Cold War?
4. Why was Hawaii not annexed until five years after the revolt?
5. When did Hawaii become a state?

The Philippine Islands

In the late nineteenth century, the United States was becoming one of the leading naval powers of the world. We began to build up a large and powerful fleet of warships. At that time, navy ships were powered by coal. The ships could not carry enough coal with them to allow them to operate at sea for long periods of time without being re-supplied. To solve this problem, the United States began looking for naval bases around the world where her ships could be supplied.

In 1867, the United States began acquiring several islands in the Pacific Ocean. These islands became important for military and commercial purposes. Midway Island, about 1200 miles northwest of Hawaii, was obtained in 1867. It became an important naval base. Midway was the site of a decisive victory against Japan in World War II. Wake Island, about 2300 miles west of Hawaii, was acquired in 1899. It was a naval base, but became important as a stopping point for commercial airplanes. Wake Island was also the site of a major battle in World War II. Guam, about 1,500 miles south of Japan and west of Wake Island, was acquired in 1898. It was an important military and commercial base. The Japanese held it during World War II. Finally, part of the Samoan Islands, northeast of Fiji in the southern Pacific, was acquired in 1899. They are still an important naval base.

Today, all these islands are still territories of the United States. Guam and American Samoa have their own legislatures and governors. However, the people are citizens of the United States. They send non-voting representatives to the U.S. Congress.

THE SPANISH-AMERICAN WAR

American Interests in Cuba

At the end of the nineteenth century, the United States wanted to expand its interests around the world. One place of

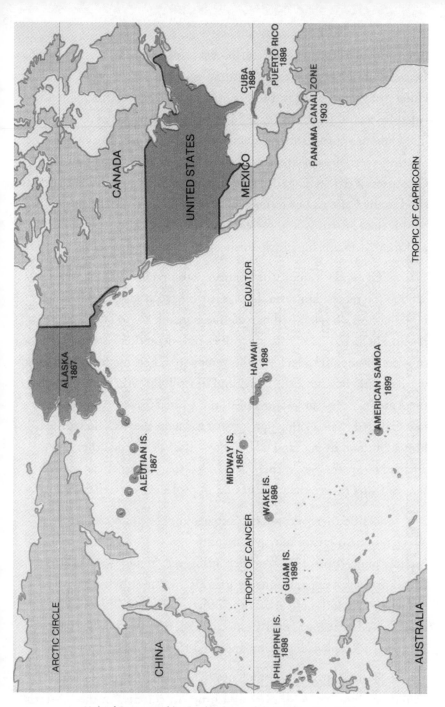

United States and its territories and dependencies, 1903

interest to America was the Caribbean, especially the island of Cuba. By the end of the nineteenth century, many Americans had gone to Cuba to live and work in the sugar industry. At this time, Cuba was ruled by Spain. Spain had ruled the island poorly for many years. The Cubans wanted independence. In 1895, an uprising against the Spanish rulers began. It was the sixth time in fifty years that the Cubans had revolted against Spain. The Spanish government tried to subdue the Cubans but to no avail. After waging a battle or making a raid, the Cubans would retreat into the mountains. It became more and more difficult for the Spanish soldiers to put down the rebellion.

General Campos, the Spanish commander in Cuba, tried to subdue the rebels. However, he was unable to do so. General Weyler replaced him. Weyler used harsher measures to try to put down the revolt. He forced hundreds of families into detention camps so that they could not aid the rebels. The camps soon became filthy and filled with disease. Sickness, suffering, and death followed. This angered the Americans on the island and in the United States. American newspapers began a campaign against General Weyler. They called him a "human hyena" and a "butcher." They demanded that he be recalled to Spain. Newspapers demanded that an American army be sent to Cuba to free the Cubans and to protect American citizens.

While there was a basis in truth for the charges against Weyler, the American newspaper campaign was an example of "yellow journalism." This was becoming very popular at this time. It meant that newspapers made little attempt to provide balanced reporting. Sensationalism was the order of the day. They used exaggerated headlines, overly emotional cartoons, and shocking details. This type of reporting appealed to millions of readers.

The Monroe Doctrine had pledged that the United States would not interfere with existing European colonies in the Western

Hemisphere. Cuba was such a colony. Therefore, the United States was obliged to maintain a neutral stand toward the disorders in Cuba. However, most Americans felt sympathy for the Cubans. In every raid, groups of Americans joined with the rebellious Cubans.

These Americans returned home with stories of the cruelties inflicted upon Cubans by Spanish officials. These stories inflamed American public opinion. Congress finally recognized the Cubans as "belligerents." This meant that rather than treating the Cubans as insurgents or rebels, the U.S. believed that Spain should treat them according to the rules of war. Prisoners of war had rights that rebels did not. Rebels could be hanged. Prisoners of war could not. The Spanish government deeply resented this action by Congress. The feeling between the two countries rose to fever heat.

Many in America and in Congress were looking for an excuse to go to war with Spain. At this point, the United States had one of the largest and most powerful navies in the world. This was due in great part to the work of Theodore Roosevelt who was the Assistant Secretary of the Navy. Spain, on the other hand, had been in decline for many decades. It had never fully recovered from Napoleon's invasion and the loss of its colonies in South America. As a result, there was little doubt what the outcome of a war between the two countries would be.

War Is Declared

Early in 1898, President McKinley sent the battleship USS *Maine* to Cuba. For several weeks, the *Maine* lay quietly at anchor in Havana Harbor. Then, on the night of February 15, 1898, the *Maine* blew up. 266 officers and men lost their lives. Years later, the explosion was shown to have been an accident. (A spark in a coalbunker was the most likely cause.) However, at the time, a court of inquiry could draw no certain conclusions. Nevertheless, the belief was that a Spanish mine had destroyed the *Maine*. Spain sought to avoid a war. However, the United States Congress demanded that Cuba be freed and Spain withdraw from the island. Congress declared war on Spain on April 25, 1898.

At the outbreak of the war, the U.S. Navy had been positioned to seize Spanish possessions both in the Caribbean and the Pacific. Commodore George Dewey was in charge of a naval force stationed in Hong Kong. He was immediately ordered to "capture or destroy the Spanish fleet." The Spanish fleet was reported to be near the Philippines. On May 1, Commodore Dewey trapped the entire Spanish fleet in Manila Bay in the Philippines. Without the loss of a single American sailor, Dewey won the battle and destroyed the Spanish fleet. Meanwhile, American marines landed. On August 13, the marines and the navy captured the Philippine city of Manila.

Soon after the victory at Manila, an American fleet under Admiral Sampson was sent to destroy the Spanish fleet in Cuba. The Spanish fleet soon became trapped in Santiago Harbor, Cuba. Though outclassed by the American fleet, the Spanish fleet attempted to break out of the American trap. The attempt failed. After a brave fight, the entire Spanish fleet was destroyed.

Although the American navy enjoyed much success, the American army was not ready for war. One group that gained fame was the legendary "Rough Riders." It was created and led by Theodore Roosevelt. It was made up of a group of cowboys and adventurers. They lent aid to the American army. The most famous of their actions was the charge up San Juan Hill in Cuba. During the charge, they stormed the fortifications of Santiago in Cuba. They forced the city to surrender. In the meantime, an American force also took possession of the island of Puerto Rico.

The Battleship *Maine* exploding in Havana Harbor, Cuba.

Peace between Spain and the United States

After the defeat at Santiago, Spain asked for terms of peace. Representatives from the United States and Spain met in Paris. They drew up a treaty that had four key points. First, Spain recognized Cuba as an independent nation under the protection of the United States. Second, Spain gave the island of Puerto Rico to the United States. Third, Spain gave the island of Guam in the Pacific to the United States. Fourth, Spain gave the Philippines to the United States in return for twenty million dollars.

In the treaty, the United States agreed to turn the government of Cuba over to the Cubans as soon as order was restored. Three years later, Cuba, with a constitution modeled after that of the United States, became an independent nation. However, it remained under the guardianship of the United States. At first the United States needed to intervene in Cuba from time to time to preserve peace and order. In 1934, Cuba was given its complete freedom. Cuba and the United States enjoyed friendly relations until Fidel Castro came to power in February 1959.

Puerto Rico

As a result of the war with Spain, the United States acquired Puerto Rico. In 1917, Puerto Ricans were granted American citizenship and the right of self-government. In 1947, they were given the right to elect their own governor. Five years later, in 1952, a new constitution was approved by Congress and by the voters of Puerto Rico. It made the island a Commonwealth under United States protection. This means that Puerto Ricans have almost all the same rights as any other American citizen. The exception is that they cannot vote in national elections and they have no vote in Congress.

President McKinley watches the signing of the U.S. peace treaty with Spain.

In the last fifty years there have been a few attempts by some to make Puerto Rico the fifty-first state. However, Puerto Ricans have voted to maintain their current status.

The Virgin Islands

In 1917, fifty years after talks to buy the Virgin Islands began, Denmark finally sold them to the United States. St. Croix, St. Thomas, and St. John are the three largest islands in the chain. Until recently, they were strategically important for American interests in the Caribbean. (They served to protect the Panama Canal.) They were, and remain, a major tourist area. St. Thomas is one of the loveliest islands in the Caribbean and a major stop for cruise ships. In 1927, the people of the Virgin Islands became U. S. citizens.

The Philippine Islands

At the end of the Spanish-American War, Spain sold the United States the Philippine Islands. This group includes 7,107 islands. Eleven islands are large enough and fertile enough to support a sizeable population. Of these, Luzon and Mindanao are the biggest.

Filipinos are almost all Catholic. In fact, in terms of population, the Philippines is the world's largest Catholic country. Sadly, the country suffers from terrible poverty. As a result, the Church there has not been self-sustaining. Therefore, it has welcomed many missionaries and resources from the United States. In turn, many Filipinos have come to the United States to seek a better life.

From 1898 to 1946, the United States ruled the Philippines. William Howard Taft, later President of the United States, was the first American governor of the islands. Under his direction, living conditions were improved. Improving sanitation was his chief goal. Streets were paved, sewers were built, and water supply systems were installed. Medical expeditions were sent to outlying districts. A practical health program among the natives was put into action.

In 1916, President Wilson increased the power of the Filipinos by giving them a larger say in their government. In 1934, Congress passed an act granting the Philippines independence in ten years. Meanwhile, the islands governed themselves except in foreign affairs. Due to the outbreak of World War II and the invasion of the islands by Japan, independence was delayed until July 4, 1946. On that day the Republic of the Philippines was born. Manuel Roxas became its first president.

In 1965, Ferdinand Marcos was elected president of the Philippines. At first, there were close ties between his government and the United States. Marcos was seen as a patriot and an anti-Communist. However, in 1972, he declared martial law and essentially seized power. Over the next decade, his government became more and more corrupt and harsh. As opposition grew to the Marcos regime, many Filipinos came to the United States as political refugees. In 1983, the main opposition leader to Marcos, Benigno Aquino, ignored warnings and went back to the Philippines from exile in the United States. He was assassinated as he was taken off the plane in Manila airport.

In 1986, Aquino's widow, Corazon Aquino, ran for president against Marcos. Marcos claimed victory but the election was rigged. He quickly lost support. Aquino was recognized as the duly elected president. Marcos fled the country. Both the Catholic Church in the Philippines and the United States supported President Aquino, a devout Catholic. Despite the efforts of Aquino, little was accomplished. She tried to reform the country and restore democracy. However, terrible poverty, government corruption, and Communist rebels slowed her efforts. Since 1986, conditions on the islands have improved little.

Spot Check

1. What are "yellow journalism" and sensationalism?
2. Why did the United States maintain official neutrality regarding the Cuban revolt?
3. What event caused the U.S. to invade Cuba?
4. What were the four important provisions in the treaty between Spain and the United States?
5. Who sold the Virgin Islands to the U.S.? When? Why?
6. Who was the first American governor of the Philippine Islands? What did he do to improve living conditions there?

THE PANAMA CANAL

The Idea of a Canal

The idea of a canal across the Isthmus of Panama was not a sudden thought. From the time Balboa crossed the isthmus and discovered what was the Pacific Ocean, many dreamed of a canal. In fact, soon after Balboa's discovery, the Spaniards began urging that a canal be cut to connect the two great bodies of water. However, it was an extremely difficult and expensive project. In the end, Spain was not willing to undertake it.

When gold was discovered in California, people again saw the need for a canal across Panama. The long, hazardous trip around Cape Horn and the dangerous journey overland created new interest in a canal. Great Britain also became interested in a canal. England wanted to shorten the traveling time of ships carrying cargoes and passengers from the Atlantic to the Pacific. Thus, in 1850, the United States and England signed the Clayton-Bulwer Treaty. In this treaty both nations agreed that if either nation built the canal, each would enjoy equal rights in its use. However, no canal was dug. Then, with the completion of the transcontinental railroad, the United States lost interest in the project.

In the early 1880s, a French company began building a canal across the Panama isthmus. Construction was under the leadership of Ferdinand De Lesseps. He had built the Suez Canal in the Middle East. However, almost from the beginning, the French had huge problems. The hot climate made it almost unbearable for white workmen. In addition, the region was swampy. It was so infested

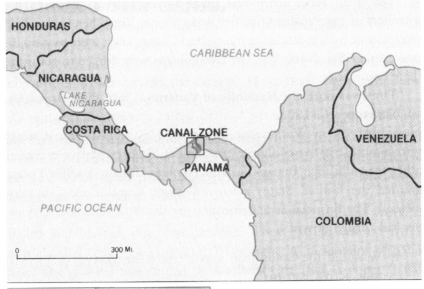

Map of Panama in Central America

Close-up of the Canal Zone

with mosquitoes that thousands of men died every year from yellow fever and malaria. After nearly eight years of work under such difficult conditions, the company went out of business. Work on the project ceased.

The U.S. and the Panama Canal

With the failure of the French company, American interest revived. Farmers, manufacturers, and businessmen all urged the building of a canal. Congress responded by authorizing the purchase of the unfinished canal from the French. Our Secretary of State, John Hay, took up the problem with England's ambassador at Washington. Together they drafted a new treaty. By the terms of this treaty, Great Britain gave up its rights under the old Clayton-Bulwer Treaty. She agreed to give the United States full control over the proposed canal. She only asked that all nations could use it on equal terms.

A treaty for the required land was drawn up by the United States and Colombia, who owned the isthmus. However, Colombia, after thinking about it, refused to ratify the treaty. Colombia claimed it was against her constitution to dispose of any land. President Theodore Roosevelt then encouraged the province of Panama to secede from Colombia. Panama declared its independence. The United States quickly recognized its independence. This prevented Columbia from attempting to regain the lost province. Later, in 1921, the United States paid Colombia twenty-five million dollars as compensation for Roosevelt's role in Panama's independence. The new Republic of Panama then signed a treaty with the United States. It granted the U.S. a strip of land ten miles wide with all desired rights and privileges. In return, the U.S. paid Panama ten million dollars. We also agreed to pay $250,000 every year we owned the canal.

With his characteristic energy, President Roosevelt began the venture. Work began on the canal in May 1904. It was expected to take twelve years to build. John Frank Stevens, a railroad designer, was made chief engineer. However, he abruptly resigned in 1907 for personal reasons. Roosevelt then appointed Colonel George W. Goethals as chief engineer.

One of the most important people on the project was Colonel William C. Gorgas. He was the chief sanitary officer. Gorgas was an excellent doctor. He knew that the mosquitoes carried the yellow fever and malaria. Thus he ordered that the swamps be drained and the areas sprayed to kill the mosquitoes. He installed mosquito netting and public water systems. He was thereby able to protect the health of the workers. This made the completion of the canal possible.

The building of the Panama canal was an incredible task. Nothing like it had ever been done. More than thirty-five thousand men labored ten years. A mountain was removed at Culebra Cut. Another was built to dam the Chagres River from the great Gatun Lake. Since the Pacific is eighty-five feet higher than the Atlantic,

Colonel George W. Goethals

Colonel William C. Gorgas

several locks were built to raise and lower the ships on the way through the canal.

On August 15, 1914, just at the beginning of the First World War, the fifty-mile Panama Canal was finished and opened to ships. What Spain had only talked about and France could not do at all, America had done in just over ten years—two years ahead of schedule. Travel by sea between New York and San Francisco was now 7,000 miles shorter. All nations were guaranteed equal access. The United States reserved the right to close the canal to any nation's commerce only in wartime. To provide for its upkeep, vessels passing through the canal pay a toll. Even today, almost one hundred years later, it is still one of the greatest engineering feats in history.

After World War II, Panama began to insist that it should own the Canal. In 1964, there were bloody anti-American riots in the Panama Canal Zone. As a result, President Johnson opened talks to revise the deals between the United States and Panama. The talks continued under Presidents Nixon, Ford, and Carter. President Carter signed a new treaty with Panama in 1977. Panama would receive the Canal on the condition it remained opened to all nations. On December 31, 1999, Panama gained complete control of the canal. In January 2000, a Hong Kong-based company began running the Panama Canal.

Today the canal enjoys fantastic success. Despite the fact that the nature of ships and shipping has changed since the Canal was created, it remains a vital part of world trade. More cargo than ever moves through the canal. Not only do cargo ships use the canal, but cruise ships take passengers through the canal simply for the experience. A cruise ship paid the largest toll ever to use the canal.

Ships pass through the Panama Canal.

Spot Check

1. Why was the building of a canal across the Isthmus of Panama considered necessary?
2. What problems did De Lesseps face in building the Panama Canal and why was he unable to complete it?
3. What did President Theodore Roosevelt do that enabled the building of the Panama Canal to continue and finally be completed?

AMERICAN INFLUENCE IN THE ORIENT

The Open Door Policy

America has been interested in the Far East since the days of the War of Independence. Yet, it was not until Japan fought and won a bitter war with China, 1894-1895, that the United States became involved in the affairs of the Orient. After that war, the vast Chinese Empire was at the mercy of Japan, Russia, Germany,

France, and England. All these countries forced the helpless Chinese government to grant them "spheres of influence." In other words, these great powers, taking advantage of China's inability to resist them, obtained control of huge parts of China. These areas contained valuable harbors, railroads, mines, and raw materials of all kinds. China's political unity, as well as her status as a nation, was threatened.

Under these conditions, there was little hope that the United States could continue the trade relations built up over the years with China. If Japan and the great nations of the world were allowed to divide China among themselves and make any trade policies they pleased in their special spheres of influence, our country would lose much of its trade with China. Our Secretary of State, John Hay, saw the danger. By the use of skillful diplomacy, he succeeded in March 1900 to persuade the nations involved to agree not to destroy the political unity of China. They also agreed not to interfere with trade passing into and out of Chinese ports. He also persuaded them not to close their own special spheres of influence to the trade of any other nation by increased rates or harbor dues. This policy of allowing all nations to trade with China on equal terms became known as the "open door policy." Credit for the open door policy belongs to John Hay. He was the one who induced the great powers to support free trade and equal commercial opportunities for all nations.

The Boxer Rebellion

Not long after Secretary Hay announced the open door policy, a Chinese society known as the "Boxers" began a movement to rid China of "foreign devils." A series of uprisings followed. Bloody attacks were made on missionaries and government representatives and their families. The Boxers also attacked those Chinese who had become Christians.

The Boxer Rebellion

To protect the lives and the business interests of their people in China, an international army of Japanese, Russians, British, French, Germans, and Americans was formed. This army quickly subdued the Boxers. China was required to compensate each nation whose citizens had lost lives or property during the Boxer rebellion. The United States received twenty-four million dollars. However, our government found that its losses were only twelve million dollars. Congress voted to return the difference to China on the condition that the money be used to establish a fund to educate Chinese students in the United States. The Chinese were very impressed with this act of justice and charity.

Spot Check

1. What were "spheres of influence"?
2. What is the "open door policy"?

Relations with Latin America

Mexico

Mexico long suffered from revolt and changes in government. From 1823 to 1876, the country fought one civil war after another. In 1876, Porfirio Diaz seized control of Mexico. His main goal was to bring peace to Mexico. He was successful in that. However, it was at a price. By force, he created some measure of order. He suppressed the press and took control of the courts. Although he was called the president, he really ruled as a dictator from 1876 until 1911. As ruler, Diaz did much to build up Mexico. To develop the great natural resources of Mexico and to create industries, he encouraged investment by Europeans and Americans. In return, he granted land concessions.

Under the rule of Porfirio Diaz, Mexico became rich. However, the people became poor. The wealth of the nation was in the hands of a few. The people were denied political privileges. For the most part, they were reduced to desperate conditions. Much of the land was taken over by the government. The villagers became landless peons, the poorest of the poor. When once asked about the problems in Mexico, Diaz famously said: "Poor Mexico! So far from God, and so close to the United States."

Finally, in 1911, Francisco Madero led a successful revolt against Diaz. For the first time in more than a quarter of a century, a new president ruled Mexico. However, less than two years after he took office, Madero was murdered. His government was overthrown. Victoriano Huerta replaced him. However, Huerta also could not establish control.

In March 1913, Woodrow Wilson became president. He hoped to take advantage of the situation in Mexico. Wilson refused to recognize Huerta on the grounds that the people had not elected him. (A rather silly criticism since no Mexican president had ever been so elected.) Wilson told the English ambassador that he was "going to teach the South Americans to elect good men." (Wilson had

been president of Princeton for eight years; it is surprising that he did not know that Mexico was not in South America. Nevertheless, it shows the kind of thinking that the Progressive Wilson had.) So, to "teach" the Mexicans, Wilson began to arm bandits who opposed Huerta. At one point he even sent the U.S. Navy to blockade Vera Cruz to prevent a shipment of arms from reaching Huerta's forces.

Two of the bandit leaders Wilson armed were Venustiano Carranza and Pancho Villa. Carranza eventually succeeded Huerta as president. Uprisings throughout Mexico endangered the lives of natives and foreigners

Woodrow Wilson

alike. The bandits destroyed property and attacked the Church, to which they were particularly hostile. Villa became so powerful that he practically controlled northern Mexico.

In 1914, Villa and Carranza had had a falling out. After years of support for Villa, Wilson finally refused to give him more weapons. Villa felt that Wilson had betrayed him. In March 1916, Villa ordered his men to attack a town in New Mexico. Over the next four months, they also attacked Texas, killing several Americans. While Wilson was not concerned about the bloodshed in Mexico, there were voters in Texas. Wilson sent General John Pershing into Mexico with an army. Pershing was ordered to capture Villa, "dead or alive." From March 1916, until February 1917, the American army chased Villa. However, they failed to capture him.

General John Pershing

Nevertheless, the army put an end to further raids on the United States.

After several years, Carranza, a Communist, brought some peace to Mexico. However, for many years, he and his successors severely persecuted the Church. Thousands were martyred. One of the most famous martyrs of this period was Father Miguel Pro. During this time, the Wilson administration sat by quietly. As one of his close aides said, "The worst thing in Mexico is the Catholic Church. (It) must disappear." The Catholics eventually rebelled during the famous Cristeros rebellion. Peace for Catholics in Mexico did not come until about 1940 with the election of Manuel Camacho as president (1940-1946).

In the development of Mexican policy, American interests have at times been injured. In 1938, the Mexican government took over the British and American oil wells. Though the oil companies strongly protested the action, Secretary of State Cordell Hull upheld the Mexican government. He insisted the companies be paid a fair price for their holdings; however, this did not happen.

Since 1940, the government of Mexico has become more stable. The current president, Felipe Calderon (2006-), is a practicing Catholic. Although there are still anti-Catholic laws on the books, they are not enforced. The Church is strong in Mexico. The Basilica of Our Lady of Guadalupe near Mexico City is one of the most visited shrines in the world. Every year millions of people go to Mexico to visit the shrine.

The "Good Neighbor Policy"

Between 1903, when the deal was made to build the Panama Canal, and 1928, the United States intervened in several Latin American countries. We sent marines to Haiti, the Dominican Republic, and Nicaragua to protect American interests. These acts created distrust toward the United States. Some Latin American leaders thought the United States was more concerned with upholding its financial interests than in promoting justice. However, we were also protecting American lives.

When Herbert Hoover was elected president, our relations with Latin America began to improve. As president-elect, he made a good will tour to Latin America. Soon after he took office, he withdrew the marines from Haiti and Nicaragua. He began a policy of cooperation with Mexico. When he left office, our relations with Latin America were better than they had ever been up to that time.

President Franklin D. Roosevelt carried on this friendly policy. In his first inaugural address, he said that he would "dedicate this nation to the policy of the good neighbor." In addition, in 1933, Secretary of State Cordell Hull told the Pan-American Conference at Montevideo that the United States would give up the policy of intervention. He also made it clear that in the future, the Monroe Doctrine would be for the benefit of all American nations, not just for the United States.

Spot Check

1. What did Porfirio Diaz do for Mexico as its president?
2. Who was Pancho Villa?
3. How did President Wilson's plan of arming bandits backfire?
4. What is the "Good Neighbor Policy"?
5. How did President Hoover improve relations with Latin America?

CHAPTER REVIEW

1. How did the United States acquire Alaska?
2. Why was Alaska called "Seward's Icebox"?
3. Has the purchase of Alaska been good for the United States? Why or why not?
4. Why did President Cleveland refuse to annex Hawaii?
5. How was annexation finally arranged?
6. When and how did the Philippine Islands become an independent nation?
7. What were the causes of the Spanish-American War?
8. What three men were most responsible for building the Panama Canal?
9. What was the "open door policy"?
10. What is the Good Neighbor policy?
11. What was the Boxer Rebellion?
12. Who was Miguel Pro?
13. Who was the first American governor of the Philippines?
14. How did the United States acquire the following islands?
    a. Guam
    b. Puerto Rico
    c. The Virgin Islands
15. What event caused the U.S. to invade Cuba?
16. What is "yellow journalism"?

THE UNITED STATES IN WORLD WAR I

The *Rock of the Marne*, by Mal Thompson, depicts the U.S. Infantry
throwing back the Germans at the Battle of the Marne.

EUROPE AT WAR

Background of the War

When war broke out in Europe in 1914, it was not a sudden flare-up. It was the result of jealous national rivalry. Still, it came to most people as a shock. Many of the nations of Europe were seeking new markets for manufactured goods, new sources of raw materials, and new territory for their expanding populations. European nations looked for opportunities to secure colonial possessions or trade on other continents. Struggles went on in the colonies but it had been almost a hundred years since there had been a major European war. Most people thought extended and bloody conflicts like the Napoleonic wars were a thing of the past. Many people thought mankind had progressed beyond the need for war. They were wrong.

In the years before 1914, each European nation stressed its superiority over the others: the superiority of its culture, customs, and people. This was called Nationalism. The people of one country were taught to distrust the people of neighboring nations. This created bitterness and suspicion.

Due to the lack of trust, each country fortified its borders. Each nation tried to surpass the others in military training and in military spending. Each nation had a spy system. Each European nation was an armed camp. Their armies were trained to the highest efficiency and always ready for war. This state of armed readiness was known as Militarism.

To better protect against attack, nearly every major European nation had made alliances with other nations. The two most important alliances became the **Central Powers** and the **Allied Powers**, or **Allies**. Germany and Austria-Hungary were the main members of the Central Powers. (Later, they were joined in the war by Bulgaria and Turkey.) They agreed to work together in case of a defensive war. Germany dominated this alliance because she was the strongest of the three. Though these three countries did not really trust each other, they were held together because they feared the power of the members of the Allied Powers. England, France, and Russia made up the Allied Powers, which was held together by fear. It feared the might of the German Empire.

The three long-term causes of World War I were Nationalism, Militarism, and a tangling system of alliances. Europe was a powder keg. It needed only a small spark to cause a great war.

Immediate Cause of the War

In 1914, war broke out between the two alliances. The spark that was the cause for war was the assassination of the heir to the Austrian throne, Archduke Franz Ferdinand, and his wife, Sophie.

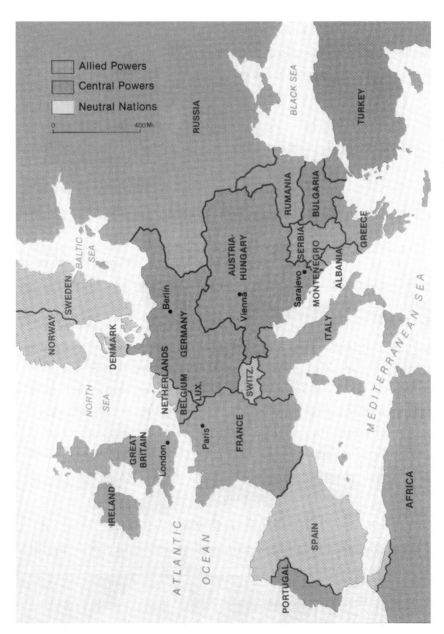

Europe at the beginning of World War I.

They were visiting the city of Sarajevo, the capital of Bosnia. Bosnia was ruled by Austria-Hungary, but contained many Serbians. They wanted Bosnia to be part of the neighboring country of Serbia. The assassin was a Serbian terrorist named Gavrilo Princip. There was reason to believe that the Serbian government had supported him. Austria-Hungary issued an ultimatum to Serbia. This was the same as a demand for Serbia to surrender. Although Serbia was too small to stand up to Austria-Hungary, the Russian empire supported the Serbians. Russia began to prepare for war against Austria-Hungary. On July 28, 1914, Austria-Hungary declared war on Serbia.

The next day, Russia called out its troops. On July 30, Germany began to get its troops ready. On August 1, France began to prepare its troops to be ready for war. Germany declared war on Russia the same day. Due to the tangling system of alliances, within weeks, almost all of Europe was at war.

Since there were no great moral issues that separated the nations, Pope Benedict XV pleaded for an end to the fighting. However, there was too much hatred between the warring nations. Only Catholic Austria-Hungary would even discuss a negotiated end to the war. The war would last from the end of July 1914 until November 1918. During those four years, more than fifteen million people were killed. World War I was one of the deadliest conflicts in history.

Spot Check
1. Which countries joined together to form the Central Powers?
2. Which countries joined together to form the Allied Powers?
3. What were the three long-term causes of World War I?
4. What incident supplied the immediate cause for the War?
5. Which pope pleaded for an end to the War?

THE UNITED STATES ATTEMPTS
TO REMAIN NEUTRAL

The Proclamation of Neutrality

When the war broke out in Europe, President Wilson issued a proclamation saying that the United States would stay neutral. He also urged the people to be neutral "in thought as well as action." However, America, bound by ties of language and culture to every nation in Europe, could not easily remain neutral. Millions of Americans had been born in one or another of the nations at war. They identified with these countries. It was difficult to remain neutral under such circumstances.

Neutral Trade and International Law

Just as the Napoleonic wars created a great demand for American products, so did the First World War. With millions of men in Europe in the armies, the production of the factories and the farms was severely cut short. The countries turned to America for supplies. Supplying those countries meant great profits. American business and industry quickly focused its attention on the European market.

In 1914, wartime trade was regulated and protected by international laws. Of these laws, four need to be understood. First, neutral ships carrying any cargo other than war supplies were free to sail wherever they pleased. Second, a neutral ship suspected of carrying military supplies could be searched. If war supplies were found on board, the ship could be seized. Third, even in a war zone, peaceful merchant ships, whether belonging to an enemy or a neutral country, should not be destroyed or sunk until safety had been provided for the passengers and crew. Fourth, it was lawful for a nation at war to blockade the ports of an enemy. However, to be lawful, the blockade had to be a real blockade. This meant that ships must be placed at the harbors and along the coasts that were declared blockaded. If this were done, neutral countries must respect the blockade. If neutral countries attempted to send ships through the blockade, they could be captured or destroyed. According to the law, it was illegal for a country at war to stop a ship in mid-ocean.

British Interference with Our Neutrality

At this time in history, Great Britain controlled the seas. Thus, it was not difficult for her to blockade the ports of Germany and the other Central Powers. However, the British fleet did not blockade only the Central Powers. It also tried to prevent American merchants from trading with neutral countries that might resell the goods to Germany.

There was no doubt that American goods were being resold to Germany. For example, we exported thirteen times more goods to Denmark after war broke out. Obviously, the Danes did not suddenly start using thirteen times as many products as they had before. They resold the American goods to warring nations. However, in preventing our trade with such countries as Denmark, Great Britain was in effect blockading neutral ports. Therefore, she was violating international law.

In a published list of articles that neutrals were not allowed to send to the enemy, Great Britain included many articles useful in war. These included such items as rubber, cotton, leather, wool, chemicals, and even wheat and other grains. To carry out this embargo, British warships forced American merchant ships bound for Europe to enter British ports. Once in port, the ship's cargoes could be searched. In spite of repeated notes of protest to Great Britain, her seizure of American merchant ships did not lessen. As a result, over time, most of our trade was diverted to the Allied Powers.

German Violations of Our Neutrality

Germany's violation of our neutrality was more serious than England's because it involved heavy loss of life. Early in 1915, Germany declared all the waters around Great Britain a war zone. Germany warned that she would destroy every ship found there. The British surface fleet was too powerful for the Germans to oppose. As a result, they attempted to impose a blockade with submarines. This was a problem. German submarines could not observe the international law of providing safety for passengers and crew. First, they were small and there was no extra room on board. Second, submarines generally attack without warning as they are underwater. Passengers have no time to evacuate.

President Wilson protested the German submarine attacks. Despite the protests, the Germans carried on their attacks. British freighters were sunk, an American ship was attacked in the war zone, and American lives were lost. Then, on May 7, 1915, an event took place that shocked the American public. The British liner *Lusitania* had left New York for the British Isles. The ship was known to be carrying war supplies. In fact, the Germans warned civilians not to travel on the ship because they considered it to be a military target. The British, for their part, were attempting to use the civilians as a shield so that the Germans would not sink the ship. When some distance off the coast of Ireland, a German submarine torpedoed the *Lusitania*. It sank in eighteen minutes. Almost everyone on board died. Among the victims were one hundred twenty-eight Americans. A wave of resentment and anger swept the United States. The American people began to demand war against Germany.

President Wilson refused to listen to those who sought war. He ran for re-election on the slogan, "He kept us out of war." In November of 1916, he won a second term. However, Wilson almost immediately changed his mind. His second term began in March of 1917. He asked for a declaration of war the next month! What had caused his change of mind?

At the beginning of 1917, Germany issued a proclamation enlarging the war zone. She also removed restrictions from German submarine warfare. She started a policy of sinking in mid-ocean almost all transport ships bound for Allied ports. She even sank ships that belonged to neutral nations. Between the start of this unrestricted submarine warfare and April 2, 1917, German submarines sank eight American ships. A large number of American lives were lost.

The decision to attack neutral ships in this manner seems not to make sense. It would certainly cause America to enter the war on the side of England. However, by the beginning of 1917, Germany was faced with a critical decision. They realized that they

This 1917 photo shows a German submarine stopping a neutral Spanish ship to inspect it.

could not win the war if Great Britain continued to receive supplies from America. Therefore, the Germans took a risk. They gambled that they could starve England into surrendering before America could send troops to Europe. Germany knew that America would be furious at the attacks on neutral shipping. She knew this would provoke America into the war. She hoped that America could not respond quickly enough. Germany was very nearly correct.

The submarine attacks began to work. The tide of war began to turn against Italy and France. British and French leaders begged the U.S. to send military help. They said that an overseas force would give their people new courage and new hope. After three years of incredibly bloody fighting, all the European nations were exhausted. They were at the point where they had no more men to throw into battle. Some historians believe that had Wilson refused to intervene, the war may well have come to an end that year. Instead, Wilson brought the United States into the war. America's entry was decisive.

Declaration of War

President Wilson appeared before a special session of Congress. There, he delivered a message listing Germany's violations of international law. He said that our country must fight not only to uphold the freedom of the seas, but also "to make the world safe for democracy." He called for an official declaration of war. On April 6, 1917, Congress declared war on Germany and her allies.

Many people responded to the declaration with great enthusiasm. Millions of Americans believed that by helping Britain and France our country was fighting for democracy and lasting world peace.

Spot Check

1. Why was it hard for Americans to remain neutral during the war?
2. What are the four wartime trade laws of international law?
3. How did Great Britain violate these laws?
4. What event led Americans to demand war against Germany?
5. When did the United States enter the war?

THE UNITED STATES PREPARES FOR WAR

Raising and Transporting an Army

With the declaration of war, the United States needed to begin the great task of enlisting, training, and transporting millions of men overseas. Careful thought was given to ways of making the draft a democratic process. To do this, Congress passed the Selective Service Act, or draft law. All men between the ages of twenty-one and thirty years were asked to register at their nearest voting place. A local draft board then proceeded to select those who were physically fit for service. The board also excused from service those with physical disabilities, dependents, or home duties. The names of the registered men were drawn by lot. They were called upon for service in the order in which their names were drawn. Nearly four million men entered the armed forces before the war ended.

Military training camps were established in different parts of the country. There the recruits were put through a rapid course of training to prepare them for service overseas. Six weeks after war was declared, the first group was ready to leave for France. This was far faster than Germany had ever expected. President Wilson placed General John J. Pershing in command of the American Expeditionary Force.

The transportation of a large army to Europe was indeed difficult. In order to speed up the moving of men and supplies to embarkation points, the national government took over the management of the railroads. Troops and supply trains had the right of way. Passenger and freight schedules were subject to government regulation. The Allies, especially Great Britain and Italy, supplied troopships to speed up the transport of American troops to Europe. More than half of the men who went overseas sailed in ships belonging to the Allies.

Organizing the Home Front

To win the war, it was necessary to organize the nation's resources. Production of food, munitions, and war equipment had to be increased with great speed. The nation's natural resources, farmlands, mineral resources, forests, and waterpower, were all given over to support the war.

An adequate food supply was necessary for the army as well as for the rest of the nation. Therefore, the president named Herbert Hoover as food administrator. Hoover appealed to the farmers to increase production. He asked the people to observe both "meatless days" and "wheatless days." On bulletin boards, in newspapers, and in magazines, he used the slogan, "Food will win the war!" The efficient organization of his campaign enabled the nation to produce the huge quantities of food necessary for the Allied nations as well as the army and the people of the United States.

Raising Money for the War

When the United States entered the war, the Allied Powers were running out of money. To aid them in their distress, the American government arranged to lend them great sums of money for the purchase of war supplies. The raising of the money needed called for the support of all Americans. Taxes were increased. War Savings Stamps were issued. Over twenty-one billion dollars' worth of war bonds, called "Liberty Bonds," were purchased by Americans.

Added to all this, various welfare organizations raised large sums to be used in the support of the war. The American Red Cross raised millions of dollars, which it used in caring for the wounded and the sick. Thousands of Red Cross workers and nurses gave unselfish service both here and overseas. Religious organizations, like the Knights of Columbus and the Salvation Army, worked to support American soldiers and sailors both here and abroad.

COMMUNISM IN RUSSIA

The War Badly Weakens Russia

With the war stalemated by late 1916, the Germans were desperately seeking a new strategy by which they could gain some advantage. The Russians were clearly the weakest of the Allies. If Germany could knock Russia out of the war, they could concentrate their forces in the West. Instead of having to fight on two fronts, Germany could fight on just one front. Germany thought this plan could win the war for them.

The war was going badly for Russia. Of all the countries in the war, it was suffering the most. Russia was a poor nation and the war made the bad conditions worse. The great loss of life and shortages of food caused the Russian people to strike and to riot.

The ruler of Russia, Czar Nicholas II, badly mismanaged the war and his nation. As a result of the strikes and riots, in March 1917, Nicholas II was forced to abdicate and a new government took over in Russia. The United States urged the new government to continue the war. The new Russian government agreed. However, the war was extremely unpopular in Russia. A radical group, called the Bolsheviks, said they would take Russia out of the war. As a result, they began to gain power and undermine the new government.

The Evil Communist Dictator Lenin Stirs up the Crowd in Russia

In an attempt to destabilize Russia, Germany agreed to transport the Bolshevik leader, Vladimir Lenin, from exile in Switzerland back to Russia in April of 1917. The Catholic Austrians protested. However, the plan went forward anyway. This decision by the German government had historic costs for the twentieth century. By November 1917, Lenin had seized control of the Russian government. He made a separate peace with Germany. Later, he would order the execution of the Czar and his entire family. Lenin planted the seeds of Communism in Russia. Communism is the greatest enemy the United States and the Catholic Church would face over the next 80 years. From Russia, Communism would spread throughout the world during most of the twentieth century.

What is Communism?

Karl Marx began Communism. Marx was a German philosopher who, in 1848, wrote a pamphlet called *The Communist*

Manifesto. In that pamphlet and other later books, he outlined a philosophy of life that is completely opposed to Christianity in almost every way. Communists believe there is no God and no afterlife. They are atheists. They believe there are no unchanging moral laws. They reject freedom for individuals. To them, people are the simply the tools of the state. Marx also thought that government should be controlled by a small group of people, the Communists. They alone supposedly know the "true principles" of society and history. As a result of this "knowledge," they will completely control every aspect of life. They will tell people what to believe, where to go to school, where to work, and so on. Communism was the worst evil to afflict the world in the twentieth century. By the end of the twentieth century, more Christians were martyred under Communism than all of the previous centuries combined.

Spot Check

1. How did the war weaken Russia?
2. Who was Vladimir Lenin?
3. Who wrote *The Communist Manifesto*?
4. What were its teachings?

America in Battle

With Russia out of the war, Germany moved its military from the eastern front to the western front. Germany launched new attacks against the Allies in the hope that she could defeat them before there were sufficient American forces in France to offer effective assistance. Germany launched two great attacks in the spring of 1918. One was intended to break through the Allies' lines and push on to the English Channel. The other meant to advance farther into France and capture Paris.

Marshal Foch, the commander of the Allied troops, directed a terrific effort to defeat the German offensive. At Amiens, France,

American soldiers before the Battle of Saint Mihiel

the German drive toward the English Channel was stopped by British troops reinforced by French and American soldiers. Then, the Germans advanced all along the western front. The courageous fighting of Allied troops, including American soldiers at Cantigny, at Belleau Wood, and at Chateau-Thierry, checked the Germans. Paris was saved.

American soldiers were still not ready for a general offensive. Most of them had been quickly transported to Europe. They had not received enough training. As a result, it was not until July that the American forces were prepared to attack. Supported by two million fresh American soldiers, Marshal Foch launched an attack all along the western front. For more than two months, the fighting raged. Finally, at St. Mihiel and in the Argonne Forest, the Americans under General Pershing drove the Germans and Austrians back beyond the Hindenburg Line into Germany. The German army was exhausted. They asked for terms of surrender. The terms were accepted. The war officially ended at 11:00 AM, November 11, 1918.

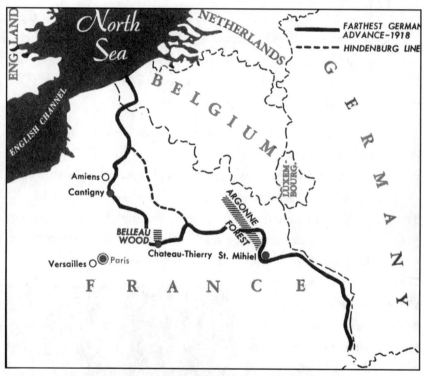

Map showing where Americans fought during World War I

The End of the War

The end of the war brought joy to the warring nations. The war had cost more than three hundred billion dollars. It had brought death, sorrow, and misery to millions. The United States had not suffered as much as other nations. However, the war had taken its toll of American lives and money. More than one hundred sixteen thousand American soldiers died during the war, and more than two hundred thousand were wounded. The war cost us almost twenty-eight billion dollars.

THE CHURCH AND WORLD WAR I

The Church Remains Neutral

Since a large number of Catholics served on both sides of the conflict, Pope Benedict XV adopted a policy of strict neutrality. The pope limited himself to appeals for peace. It was the first time that the Church did not take sides in a major European conflict. Benedict's example was followed by all of his successors.

Since he would not take sides, Benedict XV was not trusted. The peace plan he offered to the warring nations on August 1, 1917, was turned down. The plan had seven points. The pope's plan recognized that what is right and just is more important than a nation's power to impose its will. The plan said that countries should reduce the number of weapons they have, and that disputes should be resolved by appeal to an international court. The pope also said that countries should not be punished by having to pay damages to the victors. President Wilson in his *Fourteen Points*, the guide for the United States in the peace talks, included some of the pope's ideas. Later, when Wilson went to Europe for the peace talks, he visited Benedict XV in Rome. This was the first time an American president, while still in office, had visited a pope.

Pope Benedict XV

Vatican Relief Efforts

Benedict XV put the resources of the Catholic Church to work for the victims of the war. Never had so many noncombatants been uprooted and cast out of their homes. Probably the greatest service performed by the Vatican was to establish a missing-persons bureau. This organization also helped prisoners of war to stay in touch with their families. Vatican officials also helped in prison exchanges. They financed housing for the sick and wounded, and opened orphanages for children whose parents were dead or missing. Sadly, the suspicion that the warring countries had for the pope's neutrality hampered his influence on political events. The pope was not even invited to the peace conference. Yet, the pope's charitable efforts and his appeals for peace increased the Church's moral prestige after the war.

Spot Check

1. Who offered the Seven-Point peace plan?
2. Why was the Seven-Point peace plan rejected? Who used some of these points as a guide for the peace settlement?
3. In what way did Benedict XV put the resources of the Catholic Church to work for the victims of war?

THE RESULTS OF THE FIRST WORLD WAR

The Armistice

The Allied military command drew up the terms of the peace treaty that ended the First World War. This document forced Germany to surrender all her colonies, practically all of her navy, all her artillery, and most of her railway equipment. An Allied army was to occupy German territory along the Rhine River. Germany also was required to surrender all prisoners of war, all military stores, and all submarines. By the terms of the peace treaty, Germany was rendered absolutely helpless.

People celebrate the end of World War I.

Even so, Germany had no choice but to sign whatever treaty the Allies gave it.

The Treaty of Versailles

In January 1919, seventy-two delegates from the victorious nations met at Versailles, a suburb of Paris. President Wilson and four commissioners represented the United States. England, France, and Italy, the other great Allied nations, were represented by their prime ministers: David Lloyd George, Georges Clemenceau, and Vittorio Orlando. These four leaders were known as the "Big Four." Clemenceau presided at the meeting.

At the conference, Wilson tried to carry out a peace program based on the Fourteen Points that he had outlined the previous year. Among his points, Wilson wanted freedom of the seas both in time of peace and war. He sought a reduction of armaments among all nations. He wanted the removal of all economic barriers. He wanted an impartial adjustment of colonial claims. He desired the "restoration" of some countries, such as Russia and Belgium, but "readjustment" of other countries according to major nationalities. His major desire was the creation of an association of nations that would guarantee the political independence and borders of both great and small nations.

Seeing that the Americans did not wish to punish Germany in Wilson's *Fourteen Points*, Germany had agreed to the armistice. They hoped that the final peace treaty would be more favorable to Germany than the armistice. However, after months of talks, the Treaty of Versailles turned out to be no better than the armistice agreement. The leaders of France, England, and Italy did not accept many points of Wilson's peace plan. Germany was punished by having to pay huge sums of money in war damages. She also lost all her colonies as well as some of her own territory in Europe. It was truly "the peace that failed." It created a huge resentment among the Germans and destroyed the German economy.

One of Wilson's points that the peace conference accepted was the "readjustment" of nations. Austria-Hungary and the Turkish Empire were dissolved. They were divided up into smaller countries of various nationalities. Peace treaties were signed with the new governments of the new countries. Also included in the treaty was the provision for a League of Nations. The League of Nations was intended to be an international organization for the peaceful resolution of disputes between nations. Germany signed the treaty June 28, 1919.

The Treaty of Versailles

On his return to the United States, the president asked the Senate to ratify the Treaty of Versailles. However, the Senate strongly objected to joining the League of Nations. America had enough of the crusade to make the world safe for democracy. It just wanted to go back to minding its own business. The treaty was voted down. The United States never did ratify it. Later, the United States made separate treaties of peace with Germany and Austria.

The Overthrow of the Monarchies

The end of the War meant the end of the great monarchies of continental Europe. The Russian czar was overthrown in 1917. At the end of the war, William II of Germany was forced to abdicate and went to Holland. A particular tragedy was the end of Austria-Hungary and the Catholic Habsburg royal dynasty.

In the place of these monarchies, new governments were set up. In Russia, the Communists created the Union of Soviet Socialists Republics (U.S.S.R.). Germany created a republic. However, Germany was so devastated by the war that the government did not last even twenty years. Adolf Hitler came to power in 1933 and ruled as a dictator. New nations were created. Czechoslovakia and Yugoslavia were created from parts of the Austro-Hungarian Empire. They also had republican governments until after World War II when they fell under Communism. In Italy in 1922, Benito Mussolini set up a Fascist government. Although he was initially friendly to the Church, his ambition to control people's lives soon put him at odds with the pope.

The Heavy Cost of the War

Grave problems confronted the European countries after the war. Great national debts faced every country that had engaged in the war. The property loss was tremendous. Trade was at a standstill.

Germany was completely crippled. Germany was forced to assume all blame for the war and pay heavy damages to the Allies. These damages were known as reparations. The financial burden was so great that the new government in Germany appealed to the Allies in 1923 for a reduction in the reparations. The Allies responded by appointing a commission to consider the problem of reparations. The chairman of the commission was an American, Charles Dawes. The plan worked out by the commission is known as the Dawes Plan. This plan scaled the reparations down. However, before long Germany declared that she still could not make the payments. As a result, in 1929, another commission, under the chairmanship of Owen D. Young of New York, re-examined the reparations problem. It submitted to Germany the Young Plan. Though the Young Plan called for greatly reduced payments, two years later Germany again ceased making payments. The Young Plan, like the Dawes Plan, failed.

The Birth of the Soviet Union

The most lasting effect of World War I was the establishment of Communism in the Soviet Union. Some historians have said that

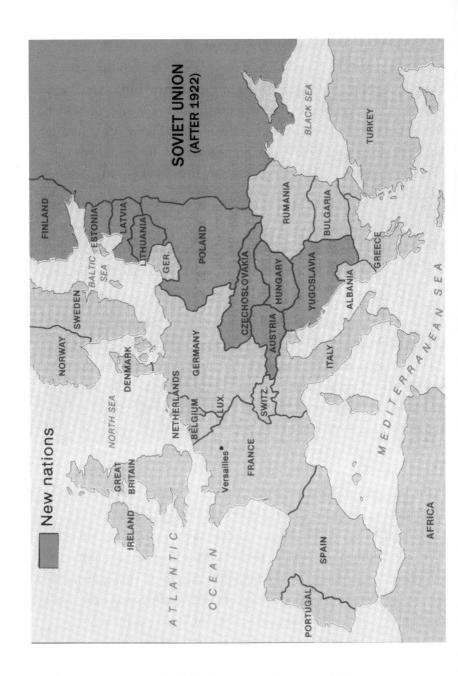

Europe in 1919. Compare to map on page 414.

the only result of World War I was the establishment of Communism, and the only result of World War II was its spread. For the next eighty years, the United States and the Church would face this horrible enemy.

Spot Check

1. What were the most important points of President Wilson's plan? Which point was used in the treaty?
2. What was the "readjustment" of nations?
3. What new nations arose out of the old Austria-Hungarian empire?
4. What happened to these new but weak republics?
5. What problems faced Europe after the war?
6. Why did the Dawes Plan and Young Plan fail?

CHAPTER REVIEW

1. What were the underlying causes of the First World War?
2. What was the immediate cause?
3. Which nations belonged to the Central Powers?
4. Which nations belonged to the Allied Powers?
5. Why was it difficult for the United States to maintain a neutral attitude?
6. How did Great Britain and Germany violate the international law of the sea?
7. Why did the United States enter the war?
8. How did the United States raise funds for the conduct of the war?
9. How did the United States raise an army?
10. How did the United States aid the Allied cause during the First World War?
11. Who was Marshall Foch?
12. When did the War begin and end?
13. What were the terms of the armistice?
14. Who were the "Big Four"?
15. Who was Karl Marx?
16. Who was Vladimir Lenin?
17. What do the initials "U.S.S.R." stand for?
18. Why was the Treaty of Versailles the "peace that failed"?
19. What was the most lasting effect of WWI?
20. Who commanded the American forces in Europe during WWI?

THE "ROARING" TWENTIES

Broadway in New York City in 1920

ATTEMPTS TO PREVENT FUTURE WARS

World War I was unimaginably horrible to those who survived it. As a result, there were several attempts to prevent any future wars. Conferences were held. Treaties were made. The League of Nations was established. Sadly, none of the attempts prevented war. As terrible as WWI was, an even more terrible war was to follow in a little more than two decades. Plato had said that only the dead have seen the end of war. Sadly, Plato was right.

The League of Nations

Even before World War I began, there were leaders who talked about an organization of nations that would try to settle disputes without resorting to war. During the war this idea took definite form in a proposal for the League of Nations, through which disputes might be resolved and wars prevented. At the Versailles peace conference, President Wilson and a representative of Great Britain, General Jan Smuts of South Africa, presented constitutions for a "League of Nations." From these proposals, the covenant (constitution) of the League of Nations, as it appeared in the peace treaty, was drafted. All the nations that ratified the Treaty of Versailles automatically became members of the League of Nations. Others could be admitted by a two-thirds vote.

In all, sixty-three nations joined the League of Nations. Although the Senate refused to ratify the Treaty of Versailles, including the League Covenant, our country usually sent unofficial representatives to the League of Nations meetings.

The Work of the League of Nations

In the end, the League failed to prevent World War II. However, it did promote cooperation in the fields of health, education, transportation, and communication. It studied such world problems as finance, labor, and drug traffic. It established the Permanent Court of International Justice, which settled several disputes between nations. It functioned until 1946 when it was replaced by the United Nations.

The Washington Disarmament Conference

The United States had maintained that the First World War was a "war to end all wars." At the end of the fighting, most Americans sincerely desired to promote peace. So, in the summer of 1921, President Warren G. Harding invited the nations of the world to send delegates to a meeting in Washington, D. C. to discuss disarming. Harding wanted the United States to be seen as doing its part to reduce the danger of wars.

The conference involved the great naval powers of the world: the United States, England, France, Japan, and Italy. In addition,

China, Holland, Belgium, and Portugal were also invited. These nations were asked to attend because of their interests in the Pacific and the Far East.

The conference resulted in two important treaties. In one, the five great naval powers agreed to scrap over one million eight hundred seventy-eight thousand tons of naval vessels. Also, no new battleships were to be built for a period of ten years. This "naval holiday" was scheduled to end in 1936. A second treaty provided for regulation of trade in China in accord with the open door policy.

When the naval holiday ended, efforts were made to extend the disarmament agreements. However, all such efforts failed. As a result, a general race in naval construction continued among the world's leading sea powers.

International Peace Conferences

Between the First and the Second World Wars, four outstanding meetings were held in the quest for peace. These were each international conferences. Two of them resulted in signed treaties: the Locarno Treaties and the Kellogg-Briand Pact. The other two meetings, the Geneva Conference and the London Naval Conference, ended in disagreement.

The Locarno Treaties

In the fall of 1925, most of the European nations met in Locarno, Switzerland. They signed a series of treaties. The signing nations promised never to fight each other. They also promised to respect each other's borders and to follow certain rules in settling disputes.

The Kellogg-Briand Pact

In 1927, Aristide Briand, prime minister of France, stated that his country would be willing to enter into an agreement with the United States to outlaw war. Thereupon, our Secretary of State, Frank Kellogg, suggested that all the leading countries of the world join in signing such a treaty. Kellogg then arranged a treaty that was acceptable to all the great nations. The treaty was quite short. The signing nations renounced war as an instrument of state policy. They resolved to settle disputes by peaceful means.

The Kellogg-Briand Pact, sometimes called the Pact of Paris, was signed by all the great powers of Europe. It was ratified by the United States Senate in 1928. Due to the number of important nations that had approved the Pact, it was considered an important step toward outlawing war. Needless to say, the attempt, while well-intentioned, had little real effect.

SPOT CHECK
1. What was the League of Nations?
2. What did the League of Nations successfully promote?
3. What replaced the League of Nations? When?
4. What was the Washington Disarmament Conference?
5. What was the Kellogg-Briand Pact? What was its effect?

THE PROBLEMS OF PEACE

Confusion and Uncertainty

The end of the First World War was followed in the United States by a period of confusion in industry, business, farming, and society. The return of nearly four million men from the armed forces to civilian life presented many problems. Factories had ramped up production for wartime. Adjustment of industry from wartime to peacetime production meant cutting production. There were strikes in the basic industries. This caused unrest and distress. Hoover had asked the farmers to increase production. At the end of the war, the storage bins were filled to capacity. Farmers could not find a market for their produce. Confusion ruled the land. The uncertainty of the markets, the idle factories, and the critical situation of the farmers made life in the United Sates unpredictable.

The "Return to Normalcy"

In 1921, a Republican, Warren G. Harding of Ohio, succeeded President Wilson. Harding had used the slogan "return to normalcy" in his campaign. He promised to cure all the ills of our ailing country and return it to the way that existed before the war. He was elected by a huge majority.

Though Harding had served as a senator from Ohio, he was not a strong leader. As a result, he became the prey of unworthy associates. Many of those he elevated to high trust stole from the public. Several scandals broke out during his administration. The most famous scandal was the Teapot Dome Scandal. The Secretary of the Interior accepted bribes of over $400,000 in return for allowing illegal oil drilling on public lands at Teapot Dome, Wyoming.

President Warren G. Harding

Harding died before the end of his first term. Vice President Calvin Coolidge was vacationing on his father's farm in Vermont when the news of the death reached him. At 2:47 in the morning, August 3, 1923, the presidential oath was administered to Calvin Coolidge by his father, a justice of the peace.

Calvin Coolidge was an honest man and a careful spender. He had a high sense of duty. He made every effort to

Calvin Coolidge is sworn into office by his father.

bring to justice those who had been guilty of fraud in Harding's administration. Though Coolidge was not especially popular, he was elected to serve another term in 1924. After completing his full term, Coolidge refused to be considered for nomination in 1928. He retired to private life.

The Election of 1928

The Republican nomination for president was Herbert Hoover. He was well known for efficiency, both as Secretary of Commerce and as the food administrator during World War I. The Democrats nominated Alfred E. Smith who had served four times as governor of New York. He, too, was popular, but he was a Catholic. Moreover, he wanted to repeal the Eighteenth Amendment (1919). This amendment created a national ban on alcohol. This ban was

President Herbert Hoover

known as Prohibition. As a result, Smith had opposition from many sides. Sadly, anti-Catholicism was still a major factor in American politics.

For the first time, radio played a large part in a presidential campaign. Millions who had never heard a presidential candidate listened to Smith and Hoover. Smith received the largest number of popular votes given to a Democratic candidate up to that time. However, Hoover received more votes.

Harding, Coolidge, and Hoover all worked to reduce government spending. They tried to increase the tariff and decrease taxes. They worked to reduce how much the government money the government borrowed.

The "Roaring Twenties"

Growth of the American Economy

World War I had seriously slowed the industrial and agricultural production of Europe. As a result, the United States made a great deal of money supplying the European countries. Also, new industries began at this time as a result of new technologies. The automobile, the radio, the phonograph and all sorts of new goods became available to consumers. Thus, the 1920s were a time of great wealth and luxury in the United States.

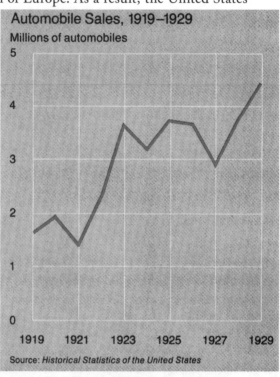

Automobile Sales, 1919–1929
Millions of automobiles

Source: *Historical Statistics of the United States*

Political Conservatism

In politics, the result of this newfound wealth was a more conservative approach. Americans were more happy and prosperous than ever before. They did not want to do anything that might change that. After women were given the right to vote in 1920, the reforms of the Progressives ended. The Progressives were those who wanted to make radical changes in the nation. Progressives, like Woodrow Wilson, lost power. The Republicans of the 1920s felt that the government's job was simply to provide an atmosphere in which people and businesses could create wealth. The Progressives wanted government to redistribute the wealth.

Social Transformation

The growth of luxury also had a deep impact on society. American society had always been influenced by a strong Puritan tradition in which leisure and luxury had been suspect, if not sinful. This tradition began to disappear rapidly under the temptations of material goods. Catholics had always viewed leisure as good and vital. Indeed, Puritanism was a heresy that denied much that was good in human nature. However, perhaps the change came about too quickly. Old social practices were overthrown so quickly that Americans did not know when to stop. Concern for one's own pleasure became a common attitude. Among other things, divorce

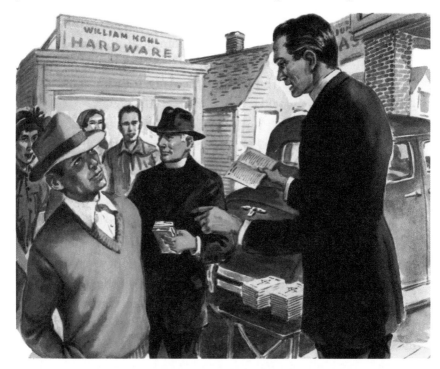

During these times, the Church continued to work to spread the Faith.

became more accepted. Between 1910 and 1928, the divorce rate doubled.

The Rise of the Mass Media

The development of radio, motion pictures, and national magazines had a tremendous effect on American society. The rise of the consumer society meant the rise of consumer advertising. The radio and magazines were obvious ways to reach large numbers of people with advertisements. These commercials urged the audience to buy the sponsor's product. They increased the desire for greater personal satisfaction.

The growing popularity of movies ensured that Hollywood would be a leading cultural influence. This became even truer in 1927 when the movie *The Jazz Singer* introduced sound to film. The national nature of movies and radio also broke down regional differences. Americans began to develop a national culture. Films from Hollywood and magazines from New York City controlled the new national culture.

New labor saving machines of the Twentieth Century reduced the need for labor in the factory and on the farm. A growing class of people who no longer worked in these two major industries began to grow as the need for laborers lessened. The industrial age was coming to an end. It would be eventually replaced by the information age. The number of pamphlets and digests grew enormously during the 1920s. A great emphasis was placed on education.

Prohibition and Lawlessness

Many Americans had believed that government could solve the problem of drunkenness. The result was the Eighteenth Amendment, which created Prohibition. However, not long after the Amendment was ratified, it was clear that it created more problems than it solved. The years that followed the passing of the Prohibition Amendment were filled with lawlessness. The Amendment not only failed to achieve its purpose, but contempt for laws actually increased. Gangsters grew rich and powerful through "bootlegging." This is the illegal making, selling, and transporting of alcoholic liquor. They also ran "speakeasies," places where alcoholic drinks were illegally sold. Gangsters fought for control over who would control the supply of illegal liquor to a certain city or region. Robbery, extortion, kidnapping, and murder became common.

The automobile greatly increased the mobility of the gangsters. It allowed bootleggers to move quickly from state to state. This made it difficult for the police in any one state to fight crime as they had done in the past. The Federal authorities had to become involved. It was during these "Lawless Years" that the Bureau of Investigation (BOI) rose to importance. In 1935, the bureau became known as the FBI, the Federal Bureau of Investigation.

The 1920s were a decade when people were enjoying the good times. The war was over. Life was good. It was a time of new entertainment. There were movies and radio. There was a new kind of music: jazz. It was bright and lively. There were laws against alcohol but they were almost universally ignored. This disregard for laws, even for the moral laws of God, is a major reason the decade was known as the "Roaring Twenties."

Spot Check

1. Why were the 1920s so prosperous and luxurious?
2. What was the cause of political conservatism in the 1920s?
3. What inventions assisted in the development of an American national culture?
4. What was the Eighteenth amendment? Why did it create more problems than it solved?

THE GREAT DEPRESSION

The "Crash" of 1929

Early in 1929, there were signs of a down turn in business. However, the public did not heed the warning signs. In fact, the stock market rose to new heights. Huge profits were reported. A new wave of gambling in stocks followed.

Then came the "crash" on October 24, 1929. Stock prices suddenly dropped sharply. People started to sell their stocks. Five days later, October 29, came the greatest panic in the history of the stock exchange. On that day alone, more than sixteen million shares were sold on the market for anything that they might bring. Millions of people lost their life savings. For the next two-and-a-half years, the stock market continued to drift lower and lower.

The Great Depression

Economic depression followed the stock market panic. The prices of goods declined, foreign trade fell off, and there was less buying. Factories closed their doors. Wages and salaries declined. Unemployment became widespread. People began to withdraw money from banks in order to pay their bills. Many banks could not meet the demand for cash because money was out on loan. Many banks began to fail. Money became hard to get. Families could no longer pay their rent or mortgage and lost their homes. The economic depression was accompanied by a depression of spirit. Investors who had lost their fortunes committed suicide. Despair could be found almost everywhere. In many places, long bread lines told the story of hunger and unemployment.

The people in the cities suffered most during the Depression, but the farmers also shared in the suffering. The prices of farm products fell off sharply. Most farmers were unable to pay their taxes, their mortgages, and the interest on loans. As in other industries, farmers had invested heavily in machinery in order to produce more for the war effort. They had expanded their farms and invested in larger herds of livestock. Overproduction and surplus stocks of crops paralyzed the market. Between 1929 and 1933, thousands of farmers saw their mortgages foreclosed. Farms were put up for auction to

Long bread lines told the story of hunger and unemployment.

satisfy both taxes and debts. To add to the problem, a drought hit large parts of the nation beginning in 1930. So many dust storms struck the area between Texas and the Dakotas that the area was called the "Dust Bowl."

REACTION TO THE DEPRESSION

Government Efforts to Help the Situation

President Hoover was slow to try to restore public confidence until conditions became very bad. He believed the economy worked best when the government stayed out of it. However, late in 1931, the continuing crisis forced him to intervene. Hoover tried to restore the confidence of the American people in our economic system by setting up the two billion dollar Reconstruction Finance Corporation (RFC). The RFC made loans to banks, insurance companies, railroads, and mortgage companies that were close to failing. Congress also provided money for public works and made loans to states for relief. Federal Home Loan Banks were established to aid homeowners and farmers in trouble.

To the very end of his term, President Hoover believed that the Depression would not last long. He opposed large-scale federal relief on the grounds that it would further damage the economy. Some people called for government work programs. However, the Republicans viewed that as a socialistic solution that would not work. Nevertheless, through the efforts of a group of liberal congressmen, a public works program was created to provide work for millions of the unemployed. Loans and direct grants of money were made to states for the construction of bridges, roads, highways, and public buildings. This program brought temporary relief. However, it increased taxes and did not stop the Depression.

The Election of 1932

The Republicans nominated Herbert Hoover for a second term as president. However, there were few who thought that he could win. Most people blamed his administration for the Depression. The Democrats nominated Franklin D. Roosevelt of New York for the presidency. Roosevelt was from a very privileged family. Private tutors provided his early education. He attended Harvard University and received his law degree from Columbia University. He had served in the Wilson Administration. In 1928, he was elected governor of New York. Franklin Roosevelt had

President Franklin D. Roosevelt

a winning smile and a warm public manner. However, he did not have a clearly thought-out plan to deal with the Depression at the time of his nomination. In his speech to accept the nomination for president he promised "a new deal for the American people." He did not spell out what he meant, but people liked the sound of "a new deal."

Franklin Roosevelt won a landslide victory in 1932. This victory signaled the start of the longest time in office of any president in American history. He is the only president to be elected to four terms. He is also one of the most controversial presidents because of the far-reaching changes that he made during his term in office.

Spot Check

1. How did the stock market panic cause economic depression in the United States?
2. How did it affect American families?
3. How did the Depression affect agriculture?
4. How did President Hoover try to restore the confidence of the American people?
5. What was the Public Works program? Was it successful in its attempt to stop the Depression?
6. Why was Franklin D. Roosevelt's presidency unique?

CHAPTER REVIEW

1. What was the Kellogg-Briand Pact?
2. What were the main policies of Harding, Coolidge, and Hoover?
3. Why was Alfred E. Smith's nomination for president in 1928 controversial?
4. Why were the 1920s politically conservative?
5. What effect did the development of radio and movies have on American culture?
6. What was Prohibition?
7. Why was it started?
8. What was the "Crash" of 1929?
9. What were some of the reasons for the Great Depression?
10. How did President Hoover combat the Depression?
11. Who won the election of 1932? Why is this president considered controversial?

America Gets a New Deal
and Becomes Involved in World War II

President Franklin D. Roosevelt prepares to start his first Fireside Chat to the
American people on March 12, 1933.

Money and Banking

The "Bank Holiday"

When Franklin D. Roosevelt was inaugurated as president on
March 4, 1933, the economic depression had reached major proportions.
Banks throughout the country had closed. State and local relief funds
were nearly gone. Business was virtually at a standstill. There were
over ten million people unemployed. However, the people believed in
President Roosevelt. They placed their hopes in him and his platform.

In his inaugural address, President Roosevelt pleaded with the people not to be overcome by fear. He said: "The only thing we have to fear is fear itself." He promised prompt action and a program that would furnish jobs for the unemployed. He spoke of recovery measures to end the Depression and a New Deal for all people. The promised measures meant that the federal government would assume responsibility for the general welfare of the people on a scale never before seen in the United States. The series of laws that Roosevelt proposed and Congress passed in the first hundred days of his first term profoundly changed American life.

Roosevelt's first act was to declare a "bank holiday." The banking situation was so bad that drastic action was necessary. He ordered all the banks in the country to be closed. The purpose of the holiday was to give the federal government time to determine which banks were sound and which were not. Only those banks that were found to be solid were to be allowed to reopen. All the others were to remain closed. In a very short period of time, the banks found to be in good shape were reopened. Confidence in the banks was restored. People stopped withdrawing money.

Banking Legislation

To cure the money and banking problems, Congress passed a number of laws. The law with the most impact was the Banking Act of 1933. The Banking Act set up a Federal Deposit Insurance Corporation (FDIC). The FDIC provided insurance on deposits for member banks of the Federal Reserve System and for state banks. This protected the money people deposited in banks.

Another act reorganized the Federal Reserve System under a Board of Governors. This Board was given extensive authority to regulate the business of banks. The board was given the authority to regulate the buying and selling of government bonds through the

Federal Reserve Banks. Thus, the board could control money and the use of bank deposits.

To protect the people further, Congress passed two acts dealing with the stock market. These provided more effective federal supervision of the stock exchanges. They also required that all issues of stocks and bonds be filed with a government commission known as the Securities and Exchange Commission.

Farm Relief and Homeowners' Relief

The Agricultural Adjustment Act

The Agricultural Adjustment Act was passed to relieve the farming situation. This was even worse in 1933 than it had been in 1929. The chief purpose of the act was to raise the price of farm crops by cutting production. The act set up an Agricultural Adjustment Administration (AAA). The AAA had the power to make contracts for the reduction of crops. Farmers who cut production of certain crops, among which were cotton, corn, rice, and tobacco, were given benefit payments. The farmers responded well. The financial returns brought them new hope. Although it helped the farmers, higher crop prices did not help the urban poor who were struggling to buy food.

This act was later declared unconstitutional. However, Congress then passed the Soil Conservation Act. By this act, farmers were paid for planting crops that would conserve natural resources rather than paying them not to plant at all. Under this act, many activities formerly carried on under the Agricultural Adjustment Act were continued.

A number of other acts were passed to help the farmers. The Farm Mortgage Foreclosure Act was passed to prevent farmers from losing their farms because they could not pay their mortgages. The Farm Tenancy Act provided tenant farmers with money to buy farms. This act established the Farm Security Administration. Needy tenant farmers were given a chance to obtain small loans for the purchase of work animals and equipment. The Farm Mortgage Refinancing Act provided money for refinancing farm mortgages at low interest.

The Home Owners' Loan Corporation

Homeowners as well as farmers needed help during the depression. As a result, the Home Owners' Loan Corporation (HOLC) was established. Through the HOLC, homeowners could obtain long-term mortgage loans to save their homes from being lost.

Federal Housing Administration

The Federal Housing Administration (FHA) was set up to make it possible for a greater number of people to own their own homes. The FHA insured banks and loan associations against some of the loss that they might suffer if the people to whom they have loaned money cannot repay the loan. The FHA made it possible for many people to buy homes who otherwise would have been unable to do so.

Spot Check

1. What was the "bank holiday"?
2. How did the Banking Act of 1933 strengthen banks in the United States?
3. How did the Home Owners Loan Corporation help homeowners save their homes?
4. How does the Federal Housing Administration (FHA) enable more people to own their own homes?

REGULATION OF LABOR AND INDUSTRY

Labor Legislation

The first efforts of the Roosevelt administration were centered on relief for farm and homeowners. However, before long, laws dealing with industry and labor were passed. Prior to the New Deal, labor legislation had been regulated by the states. The New Dealers sought federal laws to regulate labor, as well as wages and working hours. The New Dealers supported unions. They encouraged people to join unions. The Roosevelt administration worked to strengthen unions at the cost of private enterprise.

In June 1933, Congress passed the National Industrial Recovery Act (NIRA). This act gave the federal government control over industry for two years. However, in May 1935, the Supreme Court declared this act unconstitutional. The Court said that the act attempted to regulate wages and hours within the individual states. This was declared to be beyond the powers of Congress. In response to the Court's decision, Congress enacted the National Labor Relations Act. This act was actually more favorable to labor and was within the powers of Congress.

In 1938, Congress passed the Fair Labor Standards Act (FLSA), the so-called Wages and Hours Law. The purpose of the law was to create jobs. To that end, it created a workweek of no more than forty hours per week. Workers who worked more than forty hours were to be paid "time and one-half" for all overtime work if they worked in industries affecting interstate commerce. The idea was that an employer would hire two people rather than pay one worker time and a half. The FLSA also prohibited child labor in interstate industries. It also provided for a minimum wage. Since the time of its passage, the FLSA has had one of the greatest impacts on American businesses.

Regulation of Transportation and Communication

In 1933, a transportation act was passed. This act ordered that transportation service be improved. It also called for the reduction of rates and fares. The Communications Act created the Federal Communications Commission (FCC). The FCC regulates foreign and domestic communications by telephone, telegraph, cable, radio, and, television.

Electric Power and the People

By 1930, almost half the electric power produced in the nation was controlled by five of the largest utility companies. High power rates limited the use of electricity. Poor people could not afford electricity. Roosevelt concluded that the states could not regulate power production adequately. He believed that greater federal control was needed.

In 1933, Congress established the Tennessee Valley Authority (TVA). This was a vast government project designed to generate and sell electricity. (The TVA still exists today.) The TVA could sell electricity at a very low rate. If it sold to private companies, it could set the rates at which they could resell. The TVA was an enormous effort to develop the entire Tennessee River region. This region includes parts of Tennessee, Kentucky, North Carolina, Virginia, Mississippi, Alabama, and Georgia. Since the TVA is a

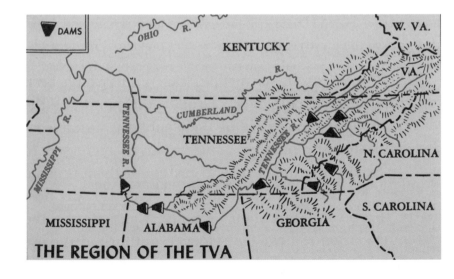

THE REGION OF THE TVA

land developer, it also has the right to control flooding, improve river navigation, and irrigate land. These various projects greatly improved the economy and social welfare of the people in the Tennessee Valley. Its success caused the TVA to become a model for similar river projects around the world.

Power companies bitterly opposed the TVA project. They saw it as interference in private enterprise. The TVA was challenged in court. However, the Supreme Court upheld its legality.

UNEMPLOYMENT RELIEF AND SOCIAL SECURITY

Relief Measures

In every society, there have always been some people who are unemployed. Usually their family, the local churches, or the local community supported them until they found work. However, during the Depression, the number of unemployed increased to such an extent that the burden of caring for them became too great for families or the local community. It was decided that state aid was needed to prevent starvation. Congress, on the advice of President Hoover, authorized the use of federal funds to aid the states in granting relief.

When Roosevelt became president, federal aid for unemployment relief was continued. Moreover, new agencies for directing relief to this growing mass of unemployed were created. These agencies gave thousands of people useful jobs at a time when they otherwise could not have found work.

Of particular interest is the Civilian Conservation Corps (CCC). The CCC was established to care for the employment and training of jobless youths. Under the direction of the CCC, unemployed young men were housed in camps, clothed and fed, and given a salary of one dollar a day. The work of the CCC was confined to public lands. The young men made trails, cut fire lanes, planted trees, fought plant pests, and built dams. However, the CCC did more than employ jobless youth. It built morale, gave youth a new outlook, and re-established their faith in America.

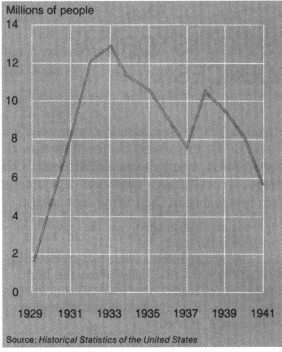

Millions of people

Unemployment statistics, 1929 - 1941

The welfare of young Americans was also protected by the National Youth Administration (NYA). Under this agency, the government paid needy students between the ages of sixteen and twenty-five for part-time work. This allowed them to continue their high-school and college educations.

Social Security

The most far-reaching measure of this period was the creation of Social Security. Recovering from the Depression was not the only goal of the Roosevelt administration. They also wished to enact permanent social programs that would prevent similar disasters in the future. For that reason, on August 14, 1935, Congress passed the Social Security Act. This far-reaching Act provides security for a number of people. It provides security for the aged, the unemployed, and the handicapped. It also furnishes care to needy children and the blind as well as public health services. It also provides unemployment insurance. The money to pay for the act is paid by a payroll tax on employers and employees. The Act has been extended and modified since it was originally passed.

Spot Check

1. What was the National Industrial Recovery Act? Why was it ruled unconstitutional?
2. What does the FCC do?
3. Why did power companies oppose the TVA?
4. What is the Social Security Act?

OPPOSITION TO THE NEW DEAL

Despite the popularity of Roosevelt, there was opposition to the New Deal. It came in the form of two arguments. One argument was constitutional. Many people thought that the federal government had gone far beyond its authority and was controlling and interfering in many aspects of the people's lives. The other argument was economic. Such vast government control was bad for the economy.

Economic Issues

Economists still argue over the effects of Roosevelt's policies. Many believe that his policies extended and deepened the Depression for many years. They reason that the government does not create wealth. It only redistributes and consumes it. The increases in taxation and government work programs took vital resources away from the private sector and prevented it from recovering. When there is widespread unemployment, labor is cheap. New business and industries are able to take advantage of this cheap labor. Government programs kept wages artificially high. This prevented private business from growing as they might have.

However, other economists insist that Roosevelt's actions had positive results. They believe that his actions prevented greater suffering that would have resulted had such drastic measures not been taken. Certainly the people who were helped by these social programs believed that the New Deal was a good thing.

Constitutional Issues

The constitutional issues that were raised by the New Deal are very important and long lasting. According to the Constitution, the federal government is one of limited powers. This means that it has only those powers that are expressly given to it or are implied as necessary to carry out those express powers. The Great Depression caused some people to reject this idea. They thought that the federal government should be responsible for many of the improvements needed in society. Sadly, they were not concerned whether these powers were in the Constitution or not.

The Court Packing Plan

As noted earlier, the Supreme Court declared some of the New Deal laws to be unconstitutional. These rulings caused public debate, as well as a power struggle within the national government. Supreme Court justices are appointed for life. Roosevelt, despite his popularity and support in Congress, was not able to control the Court. Moreover, he was not able to appoint a new justice until an old one retired or died. In 1937, after repeated rejection of some of his programs, Roosevelt fought back. He proposed the enlargement of the Supreme Court and a reorganization of the Federal courts. This would allow him to appoint several new Supreme Court justices. He could appoint judges who would support him. Thus he could gain control of the Court. This scheme to add more Justices was known as the "Court Packing Plan."

Many in Congress saw Roosevelt's idea as a serious threat to the checks and balances among the three branches of government. If every new president expanded the Court when he came into the office, the Supreme Court would lose much of its power. As a result, Congress rejected the plan.

The Effectiveness of the New Deal

New Deal programs swelled the federal government from 600,000 to 3,800,000 employees. The national government became a very big business. Yet, many of the rules it issued discouraged the private businesses which were needed to improve the economy. In the end, this new larger government and its programs failed to end both large-scale unemployment and the Depression. It was World War II that ended the Depression. Also, the New Deal programs failed to markedly reduce rural and urban poverty.

On the other hand, Roosevelt succeeded in giving people hope. After all, he was the only president to be elected four times. Also, he created many policies that today are part of the fabric of American society. These include such programs as social security and certain labor rights. Finally, the New Deal programs did improve the physical condition of the country. The programs preserved and enhanced the nation's roads, bridges, power and water supplies, and public buildings.

SPOT CHECK
1. What were two different arguments against the New Deal?
2. Why did Congress reject President Roosevelt's plan to expand the United States Supreme Court?
3. What were some of the negative effects of the New Deal?
4. In what ways did the New Deal improve the physical condition of the country?

Relations with Other Nations in the Years Before World War II

Reciprocal Trade Agreements

In 1934, Congress passed the Reciprocal Tariff Act. This act gave the president the power to make special trade deals with other countries without consulting the Senate. It also allowed him to lower tariff rates for nations willing to lower their rates on American-made goods. These reciprocal trade agreements resulted in a large increase of our exports. It did much to improve friendly relations with other nations.

Neutrality Policy

In 1935, Congress passed a Neutrality Act. It was intended to keep America from becoming involved in foreign wars. The Act forbade the sale or transport of munitions to any warring nation. To further protect our nation, Congress passed another act in 1936 prohibiting loans to warring nations. The next year, Congress passed an even stronger neutrality act. This law banned American ships from carrying goods to warring nations. It also barred Americans from traveling on ships of nations at war. These acts were passed in an attempt to avoid the causes that led to our entering the First World War.

Repeal of the Arms Embargo

When World War II broke out in 1939, President Roosevelt again declared American neutrality. However, it was clear that a Nazi victory would be a worldwide disaster. Our hope lay in a victory for those nations, the Allied Powers, who opposed the Nazis. Aware of the need to defeat Nazi Germany, Congress passed the Neutrality Act of 1939. This Act changed previous law. It permitted the sale of arms to nations at war on a "cash and carry" basis. By this arrangement, it became possible for the United States to sell war materials to the Allies.

Plans for Defense

In September 1940, Congress passed the Selective Training and Service Act. This Act created the first peacetime draft in the history of our country. Within a month, more than sixteen million young men between the ages of twenty-one and thirty-five registered for service. Training camps were established around the country. Training began early in 1941.

In November 1940, Roosevelt was re-elected for the third time. He was the first president to break the tradition of two terms that George Washington had started. A Roman emperor had once said that once you have been emperor, it is hard to stop being emperor. Franklin Roosevelt was as close as America came to having an emperor.

To make our national defenses strong, Roosevelt recommended a budget of over seventeen billion dollars. This was by far the largest budget in our peacetime history. The plans for defense called for a two-ocean navy, a large army, and an air force that would be the best in the world.

Aid to England

Meanwhile in Europe during 1940, Nazi Germany was winning the war. Germany had conquered Norway and Denmark. She had invaded the Netherlands, Belgium, and Luxembourg. France had fallen in June. The British had barely been able to rescue their army from Dunkirk. England had sent every ship that could float to take its men off the beaches at Dunkirk. The army was forced to leave all its equipment behind. The dramatic retreat from Dunkirk and the fall of France made the danger of a Nazi victory seem imminent.

The Nazi victories woke up the American people. They realized that if England fell, the Western Hemisphere would be next on Adolf

The Retreat from Dunkirk

Hitler's list for conquest. There was a great sentiment in America to aid Britain just "short of war." Consequently, our government sold ammunition, rifles, machine guns, ships, fighter planes, and bombers to Britain in ever-growing amounts. The United States also gave Britain fifty out of date destroyers in exchange for naval and air bases in Canada and the Caribbean.

The Lend-Lease Act

The financial cost of fighting the Nazis was very high for Britain. In early 1941, England told the American government that it would not be able to continue much longer to pay cash for its purchases. The Chinese were also running out of cash in their war against Germany's ally, Japan. To meet these needs, President Roosevelt suggested that we lend goods instead of dollars, and accept goods as repayment. Thus, the Lend-Lease bill was proposed to Congress.

The Lend-Lease bill gave the president the right to lend or lease weapons and war materials to any government whose defense he considered important to our country. There was strong opposition to the bill by a large group in Congress. This group claimed that the bill made the president a dictator. They also feared that the bill would draw us into the war. Nevertheless, the bill was passed in March 1941. Passage of this bill really meant the end of American neutrality. The United States was definitely on the side of the Allies. We just were not yet involved in the actual fighting.

In November 1941, the last restrictions of the Neutrality Act were repealed. At once, the president also proposed to protect the Lend-Lease cargoes. American ships were armed and ordered to shoot on sight. Ten Coast Guard cutters and twenty mosquito boats were assigned to patrol service. The United States had assumed the responsibility of limited armed intervention.

Spot Check

1. What was the Reciprocal Tariff Act?
2. What was America's Neutrality Policy?
3. What was the Lend-Lease bill? Why was it proposed and passed?

CHAPTER REVIEW

1. What was the bank holiday?
2. What were some of the measures taken to relieve the condition of the American farmer?
3. How were homeowners aided during the Depression?
4. Name some of the New Deal labor laws.
5. What important service does the Tennessee Valley Authority perform?
6. Why was the Social Security Act passed?
7. What does Social Security do?
8. What was an important result of the reciprocal trade agreements?
9. How did the Lend-Lease Act help Britain?
10. What was the Court-Packing Plan?

AMERICA IN WORLD WAR II

German Submarine attacks Allied Cargo Ship

Adolf Hitler

Adolf Hitler became the leader of the National Socialist Party (the Nazis) in Germany long before World War II began. Even then, he planned to conquer the whole world. The Treaty of Versailles had crushed Germany's pride and caused an economic depression. Hitler promised the German people to restore the greatness of Germany. He promised to restore its prosperity and power. Germany readily responded to Hitler's promises. He quickly became popular. Sadly, he was an evil, cruel, ruthless man who led the world to the edge of destruction.

In 1933, Germany elected Hitler chancellor of Germany. As soon as he gained control of the government, he set up a military dictatorship. As dictator, Hitler began to build the world's strongest war machine. He updated his army and built up his air force and navy. He also organized the German youth. He wanted to fill their impressionable minds with his beliefs so that his policies would be put into action for years to come.

Next, Hitler allied himself with Benito Mussolini, the dictator of Italy. This alliance came to be known as the Rome-Berlin Axis, or more simply "the Axis Powers." At this time, Japan was seeking

Pope Pius XI, who was pope from 1922 until 1939, opposed the Nazis.

to expand its power in Asia. Japan entered into an understanding with the Axis nations. Thus, by the end of 1940, these three nations, motivated by desire for more power, more land and raw materials, had formed a strong and menacing alliance. This gave these nations a feeling of strength that made their foreign policy much bolder.

In 1938, Hitler's huge war machine began to move. In that year, it conquered Austria. Then in 1939, he seized Czechoslovakia. Meanwhile, Mussolini conquered Ethiopia and Albania. France and Britain reluctantly accepted Hitler's conquests in return for assurances that he did not conquer any more territory. This was a grave mistake as it emboldened Hitler to conquer more.

Hitler then signed a secret non-aggression pact with the Soviet Union's brutal and malevolent dictator, Josef Stalin. On September 1, Hitler attacked Poland. England and France had promised Poland they would defend her if she were attacked. Though unprepared for war against the Nazi war machine, England and France declared war on Germany on September 3, 1939. Meanwhile, Hitler and Stalin marched into Poland. They divided it between them. The Western allies were able to offer no more than token aid to Poland. The conquest of Poland took several months because of the brave resistance of the Poles. However, they did not have the training and equipment of the German army.

After conquering Poland, Hitler's troops suddenly overran Denmark in April 1940. Within a month, they subdued Norway. On May 10, the German army invaded the Netherlands, Belgium, and Luxembourg. In less than a month, Hitler's forces had crushed France and driven the British Expeditionary Force off the continent.

Hitler knew his navy could not defeat the British navy. Germany had lost too many ships fighting Norway. Instead, Hitler began a massive air attack on England that he hoped would make

England surrender. However, the new leader of Great Britain was Winston Churchill. He told his people that they would fight on the beaches and in the hills. They would never surrender. He inspired the English to fight. At the start of the war, Germany's air force was better than the British Air Force. However, Hitler underestimated the daring of British pilots. His attempt to force Britain to surrender was unsuccessful. This air conflict came to be known as

Winston Churchill

the Battle of Britain. It lasted from July 10 until October 31, 1940. It is considered a turning point in the war.

Having failed to conquer Britain, Hitler attacked the Soviet Union. He needed the oil that was in the Soviet Union. Despite his secret peace treaty signed two years earlier, Hitler's army went storming into the Soviet Union on the pretense of destroying Communism. The invasion began June 22, 1941. Joseph Stalin and his generals were taken by complete surprise.

Suddenly Joseph Stalin, a Communist dictator every bit as bad as Hitler, became an ally of Britain and the United States. The United States pledged material to aid the Soviets to fight Germany. Great Britain and the Soviets signed a treaty of mutual aid. In this treaty, each promised not to conclude a separate peace with Germany. Thus, they would all be allies until the end of the war. Many Christians hated the idea of aiding Communism or being allied with it. However, Hitler was a more immediate threat to Europe. Now that Hitler had attacked the Communists in the Soviet Union, the Soviets were needed to win the war. Winston Churchill, England's great prime minister, and one of the greatest anti-Communists of the century, summed up the attitude of most people. Churchill said, "If Hitler invaded Hell, I would make at least a favorable reference to the devil in the House of Commons."

The early stages of the German-Russian war looked like another Hitler victory. For five months, the Germans advanced eastward. They drove the Russian army back to Moscow. They occupied the Baltic States. Finally, they besieged Leningrad. In the south, they overran most of Ukraine and the Crimean Peninsula. However, with the coming of winter, the tide turned. The German army was forced onto the defensive along most of the front. The Russians took the offensive and kept it throughout the winter.

Spot Check

1. What does "Nazi" mean?
2. Which nations formed the Axis Powers?
3. What was the Battle of Britain?
4. Why did Britain and the United States become an ally with the Soviet Union?

The United States Declares War

During this time, the United States had begun to mobilize her resources. The Lend-Lease Act was in operation. The national draft was in high gear. Our ships were being sunk, and an undeclared naval war was going on. America was rapidly headed for open war with the Axis.

On a quiet Sunday morning, December 7, 1941, the residents of the naval base at Pearl Harbor in Hawaii were suddenly awakened

USS *Shaw* exploding at Pearl Harbor, December 7, 1941

by the sounds of Japanese planes dropping bombs. The surprise
was complete. The American fleet was lined up at the dock. Several
battleships and destroyers were sunk. Many others were put out of
action. Over 2,300 American soldiers were killed and more than 1,200
were wounded. It was the worst attack on American soil until the 9/11
attacks on New York and the Pentagon.

The next day, Congress declared war on Japan. On
December 11, Germany and Italy retaliated by declaring war on the
U.S. The same day, Congress declared that a state of war existed
between the United States and Germany and Italy.

The First Year of War in the Pacific

The first months after Pearl Harbor were marked by continued
Japanese victories. At Pearl Harbor, they had succeeded in sinking
or disabling twenty-one ships, of which eight were battleships. This

disaster temporarily crippled our Pacific fleet. More losses followed. The Japanese took Guam on December 10. Wake Island fell on December 23. On January 2, 1942, Manila in the Philippines fell to Japan. The Bataan Peninsula held out for three more months. Finally, the island fortress of Corregidor, the last stronghold, was forced to surrender in early May.

In the meantime, England lost to Japan Hong Kong, the Malay Peninsula, and most of Burma in Southeast Asia. The Japanese also took most of the islands of the Dutch East Indies, one of the richest storehouses of raw materials in the world. With this victory, the Japanese had enough rubber, tin, and oil to wage a long war.

The conquest of the East Indies by Japan posed a serious threat to Australia and New Zealand. These were the last valuable bases against Japan. The United States recognized this danger. The U.S. did everything possible to keep the shipping lanes open to the land "down under."

The first setback for Japanese forces came in May 1942. American naval and air forces met the Japanese fleet in the Coral Sea, not far off the coast of Australia. During four days of intense fighting, our forces sank seven Japanese warships, including a small carrier and several transports. American losses were the carrier *Lexington* and two other vessels. The Allies had finally stopped the Japanese advance south towards Australia.

Early in June, in the northern Pacific near the coast of Alaska, the Japanese took two of the Aleutian Islands. The invasion followed an air attack on Dutch Harbor, the naval base in Alaska. This was the closest to the mainland the Japanese enemy reached during the war.

In June, a strong Japanese naval force moved toward Hawaii. They planned to seize Midway Island and use it as a base for further

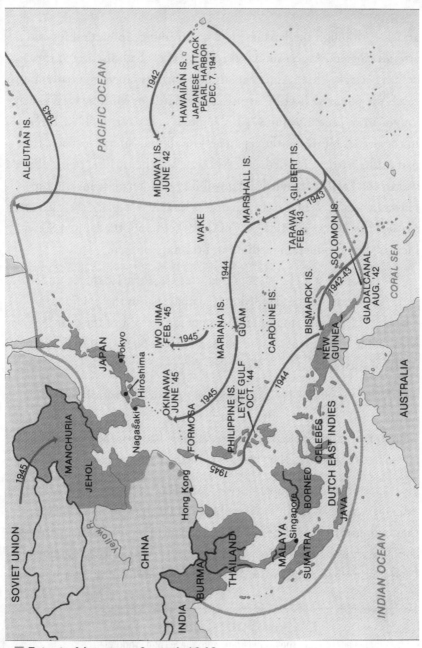

■ Extent of Japanese Control, 1942
⟶ Allied Advances

The War in the Pacific

attacks. Although the Japanese had an advantage in battleships and aircraft carriers, American naval code breakers had discovered the coming attack. Three American aircraft carriers sailed in an attempt to catch the Japanese fleet by surprise. The Battle of Midway was fiercely fought from June 4 to June 7. The United States lost the USS *Yorktown* in the battle. However, the Japanese lost all four aircraft carriers they had in the battle. The victory at Midway was the turning point of the war in the Pacific. It ended the possibility of a Japanese invasion of Hawaii and the West Coast. Japan was unable to replace the men and carriers that it lost at Midway. On the other hand, the United States increased its production of ships and training of men.

In August 1942, the counterattack against Japan got under way. American marines landed on Guadalcanal in the Solomon Islands. The marines fought desperately for the rest of the year. Meanwhile, the Japanese were pushed back in New Guinea, an island north of Australia.

At the end of 1942, the first year of our war with Japan, the Japanese still held most of the land that they had conquered and that were so rich in raw materials. However, they had lost their initial advantage of surprise. They had also lost their air and naval superiority.

Moreover, the superiority of American industry was becoming evident. American factories were able to build ships and planes faster than our enemies could destroy them. Japanese industry was unable to compete with the massive American industrial machine. The attack on Pearl Harbor had awakened a sleeping giant and filled him with a great resolve.

Spot Check

1. What event brought the United States into the Second World War?
2. Why is the Japanese conquest of the Dutch East Indies important?
3. Why is the Battle of Midway important?

The North African Campaign

In the fall of 1940, an Italian army had invaded Egypt to gain control of the Suez Canal. The Italians were no match for the English soldiers who had beaten them back. However, a few months later, the Germans aided their Italian allies. The Germans drove the English back to Egypt. Northern Egypt changed hands several times. In the early summer of 1942, a successful German attack advanced almost to Alexandria, Egypt. However, three months later the British forced the Germans to retreat.

The Allied forces sail through the Straits of Gibralter to land in North Africa.

On November 8, 1942, a large American force landed on the coast of French North Africa, between Casablanca on the Atlantic and Algiers on the Mediterranean. General Dwight D. Eisenhower commanded this American army. It soon gained control of the northwest coast of Africa. British land forces joined the Americans a few days later. These Allied forces were further strengthened by several groups of "Free French." These were Frenchmen who had refused to accept France's surrender. They were not in sympathy with the new French government. The French people continued to fight against the Germans.

The Allied forces continued to push German forces out of Africa from Morocco in the west and from Egypt in the east. The aim of this two-fold attack was to drive the Axis forces out of Africa and thus gain bases for an invasion of Europe from the South. At the end of January 1943, the English took Tripoli on the coast of Libya. The German army had retreated over 1,300 miles; however, it was still intact. The battle for Tunisia flared into a fierce fight. Both sides suffered heavy losses. In early April, the British forces from the east joined with the Allied forces from the West. Finally, in May 1943, the Axis forces surrendered. All of Africa was freed and under Allied control.

The Surrender of Italy

Two months after the Allied victory in North Africa, General Eisenhower prepared to invade Italy. On July 10, 1943, American, British, and Canadian troops landed on the southeastern coast of the island of Sicily. The Allies met only weak resistance from the Italian troops in Sicily. However, the German troops there fought hard. Losses were heavy. By the middle of August, the Allies had captured the island.

Meanwhile, the Allies had carried out heavy air attacks against Italy. By this time, the Italians had grown tired of the war and unhappy with Mussolini. They were ready to give up. In July, they forced their dictator Mussolini to resign. Marshal Pietro Badoglio was chosen as the new leader of Italy. Within a few days, Badoglio agreed to Eisenhower's demand for unconditional surrender. He signed an armistice with the Allies in September of 1943. Soon afterwards, the Italians surrendered their fleet to comply with the terms of the armistice. The surrender actually made little difference since the Germans continued to occupy most of Italy anyway.

The Nazis and the Soviets at War

The winter of 1942 was marked by Soviet victories. However, with the coming of spring, the German army was able to go on the offensive. The Germans took Sevastopol on the Black Sea and pushed the Soviet armies back toward the Volga River and the oil fields of the Caspian Sea. The oil fields were the Germans' goal. However, the Nazis never reached the Caspian. The tide of the war on the eastern front turned at Stalingrad in February 1943. At Stalingrad, the Soviet army won a decisive battle over the Germans. The Soviets refused to allow their soldiers to retreat. Any soldier retreating was shot. Hitler refused to allow his army to retreat as well. Unable to retreat, the soldiers in the German army were either killed or forced to surrender. It was a crippling blow to the Nazis.

The War in the Pacific in 1943

During 1943, Japan was on the defensive. Japan suffered heavy losses in shipping. Naval power in the Pacific shifted in favor of America. Under General Douglas MacArthur, the supreme Allied commander in the Pacific, the American forces began "island hopping" toward Japan. Marines took New Guinea and New Britain. They continued their campaign to recapture the Solomon Islands.

The Cairo Conference

In November 1943, President Roosevelt, Prime Minister Churchill, and General Chiang Kai-shek, the leader of China, held a five-day conference in Cairo, Egypt. The conference was to discuss plans for the unconditional surrender of Japan. The leaders issued a statement declaring that Japan should be deprived of all islands seized since 1914 and all lands taken from China.

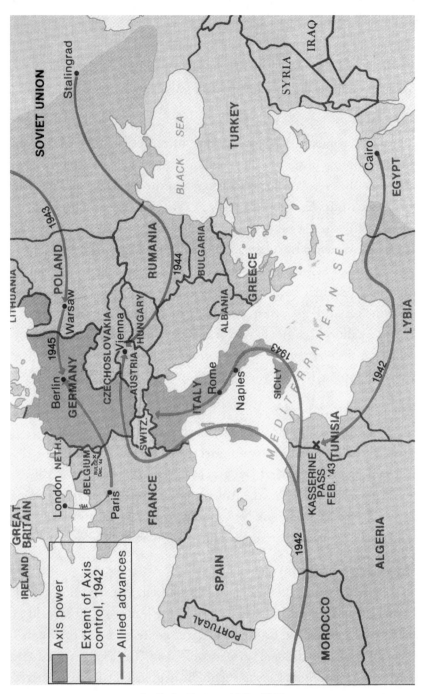

Battle for Europe, 1942 - 1945

478

The Teheran Conference

At the end of November 1943, Roosevelt and Churchill met Stalin in Teheran, in Iran. It was their first meeting with the Communist dictator. At the meeting, they laid plans for Hitler's defeat and unconditional surrender. At the time, Germany occupied all of Eastern Europe. In the west, Germany still controlled France, Belgium, and the Netherlands. In the north, it still controlled Denmark and Norway. In the south, it still held much of Italy.

The Italian Campaign

In September 1943, just before Italy's surrender, Allied troops had landed in Italy. They had encountered light resistance from the Italian army. However, after the Italian surrender, the Germans rushed troops to Italy. Within a month, the Germans moved into northern and central Italy, including Rome. The Allies controlled only the lower part of the Italian boot. For the next several months, the allies tried desperately to advance toward Rome. They gained control of Salerno and Naples. They opened up a new beachhead at Anzio, south of Rome. However, the Germans held fast to all the land they occupied.

It seemed a fierce battle was going to be necessary to take Rome. Fortunately, the German commander in Rome withdrew his troops without a fight. Rome was declared an "open city." Allied forces marched into Rome on June 4, 1944. The people of Rome rejoiced in a public parade. The city was saved.

By the end of the year, the Allies occupied most of Italy. However, the Germans still controlled the industrial north. Finally, in April 1945, the Allies launched a decisive attack on the German lines. Their defenses collapsed. Early in May, the German armies in Italy surrendered to the Allies. Shortly before the war ended in Italy, freedom-loving Italians captured Mussolini and killed him.

Spot Check

1. Why was the North African campaign so important?
2. Who were the "Free French"?
3. How was Rome saved from a fierce battle and freed from German rule?
4. What happened to the Italian dictator, Mussolini?

Plans for a "Second Front" in Western Europe

At their Teheran meeting in November 1943, Roosevelt, Churchill, and Stalin had planned for a major invasion of Western Europe. This invasion would coincide with a major Russian offensive to push Germany out of Eastern Europe. However, at that time neither the United States nor England could invade France. They did not have enough equipment or men to invade. The opening of a second front had to wait. Meanwhile, the Allies geared up production, stepped up military training, and built up their supply centers in order to undertake this tremendous task.

In the months that followed, the British Isles became a vast storehouse for military supplies. A steady stream of ships from the United States brought weapons and supplies of every description. Sixteen million tons of arms, ammunition, and equipment were gathered together. Thousands of ships were assembled. More than two million American and English soldiers prepared to cross the English Channel and invade the Continent.

The Air War over Europe

In the beginning of the war, Germany's air force was superior to Britain's Royal Air Force (RAF). However, after England's success in the Battle of Britain, Hitler was no longer able to send his planes to attack England. By the spring of 1942, the damage to British war production had largely been overcome. Increased production at home and planes sent from the United States enabled the British to launch a strong air offensive over Europe. In May, the English RAF was able to send 1,000 planes to raid the industrial city of Cologne. [The magnificent Cologne cathedral was severely damaged. The stained glass windows had been removed from their frames and buried. Thus they were saved.] Meanwhile, America had been building up air forces in Britain. In the fall of 1942, the American air force began to bomb Germany. The power of the American bombers was soon felt.

During 1943, seventeen industrial cities in northeastern Germany were bombed and severely damaged. In the fall, the Allies announced their plans to destroy Berlin, the center of the German government. The city was bombed over and over. By the spring of 1944, Berlin had become a dying city. Almost nothing is left in Berlin that was built before 1940. By 1944, the American bombers were carrying out daylight precision bombing missions while the

Allied bombers attack Germany.

RAF did night bombing. In this way, they could bomb Germany "around the clock."

D-Day: The Invasion of Normandy

By the spring of 1944, heavy Allied bombing raids had damaged the German defenses along the Atlantic coast. Sufficient men and material had been gathered in England for the projected second front. Under the command of General Eisenhower, the Allies were poised for the invasion of the coast of France at Normandy. Finally the long awaited day arrived. Before the sun rose on the morning of June 6, 1944, hundreds of thousands of troops began landing on the beaches of Normandy. Allied planes formed an umbrella of protection over the ships and beach. Battleships shelled the German defenses. Paratroopers landed behind German lines. This was "D-Day."

The German troops fought desperately to keep the Allies off the beaches. However, the Allies were able to hold and expand their positions. After heavy fighting, the Allies finally broke through the German defenses. The Allies recaptured Paris on August 25. In early September, they entered Belgium, the Netherlands, and Luxembourg, freeing them from Nazi control.

Meanwhile, an American army had landed in southern France. The troops advanced rapidly, and on September 11, they joined the northern Allied forces. Thus, by the middle of September, the Allies had driven the Germans out of most of France. They were fighting along the German border, from the Netherlands in the north to Switzerland on the south. In December, the Germans launched a violent counterattack. This attack carried the Germans back into Belgium and Luxembourg. Allied reinforcements finally stopped them at the Battle of the Bulge (so named because of the bulge that it caused in Allied lines). The Germans were forced to retreat. The Allies opened a drive along the entire front. However, they were not able to break through the German lines until spring.

The Yalta Conference: The Sellout of Eastern Europe

In February 1945, Roosevelt, Churchill, and Stalin met at Yalta in the Crimea. Roosevelt was dying. He had been elected to a fourth term in November 1944. However, those close to him knew he would never complete his term. [In an age before television, the obviously dying Roosevelt could be elected. It is doubtful the American people would elect such a clearly ill man today.] At this meeting, policies were established for the occupation of Germany. Plans were drawn up for a conference in San Francisco and for a new world organization to replace the League of Nations.

Churchill, Roosevelt, and Stalin at Yalta. Note how thin and sickly Roosevelt looks.

At Yalta, Roosevelt agreed to give Eastern Europe to Stalin. The Soviet armies would remain in Eastern Germany and all the lands that they had taken from the Nazis. World War I had given birth to Communism. World War II and the Yalta conference had allowed communism to spread like a plague across the face of Eastern Europe. Roosevelt would die a few months after Yalta. Millions would die because of what he did at Yalta.

Victory in Europe

In early March, the Allied armies reached the Rhine River in several places. American troops took Cologne on March 6. The next day they crossed the Rhine at Remagen. After heavy fighting, more and more Allied soldiers reached the highways leading into the heart of Germany. One large German city after another surrendered to the advancing armies. The number of prisoners grew steadily. The fighting strength of Germany shrank daily.

Meanwhile, the Russians were attacking Germany from the east. Nazi Germany was soon caught between the power of two great armies. On April 25, the two armies met, cutting Germany in two. Five days later, Hitler was dead. He had committed suicide when he saw that defeat was certain. On May 2, Berlin surrendered to the Russians. On May 7, 1945, Germany surrendered unconditionally at General Eisenhower's advanced headquarters in Reims, France.

Nazi Atrocities Revealed

During the war, word had reached the Allies that the Nazis were engaged in mass murder. However, the extent of it did not come to light until the Allies entered German controlled territory. The Nazis had set up huge camps for the purpose of murdering those they considered racially inferior or who opposed Nazism. As a result of Hitler's hatred for the Jews, they were the primary targets of these death camps. Six million Jews died in the camps. The world called this plan of mass murder the Holocaust. However, millions of other Europeans were killed as well. Among them were Poles, Russians, and Gypsies, as well as anyone who spoke out against the Nazis.

There are two notable saints who died in the Nazi death camps. They are Maximilian Kolbe (January 8, 1894-August 14, 1941) and Edith Stein (October 12, 1891- August 9, 1942). Maximilian Kolbe was a Polish Franciscan friar. He volunteered to die in place of a stranger in the Auschwitz death camp in Poland. Pope John Paul II canonized him in 1982. He is the patron saint of political prisoners, families, and the pro-life movement. Pope John Paul II declared him "The Patron Saint of Our Difficult Century."

Saint Edith Stein was a German Jew who became a Catholic. Born into a Jewish family, she lapsed into atheism in her teenage years. In 1922, she converted and was baptized a Catholic. In 1934, she joined the Discalced Carmelite Order, the same order as St. Teresa of Avila. To avoid Nazi persecution, she moved from Germany to the Netherlands. However, in 1942, the Nazis arrested her. They sent her to Auschwitz where she died in the gas chamber. In 1998, Pope John Paul II canonized her as Saint Teresa Benedicta of the Cross (her monastic name).

Spot Check

1. What were the plans made at the Teheran meeting?
2. What was D-Day? What was the date of D-Day?
3. Which three world leaders were present at the Yalta Conference? What was their purpose in meeting?
4. When did Germany surrender? What events led to this surrender?
5. What is the "Holocaust"?
6. What two saints died at Auschwitz?

The Campaign in the Pacific

Early in the war, Japan had been on the offensive. However, after 1943, American marines began to take one Japanese outpost after another. By the end of 1944, the marines, aided by the Australians, had taken the Marshall Islands, Saipan, Guam, New Guinea, and New Britain.

In October 1944, the Americans landed on Leyte, one of the Philippine Islands. On October 23, a tremendous three-day naval battle began. The Allied victory at the Battle of Leyte Gulf gave General MacArthur control of the seas around the Philippines. It spelled the end of the Japanese navy. Early in February 1945, the Allies entered Manila, the capital city. The same month, the American forces retook Bataan. In March, they recaptured Corregidor. However, it was not until July when MacArthur announced the liberation of the Philippines.

The Battle for Iwo Jima

While General MacArthur's troops were recapturing Luzon, the largest of the Philippine Islands, American marines landed on the island of Iwo Jima. The Japanese had used this island as a base for air attacks. It was very heavily defended. The battle to capture it was one of the fiercest and bloodiest of the war. In fact, the Japanese fought almost to the last man. Even when the battle was clearly lost, they refused to surrender. By taking this island, which is located less than 800 miles from Tokyo, the Americans were able to carry out large-scale bombing of Japan.

The Battle of Okinawa: The Typhoon of Steel

On April 1, American soldiers landed on the island of Okinawa. This island is 400 miles closer to the Japanese home islands. As a result, the Japanese again fought like mad men. Tens of thousands of soldiers were killed or wounded on both sides. Thousands of civilians also perished in the fighting. Once again, despite the fact that the battle was lost, the Japanese fought on. There were so many bullets flying and bombs exploding that the battle became known as the Typhoon of Steel. The stiff resistance by the Japanese postponed the final American victory over the island until June 21. The capture of Okinawa provided bases from which to carry out the final defeat of Japan.

The Death of Roosevelt

On April 12, 1945, less than six months after his election to a fourth term, and only a month after his term began, President Roosevelt died. In his twelve years as president, Roosevelt made many changes affecting domestic and foreign policies. He had led the nation through three and one-half years of global war. He died just a few weeks before Victory in Europe, or V-E Day. Vice President Harry S. Truman succeeded him as president.

On taking office, President Truman stated that he would continue the policies of his predecessor. His fearlessness and willingness to meet problems gave the nation confidence. People felt Truman was a man they could trust.

The Potsdam Conference

In July 1945, Truman, Churchill, and Stalin met at Potsdam in suburban Berlin. (Clement Attlee would later succeed Churchill as Prime Minister of Great Britain and replace him at the conference.) The leaders talked about defeated Germany and undefeated Japan. Far-reaching decisions were reached regarding the future of Germany and Eastern Europe. At Potsdam, Truman learned that Roosevelt had sold out Eastern Europe to the Soviets. The three leaders, with the okay of Chiang Kai-shek, agreed that Japan must surrender unconditionally. The Japanese were informed that if they did not so surrender, they would suffer vast destruction. Also, the Soviet Union promised to join in the war against Japan in exchange for land in the Pacific. Though this deal was kept secret, the Soviets declared war on Japan on August 8, 1945. This was just days before Japan surrendered.

The Atomic Bomb

The destruction and death caused by air raids in Europe was almost immeasurable. To this day, churches in Germany have pictures showing what they looked like before they were bombed. Almost every church built before 1940 contains such pictures. Nevertheless, the devastation of these bombs cannot be compared with the effects of the single atomic bomb that was dropped on Hiroshima, Japan, on August 6, 1945. That bomb was so powerful that it destroyed a major portion of the city. A second atomic

President Harry S. Truman

bomb was dropped on Nagasaki, Japan, on August 9. In that city, only a Catholic church was miraculously saved from destruction.

The decision to use the atomic bomb was not made lightly. Had the bomb not been dropped, the main islands of Japan would have had to be invaded. By August 1945, Japan had lost the war. However, when they knew that they had lost the battles of Iwo Jima and Okinawa, they still fought until virtually the last man was dead or wounded. His advisors told Truman that it would take eighteen months and cost a million Allied lives to conquer Japan. It would cost countless civilian lives as well. Another option would have been to show the Japanese the power of the atomic bomb by means of a demonstration. However, there were only two bombs. If the demonstrations failed to work or convince the Japanese, we would have lost the opportunity to use them as bombs. Truman used the bomb, he said, "in order to save the lives of thousands and thousands of young Americans." America is the only country ever to use atomic weapons in war. We must all pray they are never used ever again.

The End of the War

On August 10, the Japanese offered to surrender to the Allies. The Japanese asked that their emperor be permitted to keep his throne. The Allies agreed but said that he must be subject to the orders of the supreme Allied commander. Four days later, on August 14, the Japanese accepted the Allied terms of surrender. On September 2, 1945, the formal terms of surrender were signed aboard the USS *Missouri* as she sat in Tokyo Bay.

The war was over. It had been the most destructive combat in history. Perhaps as many as fifty million people had lost their lives. On the deck of the *Missouri*, General MacArthur asked that everyone pray for peace and that God preserve it.

The United States was merciful and generous to its defeated enemies in a way unmatched in the history of war. Many of the war leaders of Germany and Japan were quite rightly charged with war crimes. However, they were given fair trials. The Allied armies of occupation worked seriously to reconstruct the defeated countries. The reconstruction administration of General MacArthur in Japan stands out as a humane and successful rebuilding of a beaten foe.

Spot Check

1. Why was the capture of the island of Iwo Jima important?
2. Why was the capture of the island of Okinawa important?
3. Who became president after Franklin D. Roosevelt?
4. What policies were made at the Potsdam Conference? Why were some of these policies bad?
5. On which two Japanese cities was the atomic bomb dropped?

CHAPTER REVIEW

1. How did Hitler rise to power in Germany?
2. What countries did Hitler seize before he attacked Poland?
3. What event caused the United States to declare war on Japan? What was the date of this event?
4. How did Japan's conquests during the first year of the war help her to continue the struggle for almost three more years?
5. What was the Battle of Midway?
6. What is the Battle of Britain?
7. Who was Josef Stalin?
8. Why did the U.S. and Britain become allies of the Soviet Union?
9. What was the chief purpose of the Allied campaign in North Africa?
10. What was the importance of the Battle of Stalingrad?
11. What is D-Day? What date did it occur?
12. Who was Dwight D. Eisenhower?
13. Who was Winston Churchill?
14. Why is the Battle of Leyte Gulf important?
15. How did Harry Truman become president?
16. On which two Japanese cities did Truman drop the atomic bomb?
17. Why was the capture of Okinawa important to the United States?
18. Why did Truman decide to drop the atom bomb?
19. Where did Japan sign the formal terms of surrender?

THE COLD WAR BEGINS

**People in West Berlin watch as an American plane
delivers supplies during the Berlin Airlift.**

THE UNITED NATIONS

Planning for Peace

Long before the end of the World War II, many of the world's
leaders were thinking of ways to build lasting peace. They were
thinking in terms of a worldwide organization of nations. It would
promote peace and work to avoid another world war. Although the
League of Nations had been a failure, it was hoped that with American
support another such organization might be more successful. In
September 1943, the U.S. House of Representatives passed a vital

resolution. It approved an international organization strong enough to promote and maintain lasting peace. It also promised to fully cooperate in such an organization.

In 1943, three conferences were held that were instrumental in laying the groundwork "for international cooperation and lasting peace." After these conferences, the Senate passed a resolution calling on the United States to join in establishing an international organization. In the summer of 1944, delegates from the United States, the Soviet Union, Britain, and China met in Washington to draw plans for a world organization. After seven weeks of talks, they presented a rough draft of their plan. Though the plan was incomplete, it became the basis for the United Nations (UN) charter.

The San Francisco Meeting

At the Yalta meeting, Roosevelt, Churchill, and Stalin agreed to call a United Nations conference in San Francisco in April 1945. Roosevelt died on April 12. However, the San Francisco meeting met two weeks later on April 25, 1945. Delegates from fifty nations attended the meeting. They hammered out the final charter that would be presented to each of the countries for approval. [It was later discovered that the person who mainly shaped the United Nations Charter was Alger Hiss, the Communist spy.]

After weeks of talks, the UN charter was completed. However, the UN was not yet a reality. It still needed to be ratified by the "Big Five:" the United States, the Soviet Union, England, France, and China. Also a majority of the other fifty nations that had signed the charter needed to ratify it as well. By October, this was accomplished. The United Nations came into existence. Truman signed the charter on October 24, 1945.

Organization and Structure

Six major agencies or divisions were created to carry out the plan and work of the United Nations: (1) the General Assembly; (2)

the Security Council; (3) the Economic and Social Council; (4) the Trusteeship Council; (5) the International Court of Justice; and (6) the Secretariat. The General Assembly and the Security Council are the two most important agencies.

The General Assembly consists of representatives from each of the member nations. Each member nation has only one vote. The General Assembly does not have the power to pass laws. It does allow the delegates to make recommendations to the other divisions. It serves as an open forum for discussion. The General Assembly may consider general principles of cooperation in maintaining international peace and security. It may make recommendations to the Security Council for carrying out these principles.

The Security Council is composed of eleven members. There are five permanent members: the United States, England, the Russian Federation (formerly the Soviet Union), France, and China. There

The Empire State Building (left), the United Nations (middle),
and the Chrysler Building (right)

are six other members chosen by the Assembly. The Security Council has authority to investigate international disputes, to foster peaceful settlements, and to take military action against an aggressor nation. However, it can act on matters of peace and security only by an affirmative vote of at least seven members, including all of the "Big Five." Each of the five permanent nations was given a veto power over the actions of the Security Council. In other words, the actions of the Council may be blocked by the use of the veto, or negative vote. This insured each of the great powers that the United Nations force could never be used against it. Thus, the Security Council was not able to act against the many years of aggression of the Soviet Union.

The Economic and Social Council studies economic, social, cultural, and health problems around the world. It then makes recommendations to the General Assembly or to the member states of the United Nations for their solution. The Trusteeship Council looks after the welfare of the peoples in territories held in trust by the UN and advises on the supervision of these lands. The International Court of Justice is the main judicial organ of the UN. It decides the legal aspects of international disputes that are submitted to the court. However, the Court cannot enforce its decisions. Its influence depends upon world opinion. The Secretariat carries on the administrative work of the UN. The chief officer of the United Nations is called the Secretary-General.

Effectiveness of the UN

Not long after the United Nations was organized, it became clear that the Soviet Union would not cooperate with the West in the UN or in any other way. Since the Soviets had a permanent veto in the Security Council, the United Nations could not make the Soviet Union live up to its obligations nor halt its aggression. As a result of the veto, many agree that the UN lacked the power to respond effectively to the crises that arose from 1946 to 1990. Nevertheless, in the last 65 years, the UN has been a major presence on the world scene. Most people agree that some world organization is necessary in an increasingly interconnected world. However, there is huge difference of opinion on how effective the UN has been in its many activities. It is clear that the UN has been unable to maintain world peace. Many also feel that it has added to the spread of Communism.

The Nation of Israel is Founded

The first major problem facing the UN was the conflict between the Arabs and Jews in the area of the Middle East known as Palestine. Hundreds of thousands of Jewish refugees from Europe were trying to enter Palestine. England, which had controlled the area since 1917, had pledged to support a Jewish homeland there. However, England had also promised to support the rights of the non-Jewish people in the area.

In 1947, England had turned the Palestine question over to the UN. In November, the UN had voted to create two states in Palestine: one for Jews and one for Arabs. The Jews agreed to this but the Arabs did not. They insisted that all of Palestine was theirs.

On May 14, 1948, the state of Israel proclaimed its independence. Within minutes, President Truman recognized the diplomatic existence of the state of Israel. The next day, a coalition of Arab nations invaded Israel. The fighting lasted until 1949 when a truce was declared. However, there has yet to be a lasting peace between the Arabs and the Israelis. The basic problem remains: the Arab nations refuse to accept Israel's very existence. The Arabs believe that all of Palestine is rightfully theirs.

Spot Check

1. Why was the United Nations started?
2. Which part of the UN can take military action?
3. When was the nation of Israel founded?
4. Why is there no peace between Israel and the Arab nations?

STALIN TAKES CONTROL OF EASTERN EUROPE

America as World Leader

After the end of World War II, America took the lead in world affairs. We were the strongest nation in the world. We had the strongest military and economy. Unlike the European nations the fighting of the war had not devastated us. World War II had ended the Depression and made America the world's first superpower.

However, this new role brought us into conflict with the Soviet Union. The Soviet Union wanted to rule the world. For the next forty-five years, the United States and the Soviet Union would attack each other in a war of ideas and propaganda. This war of ideas became known as the **Cold War**. The Soviets offered Communism, atheism, and oppression. However, they did not say that. They spoke of a worker's paradise. The United States offered capitalism and freedom, and that is what we said.

Stalin's Plans

By late 1943, it was clear that the German army would fall before the combined strength of the United States, the Soviet Union, and England. Having come to this insight, Josef Stalin devoted his efforts to securing an advantage for Communism by the end of the war. As the Soviet army pushed Hitler's forces back in Eastern Europe, Stalin had a plan. He planned to use his power to conquer nations and establish governments friendly to him.

Stalin as Soviet Dictator

Josef Stalin was the dictator of the Soviet Union from 1929 to 1953. He ruled by terror during his years as dictator. He allowed no one to oppose his decisions. He killed millions of his own people. He had periodic purges during which he jailed or killed those who helped him gain or preserve power because he feared they might threaten his rule. During some of these purges, Stalin would have "show" trials where Communist officials were forced to confess to crimes they did not commit. Such was the madness of the terror by which he ruled the land.

Under Stalin, the Soviet Union operated a network of Communist parties around the world. These parties worked to promote Communism. During the 1930s and World War II, the Communist Party in the United States was able to deceive some Americans. They fooled these people into believing that Stalin was a great and good man. They also tricked some people into thinking that Communism was good.

The Baltic Republics

On August 23, 1939, Stalin had divided Poland with Hitler. Then Stalin had annexed three countries on the Baltic Sea along the western border of the Soviet Union. These are the Baltic Republics: Lithuania, Estonia, and Latvia. These countries were small and were unable to resist Soviet occupation and annexation. During World War II, Germany invaded the Baltics and pushed the Soviet troops out. After the defeat of Germany, Stalin reoccupied the Baltic Republics.

Poland

The nation that Stalin most wanted to control was Poland. He had annexed much of eastern Poland during his deal with Hitler and Stalin wanted to keep it. At the Teheran conference, Stalin convinced Roosevelt and Churchill that he should keep the eastern third of Poland. In exchange for loss of territory in the east, Poland would gain land in the west from defeated Germany. The entire country simply "moved" westward two hundred miles. However, one cannot suddenly call Germans, "Poles." It meant terrible uprooting for thousands of Germans already devastated by the Allied bombing.

In addition, Stalin also acted to see that Poland would be in no position to challenge this action. Early in the war, the Soviets had secretly murdered more than 20,000 Polish soldiers, including about

4,500 Polish officers in the Katyn Forest. They had been captured as prisoners of war. This was an attempt to ensure that the army lost its leadership forever. Still, the Poles were able to put together an underground army to oppose the German occupation. When the Soviet Army reached the outskirts of Warsaw, the Polish Home Army rose in rebellion against the Germans in August of 1944. Rather than taking advantage of this, Stalin ordered the Soviet army to halt outside of Warsaw. The Soviet army made no attempt to take the city or aid the Poles. The Poles were armed with captured weapons, old revolvers and homemade explosives. They were no match for the Germans. For two weeks, the Soviet army waited while the Germans crushed the rebellion. Churchill and Roosevelt begged Stalin to intervene, but he refused. The Western Allies tried to drop ammunition and weapons into Warsaw, but Stalin would not even permit Allied aircraft to refuel at his airbases. Not until Warsaw had been leveled and all its defenders killed, did

Monument in Wroclaw, Poland, dedicated to the Polish soldiers murdered by Stalin.

Stalin send his army to occupy the city. Stalin had made sure that there was no military force left to oppose his own occupation.

There was a young priest in Poland who saw these horrors. He saw the terrible things that the Nazis did. In fact, he was almost captured by the Nazis. He hid in the bishop's palace to escape them. When the Communists drove out the Nazis, he saw that as well. He lived under Communist oppression for decades. His name was Karol Jozef Wojtyla. As Stalin had brought Communism to Poland, he would do much to end it.

Spot Check

1. Who was Josef Stalin?
2. How did he rule the Soviet Union?
3. What was the Cold War?
4. How did Stalin gain control of Poland?

Other Countries of Eastern Europe

Bulgaria, Rumania, Hungary, Czechoslovakia, Albania, and East Germany all were forced to follow a similar pattern of surrender to the Soviets. The Soviet army, in pushing the Germans west, occupied these countries. Once they defeated the Germans, the Soviet army simply stayed. The poor people of these countries traded Nazi oppression for Communist oppression. The Soviet army, along with the local Communist parties, arranged for the Communists to take control of the post-war governments in these countries by 1949. "Elections" in these countries gave the impression that Communists were legitimately voted into power. In fact, the Communist victories were the result of manipulation, force, and fraud.

The nations of Eastern Europe remained free in name only. By the late 1940s, they were completely dominated by the Soviet Union. They became known as Soviet satellites.

Greece

In Greece, Stalin supported the local Communists. He hoped that they could establish a Communist government as the Germans withdrew. However, he encountered stiff resistance. Churchill also sent British troops into Greece because he considered it part of the British sphere of influence. The English troops prevented the Communist "People's Liberation Army" from gaining control.

The Yalta Conference

In February of 1945, with the German defeat only months away, Stalin, Roosevelt, and Churchill met at Yalta to discuss post-war arrangements. Stalin suggested that Germany be divided. Roosevelt agreed, but Churchill would not. Sadly, Churchill was outvoted. This ensured that Stalin would gain control of at least a part of Germany.

Stalin obtained a promise from Roosevelt that all Soviet citizens and Eastern European refugees would be returned to the Soviet Union, by force, if necessary. Many anti-Communists had fled during the German occupation. Stalin feared that they could stir up trouble against him. As a result, he was determined to get them back under his power. There were also millions of refugees who had simply been forced from their homes. Churchill and Roosevelt both knew how disgusting this promise was. It was made in secret and was kept a secret for fifty years. Most people agree it was one of the most horrible things an American president has ever done.

The name for the plan of forced return was "Operation Keelhaul." Keelhauling was a cruel form of corporal punishment used in the Dutch navy during the era of sailing ships. It involved dragging a sailor under the keel of the ship. It was especially brutal and dangerous. (The name was chosen by the army out of disgust for what they were about to do.) During *Operation Keelhaul*, millions who were already in the lands of freedom were deported by brutal force to concentration camps. There they were tortured and killed. Clearly, in all of our history, this action is one that simply cannot be defended.

WESTERN RESPONSE TO COMMUNISM

The Iron Curtain

By force and deceit, Stalin emerged from World War II either in control of or poised to take control of many nations in Eastern Europe and Asia. Many people in the West sincerely hoped for peace. They hoped that the Communists would become decent members of the international community. Soon, however, Stalin's lust for power could leave no objective observer in doubt as to his goals.

After the war, Winston Churchill had been voted out of office. However, he did not retire from public life. On March 5, 1946, he delivered a speech at Westminster College in Fulton, Missouri. The speech seemed to wake the free world from its hopeful outlook about Communism. Churchill told the world that from the Baltic to the Adriatic, "an iron curtain has descended across the continent." He warned that the Communists were not going to stop at Eastern Europe. He said that "Communist parties . . . are seeking everywhere to obtain totalitarian control."

Churchill in Fulton, Missouri

The Truman Doctrine

By the fall of 1946, it was evident that Roosevelt's policy of trying to appease the Soviet Union had failed. The "iron curtain" of

Communism was, indeed, falling across Europe. Truman, therefore, decided on a new course of action. The first evidence of America's change in policy was the crisis in Greece. Britain had been giving military aid to the anti-Communist government in Greece. However, Britain was nearly bankrupt. In February 1947, the British informed Truman that they would need to stop the aid at the end of March.

On March 12, 1947, in response to the situation in Greece, President Truman spoke to a joint session of Congress. He announced what came to be called the Truman Doctrine. The intent of this doctrine was to contain Communism. America's new policy would be to aid democratic governments that were threatened by Communist takeover. Truman was not going to take back lands that the Communists already had, but he was not going to let them take more nations. The president asked for funds for this purpose. In support of this plan, Congress gave $400,000,000 to Greece and Turkey to build up their armed forces.

The Truman Doctrine had three basic goals. First, it aimed to stop Soviet expansion. Second, it wanted to weaken Communist influence around the world. Third, it hoped to encourage democracy.

The Marshall Plan

In June 1947, Secretary of State George C. Marshall gave a speech at Harvard University where he outlined a plan to rebuild Europe. He said that the United States should do whatever it is able to do to help the return of normal economic health in the world. This meant giving billions of dollars to Europe. This would restore economic independence to Europe. He said that only by giving Europe the money to rebuild its farms and factories could it recover from the terrible effects of the war. The Soviet Union and the nations it controlled rejected Marshall's plan. However, sixteen nations of Western Europe did accept it.

Stalin retaliated by forming a bloc of Communist nations. As part of his plan, he set up the "Cominform" (Communist Information

Bureau). The Communist parties of nine European countries organized the Cominform. Its aim was to coordinate the activities of Communist parties around the world.

This Soviet action brought a quick response from the United States. Congress appropriated seventeen billion dollars. By midsummer 1948, the European Recovery Program, or the Marshall Plan as it was commonly called, was in operation. It was a great success in two ways. First, it reduced the threat of Communism in Europe. Second, it helped to re-establish Europe's faith in America. For his work in rebuilding Europe, George Marshall received the Nobel Peace Prize in 1953.

Spot Check

1. What was Operation Keelhaul?
2. Who first spoke of Communism as an "Iron Curtain"?
3. What was the Truman Doctrine?

THE COLD WAR HEATS UP

The Berlin Air Lift

After World War II, Germany had been divided into four sections. Each section had been occupied by one of the leading powers. Berlin had also been divided into four sections. However, the city itself lay in the eastern, or Soviet-controlled section. In the summer of 1948, Stalin decided to turn up the heat in the Cold War. The place he chose to apply the flame was Berlin.

In an attempt to force the Americans, British, and French to give up Berlin, Stalin established a blockade of the city. By cutting off rail, water, and road traffic, the Soviets were giving the Western powers notice to leave or to let Berlin starve. However, this did not stop the Western Allies. They set up the famous "Berlin air lift." The Western Allies flew thousands of tons of supplies into Berlin each day for almost a year. The airlift showed that the West would not

Planes are filled with supplies for West Berlin.

knuckle under to Communist threats. It raised the prestige of the West throughout Europe. In the fall elections of 1948, 80 percent of the people of western Berlin rejected the Communist candidates for office. After maintaining the blockade for almost a year, in May 1949, the Soviets finally agreed to let the Western Allies resume land traffic with Berlin. The blockade had backfired. It convinced the West that the Soviets were a serious threat to world peace.

The North Atlantic Treaty Organization (NATO)

The blockade of Berlin was a sign to the people of Western Europe, Canada, and the United States that it was time to develop a military alliance for their mutual defense. To this end, twelve nations signed the North Atlantic Treaty on April 4, 1949. The nations the signed were the United States, England, Canada, Iceland, France, Portugal, Belgium, the Netherlands, Denmark, Norway, Italy, and Luxembourg. [Greece and Turkey joined NATO in 1952. West Germany joined in 1955.] The treaty went into effect in July 1949.

The member nations of NATO pledged to settle all disputes under the direction of the United Nations. They further agreed that, if any member were attacked, the other members would come to the aid of the country being attacked. Of course, the Soviets called this defensive pact "aggressive." They declared that it was aimed at the Soviet Union. On the other hand, the American people very much favored the treaty. Congress appropriated a billion dollars for military aid to the member nations.

THE COLD WAR BECOMES A HOT WAR IN ASIA

Communists Come to Power in China

One of the greatest disasters for the cause of freedom was the Communist takeover of China in the late 1940s. Sadly, the United States must bear some of the responsibility for the loss of China to the Communists. During this time, there were many in the State Department who were pro-Communist. They were working to see China become Communist. Many anti-Communists in the government, like Truman and Marshall, looked to these bad men for advice about China. Unhappily, the good men listened to the bad men far too often.

Since the early 1930s, the Nationalist Government of Chiang Kai-shek had been at war with Chinese Communists who were led by Mao Tse-tung. However, when Japan invaded China, the civil war entered a new phase. Chiang and Mao worked both to defeat the Japanese and each other.

On August 15, 1945, the Allies announced the surrender of Japan. The surrender brought an end to the war between Japan and China. However, it did not bring peace to China. When the Soviet Army entered the war against the Japanese, there was a Japanese army of some one million men in China. When Japan surrendered, much of this well-armed force ended up in the hands of the Soviet army. All of the captured arms and equipment were given to the Chinese

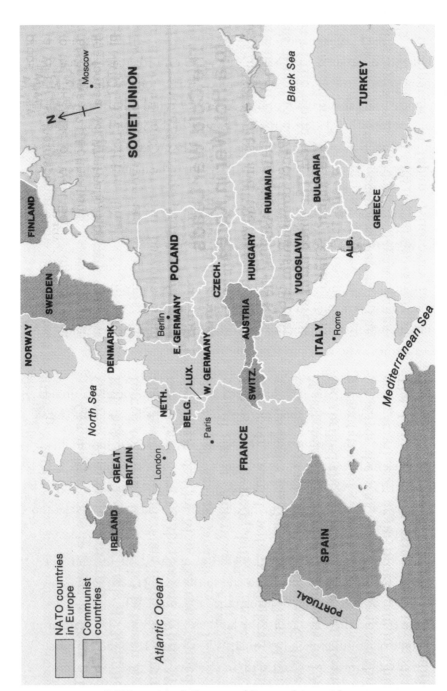

NATO countries in Europe and Communist countries

Communists. The Chinese Communists emerged from World War II better than before the war. They seized Manchuria and parts of northern China.

In the winter of 1945, General George C. Marshall went to China to try to convince Chiang Kai-shek to accept the Communists into his government. Chiang knew what such a move would mean. The Communists would take over the country. He wisely refused Marshall's idea.

In March 1946, the Soviet Army withdrew from Manchuria, the richest and most industrialized part of China. The Chinese Nationalists controlled the South of Manchuria, while the Communists controlled the North. In between lay the important industrial city of Changchun. The Communists immediately moved to seize this city. After several days of fighting, the city fell to the Communists. Chiang Kai-shek ordered an immediate attack to retake the city. However, General Marshall warned him that such a move would mean risking the disfavor of the United States.

At first, Chiang canceled the attack. However, he soon came to believe that America was forcing him to fight a purely defensive war. He believed the U.S. would not let him attack, since the U.S. hoped he would allow the Communists into his government. On the other hand, the Communists were able and willing to continue their attacks. Moreover, the Communists were receiving aid from the Soviet Union. Chiang Kai-shek decided that he could not wait. It might mean the end of American aid, but he believed that the only way to win was to launch an offensive to destroy the Chinese Communists while he still had the strength.

American Arms Embargo

In June 1946, the Nationalist Army under General Chiang Kai-shek attacked the Communist military forces. In response, General

Marshall suggested a total arms embargo against China. Of course, this only affected the Nationalists because the Communists did not receive American weapons. President Truman agreed with Marshall and American aid stopped.

The Nationalist attacks were very successful. Chiang's forces drove the Communists back. They liberated great stretches of China that the Communists had controlled for years. However, by March 1947, the offensive ground to a halt. After ten months of heavy fighting without outside aid the Nationalists were almost out of ammunition and other supplies. However, there was still a flicker of hope. In March of 1947, Truman unveiled the Truman doctrine.

By the summer of 1947, the shortages in the Nationalist army had become acute. Meanwhile, the Chinese Communists continued to receive plenty of aid from Stalin. Finally, the arms embargo was partially lifted. However, large scale American aid did not resume. As a result of U.S. policy, the military balance shifted decisively in favor of the Communists.

Finally, Truman acted. In February of 1948, he proposed economic, but not military aid to the Nationalists. Anti-Communists in Congress were outraged. They insisted on providing $150 million in military aid. Truman continued to drag his feet. Despite the appropriation, little military aid was sent to the Nationalists. It is suspected that Soviet agents in the U.S. government influenced the way Truman perceived events.

The Presidential Election of 1948

The situation in China continued to deteriorate throughout 1948. The Republicans made China an issue in the elections that year. They promised large-scale aid to the Nationalists if their candidate, Thomas Dewey, were elected president. Truman was re-elected and his policies continued. During 1949, the last great battles of the Chinese war took place. With the Chinese Communists victorious in these battles, the fate of China was sealed. Chiang Kai-shek gathered up the remnants of the Chinese anti-Communists and fled to the island of Taiwan.

On mainland China, Mao Tse-tung established a Communist regime called the People's Republic of China. Many called the nation "Red China," because it was Communist. For years, the United States only recognized Chiang's government as the rightful government of China. However, in the 1970s the U.S. recognized two separated Chinas.

Spot Check

1. What was the Berlin Air Lift?
2. What is NATO?
3. Who were Chiang Kai-shek and Mao Tse-tung?
4. Why is the People's Republic of China often called "Red China"?

CHAPTER REVIEW

1. When was the nation of Israel founded?
2. What was the first nation to recognize Israel's existence?
3. What was Operation Keelhaul?
4. How did Stalin take over Eastern Europe?
5. What was the immediate reason for the Truman Doctrine?
6. What were the three objectives of the Truman Doctrine?
7. What was the Berlin airlift? Why was it needed?
8. How did Chinese Communists become more powerful as a result of World War II?
9. Why was the United Nations established?
10. Why did Chiang Kai-shek launch an offensive despite U.S. disapproval?
11. What was the result of the American Embargo against China?
12. Why was the American presidential election in 1948 important for the future of China?
13. What was the purpose of NATO?
14. Who was the Communist leader of China during this period?
15. What was the Marshall Plan? Was it successful?
16. How did Stalin react to the Marshall Plan?

THE COLD WAR TURNS RED HOT

Break Through at Chipyong-Ni, by Hugh Charles McBarron. This painting depicts U.S. troops surrounded by Red Chinese Communists during the Korean War. The Americans fought for four days before finally breaking free of the entrapment.

COMMUNISTS IN AMERICA

Stolen Atomic Secrets

At the beginning of the Cold War, the West possessed a great advantage over the Soviet Union because we had atomic weapons. American and British scientists had developed the atomic bomb towards the end of the war. The work on the atomic bomb was known as the Manhattan Project. The Western Allies counted on having an atomic superiority for years to come. Little did they know that Soviet spies had been watching the project from its earliest days.

In Roosevelt's desire to work with Stalin during World War II, the United States government had failed to take the proper safety measures to stop Communists from working on the Manhattan Project. One of the scientists who worked on it was a Communist named Klaus Fuchs. Before the first bomb was even dropped on Japan, Fuchs had already given the Soviets detailed information on how to build an atomic bomb. With the aid of Fuchs and a virtual army of spies in the U.S. government, the Soviets received a boost to their atomic program. In August 1949, Stalin shocked the world by detonating the Soviets' first atomic bomb. This came years ahead of when the West expected Stalin to develop nuclear weapons.

The Hydrogen Bomb

Even before the first detonation, it was known that the Soviets were conducting experiments leading toward the creation of atomic weapons. As a result, the United States felt it was necessary to develop even more powerful weapons in order to discourage any Soviet attacks. Thus, our government began to develop a hydrogen bomb. This terrifying weapon was expected to be more than a thousand times more powerful than the atomic bomb. Finally, scientists found a way to produce a hydrogen explosion. A successful test was conducted far out in the Pacific Ocean late in 1952. Sadly, Soviet spies were gathering information about these experiments as well. Less than a year later, the Soviet Union announced that it had also made and exploded a hydrogen bomb.

The Government Investigates Spies

In 1945, a Soviet spy who worked in Canada defected, that is, he changed sides. He turned over more than one hundred documents that proved the existence of a Communist spy ring in North America. This spy ring had worked to steal atomic secrets and give them to the Soviets. As a result of this defection, the American government began to investigate whether there were Communists in high government positions.

In 1938, the House of Representatives established a committee to investigate un-American activities. In 1948, the House Un-American Activities Committee announced that charges of spying had been brought against a trusted government official. His name was Alger Hiss. A former American Communist named Whittaker Chambers had converted to Christianity. Chambers had come forward to identify a number of other American Communists. One of these was Alger Hiss.

Hiss had been an influential assistant to the Secretary of State. He had been present at Yalta and had been a leader in setting up the United Nations. The House Un-American Activities Committee investigated Chambers' claims against Hiss. The two lawyers in charge of the investigation were Richard Nixon and Robert Kennedy. The evidence against Hiss included testimony and secret papers that Hiss had passed to Chambers. The evidence was clear. Hiss was convicted of perjury and sent to prison.

Senator Joseph McCarthy

One of the leaders attempting to discover Communist agents was Joseph McCarthy. McCarthy was a Wisconsin senator who had been elected in 1946. McCarthy looked into Communist influence in government, as well as in important non-government jobs. Both known and suspected Communists were called before his committee and were asked about their activities. The revelations about Hiss and Fuchs had been troubling. For a time, McCarthy enjoyed widespread support. However, eventually the media and Democrats harshly attacked him.

McCarthy was basically a good man. He was trying to protect this country. However, he often accused people who engaged in pro-

Communist activity of being Communists, when there was little evidence that they were anything more than foolish. This led many people to question the validity of his claims. When McCarthy began to ask about Communist influence in the army, he began to lose support. The army was an obvious place for the Soviets to place agents. However, McCarthy was seen as attacking a great patriotic institution. His opponents began to use a new term, "McCarthyism," to denote attacks that were unfounded or intended to silence opponents by questioning their loyalty. However, McCarthy was a good Catholic

Joseph McCarthy in his Marine Captain's Uniform

who attended daily Mass. Many Catholics still remember him as someone who sacrificed his career to help the nation.

THE KOREAN WAR BEGINS

The Causes of the Korean Crisis

Since 1910, Korea had been ruled by Japan. After the defeat of Japan in 1945, Soviet and American armies occupied Korea. The Communists occupied northern Korea and American forces occupied southern Korea. Although the Soviet Union and the United States had agreed to establish a unified government in Korea, the Soviets refused to keep their word. The friendly agreements made between the two countries when they were allies were ineffective in peace. Stalin did not keep his agreements with the Allies. Instead, he imposed a Communist government on Soviet occupied North Korea. In South Korea, elections were held in 1948. The elections created the Republic of Korea and placed its capital at Seoul. Thus, there were two governments in Korea. In the north, there was a Communist government. In the south, there was a democratic government.

In June 1949, both the United States and the Soviet Union had withdrawn their forces from Korea. North and South Korea, as the two countries are now known, were left to defend themselves. On June 25, 1950, without warning, North Korea invaded South Korea. This was a brutal blow to world peace. The United Nations lost no time in branding the action of North Korea as a breach of the peace. The United States sought Soviet cooperation in restoring the peace. However, the Soviet Union and China supported the aggression of North Korea.

President Truman immediately sent the Secretary of State, Dean Acheson, to the United Nations Security Council. Acheson asked the Council to pass a resolution allowing forces under the flag of the United Nations to intervene in the conflict. The Soviets would have used their veto power but they had walked out of the Council six months earlier in protest over the UN failure to recognize the government of Communist China. Thus the measure passed the Security Council. On June 27, the UN called on its members to aid South Korea in repelling the invaders. Although other nations sent some soldiers, the vast majority of the soldiers who fought in Korea, other than South Koreans, were Americans.

During the summer of 1950, the North Koreans pushed back the Americans and the South Koreans. The Americans and South Koreans were forced to retreat before the larger Communist

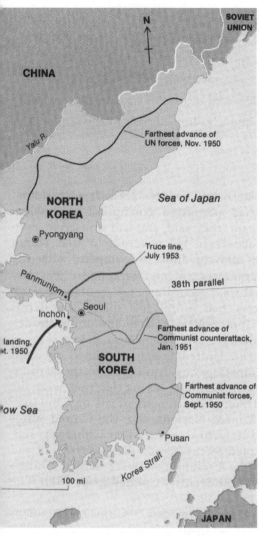

Map of Korea during the Korean War

army. Almost all of South Korea fell to the North. Then, in September, the U.S. marines arrived in Korea. On September 15, the American commander Douglas MacArthur used the marines for a daring amphibious landing at Inchon behind the Communist lines. The marine landing was a success. The American army quickly re-captured the capital of Seoul and cut the Communist forces into two. The defenders in the south were able to attack the surprised Communists.

By October 1950, the Americans took back all of South Korea and turned north to destroy the Communists and reunite the country. By November, MacArthur's troops had taken over most of North Korea. To many, it appeared that the war had been won. They had not taken into account Mao Tse-tung, the Communist leader in China. With the fall of North Korea pending in late November, Mao ordered a massive Chinese invasion.

The Chinese Attack

On November 25th, 1950, the Chinese army struck the UN forces with a devastating attack. The Americans were taken by surprise as Chinese soldiers swarmed across the border. The marines, who had been the spearhead of the American advance, were surrounded by the Chinese at the Chosin Reservoir in the mountains of central Korea. The marines were outnumbered 10 to 1.

The surrounded marines were the First Marine Division. This Division was composed of veterans from World War II as well as new recruits. This was the finest group of fighting men that been in battle since the days of the Roman legions. Outnumbered and surrounded, the marines did the only thing they could do. They attacked! When the marines finally emerged from the mountains, they had not only destroyed eight Chinese divisions but had brought out every wounded marine and even all their dead. They left nothing for the Chinese.

The Chinese forces pushed the Americans all the way back down the peninsula. The marines fought their way to the sea. They were evacuated and transferred back to Allied lines in the south. The Soviets were now providing the Chinese and North Koreans with large numbers of jet fighters. The air superiority, which the Allies had in the early part of the war, disappeared. Only in naval forces did the Allies enjoy a significant advantage.

As the Chinese soldiers continued to pour into Korea, MacArthur said that it was "an entirely new war." He wanted to blockade the Chinese coast and bomb their supply lines in Manchuria (China). The head of the armed forces, General Omar Bradley, said that this was a bad idea. President Truman agreed with him. Truman believed bombing would widen the war, not help to resolve it. Thus, Truman would not allow bombing. He told

General Douglas MacArthur (holding binoculars) at Inchon Landing

MacArthur to fight a limited war aimed at just freeing South Korea from the North.

General MacArthur was furious. He publicly criticized President Truman as pursuing a no-win policy. He said that we could not fight a war with "one hand tied behind our back." MacArthur said that if he could not attack bases in China, the Communists had a protected refuge from which to attack. He publicly called for an attack against mainland China.

President Truman felt that General MacArthur had gone too far in publicly criticizing him. Thus, on April 11, 1951, Truman fired MacArthur. He replaced him with General Matthew Ridgway.

MacArthur's Return

General MacArthur returned to a hero's welcome in the United States. Truman's decision to fire him had not been popular. MacArthur came to Washington to deliver an address to Congress. His speech, which he concluded with the words "Old soldiers never die, they just fade away," became one of the most famous speeches in American history.

Truce Talks Begin in Korea

Under the leadership of General Ridgway, the UN troops fought a limited war in Korea. Neither side gained much. The war became a stalemate. In June 1951, the Soviet ambassador suggested that a resolution was possible. Truce talks began the next month.

The most difficult question to be resolved in the truce talks was what to do with the many Chinese and North Korean prisoners of war (POWs) who did not want to go home to live under Communism. The Communists insisted that all POWs be returned. The United States had discovered that the majority of the POWs did not want to return home. The United States wanted to honor the wishes of the POWs. Many remembered that the Allies in World War II forced Russian soldiers to go back to the Soviet Union against their wishes in Operation Keelhaul. Those returning soldiers faced imprisonment and execution.

The talks dragged on for several months. However, eventually, Stalin died. Also, the United States threatened to use atomic weapons to end the war. Finally, the Communists agreed to the American position on POWs. A neutral commission was set up to determine which POWs did not wish to return. Seventy-five percent of the Chinese and fifty percent of the Koreans refused to return.

Spot Check
1. Why were two governments established in Korea?
2. Who was General Douglas MacArthur? How was he able to force the North Korean army back and almost defeat it? Why was he fired?
3. Describe the heroism of the First Marine Division during the Korean War.

PRESIDENT EISENHOWER

The Election of 1952

As the end of President Truman's second term approached, it became clear that he had lost most of his popular support. His party was blamed for the loss of Eastern Europe and China. Even in Korea, he was blamed for pursuing a policy of containment rather than victory. In March 1952, Truman decided not to run for re-election.

The Democrats nominated Adlai Stevenson, the Governor of Illinois for president. He promised to continue the New Deal and other policies of Roosevelt and Truman. As a result, he had the support of Truman.

The Republican Party nominated General Dwight Eisenhower, the commander of Allied Forces in Europe during World War II, as their presidential candidate. Eisenhower was hugely popular. At the party's convention, the delegates all shouted "We like Ike." Eisenhower's running mate was Senator Richard Nixon who had played such a prominent role in the Alger Hiss case. Eisenhower was elected president in a landslide victory.

The Korean War Ends

As candidate for president, Eisenhower had said he would "go to Korea." Most Americans had taken this to mean that he would end the war. In December 1952, while still only president-elect, he had fulfilled his promise. Finally, in July 1953, a peace treaty was signed.

The quick action of the United States had saved the South from Communist aggression.

The French Leave Vietnam

After the Korean truce in 1953, Mao Tse-tung turned his attention to Southeast Asia. He put pressure on Indochina, a French colony in Southeast Asia on a peninsula south of China.

In early 1954, a Communist army in Vietnam had isolated a major French base at Dien Bien Phu. The fall of this base would probably spell the end of French involvement. France appealed to the United States for help, for air support if nothing else. Eisenhower had said that he opposed Communism. Thus, the French were shocked when they received so little aid from the U.S. Dien Bien Phu fell. The French were forced to withdraw from Vietnam. The country was broken up into two parts. The Communists controlled North Vietnam while anti-Communists established a government in the South Vietnam.

President Dwight Eisenhower

Following the pullout of French troops and the division of Vietnam in 1954, the United States became the protector of South Vietnam. When the split was announced, about a million people, mostly Catholics, fled from the north to the south. The poor people left in the North suffered horribly under the Communist dictator Ho Chi Minh.

The Suez Crisis in the Middle East

Since 1888, the Suez Canal had been open to all nations in war and peace by international treaty. However, in July 1956, Gamel Abdel Nasser, the president of Egypt, seized the Suez Canal. The canal was in Egypt but was owned by an international company.

Gamel Abdel Nasser had come to power in 1952 when he overthrew the monarchy in Egypt. In order to obtain his good will, both the United States and the Soviet Union offered him money for various projects. The United States offered to help build a dam on the Nile River. The Soviets made an agreement to trade weapons for Egyptian cotton. As Nasser became friendlier with the Soviets, the United States decided to stop the dam deal.

At this point, Nasser seized the Suez Canal. He expelled foreign employees and took control of the canal from the corporation that owned it. He also began collecting the tolls for himself. Next he announced that Israeli ships would no longer be allowed to use the canal. This was a breach of international law. The French and British feared that they would also be denied access. They demanded that canal traffic be unimpeded. When Nasser refused to listen, the French and British suggested to President Eisenhower that force should be used to seize the canal. Eisenhower refused to go along with this plan.

Meanwhile, the situation became worse. On October 29, 1956, Israel attacked Egypt. Two days later, Britain and France joined Israel. They were determined to take the Suez Canal by force. The United States refused to support the English and French because they took action without consulting the United Nations. In fact, Eisenhower instructed the U.S. delegate at the United Nations to vote to condemn the attack. The British and French vetoed the resolution. The United States next put pressure on Israel, threatening to stop all aid if she did not withdraw her forces.

Noting that the U.S. had committed itself not to support its Allies, the Soviet Union became more supportive of Nasser. The Soviets hinted that they would not be against using nuclear weapons in the conflict. Without American support, the British and French had no choice but to withdraw their forces. The issue caused resentment lasting for years. It was many years before open navigation of the Suez Canal to all ships was reestablished.

The Hungarian Revolt

At the very same time as the Suez crisis, in October 1956, Hungary revolted against the Communists. Hungarian freedom fighters demanded that the Soviet troops be withdrawn. The brave Hungarians demanded that they be allowed to elect a democratic government.

Ever since the Communists seized Hungary in 1945, the Church suffered persecution. Over 400 priests and 3,000 religious had been imprisoned or sent to slave labor camps. Almost all Catholic seminaries, schools, and hospitals had been closed or taken over by the government. The Communists had sought to replace true bishops with men whom they appointed in order to control the Church.

In 1948, the leader of the Church in Hungary, Joseph Cardinal Mindszenty, protested the Communist takeover of Catholic schools. He was arrested as a spy. He was tortured and forced to sign a false confession. In 1949, the Communists imprisoned him for life.

In 1953, Josef Stalin died. In Eastern Europe, there was hope that his death would mean greater freedom for their nations. Indeed, in the spring of 1956, millions of political prisoners were freed. Another factor that caused both hope and unrest in Eastern Europe was the increased anti-Communist talk from the Eisenhower administration. There was talk of attempting to push back Communism when ever possible. This idea was broadcast to Eastern

Hungarian Freedom Fighters pose on a Soviet tank.

Europe over Radio Free Europe. The Hungarians had every reason to expect that the United States would support their fight for freedom.

On October 23, 1956, massive demonstrations against Communism exploded onto the streets of Budapest. Army and police were sent in to disperse the people. However, the police chief and the army colonel sent to do the job joined the revolt. The Hungarian army and police would not fire on their own people. In fact, they freed Cardinal Mindszenty after seven years in prison.

The Soviet Union moved quickly to put down the freedom-loving peoples. Four tank divisions were sent to occupy Budapest.

However, they lacked infantry support. The Hungarians pelted the tanks with bottles of gasoline and nitroglycerine. The Soviets were forced to withdraw their tanks from Budapest on October 29. The Soviets gathered a force to reenter Budapest and destroy the rebellion.

Although parts of the Hungarian army had joined the revolt, the Hungarians were totally outgunned by the Soviet army. The Hungarians appealed to the West and to the United States for help. The rest of Eastern Europe watched the situation closely. Radio Free Europe broadcast encouragement. The Hungarians kept looking to the western skies for American supply planes.

A series of events seemed to conspire against any actual American support. First, this was the exact time of the Suez crisis and the split in the Western alliance. Britain and France were not being supported by the United States and there was no chance that they would take up another cause without American support. Most of Eisenhower's interest was focused on Suez. Also, he was in the middle of a re-election campaign. Although he was well ahead in the polls, he refused to take any time to deal with the Hungarian situation. He spoke some encouraging words to the Hungarians but sent no aid.

Soviet tanks waited outside the border of Hungary while the United Nations talked. When the Soviets saw that no one was going to help the Hungarians, the tanks moved into Hungary. Before the country fell, 200,000 to 300,000 refugees escaped to Austria. After two weeks, the Communists re-gained control. Hungary was placed under even harsher rule.

Despite the chance to escape, Cardinal Mindszenty remained in Hungary. He took refuge in the American Embassy in Budapest where he was forced to live for fifteen years. From this time on, Cardinal Mindszenty became a symbol of resistance to Communism. In 1971, on the orders of Pope Paul VI, he left Hungary and went into exile in Rome. He later went to Vienna, Austria, to be closer to his homeland. He died in Vienna in 1975. In 1991, his remains were reburied in Esztergom Basilica in Hungary.

Advances in Transportation Change the Way We Live

America during the Eisenhower years became more and more wealthy. Television was invented during these years and soon people began to buy TV's. More people began to buy cars. The nation began to build a network of highways extending from one end of the country to the other. The car gave its owners a sense of personal freedom that public transportation did not. Americans loved their cars! They loved the new highway system.

The car changed the way Americans lived. No longer did they need to live in the central city. They could live in the suburbs, the areas outside the city. Shopping malls were built. Movie theatres, restaurants, bowling alleys, and skating rinks all sprang up along the roadways.

The growth of commercial air travel also changed the lives of Americans. The beginning of jet travel in the late 1950s added comfort and convenience that propeller planes could not match. The country became much "smaller" as people jetted from coast to coast. Since most travelers were on business, hotel chains began sprout up, as did car rental companies. The American economy was booming. Business was booming!

The U-2 Incident

On May 1, 1960, the Soviet Union shot down an American U-2 spy plane some 1200 miles inside Soviet territory. The U-2 incident caused great embarrassment to the United States. At first, the U.S. denied that it was a spy mission. We claimed that the secret plane was studying weather patterns and had lost its way. No one believed this unlikely story. Eisenhower had to admit that it was a spy plane sent to take pictures of Soviet nuclear facilities. Eisenhower announced that such flights would stop. Despite Soviet demands, he refused to apologize for the flights.

COMMUNISM IN CUBA

Fidel Castro

In 1952, Fulgencio Batista seized power in Cuba. While his government was corrupt, the Cuban economy as a whole was in good condition. Cuba was a tourist attraction for many from the United States. There was gambling in Cuba as well as nice hotels and beaches. It was also close to the coast of Florida. Thus, many Americans vacationed in Cuba and many companies did business there.

In an attempt to challenge the Batista regime, a young revolutionary named Fidel Castro gathered a small band of fighters. At first, he had little luck. In November of 1956, he had only eighty-two men. By December of 1956, he had only fifteen.

Castro's Rise to Fame

At this point, most men would have given up. However, Fidel Castro was completely determined to achieve his goals. He decided to see what could be done with public relations. Castro contacted a left wing American journalist named Herbert Matthews. He invited Matthews to come to Cuba and do a story about him. When Matthews arrived, Castro spoke of his numerous military virtues and claimed to have hundreds of followers. Matthews returned to the United States to praise Castro in a series of stories that appeared in *The New York Times*. Matthews made Castro appear as a likable fellow. He said that Castro was a brilliant leader who could save Cuba from disaster. These accounts spread in Cuba as well and more recruits began to pour into Castro's small force.

Although Castro had not said that he was a Communist, there was ample evidence of his leanings. The U.S. ambassador to Cuba, Earl Smith, called Castro an "unstable terrorist." He said that a takeover by Castro was the worst thing that could happen to Cuba. Sadly, Smith's superior, William Wieland, refused to pass along any of the reports on Castro to his superiors at the State Department.

Cuba Falls

In March of 1958, the U.S. State Department suggested an arms embargo against Batista in order to persuade him to reform his corrupt government. However, Batista could not reform his

Catholic Cathedral in Havana, Cuba

government and focus on suppressing the violent rebels within Cuba at the same time. Ambassador Smith objected to the embargo but to no avail. Eisenhower approved the embargo. Batista, seeing that he had no support, left the country on New Year's Day, 1959.

Within a few months, Castro's Communist beliefs became clear. Hundreds of army officers were executed. Industries were nationalized. Private farms were seized and turned over to the state. Anti-Communists who had unwittingly supported Castro were put in prison. Exiles reported that his regime tortured women and the elderly. The Catholic Church in Cuba was persecuted. Thousands fled the country as refugees to the United States.

The Cuban revolution was the first Communist revolution in the Americas. Sadly, there would be more. Communism was now at America's front door. Cuba is only ninety miles from the tip of the Florida Keys.

The Cuban Invasion: The Bay of Pigs

Though history would treat him harshly during this period, Richard Nixon was one of the leading opponents of Communism in the United States. [This is one reason why his enemies would treat him harshly.] He had fought Communism as a lawyer in the Hiss case and as a senator. He continued to fight it as vice president. In 1960, he had even more influence because he had been chosen as the Republican candidate for president. Largely because of his insistence, Eisenhower approved an overthrow of Castro's regime. The government supported an invasion of Cuba by a small army of Cuban exiles. They planned to land this army in exile in Cuba to depose Castro.

Had Nixon won the election, the plan to overthrow Castro would probably have worked, despite the problems it had from the beginning. However, John F. Kennedy won the presidential election in 1960. He inherited the Cuban operation. While he never really supported it, he was afraid to cancel it. The plan called for an amphibious landing of the Cuban exiles. However, the place selected, the Bay of Pigs, was surrounded by coral reef and a true landing was not possible. Also, the exiles' ships did not have anti-aircraft guns. However, the biggest reason for the failure of the invasion was that President Kennedy failed to keep his promise to supply air cover to the Cuban freedom fighters. As a result, soon after the Cuban patriots swam ashore, the defenseless ships were attacked by Castro's air force and sunk. The brave Cuban exiles fought for as long as they had ammunition. Then they were captured or tried to escape into the swamps.

Spot Check

1. How was Castro able to gain public support?
2. What was the result of the arms embargo against the Batista regime by Eisenhower?
3. What caused the Cuban invasion to be disastrous?

CHAPTER REVIEW

1. What events led to the North Korean invasion?
2. What happened at the Chosin Reservoir?
3. Why was MacArthur relieved of command?
4. What was the result of the battle of Dien Bien Phu?
5. What led to the Suez Crisis of 1956?
6. What effect did the Suez crisis have on Britain and France?
7. Why did America not provide any aid to Hungarians fighting to establish their independence?
8. How did Castro come to power in Cuba?
9. What was the U-2 incident and why was it such an embarrassment for America?
10. What was the Bay of Pigs Invasion?
11. Who was Cardinal Mindszenty?
12. Identify the following people:
    a. Claus Fuchs
    b. Alger Hiss
    c. Whittaker Chambers
    d. Joseph McCarthy

A Nation on the Brink: The Turbulent 1960s

The Berlin Wall and the Brandenburg Gate. The Wall is at the bottom of the picture. The Wall was the ultimate symbol of the Cold War. The sign on the right warns that you are leaving West Berlin.

The Election of 1960

Richard Nixon, the Republican Candidate

Richard Nixon had been President Eisenhower's vice president for eight years. Nixon's daughter, Julie, would marry Eisenhower's grandson, David, in 1968. Yet, despite this seeming closeness, Eisenhower did almost nothing to aid Nixon's campaign. Nixon, knowing that Eisenhower was popular, campaigned on the record of the past eight years. The country was at peace and thriving. Nixon offered stability. He promised to build on the strong foundations that Eisenhower had laid.

Nixon appeared to have the political advantage over John F. Kennedy. Kennedy had less political experience. In fact, he was the youngest man ever nominated by the Democratic Party. Moreover, he was a Catholic. Some Democrats feared that his youth and religion would make his election impossible. They thought that, based upon the defeat of Al Smith in 1928, no Catholic could be elected president.

John F. Kennedy, the Democratic Candidate

John F. Kennedy's father gave his son every advantage. He was sent to the finest schools. He was groomed for politics. During the Second World War, John received a commission in the Navy. He was assigned to a patrol torpedo (PT) boat in the Pacific. On the night of August 2, 1943, while on patrol, Kennedy's boat, the PT-109, was rammed by a Japanese destroyer. As his boat was sinking, Kennedy gathered his men together and swam to a nearby island. For his bravery, he was awarded the Navy and Marine Corps Medal. Kennedy returned to the war and was awarded several more medals before he was discharged in 1945.

Returning from World War II a hero in 1946, Kennedy ran for Congress. He was elected to the House of Representatives. Among the new members to the House that year was Richard Nixon. In 1952, Kennedy was elected to the U.S. Senate. Although he did not have a notable career as a senator, he was a charismatic person. In 1960, despite his youth and inexperience, he easily received the Democratic Party's nomination for the presidency.

The Catholic Issue

In 1928, when Alfred Smith ran for president, many had rejected him because of his Catholic faith. However, since World War II, Protestants and Catholics had drawn closer together. Both Catholics and Protestants were united in their opposition to Nazism and Communism. Religious differences could be put aside when faced with the threats posed by the Cold War.

Nevertheless, Kennedy believed that he needed to address his religion. In a famous speech in Texas during the campaign, he spoke on the issue of faith. He said: "I am not the Catholic candidate for president. I am the Democratic Party candidate for president who also happens to be Catholic. I do not speak for my Church on public matters – and the Church does not speak for me." To many, this implied that his Faith would not be the basis for his policies.

Many Americans welcomed this statement. They saw it as promoting the separation of church and state. However, by the early 1960s, that had come to mean that a politician's religious beliefs should have no bearing on his political views. As Catholics, our Faith must permeate everything we do. We are not just Catholics in church, we are Catholics in society. Moreover, as Catholics our Church does speak for us. While his statement horrified some Catholics, many others saw Kennedy as a symbol of the progress that American Catholics had made since the days of Al Smith. Many young Catholics came to admire Kennedy as a Catholic hero.

President John F. Kennedy

On election day, a record number of people went to the polls. The election between Kennedy and Nixon was extremely close. Of sixty-eight million votes cast, Kennedy won by fewer than 120,000. There was evidence of voter fraud in Texas and Illinois. However, no investigation was made. John F Kennedy became the thirty-fifth president of the United States.

Spot Check

1. How did Kennedy address the question of his religious faith and politics?
2. Who was the Republican nominee for president in 1960?

THE KENNEDY ADMINISTRATION

Kennedy was very popular as president. He was handsome and had a beautiful wife. They had two children. He was the first president whose personal life fascinated the American people. However, despite his personal charm, his Presidency was rocked with foreign policy disasters. Perhaps never has the world been so close to a nuclear war than in the first years of Kennedy's presidency. The payment for Kennedy's failure to provide air support to the anti-Castro rebels was about to come due.

The Crisis in Berlin

On April 17, 1961, only three months after Kennedy took office, the invasion of Cuba was launched. Due to the lack of air support, the invasion failed. The failed invasion emboldened the Soviet Union.

The new leader of the Soviet Union, following the death of Josef Stalin, was Nikita Khrushchev. If the West thought that Khrushchev would be more open to democracy than Stalin, they were absolutely wrong. For the harsh measures that he used to crush the Hungarian revolt in 1956, Khrushchev came to be known as the "Butcher of Budapest." He was almost as evil as Stalin.

In June 1961, Kennedy and Khrushchev met in Vienna, Austria. Kennedy was shocked when Khrushchev spoke of ending the American presence in Berlin. Kennedy made it clear that he was determined to stop the Soviets from taking West Berlin. Both men had taken the measure of the other. Khrushchev apparently thought that Kennedy was weak and would not hold to his commitments. Kennedy should have known that Khrushchev was the heir to Stalin.

St. Stephen's Cathedral in Vienna, where Kennedy attended Mass before meeting with Khruschev

Since 1945, the people of East Berlin had risked their lives to flee to West Berlin. The Communists would kill or imprison anyone they caught trying to escape to the freedom of the West. Therefore, in August 1961, in order to stop East Germans from leaving, the East German government began to build a wall across the city. The West dubbed the wall "the wall of shame." It became the symbol of the

Cold War. Under the terms of the treaty between the Soviet Union and the United States after World War II, the Communists had no right to build the wall. We can never know what would have happened if Kennedy had ordered that, as the Wall was being built, bulldozers knock it down.

The Wall was built. However, America stayed in West Berlin. Kennedy did send more troops to protect West Berlin. Yet, Khrushchev was not going to stop at Berlin. Communism has always been determined to conquer the world. It was time for Khrushchev to hit a lot closer to home.

The Cuban Missile Crisis

During the autumn of 1962, American spy planes flying over Cuba had found a huge military build-up. Photographs showed that the Soviet Union was building missile bases in Cuba that could fire nuclear missiles at most of the United States. In October, Kennedy went on television. He showed the photos and told the public about the missiles. He said that he had ordered a naval blockade of the island so that no more weapons could go to Cuba. He also demanded that the Soviets remove the missiles that were already there. Lastly, he placed the American military on full alert. The world was on the brink of nuclear war.

Kennedy also had information that more missiles were headed to Cuba on Soviet ships. He clearly could not allow them to land. On October 24, Soviet ships reached the blockade. They suddenly stopped dead in the water.

Meanwhile, behind the scenes, Khrushchev and Kennedy were negotiating. Khrushchev agreed to remove the missiles if the United States agreed not to overthrow Castro. Kennedy agreed on October 27. The missiles were removed. Khrushchev backed down, but the Soviets gained significant assurances in the process. Cuban exiles continued to attack the Castro regime, but after this agreement, the American government no longer assisted them. Most importantly, the Soviets now had a base in the Western hemisphere. They would use it to launch numerous attacks against nations in the Americas.

Spot Check

1. What was the Cuban Missile Crisis?
2. How did Kennedy resolve this crisis?
3. Why was it a bad resolution?
4. What was the result of the resolution?

AMERICA BECOMES INVOLVED IN VIETNAM

The Conflict Begins

In addition to Berlin and Cuba, Kennedy had to deal with the problems in Vietnam. When the French left Vietnam in 1956, there was an agreement that an election would be held to unify the country. The South was free and the North was Communist. The election was not held because the Communists would not allow a democratic election.

During his last years in office, President Eisenhower became more and more concerned about the situation in Vietnam. He spoke of what he called the Domino Theory. He believed that a Communist victory in Vietnam would lead to the fall of every other country in the region. After all, the fall of China had quickly led to the occupation of Tibet, and to subsequent wars in Korea and Vietnam.

In December of 1960, Ho Chi Minh, the Communist leader of North Vietnam, created the National Front for the Liberation of South Vietnam. Its members became known as Viet Cong. The goal of the Viet Cong was a unified Communist Vietnam. The Viet Cong began to wage a guerrilla war against South Vietnam.

South Vietnam had established a government under the presidency of Ngo Dinh Diem. Diem was a practicing Catholic. When the Viet Cong attacks began, Diem put his brother Ngo Dinh Nhu in charge of security measures. The principal means to increase security was to gather villages into fortified groups. In this way, the government tried to protect farmers from terrorist attacks. President Diem requested and received military aid from the United States. However, he insisted that he did not want American soldiers or direct American involvement. He feared that would play into the hands of the Communists. Diem feared that he would be seen as a puppet of the Americans who did not want Vietnam for the Vietnamese.

The Tri Quang Affair

In 1960, Catholics formed about 10 percent of the population of South Vietnam. President Diem and his closest advisers were Catholics. The Communists hoped to use his Faith against him.

Thich Tri Quang was a Buddhist priest and a former member of the Communist party. On May 8, 1963, he addressed a large crowd of Buddhists. He claimed that the Diem government was persecuting the Buddhists. The crowd grew larger. Soldiers were called in to control the crowd. Two explosions erupted in the crowd. Chaos followed. When the crowd dispersed, eight people lay dead. The soldiers were blamed and accused of firing into the crowd. This was taken as proof that the Diem government really was persecuting Buddhists.

Tri Quang organized more demonstrations against the alleged persecution. On June 11, a Buddhist monk doused himself with gasoline and set himself on fire. The picture of the burning monk was front page news around the world. It was assumed that the persecution must be terrible if men were willing to burn themselves to death. The United Nations was called to investigate the alleged persecution. The UN reported that there was no persecution. However, the report came too late. Moreover, the report did not get the headlines that the suicide had.

The Death of Diem

Later that year, a group of South Vietnamese generals, unhappy with Diem, planned to overthrow his government. Early on the morning of November 1, 1963, South Vietnamese troops stormed the presidential palace. They took control of the government and killed Diem and his family.

Kennedy's Domestic Policy: "The New Frontier"

Kennedy continued the policy of expanding social programs. In this, he was following in the tradition of his Democratic predecessors, Roosevelt and Truman. He sought to reenact the early days of the New Deal. Kennedy called his new series of reforms the New Frontier. However, opponents in Congress were able to put together a coalition to stop most of these new measures. On the other hand, there was one area where Congress supported massive spending by the president. This was his goal to put a man on the moon by the end of the 1960s.

The Space Race

In October 1957, the Soviet Union shocked America by launching Sputnik I, the first manmade satellite, into space. In response, the United States sped up its own space program. In the next year, we launched the first American satellite into orbit: *Explorer I.* This competition between the Soviet Union and the United States to conquer space and put the first man on the moon became known as the Space Race.

Less than four years after the launch of Sputnik, the Soviets surged ahead again in the Space Race. A Soviet cosmonaut named Yuri Gagarin became the first man to travel in space. However, the United States was not sitting by idly. In May 1961, Alan Shepherd became the first American in space. On February 20, 1962, John Glenn became the first American to orbit the earth. The Soviets had taken a lead in the race, but America was gaining fast. Kennedy

Alan Shepard in the space capsule before launch

touched the spirit of the nation. America would be the first to put a man on the moon!

Spot Check

1. Who were the Viet Cong?
2. Why did Ngo Dinh Diem not want American soldiers or direct American involvement in Vietnam?
3. What was the Tri Quang affair? What was its result?
4. Who was the first man in space?
5. Who was the first American in space?

The Civil Rights Movement

The Civil Rights Movement is the effort of many Americans to gain equal treatment for Blacks under the law. It is their attempt to overcome segregation and discrimination. The Civil Rights Movement began in the 1950s. This is when black groups began winning legal battles over segregation.

Desegregation

According to the 14th Amendment, everyone must be treated equally under the law. In 1896, in *Plessy v. Ferguson,* the Supreme Court decided that this meant that facilities for Blacks and Whites could be "separate" so long as they were "equal." This separation of races was known as segregation. Segregation occurred in various degrees across the country. However, it was most evident in the South.

The notion of "separate but equal" seemed fair in theory. However, in practice, segregation usually meant inferior facilities for Blacks. For example, public schools that had a large black student body did not receive as much money as white schools. After World War II, more and more people began to believe that segregation was wrong. In the late 1940s, a growing movement began to push for desegregation. This movement had the support of President Truman. In fact, Truman ordered the U.S. Army to desegregate.

In 1954, the Supreme Court decided the case of *Brown v. Board of Education.* The Court ruled that laws requiring segregation in public schools violated the Constitution. The court said that "separate but equal" was in fact unequal. Seventeen states were found in violation of the Constitution. They were ordered to change their laws. In most states, there was little opposition. In others, however, President Eisenhower needed to send in federal troops to ensure that the law was followed.

In response to protests that Black citizens were being denied their rights, in 1957, Congress passed the first civil rights bill since the Reconstruction Era. Its primary purpose was to create a Civil Rights Commission. This commission was empowered to look into claims that voting rights were being denied.

The Montgomery Bus Boycott

The Civil Rights Movement used direct action to fight segregation and discrimination. Sit-ins and boycotts were organized at businesses and other public places where Blacks were segregated or refused entry or service. The most famous boycott occurred in December 1955 in Montgomery, Alabama. There, a black woman named Rosa Parks refused to give up her seat on a city bus to a white man. She was arrested and put in jail. On December 5, several thousand black people in Montgomery began a boycott of the city's buses.

The Montgomery bus boycott was led by Martin Luther King, Jr. King was a black Baptist minister. He would become the leader of the Civil Rights movement. He became well known for his use of direct action. Sit-ins and boycotts would often cause clashes with police. Violence would sometimes erupt. However, King was a firm believer in non-violent methods of direct action. No matter what violence was done to them, he told his followers not to fight back. He told them that they had to be willing to go to jail for their disobedience of unjust laws. However, if they followed his plan, they would win the support of Black and White Americans.

The Civil Rights Movement under Kennedy

During the election campaign, John F. Kennedy had pledged to end discrimination. Once he was elected, he worked to keep his promise. In 1962, he banned any form of racial or religious discrimination in housing financed by the federal government. He also ordered the Interstate Commerce Commission to end segregation on all interstate buses, trains, and planes.

New Amendments to the Constitution

The early 1960s saw two new amendments to the Constitution that were favored by the civil rights' supporters. These were the Twenty-Third and Twenty-fourth Amendments. The Twenty-third Amendment allowed residents of the District of Columbia, almost all of whom were black, to vote in the presidential election. It was ratified in 1961. The Twenty-fourth Amendment prohibited states from requiring voters to pay a poll tax to vote in federal elections. This was ratified in 1964.

The March on Washington

In June 1963, public opinion had shifted in favor of the civil rights movement. Kennedy felt the time was right to pass sweeping new federal civil rights laws. He proposed laws banning segregation in public places, speeding up school desegregation, and providing job training for unskilled black workers.

To support Kennedy's plan, Martin Luther King, Jr. organized a massive "March on Washington." Some 200,000 people attended. They marched from the Washington Monument to the Lincoln Memorial. At this event, King gave a famous speech in which he said that he had a dream of racial equality in America. He said that he had a dream where people were judged not "by the color of their skin but by the content of their character." King spoke of the American ideal of a land of freedom and equality under God.

The Death of John F. Kennedy

President Kennedy had set a dramatic goal for America: to put an American on the moon by the end of the decade. However, he did not live to see his goal fulfilled. On November 22, 1963,

President Kennedy flew to Dallas, Texas. The purpose of the visit was to build support for his up-coming re-election campaign. As he rode in an open limousine through the downtown streets, shots rang out. Bullets hit the president in his head and neck. He was rushed to the hospital but it was too late. The doctors declared him dead. Vice President Lyndon Johnson was sworn in as president aboard the president's plane.

The Dallas police searched the city for the assassin. They quickly arrested Lee Harvey Oswald, a former marine and a deranged Communist. He denied any knowledge of the murder but the evidence against him was great. Two days later, Jack Ruby shot and killed Oswald as he was being escorted by the police.

Since the time of the murders, there have been numerous conspiracy theories about the killings. Some people believe that Oswald did not shoot Kennedy at all, but that someone else did. Others think that more than one person was involved in Kennedy's murder. The Warren Commission, which was convened to investigate the killings, determined that Oswald acted alone. The most recent evidence based on computer-generated models indicates that a trained marksman like Oswald could have shot the president in the way that he was shot.

Spot Check

1. What did the Supreme Court rule in the case Plessy v. Fergusson?
2. What Supreme Court case ruled segregation as unconstitutional? What was the reaction of the states?
3. What was the Civil Rights Movement?
4. Who was Martin Luther King? What were his beliefs?
5. What was the Montgomery bus boycott?

Lyndon B. Johnson Taking the Oath of Office, November 1963

Lyndon Johnson Becomes President

When Lyndon Johnson became president, he promised to continue the policies of President Kennedy. However, unlike Kennedy, Johnson had spent decades in politics. He had first been elected to Congress in 1937. In 1948, he was elected to the U.S. Senate. Johnson was known as a man who got things done, one way or the other. The new president turned to Congress and asked for the most sweeping social programs since the New Deal. Congress went along.

The Civil Rights Act of 1964

One of the most important laws passed during Johnson's first term as president was the Civil Rights Act of 1964. Conservative senators from the South opposed the bill. They used a tactic in the Senate called the filibuster to try and stop its passage. The filibuster allows a senator to have open-ended debate and tie up the Senate. No bill can be voted on as long as the senator is talking and debating. To stop the filibuster, three-fifths of the Senate must vote for cloture. This means the Senate can limit the amount of debate on the matter under consideration. After 83 days of debate on the bill, liberal senators were able to stop the filibuster.

The Civil Rights Act of 1964 was one of the most wide-ranging laws ever passed by Congress. The Act prohibited discrimination in public places like restaurants and hotels. It ordered that all states must have the same voting requirements for Blacks and Whites. It prohibited discrimination on the basis of race or gender by anyone engaged in interstate commerce. It denied federal funds to segregated public school districts. Congress offered money to public schools to help them to desegregate.

The War on Poverty

In addition to trying to abolish discrimination, Johnson also tried to abolish poverty in the United States. In fact, in his State of the Union Address to Congress in 1964, Johnson declared war on poverty. The Congress went along with his plan and passed a massive spending bill to try to get rid of poverty. Numerous programs were created to help poor Americans.

The Election of 1964

While many people liked Johnson's plans to end poverty, many people did not because of massive spending. One of the leaders of those opposed to Johnson was a conservative senator from Arizona named Barry Goldwater. He believed that the federal government was going beyond the powers granted it in the U.S. Constitution by undertaking these vast social programs. Goldwater thought these programs were the responsibility of the states. He also believed that individual liberty was being restricted by all the government regulations.

In July 1964, at the nominating convention, the Republicans chose Senator Goldwater to be their candidate for president. Goldwater was a good man. Many regard him as the founder of present day conservative politics. However, many people thought that he was too extreme. At his speech to accept the nomination for president, Goldwater addressed the issue of his extremism. He said that, "Extremism in the defense of liberty is no vice. And … moderation in pursuit of justice is no virtue." This statement did not help him to get elected.

The Democrats nominated Lyndon Johnson. He painted himself as John F. Kennedy's heir. Thus, he easily defeated Goldwater.

The Great Society

Johnson's landslide victory caused him to call for even greater social changes. In his inaugural address, he called on Congress to pass laws that would create "the Great Society." The Democratic Congress went along with Johnson. It spent billions and billions of dollars enacting the Great Society.

The Great Society laws doubled the money spent on anti-poverty programs. It gave medical insurance to all elderly Americans in a program called Medicare. It was more even-handed in allowing immigration from all nations. More money was spent at all levels of education. Money was spent on many new plans for urban renewal and public housing projects. New programs were created to improve highways, cities, and the environment.

President Johnson was able to influence Congress to enact all of his Great Society goals into law. Many older New Dealers were amazed. They looked in awe at how the impossible dreams they had from Roosevelt's New Deal came to life in Johnson's Great Society. Yet, the new laws did not end up creating a "great society."

The Growth of Violence

By 1965, Black Americans had taken many steps toward equality. However, they still faced obstacles. Many black people lived in the decaying inner cities. These areas had poor schools and few jobs. High unemployment caused many Blacks to grow angry and despair. They felt that they were going to live all their lives in poverty.

Early in the Civil Rights Movement, some Communists had seen the movement as a way to destabilize the United States, so, they became active in the movement. A number of politicians had asked Martin Luther King to purge his organization of these people. He denied that there were Communists in the movement. Until 1964, the movement had proceeded with little violence. However, by the summer of 1964, more radical elements in the Civil Rights Movement began to suggest that reform was not coming quickly enough. They preached violence and urban guerrilla warfare. The summer of 1964 became known as the "long hot summer" because of the number of riots which occurred in northern cities.

In August 1965, one of the nation's worst riots occurred in the mostly black area of Los Angeles known as Watts. This large riot lasted six days. Fifteen thousand National Guard troops had to be sent in to restore order. At the end of the riot, thirty-four people had been killed and over a thousand had been injured. Fires destroyed about $35 million dollars of property.

Many of the Communists who had become leaders in the Civil Rights Movement began to tie civil rights to the expanding war in Vietnam. They said that supporting the Vietnamese government was the same as supporting racism. They also said that Blacks should not be forced to fight for an American government that denied them full citizenship. They pointed out that Blacks were carrying an unfair burden in the war. More Blacks were drafted than Whites because White men could avoid the draft by going to college. They urged Black men not to register for the draft and to evade the draft if possible.

AMERICA TAKES CHARGE IN VIETNAM

The Situation in South Vietnam Grows Worse

Following the assassination of President Diem, the situation in South Vietnam quickly grew worse. The head of the Communist rebels called the death of Diem "a gift from heaven." The South Vietnamese government was thrown into confusion, as was its army. Many of Diem's supporters in the army lost their positions. This further caused a breakdown in leadership.

The Communists immediately raised the level of attacks in South Vietnam. In North Vietnam, Ho Chi Minh requested and received increased aid from China and the Soviet Union. Reports came back to the U.S. that South Vietnam would fall to the Communists if the U.S. did not help. Johnson's top advisors urged that the U.S. not abandon South Vietnam. They believed that America must show that it was committed to stopping Communist aggression.

On the other hand, there were many people who wanted Johnson to end the war. They wanted him to support the establishment of a coalition government in South Vietnam that included the

Communists. However, Johnson remembered the history of Eastern Europe. There, coalition governments had quickly become Communist governments. Johnson believed that more assistance to South Vietnam was necessary. However, before he sent more aid, he wanted the support of the American people. He also wanted the support of both Republicans and Democrats in Congress. He waited for a chance to gain that support. The chance came in August.

The Gulf of Tonkin Resolution

On August 2, 1964, the destroyer USS *Maddox* was conducting electronic intelligence gathering off the coast of North Vietnam when it was attacked by North Vietnamese torpedo boats. The *Maddox* returned fire and retreated from the area. Two days later, the *Maddox* and another destroyer were sent back to the same area. What happened that night is not exactly clear. The two ships thought they were being attacked. They fired at targets on their radar. After the report of the second attack, President Johnson ordered air strikes against North Vietnamese naval bases.

On August 7, at the request of President Johnson, Congress passed the Gulf of Tonkin Resolution. The Resolution gave the president the power to take the steps that he felt were needed to prevent further attacks against the forces of the United States. Almost every member of Congress voted for the Gulf of Tonkin Resolution. Only two senators objected. It became the legal authorization for America's long involvement in Vietnam.

America Becomes More Involved in Vietnam

When Johnson became president, there were about 17,000 American military advisors in Vietnam. These were mostly U.S. Special Forces troops known as the Green Berets. Their mission was to train and advise the South Vietnamese troops and to help train and build their army. The motto of the Green Berets is "To Liberate the

Oppressed". The Green Berets fought alongside the South Vietnamese.

After the 1964 election, Communist gains in South Vietnam caused Johnson to expand the role of the United States. More advisors were sent. In February 1965, following a Viet Cong attack on American barracks, the United States began bombing raids against North Vietnam's supply lines and military bases. In March, the decision was made to send American combat troops to Vietnam. At first, marines were sent only to guard U.S. bases. However, they were soon conducting combat patrols. Bombing of North Vietnam and its supply lines steadily increased. About two-thirds of the supplies coming from the Soviet Union and China were destroyed. However, China and the Soviets simply sent more. The U.S. bombing never seriously hurt the North's ability to wage war.

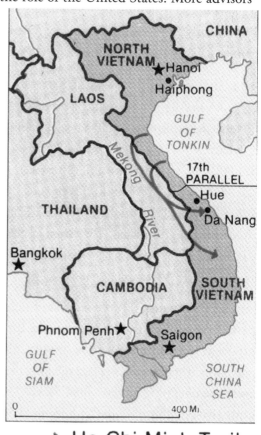

Map of the Vietnam War, 1965 to 1973

By the middle of 1966, about 265,000 American troops were in Vietnam. As more time went by and more troops were sent to Vietnam, more Americans began to question whether we should be in Vietnam. Some felt that America should not be in Vietnam at all. Others thought that Johnson was not fighting the war hard enough to win. At Christmas 1965, he called for a "peace offensive." This meant he stopped bombing the North. However, the Communists did not want to talk about peace as long as American troops were in Vietnam. Everyone knew that once the troops left, the Communists would overrun the country.

Johnson tried to keep up the pressure. He continued the heavy bombing. By the end of 1967, there were about 500,000 American troops in Vietnam.

THE TET OFFENSIVE: THE TURNING POINT

The New Year's Attack

Massive U.S. firepower was pressing the Communists to their limit. The United States was killing soldiers and destroying material just as fast as Ho Chi Minh could supply them. Communist progress in the South had been stopped cold. The American commander in Vietnam was confident of victory. The American government announced that the end of the war was in sight.

Ho Chi Minh was a dedicated Communist. He was willing to sacrifice any number of men to conquer the South. He would accept nothing less than victory. He was determined to win. Therefore, he organized the largest Communist offensive of the war. He planned to launch a countrywide attack against the Americans. The attack was scheduled to coincide with the Vietnamese New Year's Holiday called Tet.

The North began by declaring a cease-fire for the holiday. American intelligence suspected something. The top American general suggested that the South cancel the holiday and keep their soldiers on alert. However, President Thieu did not agree. As a result, when the offensive began, half the South Vietnamese army was at home celebrating the holiday.

On the night of January 30-31, 1968, Communist guerrillas launched surprise attacks throughout South Vietnam. Over 100,000 Communist troops were involved. They attacked 36 of the 43 provincial capitals.

A key battle was fought at Hue, the ancient capital of Vietnam. During the initial attacks, the North was able to seize this important town. The Communists proceeded to kill over 2,700 people accused of working with the Americans. The Communist army fortified the town and prepared to stay. The First Marine Division was called to take it back. The month long struggle that followed included fierce house-to-house fighting. However, the marines, the same corps of brave men who had fought their way out of the Chosin Reservoir in Korea, destroyed the enemy. Half the Communist army was killed and the rest were injured.

Everywhere the Communists attacked, they were thrown back. They suffered high casualties. Ho Chi Minh had hoped that many South Vietnamese civilians would join the offensive. They did not. His forces were either destroyed or forced to retreat.

The Results of the Offensive

The Tet Offensive was a major military victory for the United States and South Vietnam. Casualties for both Viet Cong and regular North Vietnamese soldiers were estimated in the tens of thousands. In fact, the Viet Cong were destroyed as an effective fighting force. From that point on, the North Vietnamese army fought a guerrilla war.

However, wars are not always won or lost on the battlefield. Recall how the Confederacy during the Civil War planned to win: wear down the Union. North Vietnam had lost a military battle but they had won a psychological victory. The fact that North Vietnam could launch such a large-scale attack convinced many in the U.S. that the end of the war was not in sight as the government had said it was. Moreover, the American media concluded that the war could not be won. Only strong leadership from the president could have ensured the needed recovery of spirit. However, President Johnson was a beaten man. On the night of March 31, he went on national television. He outlined a new policy about the war. He announced that he was limiting air attacks upon North Vietnam. He appealed to Ho Chi Minh to enter peace talks to end the war. He finished the speech by declaring that he would not seek, nor would he accept, the Democratic nomination for another term as president. Ho Chi Minh had won in the American media and public opinion what he could not win on the battlefield.

The *Pueblo* Incident

Relations between the United States and North Korea had never been good. The situation became even worse in January 1968, when North Korea seized an American naval ship, the USS *Pueblo*. The *Pueblo* was in the Sea of Japan. North Korea claimed that the ship was spying in North Korean waters. However, the United States denied this. During the capture of the ship, one American sailor was killed. Eighty-two American sailors were held hostage for nearly a year while American officials negotiated with the Communists. The hostages were finally released when American diplomats signed a false statement admitting that the *Pueblo* was spying. The *Pueblo* was never returned to the United States. Many Americans saw this incident as another example of American leaders being weak resisting Communism.

Martin Luther King is murdered

On April 4, 1968, Martin Luther King was standing on the balcony of a hotel room in Memphis, Tennessee. Shots rang out.

King was murdered. News of the murder caused rioting across the country. Black riots broke out in over a hundred cities. Rioting was the worst in Washington, D.C. The president called out thousands of troops and surrounded the White House with soldiers. After this incident, student radicals increased their protests against the Vietnam War.

The Election of 1968

The man most people expected to be the Democratic nominee for president in 1968 was Senator Robert Kennedy. He was John Kennedy's brother. Robert had worked to fight the Communists in the 1950s and had served as Attorney General of the United States during his brother's presidency. On June 4, he had won the very important California Democratic primary. That night, he gave a victory speech at a Los Angeles hotel. A little past midnight, on June 5, he was shot three times by Sirhan Sirhan. Sirhan was a Palestinian radical who was angry with Kennedy for supporting Israel. Kennedy was rushed to the hospital but the

Robert Kennedy

doctors were unable to save him. As a result of Kennedy's death, Vice President Hubert Humphrey received the Democratic nomination for president.

The Republicans nominated Richard Nixon for president. Nixon said that he could bring the country back together. He also said that the social programs of the Great Society were mostly costly failures.

He promised to end the violence in America's streets that frightened so many people. Lastly, he claimed to have a plan to end the Vietnam War honorably. He gave no specifics of the plan because he did not want to upset the on-going peace talks. Although the election was very close, Nixon was elected.

Spot Check

1. What was President Johnson's "Great Society"?
2. Why was the summer of 1964 called the "long hot summer"?
3. What was the Tet Offensive?
4. What was the *Pueblo* incident?

CHAPTER REVIEW

1. How did John F. Kennedy's war record aid him in politics?
2. How did Kennedy address the charge that his religion would affect his policies?
3. How did the United States respond when it was discovered that the Soviet Union had placed missiles in Cuba? How was this crisis resolved?
4. Who was Tri Quang and why was he important?
5. Why was the Berlin Wall built?
6. What was the result of the Kennedy assassination?
7. What was the "Domino Theory"?
8. Who was the first American in space?
9. Who was the first American to orbit the earth?
10. What was the Civil Rights movement?
11. What was the Montgomery bus boycott?
12. Who was Martin Luther King, Jr.?
13. What was the meaning of the phrase "separate but equal"?
14. Who killed John F. Kennedy?
15. What was the "Great Society"?
16. What was the Gulf of Tonkin Resolution?
17. What was the Tet offensive?
18. What was the *Pueblo* incident?
19. Why was Robert Kennedy not nominated for president?
20. Who was elected president in 1968?

THE DARK DAYS BEFORE THE DAWN

Man walked on the moon in a decade when much went wrong in America. The conquest of the moon filled most Americans with a sense of pride.

Nixon's Strategy to End the Vietnam War

When Nixon became president in 1969, he was determined to pull the United States out of Vietnam. However, he wanted an "honorable peace." This meant that he was determined to try to save South Vietnam in the process.

In the spring of 1970, Nixon ordered a ground attack on the Communist-controlled areas in neutral Cambodia. The Communists were using Cambodia as a base and refuge. The attack was the only way to halt the flow of Communist soldiers and supplies to South Vietnam. On April 30, Nixon told America about the attack. He said that he believed this would shorten the war and save American lives.

When they heard Nixon's announcement, anti-war protesters went after him with increased vigor. They accused the United States of violating the neutrality of Cambodia and widening the war. Protests broke out at over 400 colleges and universities. At Kent State University in Ohio, the National Guard was called in to restore order. In the confusion that followed, the Guard fired into the crowd. Four students were killed and others were wounded.

In February 1971, Nixon sent troops into Laos, the country north of Cambodia. His purpose was the same as before: to stop the flow of supplies into South Vietnam. However, Congress then prohibited the use of American troops in Laos or Cambodia. Despite this prohibition, Nixon was determined to do in Laos what he had done in Cambodia. Only the South Vietnamese army was to be used for the operation. However, the Vietnamese lacked the strength to carry through the operation without the help of American soldiers. Thus, the attack failed.

The Paris Peace Talks

Throughout this period, peace talks to end the war had been going on in Paris. The peace talks had begun in May 1968. At the start of the talks, the North Vietnamese refused to listen to any proposal. They simply denounced American and South Vietnamese "aggression." In May 1969, the United States proposed a withdrawal of all foreign troops from South Vietnam. Ho Chi Minh did not even consider it. Nixon was resolved to lessen U.S. involvement anyway.

Soon after taking office, Nixon announced his plan to end American involvement in Vietnam. The United States would pull out all its troops. The South Vietnamese would be trained to do all the jobs that the American military did. By the end of the summer of 1968, the withdrawal of 60,000 American troops had been announced. By early 1972, only 139,000 Americans remained in Vietnam compared with more than 500,000 when Nixon became president.

Nixon Goes to China

In July 1971, Nixon accepted an invitation from the Chinese Communist dictator, Mao Tse-tung, to visit Communist China. Since the overthrow of Chiang Kai-shek in 1949, the United States had not recognized Mao's government. However, Nixon thought that the time was right to begin a relationship with Red China. In the early 1960s, China and the Soviet Union had become less friendly with each other. Nixon saw a chance to widen the divide between the two nations. He also hoped that a better relationship with Red China could help him reach a negotiated settlement in Vietnam. He went to China in February of 1972. Diplomatic relations were begun. The two nations agreed to establish trade relations and to allow culture exchanges.

A Chinese Temple known as a Pagoda

North Vietnam responded to this act of peacemaking by launching their largest military attack. In spring 1972, North Vietnam attacked the South. Fighting raged across the country. American air power supported the South Vietnamese troops. In the northern part of South Vietnam, South Vietnamese troops suffered a serious defeat.

Nixon Accepts a Truce

Nixon responded to the attack with an all-out bombing effort against North Vietnam. He also ordered mines to be placed in the North Vietnamese port of Haiphong. The mines were intended to slow down the flow of equipment from the Soviet Union and China. This step had not been taken earlier for fear of an open dispute with the Soviets. Starting in May, Haiphong and North Vietnam's other ports were mined, effectively blocking all shipping.

In Paris, the peace talks continued. In October, North Vietnam suggested a ceasefire. According to the terms, America would withdraw all of its forces from Vietnam. In exchange, the North promised not to attack any more. However, there was to be no withdrawal of North Vietnamese troops from the large areas of the South that they now controlled. America would withdraw and get virtually nothing in return. Nevertheless, Nixon's chief foreign policy advisor, Henry Kissinger, was willing to make the deal so our troops could come home.

Thieu Refuses to Accept the Truce

However, the leaders of South Vietnam saw the truce for what it was. If American forces left and Communist forces remained, it was only a matter of time before the Communists seized the rest of the country. President Nguyen Van Thieu of South Vietnam refused to accept a ceasefire under those terms.

In mid-December 1972, North Vietnam indicated it was no longer interested in a truce. The United States increased pressure on both North and South to make further compromises. To bring the North back to the talks, the United States began constant bombing of Hanoi, the capitol of North Vietnam. More mines were dropped into Haiphong harbor. The North once again said they would accept the cease-fire. However, the South still would not because the treaty still allowed the Communists to remain in the South. Finally, Nixon told President Thieu that, whether he accepted the truce or not, the United States would sign the treaty and withdraw. Thieu had no choice but to sign the treaty, though he well knew the inevitable result.

The treaty ending the American involvement in Vietnam was signed on January 27, 1973. America's longest and most divisive war was over. More than 56,000 Americans had died in Vietnam.

As a result of the Vietnam War, Congress took measures to curb the power of the president. One of the most important of these laws was the War Powers Act. This Act limited the powers of the president when U.S. troops were engaged in combat. The Act prohibited the president from keeping troops in combat in a foreign country without permission from Congress. President Nixon considered the Act to be an unconstitutional restraint upon the power of the president, so he vetoed the bill. However, the bill was passed over Nixon's veto on November 7, 1973. Every president since its passage has treated it as unconstitutional. They have claimed that they are not bound by it. (As of 2010, the U.S. Supreme Court has not spoken on the matter.)

Spot Check

1. Why did President Nixon order a ground attack on Cambodia?
2. What did President Nixon hope to gain by going to Red China?
3. What were the terms of the truce in Vietnam that Nixon accepted?
4. Why did President Thieu of South Vietnam not want to sign the truce?

Nixon's Domestic Policies

A Man Lands on the Moon

On July 16, 1969, the U.S. launched *Apollo 11* to the moon. Four days later, the lunar module touched down on the surface of the moon. Neil Armstrong climbed out of the space ship. As he stepped on the surface of the moon, he said, "That's one small step for man, one giant leap for mankind." The astronauts planted an American flag and a plaque in the ground. The plaque summed up all that was good about America. It said: "We came in peace for all mankind."

Arms Control

In May 1972, Nixon traveled to the Soviet Union. The Soviets were concerned that America was becoming friendly with the Red Chinese. While in the Soviet Union, Nixon negotiated an important treaty with the Soviet Union. The Strategic Arms Limitation Treaty (SALT) provided for limits upon various missiles. One of the important parts of the treaty was the Anti-Ballistic Missile (ABM) Treaty. The United States had been thinking about developing a defense against nuclear attack. Many people opposed this idea. They feared it would upset the strategic balance between the United States and the Soviet Union. They were afraid that if one or both countries developed a missile defense, it would make war more likely. The treaty did allow each country to develop a small number of ABMs. However, the treaty was used by many liberal Americans to oppose the development of *any* ABM system. It soon became clear that the Soviets were violating the terms of the treaty.

The Watergate Scandal

The Election of 1972

In 1972, the Democrats nominated George McGovern as their candidate for president. The main issue of the campaign was the war in Vietnam. McGovern favored the immediate withdrawal of American forces. Many people, especially the middle class, saw him as being very radical. McGovern's association with the social radicals cost him the election. In fact, throughout the campaign, Nixon always had a large lead in the polls, so it was not a great surprise when Nixon won in a landslide. Nixon won 60.7 percent of the popular vote compared to McGovern's 37.5 percent. He also won 49 states. Only Massachusetts and the District of Columbia voted for McGovern.

The Watergate Burglary

Despite Nixon's huge lead in the polls, some of his aides decided to gain every advantage over his opponents. On June 17, 1972, a team was sent to break into the headquarters of the Democratic National Committee (DNC). The DNC headquarters were in the Watergate Hotel and Office Building in Washington, D.C. The burglars had copied campaign documents and planted listening devices. However, the police arrested the team of burglars at the Democratic headquarters. Later, the burglars were traced back to some of Nixon's aides.

By early 1973, there was call for a Senate hearings into the burglary. The hearings began in May. However, even before the hearings started, several of Nixon's top aides resigned. The hearings

Watergate Hotel, Washington Monument, and the Kennedy Center (on the right)

found that the administration had authorized spying on Nixon's political opponents. Nixon defended these activities as necessary for national security. Although he tried to protect his aides, the investigation of the break-in led to them. Under pressure from prosecutors and Senate hearings, it became clear that this spying had not only been illegal but had also involved Nixon himself.

The Watergate Tapes

On July 13, a White House official revealed to the Senate investigation that Nixon had made tapes of his own phone calls and conversations in the White House. Prosecutors asked for these tapes in the hope that they could find evidence against the president. Nixon refused to give up the tapes citing executive privilege. This privilege exempts the executive branch, the president, from having to disclose certain kinds of information. Nixon said releasing the tapes would weaken the executive branch. However, he wanted to be helpful, so instead of the tapes, he would provide an edited transcript of the tapes.

The tapes became the center of the controversy. Nixon's opponents said that this was a sign that he considered himself above the law. The public began to wonder what was on the tapes. Eventually the Supreme Court ordered the release of the tapes. The tapes indicated the president was involved in ordering illegal spying and wiretaps. After the tapes were released, many of the president's closest aides resigned or were charged with crimes.

Vice President Agnew Resigns

In October of 1973, Vice President Spiro Agnew was discovered to have accepted bribes amounting to more than $200,000 when he was governor of Maryland. This revelation led to Agnew's resignation. Nixon appointed Gerald Ford, Republican Congressman from Michigan, to fill the office. Ford had a reputation for honesty that Nixon hoped would help defuse the growing Watergate scandal.

Nixon Resigns

The release of the Nixon tapes resulted in calls for Nixon's resignation or impeachment from members of both parties. On August 5, 1974, transcripts of conversations Nixon had only six days after the break-in were released. They showed he had been involved in the cover-up from the beginning. It was now clear to him that if he did not resign from office that he would be removed. On the night of August 8, Nixon went on television and announced that he was going to resign as president. He admitted that he had made mistakes, but *not* that he was guilty of anything.

The following day, Nixon resigned. Gerald Ford was sworn in as president. He was the first person to become president without having been elected president or vice president.

Gerald Ford Takes Over

On September 8, 1974, Ford pardoned Nixon for any crimes he might have committed. This act was controversial. However, it avoided creating more dissension among the American people that

As Betty Ford watches, Chief Justice Warren Burger swears in Gerald Ford as President.

would have resulted from the prosecution of a president. Americans were beginning to put Watergate behind them. Ford wanted the "long national nightmare" to end. Even so, there were many who were angry that Ford pardoned Nixon.

Ford also moved to reorganize the old administration. He inspired a renewed confidence in the office of president. He had been an Eagle Scout and played center on his college football team. He seemed to be a "regular" person. He gave the impression that the presidency had returned to the people and was no longer controlled by elites.

The Supreme Court Legalizes Abortion

During the dark days of the Watergate scandal, the Supreme Court handed down its darkest and most erroneous decision. On January 22, 1973, the Court handed down its decision in *Roe v. Wade*. The issue before the court was "when does life begin." The majority decided that they did not need to decide when life began. Instead, they said that every woman has the "right" to destroy her unborn child during the first six months of pregnancy. During the last three months, the court ruled that the state could protect the life of the child. However, later court rulings made this very difficult.

One of the dissenting justices, Byron White, summed up the problems with the decision in *Roe*. White wrote: "I find nothing in the language or the history of the Constitution

Byron White

to support the Court's judgment. The Court simply fashions and announces a new constitutional right for pregnant mothers." White went on to say that the Court gave "scarcely any reason or authority for its action." The Supreme Court had rendered some bad decisions in its history; however, none has had the brutal impact that *Roe v. Wade* has had. Millions of unborn babies have been killed because of it.

Spot Check

1. Why did Richard Nixon win a second term as president?
2. What was the Watergate burglary? Why was it done?
3. What evidence resulted in calls for Nixon's resignation or impeachment?
4. How did Gerald Ford become president without having been elected to national office?

THE FINAL LOSS OF VIETNAM

The War Continues

Even after the American withdrawal, there was never real peace in Vietnam. 1974 was the bloodiest year in Vietnam since 1968. About 31,000 South Vietnamese died in battle that year. The North Vietnamese had about 30,000 troops in the South who were supported by hundreds of tanks. Congress cut military aid to South Vietnam to a fraction of what had been promised to President Thieu. At the same time, the Communists increased their support to North Vietnam.

In March 1975, the government of South Vietnam realized that it could not hold the entire country. The South abandoned the north of the country. It concentrated its forces around the capital, Saigon. As the North Vietnamese Army poured over the border, it was clear that even the area around Saigon could not be held for long. President Ford asked Congress for one billion dollars in emergency military aid to Vietnam. He also called for the evacuation of about 200,000 Vietnamese who had been connected with the Americans.

This evacuation proceeded very slowly and only a fraction were able to be evacuated.

The Fall of Saigon

With Saigon about to fall, President Thieu fled the country. American helicopters landed on the roof and in the parking lot of the American embassy in Saigon. They flew people to American ships. By April 29, the Communist forces had completely surrounded Saigon and were about to enter the city. Helicopters continued to lift out Vietnamese civilians. Outside the walls, thousands of Vietnamese swarmed around the embassy, the last hope of escape. Although the North Vietnamese made no attempt to interfere with the evacuation, Ford wanted to avoid confrontation. He personally called the commander of the marine guard and ordered the withdrawal of all American personnel and a halt to the evacuation. Marine Major James Kean was the last American to leave the embassy. On this last helicopter, desperate Vietnamese

Helicopters unload evacuees onto the carrier USS *Midway*.

tried in vain to hold on to the landing struts. They were willing to risk death rather than live under Communism. The next day, April 30th, the Communists occupied Saigon. For the first time in our history, the United States had lost a war. Saigon was re-named Ho Chi Minh City in honor of the war's victor. No one knows how many South Vietnamese supporters were killed.

The Communist Advances in Southeast Asia

Within a month of the fall of Saigon, Communist forces took control of Laos and Cambodia. Despite promises not to harm the South Vietnamese, the North murdered thousands. People fled from the Communists in open boats. Barely seaworthy, many of the boats sank. Pirates captured others. These "boat people" died by the tens of thousands in their desperate attempt to escape the Communists.

Communist Advances in Africa

In 1974 and 1975, the Communists seized control of three African nations: Ethiopia, Mozambique, and Angola. In Angola, in southwest Africa, there was strong opposition to the Communists. Castro sent Cuban troops to Angola to fight for the Communist government. At this point, the Communists did not control the entire country. Two anti-Communists groups, the FNLA and UNITA controlled much of the country. Most of the Angolan people supported UNITA.

Senator Dick Clark pressed Congress to prohibit American involvement in Angola. He wanted to avoid a repeat of Vietnam. The senate approved the "Clark Amendment" by a large margin. It made it illegal for American funds to be used in support of anti-Communist movements in Angola. The civil war continued for many years. However, without significant outside aid, the unarmed anti-Communists had little chance of success.

Spot Check

1. What action did President Ford take concerning Vietnam?
2. What events led up to the approval of the "Clark Amendment"? What effect did this amendment have on the spread of Communism?

JIMMY CARTER AS PRESIDENT

Election of 1976

In 1976, the Republican Party nominated Ford for another term. However, the Republican Party was so weakened by Watergate that Ford faced an uphill battle from the start. The Democratic challenger was Jimmy Carter, the Governor of Georgia. He ran as an outsider and made a great deal of his Christianity. He promised a return to honesty in Washington and promised many new programs to help the common people. The election was very close. Carter won 50 percent of the popular vote to Ford's 48 percent.

Jimmy Carter

The Panama Canal

In 1978, Carter agreed to a treaty to return control of the Panama Canal to Panama. The treaty declared that the canal would remain neutral to all shipping, even during war. However, the treaty allowed the United States to defend the canal if it were threatened. At noon on December 31, 1999, Panama took control of the Canal.

The Camp David Accords

Despite several failures, Carter had one notable success: a peace agreement between Egypt and Israel in the Middle East. The Middle East had been a major concern to America for three reasons. First, America supported the existence of the state of Israel. In fact, the U.S. was the first nation to recognize Israel's existence. Second, the Middle East has a huge amount of oil. Oil is a vital resource to the industries of the United States. Since we do not produce enough in the United States, it must be imported. Much is imported from the Middle East. Third, since America supported Israel, Egypt had come under the influence of the Soviets during the Cold War.

Egypt and the rest of the Arab nations had refused to recognize the state of Israel in 1948. For almost thirty years, Arab hostility was intense. If there was not open war, there was constant terrorist activity against Israel. By 1977, Israel occupied parts of Egypt as a result of several wars between the two nations.

However, by 1977, both the president of Egypt, Anwar Sadat, and the prime minister of Israel, Menachem Begin, were willing to talk to each other. In November 1977, Sadat stunned the world by flying to Jerusalem. No Arab leader had even recognized that Israel existed. This was an incredible moment. Sadat met with Begin and even spoke before the Israeli Parliament. Sadat called for diplomatic relations and a peace treaty.

However, the resolution of differences between the two nations still seemed overwhelming. The talks between the two began to break down. At this point, Carter entered the picture. He invited Sadat and Begin to the presidential retreat of Camp David, Maryland. He offered to help them negotiate a treaty between their two countries. In early September 1978, the three men met at Camp David. After twelve tense days, Carter produced a diplomatic "miracle." Sadat and Begin agreed to the basics of a treaty. The treaty was signed at the White House in March in 1979. Egypt became the first Arab nation to officially recognize Israel.

Red China

On January 1, 1979, the United States officially recognized the government of Red China. The next year, the two nations signed a trade agreement. Very quickly, the United States began doing major business with China. Over time, China began to loan huge amounts of money to the United States. Many feared that the Chinese would not conquer the United States in battle; they would just buy the U.S.

The Iranian Hostage Crisis

One of the main points of Carter's foreign policy was concern for human rights. He refused to support any regime that he viewed as violating the human rights of its citizens. This seems very noble. However, sometimes it is necessary to support a government that does a few bad things in order to stop an even worse government from coming to power. In South Vietnam, the government was not perfect, but when we left, it was taken over by a Communist government that was much, much worse. Due to this nature of foreign governments, Carter's policy often backfired. The most obvious failure was in Iran in the Middle East.

Iran was an important country to America. It is strategically located between the Soviet Union and the Middle Eastern oil fields. Iran itself is a major oil-producing nation. At the beginning of Carter's presidency, the United States and Iran had a good relationship. A king, called the Shah, ruled Iran. He was a longtime ally of the United States. He was working to modernize his nation as well as grant greater freedom to his people.

However, there was a movement in Iran by Muslim extremists to take control of the government. The Shah opposed these extremists, often brutally. This brutality caused Carter to withdraw American support from the Shah. Without American aid, the Shah could not remain in power. In January 1979, he was forced to flee to Egypt. A revolutionary government under a Muslim religious leader took power in Iran. The new government demanded that the Shah be returned to Iran for trial. In October, the Shah was allowed to come to the United States for medical treatment.

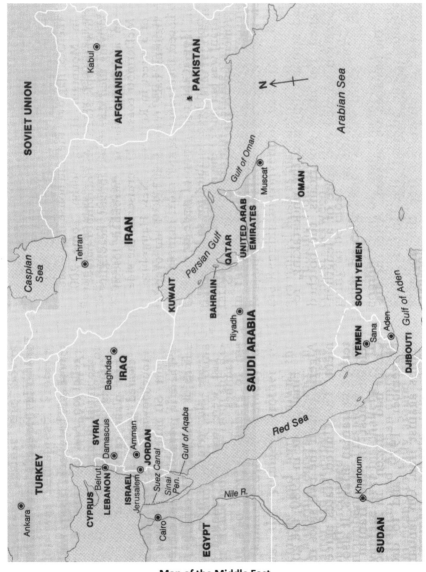

Map of the Middle East

On November 4, an Iranian mob seized the American embassy in Tehran, the capital of Iran. The mob demanded the return of the Shah. Over fifty Americans were taken hostage. They would remain hostage for 444 days. The new government supported the hostage takers. Carter responded with economic sanctions and negotiation. However, he took no military action.

Carter finally launched a secret rescue mission in April 1980. Sadly, the rescue failed when two American aircraft collided in the Iranian desert. This failure insured that the hostage crisis would continue to be an embarrassment to Carter for the entire 1980 presidential campaign.

The Soviet Invasion of Afghanistan

Afghanistan is a very poor nation. It is mostly mountains. It is surrounded by Iran, the Soviet Union, and Pakistan. As a result of its location and poverty, few Westerners had much contact with it. In 1978, the small Afghan Communist Party seized power in the capital of Kabul. However, in the countryside, there was substantial opposition to the Communists. In the countryside, the anti-Communist revolts grew more severe. In order to put an end to the revolts, the Soviets planned a large-scale invasion of Afghanistan.

The Afghan Communist president rejected the idea of a Soviet invasion. He said that the Afghan Communists would not support it. Despite this, on December 27, 1979, the Soviet Army began its invasion. The small Afghan army fought heroically. However, it was quickly overwhelmed.

The American Response

In response to the invasion, Carter announced a number of economic sanctions. He also placed an embargo on all American grain to the Soviets. He decided that the United States would boycott the 1980 Olympics that were held in Moscow. The United States also provided some weapons to the anti-Communist resistance. This aid was very small. It was simply intended to make the Soviets pay a slightly higher price for control of Afghanistan.

In the five years after the fall of Vietnam, Communists had managed to capture new countries on three continents. In 1980, Communism was stronger and controlled more of the world than ever before. On the other hand, the strength and prestige of the United States had reached a new low. Many thought that the sun was setting on all that had made America great. However, a man was about to become president who believed that it was still morning in America.

Spot Check

1. Briefly describe the events of the Iranian Hostage Crisis.
2. Was there any opposition when the Communists seized power in Afghanistan in 1978?
3. Why did the Soviets invade Afghanistan?

CHAPTER REVIEW

1. How did Nixon hope to end the Vietnam War?
2. What effect did Nixon's visit to China have on Vietnam?
3. What were the terms of the ceasefire truce between North Vietnam and the United States?
4. Why did President Thieu of South Vietnam refuse to accept the truce?
5. Why was he eventually forced to sign it?
6. What was the result of the Roe v. Wade decision?
7. What was the Watergate scandal?
8. Why did President Ford pardon Nixon?
9. What were the effects of the Iran hostage crisis?
10. Why were the Camp David Accords a major success for Carter?
11. Identify the following people:
    a. George McGovern
    b. Anwar Sadat
12. Why did the Soviet Union invade Afghanistan?
13. How did the U.S. respond to the invasion of Afghanistan?

MORNING IN AMERICA: THE REAGAN PRESIDENCY AND THE FALL OF THE SOVIET UNION

In one of the most important moments of his presidency, President Reagan speaking in Berlin, calls for the Berlin Wall to be torn down.

The Election of 1980

In 1980, the Republicans chose Ronald Reagan to be their candidate for president. He had been born in Tampico, Illinois, on February 6, 1911. Starting in 1937, he appeared in many films. One of his best roles was in the film *Knute Rockne, All American*. In that film, Reagan played the part of George "The Gipper" Gipp. His fans and supporters would affectionately call Reagan "the Gipper" for the rest of his life. His "big break" came in the film *King's Row*. This was a very good film and Reagan was very good in it. However, the film was made as World War II was breaking out. Like many film stars, Reagan enlisted in the armed forces. During the war, he was assigned to make films for the army. His unit made several hundred films.

Following the war, Ronald Reagan continued his career in films. However, he never received roles as good as those he had before the war. He made the move to the new medium of television. He had great success as the host of *General Electric Theatre*, a weekly program. During this time, he testified before the House Committee investigating Communism. For his entire life, Reagan was a dedicated anti-Communist. During this time, he gave a number of speeches for General Electric. He spoke in favor of business and against big, expensive government.

When he was a young man, Reagan had admired Franklin Roosevelt. In fact, he was a member of the Democratic Party until 1962. However, he came to realize that Roosevelt's policies hurt the economy and destroyed individual responsibility. In 1964, Reagan campaigned for Republican presidential candidate Barry Goldwater. On October 27, 1964, Reagan gave a speech that forever changed his life. It was known as the "Time for Choosing" speech. In it, he said that America had come to a time when it must choose between big government and the Democrats, or small government and the Republicans. The speech put Reagan on the political map.

In 1966, Reagan ran for governor of California. He was elected and then re-elected in 1970. During his terms as governor, he became known as one of the leading conservatives in the nation. Already known for being a strong anti-Communist, he now became known for his support of Christian moral values.

In 1976, Reagan ran for the Republican nomination for president against Gerald Ford. However, Ford narrowly defeated him. Jimmy Carter defeated Ford in the general election.

In 1980, Reagan again sought the Republican nomination for president. This time George H.W. Bush challenged him. Reagan used the solid base of supporters that he had established in 1976. He also had the active support of traditional Christians. Thus, Reagan received the nomination. He named George Bush as his running mate.

In the general election, Ronald Reagan faced Jimmy Carter. Carter had been weakened by a poor economy and the weakness of America overseas. He had been weakened also by a serious challenge in his own party. Edward Kennedy had entered the Democratic primary. Kennedy argued that Carter had not provided the leadership the nation needed. As a result, Reagan easily won the national election. Reagan claimed that he had a popular mandate from the people. They wanted him to cut taxes and cut spending. They wanted America to oppose Communism.

President Ronald Reagan

They wanted to see America return to her Christian roots and Christian values.

REAGAN'S DOMESTIC POLICIES

Economic Policy: Reaganomics

When Reagan became president, the nation faced many economic problems. One of the worst was high unemployment. He wanted to do something to speed up the economy and put people back to work. He believed that the best way to do this was to cut taxes. This allowed more money to stay in private business. It would help the economy to grow. As the economy grew, government income from taxation would also increase. Reagan believed this would allow the government to meet its demands without damaging the economy. The theory was known as "Supply Side Economics" because it placed more control in the hands of suppliers of goods. His critics labeled his concepts "Reaganomics." They did not understand that these were the very principals that had made America great.

For the first two years of Reagan's presidency, the economy remained sluggish. Unemployment and interest rates stayed high until 1983. However, after that, the economy began to grow. The economy was so strong in 1984 that it was a major factor in Reagan's landslide re-election. The Reagan years were the longest period of constant economic growth since World War II. This was the result of lower taxes and less government regulation.

Reagan is Shot

On March 30, 1981, as Reagan was leaving a Washington, D.C. hotel, a crazy man shot him. He was rushed to the hospital. Reagan's courage and good humor were never more on display than as he lay on the operating table. He turned to his doctors and said that he hoped that some of them were Republicans. The surgeon replied that "Today Mr. President, we are all Republicans." Later, when his wife Nancy came to visit him in the hospital, he told her that he "forgot to duck." Two weeks later, he was back at work.

Triumph and Tragedy in Space

In April 1981, the space shuttle *Columbia* completed 36 orbits of the earth and landed safely in California at an Air Force base. *Columbia* was the world's first reusable space ship. NASA hoped that *Columbia* and the other shuttles could be used to put satellites in space. They hoped that the space shuttle program could actually make a profit.

The Space Shuttle *Challenger* successfully lifts off on April 4, 1983.

Then on January 28, 1986, tragedy struck. After twenty-four shuttle launches, the shuttle *Challenger* lifted off from Florida. On board were seven men and women. As millions watched on television, the shuttle exploded. Reagan went on television to console a grieving nation. He said that America would continue to explore space. Of the astronauts, he said, "We will never forget them nor the last time we saw them this morning as they prepared for their journey and waved goodbye and 'slipped the surly bonds of earth to touch the face of God'."

Spot Check

1. What was the "Time for Choosing" Speech?
2. What were Ronald Reagan's chief political beliefs?

REAGAN'S FOREIGN POLICY

The Reagan Doctrine

When Reagan took over as president, our military was at the weakest it had been in many years. President Carter had made deep cuts in military spending. He preferred to negotiate arms limitations with the Soviets in an attempt to ensure American security. Reagan believed that nothing could be gained by negotiating from a position of weakness. He began a massive rebuilding of the American military. His plan called for more than doubling the military budget within five years.

Critics of his plan accused Reagan of starting an arms race with the Soviets. Reagan said, "We're already in an arms race but only the Soviets are racing!" He believed that America could win the arms race. If forced to match our new weapons with new systems of their own, then the Soviets' economy could not bear the strain. The Soviets would be forced either to admit defeat or request serious arms control measures. If that happened, then the United States could deal from a position of strength.

Early in his term of office, President Reagan announced a new policy. The United States would no longer be content merely to assist countries seeking to avoid Communist takeover. America would actively support anti-Communists who sought to oppose existing Communist governments. This policy was known as the "Reagan

Doctrine." It was the first time that the United States had officially called for the overthrow of established Communist governments. His policy gave hope and support to people around the world in their struggle against Communism.

Crisis in Communist Poland

In 1978, Cardinal Karol Wojtyla was selected as the first Polish pope. He took the name Pope John Paul II. The election immediately brought new hope into Poland which had remained staunchly Catholic despite thirty-five years of Communism. There had always been great discontent with the Communist system and with the attempt to undermine the Faith of the country. In August of 1980, a strike broke out at the shipyards in Gdansk in northern Poland. The strikers were led by Lech Walesa (va len sa).

Lech Walesa

The strikers refused to work until their demands for more freedom were met. They especially wanted the freedom to set up their own union free of the Communists. As the strike progressed, the workers also demanded access to the media for the Church. They also wanted the government to promise that it would not seize private property.

The Polish government was forced to agree to these demands. In September 1980, the first independent labor union in the Communist world was created. The new union was called Solidarity.

It was not limited only to shipyard workers. It included workers from all over the country. The Poles joined this union in massive numbers. Within three months, Solidarity membership included one third of the entire population of Poland. In 1980, the new freedom created by Solidarity made it possible for the Mass to be broadcast in Poland. It was the first time since the Communists took over in the 1940s.

Solidarity quickly became a major political force in Poland. In December 1981, Solidarity called for a vote on whether Poland should remain a Communist country. This was too much for the Communists. In response, they declared martial law (military rule) and shut down Solidarity. They rounded up the members of Solidarity to be put in prison, tortured, and killed. The Soviet Union then claimed that the crisis in Poland threatened its security. Therefore, the Soviets began building up troops along the Polish border. There was

President Reagan meets with Pope John Paul II at the Vatican, Rome, June 7, 1982.

fear that they would invade Poland. However, two men stood in their way.

The first man was the newly elected president: Ronald Reagan. He expressed support for Solidarity. He warned the Soviets not to invade Poland. He blamed them and the Polish government for repressing Solidarity. The prospect of a united Western response led by Reagan discouraged the Soviets.

The second man was a simple Polish Catholic priest: Karol Wojtyla. Of course, the simple priest was now pope. He had lived under the Nazis and the Communists. During his pontificate, he would visit almost every nation on the planet. But his heart never left Poland. The Holy Father warned the Soviets that if they invaded, he would return to Poland and personally stand before the Soviet tanks!

In the face of Western opposition and the courage of the Holy Father, the Soviets backed down. They did not invade. However, they did push the Polish government to take steps against the union. The next year, Solidarity was declared illegal. Although weakened, Solidarity was not ended by this action. The movement went underground waiting for the day that it could again emerge. Reagan directed that money be provided to the organization to help it survive. Poland remained a source of concern to the Soviets.

The Invasion of Grenada

In addition to aid, Reagan was also willing to use the military against Communist regimes. In 1979, Communists had seized the small Caribbean island of Grenada. The regime quickly became friendly with Cuba and the Soviets. The Communists began the construction of a very large airport. It appeared that the Cubans and Soviets hoped to establish an air base on Grenada. The people of Grenada and the surrounding islands asked the United States for help. When an American medical school on the island became threatened, Reagan ordered marines to seize the island. The surprise attack was successful. The Cubans were ousted and a friendly government was established. Then the American forces withdrew.

Central America

When Reagan came into office, Soviet weapons were pouring into Nicaragua in Central America. From there, the weapons went to Communist rebels in El Salvador. Reagan asked Congress for aid for the government of El Salvador to resist these rebels. Despite some opposition to his plan, President Reagan was able to obtain the aid. He also sent a small number of military advisors to help train and plan the war effort.

In Nicaragua, a small group of freedom fighters had begun armed resistance to the Communist government. The Communists were called Sandinistas. In accord with the Reagan Doctrine, the United States began to recruit and arm the freedom fighters. They were called the Contras. At first, the goal was just to stop the flow of arms to El Salvador. However, the Contras made it clear that they planned to overthrow the Sandinistas. By 1985, the Contras were a strong force. They were able to inflict major damage on the Sandinistas.

The Election of 1984

When Reagan accepted the Republican nomination for president in 1984, he proclaimed that it was "morning again in America." The Democrats ran Walter Mondale. Mondale tried to use Reagan's age against him in the election. However, Reagan was one of the finest speakers ever to be president. During his second debate with Mondale, he said that he would not make age an issue in the campaign. He said, "I am not going to exploit, for political purposes, my opponent's youth and inexperience." Everyone laughed, including Mondale. Reagan won in a landslide. Only Minnesota, Mondale's home state, voted for him.

The Iran-Contra Affair

Throughout this period, President Reagan had trouble with the Democrats who controlled Congress. Congress repeatedly cut off aid to the Contras, then renewed aid later on. At one point, Congress passed the "Boland Amendment." This prohibited the president from using American funds to aid the Contras. Reagan believed that the Boland Amendment was unconstitutional since it restricted the president's power to act freely in foreign affairs. Reagan had a good case that the Boland Amendment was unconstitutional and had no force of law. However, he failed to make the case very strongly. Despite the restriction, Reagan wanted to aid the Contras.

Thus, foreign nations were approached and asked to give money to the Contras. Members of the president's staff developed the idea of secretly selling arms to Iran, which was at war with Iraq. Neither country was particularly friendly with the United States. However, the profits of the sale would be used to support the Contras. In 1986, this deal was discovered. This episode weakened his administration.

Spot Check

1. What was the "Reagan Doctrine"? How did it differ from the policies of previous presidents?
2. What was Solidarity?
3. Who was Lech Walesa?
4. Why did the U.S. invade Grenada?
5. Who were the "Contras"?
6. What was the Boland Amendment? Why did Reagan believe it was unconstitutional?

The Beginning of the End of the Cold War

A New Kind of Soviet leader

In 1985, Mikhail Gorbachev became the head of the Soviet Union. At first, he took the standard Communist approach to things. Massive reinforcements were sent into Afghanistan in an attempt to end the war quickly. It was the bloodiest year of the entire war. The Soviets very nearly destroyed the resistance. However, they failed. The war in Afghanistan had left the Soviet Union exhausted. It was clear that a change in policy was needed.

In 1986, Soviet President Gorbachev began a series of reforms in an attempt to strengthen the Soviet Union. His first reform was called "perestroika." This Russian word means "restructuring." Gorbachev hoped to rebuild the Soviet Union's economy and political system on a more democratic, free enterprise model. These reforms gave more economic freedom to its citizens. Gorbachev hoped that this would grow the Soviet economy.

With the increase in free enterprise came an atmosphere of more open discussion about political life. This "openness" was called "glasnost." More criticism of government inefficiency was allowed. This spirit spread to Eastern Europe. With the support of the Holy Father and the United States, Solidarity again rose to prominence in Poland. Other political parties in Eastern Europe began to emerge. In addition, Soviet troops were withdrawn from Afghanistan. This showed people that determined opposition could defeat the Soviet army.

The Iron Curtain is Lifted

Most of Eastern Europe had never truly embraced Communism. They were only held captive by fear of the Soviet army. By 1989, the Communists had begun to lose control of these Eastern European nations. These nations realized that their freedom movements would not be crushed by Soviet tanks.

Events began to move quickly. In June 1989, opponents of Communism gained control of Poland's government. Hungary declared its independence in October. In November, Czechoslovakia rose against the Communists.

The Fall of the Berlin Wall

Since its construction, the Berlin Wall had been a symbol of the Cold War and Communist oppression. On June 12, 1987, President Reagan had gone to West Berlin to speak in front of the Wall. He challenged Gorbachev to "tear down this Wall."

In September 1989, massive demonstrations began to take place all over East Germany. The people demanded political reform. Gorbachev informed the East German president that Soviet

A crane removes part of the Berlin Wall near the Brandenburg Gate as East Berliners watch.

troops could not and would not be used to crush dissent. The demonstrations continued. On November 4, 1989, half a million residents of East Berlin marched in the streets demanding freedom. In an effort to stop the protests, East Germany decided to allow free travel between East and West Germany. Finally it was announced that the Berlin Wall would be taken down. People joyfully began to smash the wall with sledge hammers. On October 3, 1990, East and West Germany were reunited.

Freedom in Eastern Europe

The collapse of the Berlin Wall caused elation all over the world, but mostly in Eastern Europe. The people there thought that if the Soviets would allow the Wall to fall in East Berlin, then they would not interfere in other nations. All through Eastern Europe, Communist governments collapsed and were replaced by anti-Communist ones. Even in Bulgaria, where there had been little public dissent, huge demonstrations caused the government to collapse.

In Romania, the Communist dictator Nicolae Ceausescu said that he would never relinquish power. Nevertheless, in December, mass demonstrations began in Romania. Ceausescu ordered the army to fire on the crowd. Thousands of people were killed or injured. Yet, in the next few days, people returned to the streets to continue the protest. In fact, the massacre encouraged demonstrations in other cities. It was clear that only the murder of the entire population could stop the determined Romanians. Finally, the army revolted against Ceausescu. The evil dictator was captured and executed on Christmas Day, 1989.

Between 1990 and 1991, the Baltic Republics of Latvia, Lithuania, and Estonia, which had been annexed by Stalin during World War II, declared their independence. These republics were part of the Soviet Union itself. Gorbachev imposed economic sanctions on them. He even threatened direct action if these small republics did not reverse their declarations. However, he did not use force. The way was open for other Soviet republics to follow suit. By 1991, every East European nation considered itself free of the Soviet Union.

The Collapse of the Soviet Union

On May 29, 1990, Boris Yeltsin, a reformer, was elected president of the Russian Republic by its Parliament. In July, he left the Communist Party. Less than a year later, in June 1991, the Russian Republic declared that it was an independent state. For all practical purposes, the Soviet Union had ceased to exist. Gorbachev tried to save what was left of Communism. However, he had little success.

The Failed Coup of 1991

In August 1991, a group of Communists in the army and secret police tried to seize control of the Soviet Union and restore Communism to its former strength. Gorbachev was taken prisoner. A state of emergency was declared. Although there were confrontations in other cities, the most important events occurred in Moscow. As long as the Russian Republic maintained its independence, there could be no Soviet Union. The Communists surrounded the Russian parliament building with tanks. Boris Yeltsin, hearing of the attempted coup, went to the Parliament building. He climbed onto a tank and addressed the assembled mob. He declared that he would fight to the end. The standoff lasted for some days. However, the Communists found little support and were forced to back down.

Boris Yeltsin

The End of the Soviet Union

In December 1991, eleven of the former Soviet Republics banded together to form the Commonwealth of Independent States (CIS). On Christmas Day, Gorbachev resigned as Soviet President. The Russian government took over. The Soviet Union ceased to exist as a nation.

There are two great Faiths in our world: Faith in God and Faith in Man. Communism is the "religion" of the latter. Catholicism is the religion of the former. Only one will stand the test of time. Only one is eternal. Only one was founded by God Himself. The Soviet Union had been started in 1917. It had not lasted even to the end of the century. That Gorbachev should resign on Christmas Day is notable. The day Our Lord was born was the day the Soviet Union died. This is the difference in the two Faiths. One is about life everlasting. One is about death.

Reagan's Achievement

When Reagan came to office in 1981, Communism had just won several major victories. In fact, it was stronger than it had ever been. Yet, Reagan challenged the Soviet Union on every front: political, economic, military, and rhetorical. The Soviet Union simply was unable to compete. By the late 1980s, the Soviets were being pushed to their limit. Engaged in costly wars around the globe and in an arms race with the United States, the Soviets were pushed beyond their capacity. Reagan had been right that America would win the race. In the United States, the economy was stronger than it had ever been. It was clear that America was able to afford to continue the Cold War for the foreseeable future. When Reagan left office in 1989, the days of the Soviet Union were already numbered. The defeat of the Soviet empire ranks as one of the greatest achievements of all time. Ronald Reagan deserves a good deal of credit for it.

Pope John Paul II and Mikhail Gorbachev also played important roles in the fall of Communism. Pope John Paul II bravely backed up Solidarity and the people of Poland. His travels as pope to Poland encouraged and strengthened the Poles in their fight for freedom. Mikhail Gorbachev had the vision to see the military failure in Afghanistan. He saw also the inner decay of the Soviet system. Thus, when dissent did occur in Poland and in East Germany, Gorbachev did not authorize the use of the Soviet army to suppress it.

Spot Check

1. Who was Mikhail Gorbachev?
2. What do the words "perestroika" and "glasnost" mean?
3. How was the collapse of the Berlin Wall instrumental in the collapse of the Soviet Union?
4. Who was Boris Yeltsin?
5. Who should receive a great deal of credit for the collapse of the Soviet Union and why?

CHAPTER REVIEW

1. After he was elected, what four tasks did Reagan say were his "popular mandate"?
2. How did Reagan become one of the nation's leading Conservatives?
3. Why was President Jimmy Carter a weak candidate against Ronald Reagan?
4. What was Reagan's economic plan? How did it work?
5. What was the "Reagan Doctrine"?
6. Why did Reagan build up the American military?
7. What was Solidarity?
8. Why didn't the Soviet Union invade Poland and crush Solidarity?
9. Why did the U.S. invade Grenada?
10. What was the "Iran-Contra Scandal"?
11. Who was Mikhail Gorbachev?
12. What was "perestroika"?
13. What was "glasnost"?
14. Describe the events in Eastern Europe from September to December 1989.
15. By what year did every East European nation consider itself free of the Soviet Union?
16. Who was Boris Yeltsin?
17. What three men played the most important roles in the fall of Communism?

AMERICA ENTERS THE NEW MILLENNIUM

Statue of Liberty Unveiled (October 28, 1886), by Edward Moran

PRESIDENT GEORGE HERBERT WALKER BUSH

The Election of 1988

The presidential election of 1988 pitted Republican George Herbert Walker (H.W.) Bush against Democrat Michael Dukakis. Bush ran as the natural successor to Ronald Reagan. Many people wished that Reagan could run for a third term, so they saw Bush as the closest they could get. At the 1988 Republican National Convention, Bush delivered what was known as the "thousand points of light" speech. In the speech, he described his vision of America. He supported prayer in schools, capital punishment, and gun rights. He also said he opposed abortion. In a famous phrase, he promised no tax increases when he said "Read my lips, no new taxes." On election night, Bush received 53.4% of the votes to Dukakis' 45.6%. Bush became the forty-first president.

Bush's Economic Policy

After struggling with Congress, Bush was forced by the Democrats, who were in the majority, to raise taxes. As a result, many Republicans felt betrayed. They recalled Bush's campaign promise of "no new taxes." Bush accepted the Democrats' demands for higher taxes and more spending. This put him on bad terms with other Republicans. As a result, his popularity sharply decreased. His agreement with the Democrats in Congress proved to be a turning point in his presidency. His popularity among Republican voters never fully returned.

The Invasion of Panama

In the early 1980s, Manuel Noriega, a Panamanian general, became the dictator of Panama. In the beginning, he supported American efforts against the Communists in Nicaragua. However, before long, he began to deal in drugs. He also became friendly with Cuba. Over time, his regime became more oppressive. He beat and murdered those who opposed him. At that time, President Reagan had tried to remove him from power. Reagan imposed economic sanctions on Panama. Reagan also sent more than two thousand U.S. troops to Panama. Sadly, Noriega was too powerful for the sanctions to work.

In May 1989, Panama held elections. The results showed that Guillermo Endara, who had the support of the Church, was elected president. However, Noriega voided the results. The bishop of Panama and others denounced Noriega for stealing the election. Bush responded by imposing more sanctions. He also sent more troops to the country to prepare the way for an upcoming invasion.

President George H. W. Bush

In October, Noriega put down an attempt by some in his own military to remove him. He also put down massive popular protests in Panama against him. The breaking point came in December when Panamanian forces shot an American soldier. Bush ordered an invasion of the country. His goal was to remove Noriega from power. U.S. forces took control of Panama and Endara assumed the presidency. Noriega was convicted and put in prison in April 1992 for drug dealing and other major crimes.

The Persian Gulf War

On August 2, 1990, Iraqi forces, commanded by Saddam Hussein, invaded Kuwait, its oil-rich neighbor to the south.

Bush immediately condemned the invasion and began gathering opposition to Iraq in the U.S. and among our allies. Saudi Arabia requested U.S. military aid in the matter as they feared Hussein might invade them as well. The U.S. sent fighter jets to aid the Saudis. Iraq then made attempts to negotiate a deal with the U.S. that would allow Iraq to take control of half of Kuwait. Bush rejected this proposal. He insisted on a total withdrawal of all Iraqi forces from Kuwait.

Military plans to free Kuwait were made in August 1990. The forces going into Kuwait would be mostly Americans with some allied troops. The army would be led by General Norman Schwarzkopf. Bush spoke before a joint session of the U.S. Congress asking for authority to launch the attack. The attack into Kuwait would have four goals. First, Iraq must withdraw from Kuwait. Second, Kuwait's legitimate government must be restored. Third, security and stability of the Persian Gulf must be assured. Lastly, American citizens abroad must be protected. Congress authorized the use of military force against Iraq.

Early on the morning of January 17, 1991, allied forces began the attack on Iraq with massive bombing runs. This incredible bombing campaign continued for the next four weeks. On February 24, the ground invasion began. Allied forces sliced through Iraqi lines and pushed toward Kuwait City, the capital. Meanwhile, on the west side of Kuwait, forces intercepted the retreating Iraqi army. Bush stopped the ground offensive after only one hundred hours. Kuwait was free.

The decision to stop the attack so soon was controversial. Some said Bush acted too quickly. They pointed out that hundreds of Iraqi solders had escaped. Bush said that he wanted to minimize U.S. casualties. Others said that Bush should have pushed Hussein's army back into Baghdad and removed Hussein from power. Bush explained that he did not overthrow the Iraqi government because the cost would have been too high in terms of American losses.

The 1992 Presidential Campaign

In early 1992, George H.W. Bush said that he would seek re-election. The victory in the Persian Gulf War and his high approval ratings at first made his re-election seem likely. However, the economy began to worsen. Questions were raised as to whether he ended the Gulf War properly. These factors slowly reduced his popularity. Then, conservative political columnist Pat Buchanan challenged Bush for the Republican nomination. When Buchanan did better than expected in the primaries, Bush had to adopt more conservative positions on issues to try to win Buchanan's supporters.

Once he had won the Republican nomination, Bush faced Democrat William (Bill) Clinton in the general election. Clinton attacked Bush for not doing enough to assist the working middle-class. Clinton also said Bush was "out of touch" with the common man.

In early 1992, the presidential race took an unexpected twist. Texas billionaire H. Ross Perot entered the race as a third party candidate. Perot claimed that neither Bush nor Clinton could make government more efficient or pay down its debt. His message appealed to many voters who were angry at the way the two major parties seemed to tax and spend money without care or thought. Perot bowed out of the race for a while, but reentered it.

Clinton won the election. He defeated Bush 43% to 38% in the popular vote. Perot received 19% of the popular vote. This was one of the highest totals for a third party candidate in U.S. history.

Spot Check

1. Who ran against George H.W. Bush for president in 1988?
2. Who was Manuel Noriega? Why did Bush remove him from power?
3. Who was Saddam Hussein?
4. Who was Norman Schwarzkopf?
5. Why did the U.S. invade Iraq?
6. Who ran for president in 1992?

President William Jefferson "Bill" Clinton

The election of William Jefferson "Bill" Clinton ended twelve years of Republican control of the White House. The Democrats also gained full control of the United States Congress. It was the first time this had occurred since Jimmy Carter had been president.

National Health Care

One of the biggest efforts of Clinton's presidency was to enact national health care (socialized medicine). Conservatives warned that the average person would pay higher taxes and receive poorer care. This is what has happened in the nations that have socialized medicine. Congress debated the plan and finally defeated it.

NAFTA

In 1993, Clinton encouraged the Senate to ratify the North American Free Trade Agreement (NAFTA). NAFTA actually had its birth in 1988. The United States and Canada saw how successful European nations worked together without tariffs. Desiring the same benefits, Canada and the U.S. made a free-trade agreement in 1988. NAFTA grew out of this union when Mexico was included in the deal. All three countries ratified the treaty in 1993. It went into effect on January 1, 1994.

The goal of NAFTA was to eliminate trade restrictions between the three nations. However, it was and remains controversial. Opponents argued that NAFTA would cause the loss of American jobs. Supporters claimed it would create jobs. It seems that both sides were correct. Employment during the first five years of NAFTA increased. However, there were a number of losses in high paying manufacturing jobs.

The Battle of Mogadishu

The Battle of Mogadishu occurred in Somalia (Africa) in 1993. The battle began when two U.S. helicopters were shot down by the Somalis. American soldiers were trapped behind enemy lines. A rescue mission was mounted to get them. In the fight that followed, eighteen American soldiers died, seventy-three others were wounded, and one was taken prisoner. The U.S. inflicted heavy losses on the Somalis. The disgraceful Somalis dragged the dead bodies of the brave American soldiers through the streets. They broadcasted this vile act on television news programs. As a result of the battle, U.S. forces were withdrawn from Somalia. Somalia remains a rogue nation and a haven for pirates.

The Election of 1996

In 1996, Clinton was re-elected president. He received 49.2% of the popular vote. His Republican challenger, Bob Dole, received 40.7%. Ross Perot received 8.4%. This made Clinton the first Democrat since Franklin Roosevelt to win the presidential re-election.

The Impeachment of Bill Clinton

Clinton's years in office were rocked by numerous scandals and controversies. One scandal was so serious that it led to Clinton's impeachment. A woman named Paula Jones sued President Clinton for alleged misconduct that occurred when he was governor of Arkansas. During testimony for the Jones lawsuit, Clinton denied his bad behavior. This denial became the basis for the impeachment charge of perjury.

In 1998, the House of Representatives voted to impeach Clinton. The House said that Clinton had lied in his sworn testimony in the Paula Jones lawsuit. This made Clinton only the second U.S. president to be impeached, after Andrew Johnson. The House also said that Clinton had obstructed justice by making it difficult for the House to determine whether or not he had committed perjury. Thus, the president was impeached for perjury and obstruction of justice.

President Bill Clinton

Clinton was then tried before the Senate. The Senate held a lengthy trial. On February 12, 1999, the Senate later voted to acquit Clinton on both charges. The final vote was generally along party lines. No Democrats voted guilty. Some Republicans voted not guilty for both charges.

The Growth of Terrorism

During the Clinton presidency, there was an increase in the number of terrorist attacks on the United States. We were attacked both at home and abroad. In 1993, the World Trade Center in New York City was bombed. American embassies in Kenya and Tanzania in Africa were attacked in 1998. The USS *Cole* was attacked in Yemen in 2000. However, the greatest attack in America's history would occur during the presidency of George W. Bush. It would be the defining moment of his presidency.

Spot Check

1. Why was Clinton's health care plan defeated?
2. What is NAFTA?
3. What was the Battle of Mogadishu?
4. What were the two charges against Bill Clinton at his impeachment trial?

PRESIDENT GEORGE WALKER BUSH

The Presidential Election of 2000

The presidential election of 2000 was between George Walker (G.W.) Bush and Al Gore. Republican Bush was the two-time governor of Texas and the son of the forty-first president. During the campaign, Bush portrayed himself as a "compassionate conservative." He said that he would increase the size of the United States armed forces, cut taxes, and improve education.

Bush's opponent in the election was incumbent Vice President Al Gore. Before becoming vice president, Gore had been a senator from Tennessee. Bush campaigned across the country pointing to his accomplishments as two-term Governor of Texas. He said that Gore would raise taxes.

When the votes were counted on November 7, Bush won thirty states, including Florida. However, the vote in Florida was so close that there needed to be a recount. The first two recounts (and all later recounts) went to Bush. However, Gore tied up the outcome in the courts for a month. The case finally went to the U.S. Supreme Court. On December 12, the U.S. Supreme Court ordered all the recounting to stop because it was unconstitutional. The count showed that Bush had won the Florida vote by a margin of 537 votes out of six million cast. Bush received 271 electoral votes to Gore's 266. However, he lost the popular vote by about five hundred thousand votes. It was not the first time a president had been elected after losing the popular vote. On January 20,

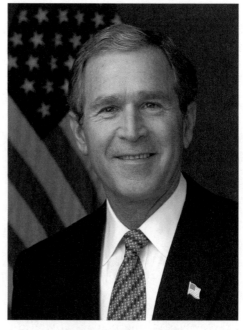

President George W. Bush

2001, George W. Bush was sworn in as our forty-third president.

THE WAR ON TERROR

The 9/11 Attacks on America

On September 11, 2001, the United States was attacked by terrorists in New York City. It was the largest foreign attack on American soil since Pearl Harbor. The man behind the attack was an Islamic militant named Osama bin Laden. His terrorist organization is called Al-Qaeda. The events of 9/11 marked an escalation of terror attacks around the world. It made most Americans realize that we were in a global war on terror.

The 9/11 attacks began when four airplanes were hijacked by nineteen Islamic terrorists. These terrorists targeted key cities in America. Two of the planes were sent to destroy the World Trade Center's Twin Towers in New York City. (The World Trade Center had been attacked before in 1993.) Just before 9 o'clock on the morning of September 11, when most of the people had arrived for work, the first jumbo jet crashed into the North Tower. Fifteen minutes later, a second plane crashed into the South Tower. Emergency crews rushed to the scene. The people in the towers tried to escape. By 10:30 A.M., both towers had collapsed. Over 3,000 people died in the attack including 400 brave police and firemen who ran into the burning buildings.

Meanwhile, in Washington D.C., a third plane was flown into the Pentagon. The Pentagon is the national headquarters for our military. 184 people died in the attack.

On board the fourth plane, *United Flight 93*, an act of bravery was taking place that would have warmed the heart of the greatest of the Spanish men and women who fought for 770 years to rid Spain of the Muslims. On that flight, terrorists had taken control of the plane. They were planning to fly it to Washington D.C. as well and crash it into the White House or the Capitol. The hijackers had murdered the pilots. The only ones on the plane who could fly it were the terrorists. The passengers got on their cell phones and called their loved ones. Tearfully they said good-bye. They asked their loved ones to pray for them. They asked for prayers for what they were about to do.

The passengers had no weapons. The terrorists had managed to sneak box cutters on the plane. The passengers made weapons from what was available. They boiled water. With pots of boiling water, they stormed the cockpit. They threw the boiling water into the faces of the terrorists. They killed the terrorists and took control of the plane. However, they could not fly it.

As a result, the plane crashed in a remote field in Pennsylvania. Everyone on board was killed, but these brave men and women had saved the lives of perhaps hundreds or thousands of others. Today there is a monument in that remote field honoring the sacrifice of these heroic men and women.

Monument Honoring the Heroes of *United Flight 93*

The 9/11 attacks were the turning point in George Bush's presidency. That evening, he addressed the nation from the Oval Office. He promised a strong response to the attacks. He emphasized the need for the nation to come together and comfort the families of the victims. On September 14, Bush visited Ground Zero (the site of the attack). He met with New York City Mayor Rudy Giuliani and firefighters, policemen, and volunteers. While standing on a heap of rubble, Bush addressed the shouting crowd: "I can hear you. The rest of the world hears you. And the people who knocked these buildings down will hear all of us soon."

In a speech on September 20, Bush condemned Osama bin Laden and Al-Qaeda. He issued an ultimatum to the Taliban regime in Afghanistan. The Taliban was Afghanistan's strict Islamic government. Evidence convinced American leaders that Al-Qaeda, which was based in Afghanistan, was behind the 9/11 attacks. Bin Laden was believed to be hiding in Afghanistan. He told the Taliban to "hand over the terrorists, or...share in their fate."

THE WAR ON TERROR BEGINS

Afghanistan

The Taliban regime did not hand over Osama bin Laden. So in October 2001, the U.S. and allied forces began a bombing campaign against suspected terrorist bases in Afghanistan. Bush later ordered the invasion of Afghanistan. The invasion had three goals. First, defeat the Taliban. Second, drive Al-Qaeda out of Afghanistan. Third, capture key Al-Qaeda leaders. In December, the Pentagon reported that the Taliban had been defeated. However, the military cautioned that the war would continue in order to weaken Al-Qaeda.

Despite the initial success in driving the Taliban from power, by early 2003, the Taliban was reorganizing. Over the next three years, the Taliban grew larger, stronger, and more organized. As a result, in March 2007, President Bush sent 3,500 more troops to Afghanistan. As of 2010, the war in Afghanistan is still going on.

Despite its best efforts, the military was unable to kill or capture Osama bin Laden. In December 2001, the military thought he was hiding in a cave in the mountains of Tora Bora. Troops attacked the location. However, he apparently had escaped from his hiding place.

"The Bush Doctrine"

In his 2002 State of the Union address, Bush asserted that an "axis of evil" consisting of North Korea, Iran, and Iraq was threatening world peace. He said that these nations posed a grave and growing danger. He also said that America had the right to, and would, engage in preemptive strikes in response to apparent threats. This idea became known as the Bush Doctrine.

Iraq War

Starting with his 2002 State of the Union address, George Bush began publicly focusing on Iraq. Saddam Hussein had failed to comply fully with the UN restrictions that had been placed in his country following the Persian Gulf War. Part of the cease-fire agreement was that he destroy all of his **weapons of mass destruction** (WMDs). UN inspectors found WMD's and the means to create more. Hussein closed his nation to more UN weapons inspectors.

After the 9/11 attacks, Bush came to believe that Saddam Hussein was not complying with the UN requirements that had been placed on Iraq. Intelligence reports indicated that Hussein intended to re-start Iraq's nuclear weapons programs. The reports also showed that he was not getting rid of his WMDs. Hussein could not account for all of Iraq's biological and chemical weapons. Finally, Bush believed that he was supporting the Al-Qaeda terror network.

On March 17, 2003, Bush gave Hussein an ultimatum. Hussein must leave Iraq within forty-eight hours. If he did not, then the United States would force him from power. When Hussein refused to leave, the United States, Great Britain, and several other nations invaded Iraq. President Bush explained that his reasons for invading Iraq were to "disarm Iraq, to free its people, and defend the world from grave danger."

Many disagreed on whether the United States had enough evidence to invade Iraq. The argument was based on the claim that that Hussein had dangerous stockpiles of WMDs. However, it was clear that Hussein was in direct violation of the terms of the cease-fire of the first Gulf War. Moreover, he had used WMDs in the past. He had used poison gas against the Kurds (a minority group in Iraq). He was guilty of committing genocide in his attempt to wipe out the Kurds. If Hussein did not at that time have dangerous stocks of WMDs, it was because he had used them.

The invasion of Iraq began on March 20, 2003. Despite having one of the largest armies in the world, the Iraqi military was quickly defeated. The capital, Baghdad, fell on April 9, 2003. On May 1, Bush declared the end of "major combat operations" in Iraq. The initial success of the war increased his popularity. However, the U.S. and allied forces faced a growing insurgency led by various religious sects. His "Mission Accomplished" speech was later criticized as premature.

Even with the end of Saddam Hussein's reign, the war in Iraq did not end. Allied forces continued to face Iraqi rebels. These rebels were mostly Hussein supporters, radical Muslims, and other Islamic fighters from around the world. On December 13, 2003, Hussein was captured. He was tried and convicted of crimes against humanity. On December 30, 2006, he was hanged.

From 2004 through 2007, the situation in Iraq became worse. On January 10, 2007, President Bush spoke to the nation about Iraq. He announced a surge of 21,500 more troops for Iraq. Despite many forecasts of failure, the surge eventually worked.

On May 1, 2007, Bush used his veto for only the second time. He vetoed a bill that set a deadline for the withdrawal of U.S. troops from Iraq.

Meanwhile, attempts were made to set up a democratic form of government in Iraq. In January 2005, free elections were held in Iraq for the first time in 50 years. Bush praised the election, saying that the Iraqis had "taken rightful control of their country's destiny." In October 2005, the Iraqis approved a constitution. A second national election for Parliament was held in March 2010. In both elections, Iraqis voted despite the threat of rebel violence. Sadly, in both elections some Iraqis were murdered.

The Election of 2004

In 2004, George Bush had broad support in the Republican Party. He promised that if he were re-elected, he would continue the wars in Iraq and Afghanistan. He also spoke of his support for the pro-life movement and the family. His opponent was Democratic senator John Kerry. Kerry was like John Kennedy in many ways. Kerry had fought in the Vietnam War. Like Kennedy, Kerry was a Catholic. Also like Kennedy, he did not want his Catholicism to get in the way of his politics. Unlike the pro-life Bush, Kerry was pro-abortion.

During the election campaign, Kerry and other Democrats attacked Bush on the Iraq War. They also said that he had failed to fuel the economy and create jobs. Bush portrayed Kerry as a life long liberal who would raise taxes and increase the size of government. The Bush campaign constantly criticized Kerry's position on the war in Iraq. Bush said that Kerry lacked the resolve and vision necessary for success in the war on terrorism. On election night, Bush won 31 of 50 states. He won a majority of the popular vote: 50.7% to Kerry's 48.3%.

Hurricane Katrina

Hurricane Katrina was one of the worst natural disasters in U.S. history. It was the costliest and one of the five deadliest hurricanes in American history. Over 1,800 people died in the storm and the floods that followed. It hit early in Bush's second term. It devastated much of the north-central Gulf Coast of the United States. Particularly hard hit was the city of New Orleans.

Hurricane Katrina formed over the Bahamas on August 23, 2005. It crossed southern Florida where it caused some damage. However, in the Gulf of Mexico, it gained strength. In anticipation of Katrina making landfall, Bush declared a state of emergency in Louisiana on August 27. The next day, he included Mississippi and Alabama. On August 29, Katrina made landfall. The storm was terrifically strong. New Orleans, which is located below sea level, began to flood due to breaches in the levees (dikes). Later that day, Bush declared that a major disaster existed in Louisiana. He

Houses in New Orleans were flooded by Hurricane Katrina.

authorized the use of federal funds to assist in the recovery effort. On September 2, National Guard troops entered New Orleans to keep order and assist with the rescue operations. The same day, Bush toured parts of Louisiana, Mississippi, and Alabama. Seeing the devastation, he declared that the success of the recovery effort up to that point was "not enough."

As the disaster in New Orleans became worse, critics blamed the president for what they saw as a poor response. Bush was attacked for having appointed apparently incompetent people to positions of authority. They also said that the federal response was limited because of the Iraq War. His critics accused the president of not acting fast enough when he received the warnings of the floods. Bush responded to the criticism by accepting full responsibility for the government's failures in handling the emergency, even though he was not fully to blame.

Stem Cell Research

Throughout his political career, George W. Bush has been pro-life. During his term in office, he worked to support pro-life and pro-family causes. In fact, his first veto as president was in defense of human life.

In 1995, Congress passed the Dickey Amendment. The law prohibited federal funds to be used for medical research that involves the creation or destruction of human embryos. Bush said that he supported adult stem cell research. Stem cells are cells whose future type has not yet been determined. When injected into human or animal bodies, they have the ability to revive damaged organs. Bush supported federal laws that would finance adult stem cell research. Research into adult stem cells has met with successful results. However, Bush did not support embryonic stem cell research.

On July 19, 2006, Bush vetoed the Stem Cell Research Enhancement Act. The bill would have repealed the Dickey Amendment. It would have permitted federal money to be used for research where stem cells are derived from the destruction of a human embryo.

The Presidential Election of 2008

The election of 2008 pitted Republican John McCain against Democrat Barack Obama. During the last months of George Bush's term in office, the economy had declined severely. Bush was blamed specifically for the decline, and the Republicans were blamed in general. As a result, Obama was elected with 53 percent of the popular vote. He is the first African American to be elected president. He is the forty-forth president of the United States.

President Barack Obama

Spot Check

1. Who ran for president in 2000?
2. How many planes were involved in the 9/11 attacks?
3. Who led the 9/11 attacks?
4. What is the Bush Doctrine?
5. What three reasons did Bush give for invading Iraq?
6. Who won the election of 2004?
7. Briefly describe Hurricane Katrina.
8. Why did Bush veto the Stem Cell Research Enhancement Act?

America's Five Living Presidents as of 2009

CHAPTER REVIEW

1. Who won the election of 1988?
2. What incident caused George W. Bush to invade Panama? What was his goal in invading?
3. What were the goals of the first Persian Gulf War?
4. Who led the American military forces during the first Gulf War?
5. Who were the three candidates in the 1992 presidential election?
6. What is NAFTA?
7. How did the Battle of Mogadishu start?
8. Who won the 1996 presidential election?
9. Why was Bill Clinton impeached?
10. Describe what happened to the four planes used in the 9/11 attacks.
11. Why did the U.S. attack in Afghanistan in 2001?
12. Why did the U.S. attack Iraq in 2003?
13. What is the "axis of evil"?
14. Who did Saddam Hussein use WMDs against?
15. Who ran against George Bush in the 2004 election? What was his religion?
16. What city was most devastated by Hurricane Katrina? Why?
17. What is stem cell research?
18. Why did George Bush veto the Stem Cell Research Enhancement Act? How many bills had he vetoed before this?
19. Who won the election of 2008?

DECLARATION OF INDEPENDENCE

A Declaration by the Representatives of the United States of America, in Congress Assembled July 4, 1776

When, in the course of human events, it becomes necessary for one people to dissolve the political bands which have connected them with another, and to assume among the powers of the earth, the separate and equal station to which the laws of nature and of nature's God entitle them, a decent respect to the opinions of mankind requires that they should declare the causes which impel them to the separation.

We hold these truths to be self-evident, that all men are created equal, that they are endowed by their Creator with certain unalienable rights, that among these are life, liberty and the pursuit of happiness. That to secure these rights, governments are instituted among men, deriving their just powers from the consent of the governed. That whenever any form of government becomes destructive to these ends, it is the right of the people to alter or to abolish it, and to institute new government, laying its foundation on such principles and organizing its powers in such form, as to them shall seem most likely to effect their safety and happiness. Prudence, indeed, will dictate that governments long established should not be changed for light and transient causes; and accordingly all experience hath shown that mankind are more disposed to suffer, while evils are sufferable, than to right themselves by abolishing the forms to which they are accustomed. But when a long train of abuses and usurpations, pursuing invariably the same object evinces a design to reduce them under absolute despotism, it is their right, it is their duty, to throw off such government, and to provide new guards for their future security. --Such has been the patient sufferance of these colonies; and such is now the necessity which constrains them to alter their former systems of government. The history of the present King of Great Britain is a history of repeated injuries and usurpations, all having in direct object the establishment of an absolute tyranny over these states. To prove this, let facts be submitted to a candid world.

He has refused his assent to laws, the most wholesome and necessary for the public good.

He has forbidden his governors to pass laws of immediate and pressing importance, unless suspended in their operation till his assent should be obtained; and when so suspended, he has utterly neglected to attend to them.

He has refused to pass other laws for the accommodation of large districts of people, unless those people would relinquish the right of representation in the legislature, a right inestimable to them and formidable to tyrants only.

He has called together legislative bodies at places unusual, uncomfortable, and distant from the depository of their public records, for the sole purpose of fatiguing them into compliance with his measures.

He has dissolved representative houses repeatedly, for opposing with manly firmness his invasions on the rights of the people.

He has refused for a long time, after such dissolutions, to cause others to be elected; whereby the legislative powers, incapable of annihilation, have returned to the people at large for their exercise; the state remaining in the meantime exposed to all the dangers of invasion from without, and convulsions within.

He has endeavored to prevent the population of these states; for that purpose obstructing the laws for naturalization of foreigners; refusing to pass others to encourage their migration hither, and raising the conditions of new appropriations of lands.

He has obstructed the administration of justice, by refusing his assent to laws for establishing judiciary powers.

He has made judges dependent on his will alone, for the tenure of their offices, and the amount and payment of their salaries.

He has erected a multitude of new offices, and sent hither swarms of officers to harass our people, and eat out their substance.

He has kept among us, in times of peace, standing armies without the consent of our legislature.

He has affected to render the military independent of and superior to civil power.

He has combined with others to subject us to a jurisdiction foreign to our constitution, and unacknowledged by our laws; giving his assent to their acts of pretended legislation:

For quartering large bodies of armed troops among us:

For protecting them, by mock trial, from punishment for any murders which they should commit on the inhabitants of these states:

For cutting off our trade with all parts of the world:

For imposing taxes on us without our consent:

For depriving us in many cases, of the benefits of trial by jury:

For transporting us beyond seas to be tried for pretended offenses:

For abolishing the free system of English laws in a neighboring province, establishing therein an arbitrary government, and enlarging its boundaries so as to render it at once an example and fit instrument for introducing the same absolute rule in these colonies:

For taking away our charters, abolishing our most valuable laws, and altering fundamentally the forms of our governments:

For suspending our own legislatures, and declaring themselves invested with power to legislate for us in all cases whatsoever.

He has abdicated government here, by declaring us out of his protection and waging war against us.

He has plundered our seas, ravaged our coasts, burned our towns, and destroyed the lives of our people.

He is at this time transporting large armies of foreign mercenaries to complete the works of death, desolation and tyranny, already begun with circumstances of cruelty and perfidy scarcely paralleled in the most barbarous ages, and totally unworthy the head of a civilized nation.

He has constrained our fellow citizens taken captive on the high seas to bear arms against their country, to become the executioners of their friends and brethren, or to fall themselves by their hands.

He has excited domestic insurrections amongst us, and has endeavored to bring on the inhabitants of our frontiers, the merciless Indian savages, whose known rule of warfare, is undistinguished destruction of all ages, sexes and conditions.

In every stage of these oppressions we have petitioned for redress in the most humble terms: our repeated petitions have been answered only by repeated injury. A prince, whose character is thus marked by every act which may define a tyrant, is unfit to be the ruler of a free people.

Nor have we been wanting in attention to our British brethren. We have warned them from time to time of attempts by their legislature to extend an unwarrantable jurisdiction over us. We have reminded them of the circumstances of our emigration and settlement here. We have appealed to their native justice and magnanimity, and we have conjured them by the ties of our common kindred to disavow these usurpations, which, would inevitably interrupt our connections and correspondence. They too have been deaf to the voice of justice and of consanguinity. We must, therefore, acquiesce in the necessity, which denounces our separation, and hold them, as we hold the rest of mankind, enemies in war, in peace friends.

We, therefore, the representatives of the United States of America, in General Congress, assembled, appealing to the Supreme Judge of the world for the rectitude of our intentions, do, in the name, and by the authority of the good people of these colonies, solemnly publish and declare, that these united colonies are, and of right ought to be free and independent states; that they are absolved from all allegiance to the British Crown, and that all political connection between them and the state of Great Britain, is and ought to be totally dissolved; and that as free and independent states, they have full power to levy war, conclude peace, contract alliances, establish commerce, and to do all other acts and things which independent states may of right do. And for the support of this declaration, with a firm reliance on the protection of Divine Providence, we mutually pledge to each other our lives, our fortunes and our sacred honor.

THE UNITED STATES CONSTITUTION

Preamble

We, the people of the United States, in order to form a more perfect Union, establish justice, insure domestic tranquility, provide for the common defense, promote the general welfare, and secure the blessings of liberty to ourselves and our posterity, do ordain and establish this Constitution for the United States of America.

Article I

Sec. I. All legislative powers herein granted shall be vested in a Congress of the United States, which shall consist of a Senate and House of Representatives.

Sec II. 1. The House of Representatives shall be composed of members chosen every second year by the people of the several States, and the elector in each State shall have the qualifications requisite for electors of the most numerous branch of the State Legislature.

2. No person shall be a Representative who shall not have attained the age of twenty-five years, and been seven years a citizen of the United States, and who shall not, when elected, be an inhabitant of that State in which he shall be chosen.

3. Representatives and direct taxes shall be apportioned among the several States which may be included within this Union, according to their respective numbers, which shall be determined by adding the whole number of free persons, including those bound to service for a term of years, and excluding Indians not taxed, three-fifths of all other persons. The actual enumeration shall be made within three years after the first meeting of the Congress of the United States, and within every subsequent term of ten years, in such manner as they shall by law direct. The number of Representatives shall not exceed one for every thirty thousand, but each State shall have at least one Representative; and until such enumeration shall be made, the State of New Hampshire shall be entitled to choose three, Massachusetts eight, Rhode Island and Providence Plantations one, Connecticut five, New York six, New Jersey four, Pennsylvania eight, Delaware one, Maryland six, Virginia ten, North Carolina five, South Carolina five, and Georgia three.

4. When vacancies happen in the representation from any State, the Executive Authority thereof shall issue writs of election to fill such vacancies.

5. The House of Representatives shall choose their Speaker and other officers; and shall have the sole power of impeachment.

Sec. III. 1. The Senate of the United States shall be composed of two Senators from each State, chosen by the Legislature thereof, for six years; and each Senator shall have one vote.

2. Immediately after they shall be assembled in consequence of the first election, they shall be divided as equally as may be into three classes. The seats of the Senators of the first class

shall be vacated at the expiration of the second year, of the second class at the expiration of the fourth year, and of the third class at the expiration of the sixth year, so that one-third may be chosen every second year; and if vacancies happen by resignation, or otherwise, during the recess of the Legislature of any State, the Executive thereof may make temporary appointments until the next meeting of the Legislature, which shall then fill such vacancies.

3. No person shall be a Senator who shall not have attained to the age of thirty years, and been nine years a citizen of the United States, and who shall not, when elected, be an inhabitant of that State for which he shall be chosen.

4. The Vice-President of the United States shall be President of the Senate, but shall have no vote, unless they be equally divided.

5. The Senate shall choose their other officers, and also a President pro tempore, in the absence of the Vice President, or when he shall exercise the office of the President of the United States.

6. The Senate shall have the sole power to try all impeachments. When sitting for that purpose, they shall be on oath or affirmation. When the President of the United States is tried, the Chief Justice shall preside: and no person shall be convicted without the concurrence of two-thirds of the members present.

7. Judgement in cases of impeachment shall not extend further than to removal from office, and disqualification to hold and enjoy any office of honor, trust, or profit under the United States: but the party convicted shall nevertheless be liable and subject to indictment, trial, judgement and punishment, according to law.

Sec. IV. 1. The times, places and manner of holding elections for Senators and Representatives, shall be prescribed in each State by the Legislature thereof; but the Congress may at any time by law make or alter such regulations, except as to the places of choosing Senators.

2. The Congress shall assemble at least once in every year, and such meeting shall be on the first Monday in December, unless they by law appoint a different day.

Sec. V. 1. Each House shall be the judge of the elections, returns and qualifications of its own members, and a majority of each shall constitute a quorum to do business; but a smaller number may adjourn from day to day, and may be authorized to compel the attendance of absent members, in such manner, and under such penalties as each House may provide.

2. Each House may determine the rules of its proceedings, punish its members for disorderly behavior, and, with the concurrence of two-thirds, expel a member.

3. Each House shall keep a journal of its proceedings, and from time to time publish the same, excepting such parts as may in their judgement require secrecy; and the yeas and nays of the members of either House on any question shall, at the desire of one-fifth of those present, be entered on the journal.

4. Neither House, during the session of Congress, shall, without the consent of the other, adjourn for more than three days, nor to any other place than that in which the two Houses shall be sitting.

Sec. VI. 1. The Senators and Representatives shall receive a compensation for their services, to be ascertained by law, and paid out of the Treasury of the United States. They shall in all cases, except treason, felony and breach of the peace, be privileged from arrest during their attendance at the session of their respective Houses, and in going to and returning from the same; and for any speech or debate in either House, they shall not be questioned in any other place.

2. No Senator or Representative shall, during the time for which he was elected, be appointed to any civil office under the authority of the United States, which shall have increased during such time; and no person holding any office under the United States, shall be a member of either House during his continuance in office.

Sec. VII. 1. All bills for raising revenue shall originate in the House of Representatives; but the Senate may propose or concur with amendments as on other bills.

2. Every bill which shall have passed the House of Representatives and the Senate, shall, before it become a law, be presented to the president of the United States; if he approve, he shall sign it, but if not, he shall return it, with his objections, to that house in which it shall have originated, who shall enter the objections at large on their journal, and proceed to reconsider it. If after such reconsideration, two thirds of that house shall agree to pass the bill, it shall be sent, together with the objections, to the other house, by which it shall likewise be reconsidered, and if approved by two-thirds of that house, it shall become a law. But in all such cases the votes of both houses shall be determined by yeas and nays, and the names of the persons voting for and against the bill shall be entered on the journal of each house respectively. If any bill shall not be returned by the president within ten days (Sundays excepted) after it shall have been presented to him, the same shall be a law, in like manner as if he had signed it, unless the Congress by their adjournment prevent its return, in which case it shall not be a law.

3. Every order, resolution, or vote to which the concurrence of the Senate and House of Representatives may be necessary (except on a question of adjournment) shall be presented to the president of the United States; and before the same shall take effect, shall be approved by him, or, being disapproved by him, shall be re-passed by two-thirds of the Senate and House of Representatives, according to the rules and limitations prescribed in the case of a bill.

Sec. VIII. The Congress shall have the power—

1. to lay and collect taxes, duties, imposts and excises, to pay the debts and provide for the common defence and general welfare of the United States; but all duties, imposts and excises shall be uniform throughout the United States:

2. To borrow money on the credit of the United States:

3. To regulate commerce with foreign nations, and among the several states, and with the Indian tribes:

4. To establish an uniform rule of naturalization, and uniform laws on the subject of bankruptcies throughout the United States:

5. To coin money, regulate the value thereof, and of foreign coin, and fix the standard of weights and measures:

6. To provide for the punishment of counterfeiting the securities and current coin of the United States:

7. To establish post-offices and post-roads:

8. To promote the progress of science and useful arts, by securing for limited times to authors and inventors the exclusive right to their respective writings and discoveries:

9. To constitute tribunals inferior to the supreme court:

10. To define and punish piracies and felonies committed on the high seas, and offences against the law of nations:

11. To declare war, grant letters of marque and reprisal, and make rules concerning captures on land and water:

12. To raise and support armies, but no appropriation of money to that use shall be for a longer term than two years:

13. To provide and maintain a navy:

14. To make rules for the government and regulation of the land and naval forces:

15. To provide for calling forth the militia to execute the laws of the union, suppress insurrections and repel invasions:

16. To provide for organizing, arming and disciplining the militia, and for governing such part of them as may be employed in the service of the United States, reserving to the states respectively, the appointment of the officers, and the authority of training the militia according to the discipline prescribed by Congress:

17. To exercise exclusive legislation in all cases whatsoever, over such district (not exceeding ten miles square) as may, by cession of particular states, and the acceptance of Congress, become the seat of the government of the United States, and to exercise like authority over all places purchased by the consent of the legislature of the state in which the same shall be, for the erection of forts, magazines, arsenals, dock-yards, and other needful buildings: And,

18. To make all laws which shall be necessary and proper for carrying into execution the

foregoing powers, and all other powers vested by this constitution in the government of the United States, or in any department or officer thereof.

Sec. IX. 1. The migration or importation of such persons as any of the states now existing shall think proper to admit, shall not be prohibited by the Congress prior to the year 1808, but a tax or duty may be imposed on such importations, not exceeding 10 dollars for each person.

2. The privilege of the writ of habeas corpus shall not be suspended, unless when in cases of rebellion or invasion the public safety may require it.

3. No bill of attainder or ex post facto law shall be passed.

4. No capitation, or other direct tax shall be laid unless in proportion to the census or enumeration herein before directed to be taken.

5. No tax or duty shall be laid on articles exported from any state.

6. No preference shall be given by any regulation of commerce or revenue to the ports of one state over those of another: nor shall vessels bound to, or from one state, be obliged to enter, clear, or pay duties in another.

7. No money shall be drawn from the treasury but in consequence of appropriations made by law; and a regular statement and account of the receipts and expenditures of all public money shall be published from time to time.

8. No title of nobility shall be granted by the United States: And no person holding any office or profit or trust under them, shall, without the consent of the Congress, accept of any present, emolument, office, or title, of any kind whatever, from any king, prince, or foreign state.

Sec. X. 1. No state shall enter into any treaty, alliance, or confederation; grant letters of marque and reprisal; coin money; emit bills of credit; make any thing but gold and silver coin a tender in payment of debts; pass any bill of attainder, ex post facto law, or law impairing the obligation of contracts, or grant any title of nobility.

2. No state shall, without the consent of the Congress, lay any imposts or duties on imports or exports, except what may be absolutely necessary for executing its inspection laws; and the net produce of all duties and imposts, laid by any state on imports or exports, shall be for the use of the treasury of the United States; and all such laws shall be subject to the revision and control of the Congress.

3. No state shall, without the consent of Congress, lay any duty of tonnage, keep troops, or ships of war in time of peace, enter into any agreement or compact with another state, or with a foreign power, or engage in a war, unless actually invaded, or in such imminent danger as will not admit of delay.

Article II

Sec. I. 1. The Executive power shall be vested in a President of the United States of America. He shall hold office during the term of four years, and together with the Vice President, chosen for the same term, be elected as follows

2. Each State shall appoint, in such manner as the Legislature may direct, a number of electors, equal to the whole number of Senators and Representatives to which the State may be entitled in the Congress: but no Senator or Representative, or person holding an office of trust or profit under the United States, shall be appointed an elector.

3. [Annulled. See Amendments, Art. 12.]

4. The Congress may determine the time of choosing the electors, and the day on which they shall give their votes; which day shall be the same throughout the United States.

5. No person except a natural born citizen, or a citizen of the United States, at the time of the adoption of this Constitution, shall be eligible to the office of President; neither shall any person be eligible to that office who shall not have attained to the age of thirty-five years, and been fourteen years a resident within the United States.

6. In case of the removal of the President from office, or of his death, resignation, or inability to discharge the powers and duties of the said office, the same shall devolve on the Vice President, and the Congress may by law provide for the case of removal, death, resignation, or inability, both of the President and Vice President, declaring what officer shall then act as President, and such officer shall act accordingly, until the disability be removed, or a President shall be elected.

7. The President shall, at stated times, receive for his services, a compensation, which shall neither be increased nor diminished during the period for which he shall have been elected, and he shall not receive within that period any other emolument from the United States, or any of them.

8. Before he enter on the execution of his office, he shall take the following oath or affirmation:""I do solemnly swear (or affirm) that I will faithfully execute the office of the President of the United States, and will to the best of my ability, preserve, protect and defend the Constitution of the United States." "

Sec. II. 1. The President shall be Commander-in-Chief of the Army and Navy of the United States, and of the militia of the several States, when called into the actual service of the United States; he may require the opinion, in writing, of the principal officer in each of the executive departments, upon any subject relating to the duties of their respective offices, and he shall have power to grant reprieves and pardons for offenses against against the United States, except in cases of impeachment.

2. He shall have power, by and with the advice and consent of the Senate, to make treaties, provided two-thirds of the Senators present concur; and he shall nominate, and by and with the advice and consent of the Senate, shall appoint ambassadors, other public

ministers and consuls, judges of the Supreme Court, and all other officers of the United States, whose appointments are not herein otherwise provided for, and which shall be established by law: but the Congress may by law vest the appointment of such inferior officers, as they think proper, in the President alone, in the courts of law, or in the heads of departments.

3. The President shall have the power to fill up all vacancies that may happen during the recess of the Senate, by granting commissions, which shall expire at the end of their next session.

Sec. III. He shall from time to time give to the Congress information of the state of the Union, and recommend to their consideration such measures as he shall judge necessary and expedient; he may, on extraordinary occasions, convene both Houses, or either of them, and in case of disagreement between them, with respect to the time of adjournment, he may adjourn them to such time as he shall think proper; he may receive ambassadors, and other public ministers; he shall take care that the laws be faithfully executed, and shall commission all the officers of the United States.

Sec. IV. The President, Vice President, and all civil officers of the United States, shall be removed from office on impeachment for, and conviction of, treason, bribery, or other high crimes and misdemeanors.

Article III

Sec. I. The judicial power of the United States, shall be vested in one supreme court, and in such inferior courts as the Congress may, from time to time, ordain and establish. The judges, both of the supreme and inferior courts, shall hold their offices during good behaviour, and shall, at stated times, receive for their services a compensation, which shall not be diminished during their continuance in office.

Sec. II. 1. The judicial power shall extend to all cases, in law and equity, arising under this constitution, the laws of the United States, and treaties made, or which shall be made under their authority; to all cases affecting ambassadors, other public ministers and consuls; to all cases of admiralty and maritime jurisdiction; to controversies to which the United States shall be a party; [to controversies between two or more states, between a state and citizens of another state, between citizens of different states, between citizens of the same state, claiming lands under grants of different states, and between a state, or the citizens thereof, and foreign states, citizens or subjects.] Altered by 11th Amendment

2. In all cases affecting ambassadors, other public ministers and consuls, and those in which a state shall be a party, the supreme court shall have original jurisdiction. In all the other cases before-mentioned, the supreme court shall have appellate jurisdiction, both as to law and fact, with such exceptions, and under such regulations as the Congress shall make.

3. The trial of all crimes, except in cases of impeachment, shall be by jury; and such trial shall be held in the state where the said crimes shall have been committed; but when not

committed within any state, the trial shall be at such place or places as the Congress may by law have directed.

Sec. III. Treason against the United States shall consist only in levying war against them, or in adhering to their enemies, giving them aid and comfort. No person shall be convicted of treason unless on the testimony of two witnesses to the same overt act, or on confession in open court.

The Congress shall have power to declare the punishment of treason, but no attainder of treason shall work corruption of blood, or forfeiture, except during the life of the person attainted.

Article IV

Sec. I. Full faith and credit shall be given in each state to the public acts, records and judicial proceedings of every other state. And the Congress may by general laws prescribe the manner in which such acts, records and proceedings shall be proved, and the effect thereof.

Sec. II. 1. The citizens of each state shall be entitled to all privileges and immunities of citizens in the several states. See the 14th Amendment

2. A person charged in any state with treason, felony, or other crime, who shall flee justice, and be found in another state, shall, on demand of the executive authority of the state from which he fled, be delivered up, to be removed to the state having jurisdiction of the crime.

3. No person held to service or labour in one state, under the laws thereof, escaping into another, shall, in consequence of any law or regulation therein, be discharged from such service or labour, but shall be delivered up on claim of the party to whom such service or labour may be due.

Sec. III. 1. New states may be admitted by the Congress into this union; but no new state shall be formed or erected within the jurisdiction of any other state, nor any state be formed by the junction of two or more states, without the consent of the legislatures of the states concerned, as well as of the Congress.

2. The Congress shall have power to dispose of and make all needful rules and regulations respecting the territory or other property belonging to the United States; and nothing in this constitution shall be so construed as to prejudice any claims of the United States, or of any particular state.

Sec. IV. The United States shall guarantee to every state in this union, a republican form of government, and shall protect each of them against invasion; and on application of the legislature, or of the executive (when the legislature cannot be convened), against domestic violence.

Article V

The Congress, whenever two-thirds of both houses shall deem it necessary, shall propose amendments to this constitution, or on the application of the legislatures of two-thirds of the several states, shall call a convention for proposing amendments, which, in either case, shall be valid to all intents and purposes, as part of this constitution, when ratified by the legislatures of three-fourths of the several states, or by conventions in three-fourths thereof, as the one or the other mode of ratification may be proposed by the Congress: Provided, that no amendment which may be made prior to the year 1808, shall in any manner affect the first and fourth clauses in the ninth section of the first article; and that no state, without its consent, shall be deprived of its equal suffrage in the Senate.

Article VI

1. All debts contracted and engagements entered into, before the adoption of this constitution, shall be as valid against the United States under this constitution, as under the confederation.

2. This constitution, and the laws of the United States which shall be made in pursuance thereof; and all treaties made, or which shall be made, under the authority of the United States shall be the supreme law of the land; and the judges in every state shall be bound thereby, any thing in the constitution or laws of any state to the contrary notwithstanding.

3. The senators and representatives before-mentioned, and the members of the several state legislatures, and all executive and judicial officers, both of the United States and of the several states, shall be bound by oath or affirmation, to support this constitution; but no religious test shall ever be required as a qualification to any office or public trust under the United States.

Article VII

The ratification of the conventions of nine states, shall be sufficient for the establishment of this constitution between the states so ratifying the same.

Amendments

The Ten Original Amendments: The Bill of Rights. Proposed by Congress September 25, 1789. Ratified December 15, 1791.

Bill of Rights

AMENDMENT I

Congress shall make no law respecting an establishment of religion, or prohibiting the free exercise thereof; or abridging the freedom of speech, or of the press; or the right of the people peaceably to assemble, and to petition the Government for a redress of grievances.

AMENDMENT II

A well-regulated militia, being necessary to the security of a free State, the right of the people to keep and bear arms, shall not be infringed.

AMENDMENT III

No soldier shall, in time of peace be quartered in any house, without the consent of the owner, nor in time of war, but in a manner to be prescribed by law.

AMENDMENT IV

The right of the people to be secure in their persons, houses, papers, and effects, against unreasonable searches and seizures, shall not be violated, and no warrants shall issue, but upon probable cause, supported by oath or affirmation, and particularly describing the place to be searched, and the persons or things to be seized.

AMENDMENT V

No person shall be held to answer for a capital, or otherwise infamous crime, unless on a presentment or indictment of a Grand Jury, except in cases arising in the land or naval forces, or in the militia, when in actual service in time of war or public danger; nor shall any person be subject for the same offense to be twice put in jeopardy of life or limb; nor shall be compelled in any criminal case to be a witness against himself, nor be deprived of life, liberty, or property, without due process of law; nor shall private property be taken for public use without just compensation.

AMENDMENT VI

In all criminal prosecutions, the accused shall enjoy the right to a speedy and public trial, by an impartial jury of the State and district wherein the crime shall have been committed, which district shall have been previously ascertained by law, and to be informed of the nature and cause of the accusation; to be confronted with the witnesses against him; to have compulsory process for obtaining witnesses in his favor, and to have the assistance of counsel for his defense.

AMENDMENT VII

In suits at common law, where the value in controversy shall exceed twenty dollars, the right of trial by jury shall be preserved, and no fact tried by a jury shall be otherwise reexamined in any court of the United States, than according to the rules of the common law.

AMENDMENT VIII

Excessive bail shall not be required, nor excessive fines imposed, nor cruel and unusual punishments inflicted.

AMENDMENT IX

The enumeration in the Constitution, of certain rights, shall not be construed to deny or disparage others retained by the people.

AMENDMENT X

The powers not delegated to the United States by the Constitution, nor prohibited by it to the States, are reserved to the States respectively, or to the people.

Further Amendments

AMENDMENT XI

The judicial power of the United States shall not be construed to extend to any suit in law or equity, commenced or prosecuted against one of the United States by citizens of another State, or by citizens or subjects of any foreign state.

AMENDMENT XII

The Electors shall meet in their respective States and vote by ballot for President and Vice-President, one of whom, at least, shall not be an inhabitant of the same State with themselves; they shall name in their ballots the person voted for as President, and in distinct ballots the person voted for as Vice-President, and of the number of votes for each, which lists they shall sign and certify, and transmit sealed to the seat of the Government of the United States, directed to the President of the Senate; the President of the Senate shall, in the presence of the Senate and House of Representatives, open all the certificates and the votes shall then be counted; The person having the greatest number of votes for President, shall be the President, if such number be a majority of the whole number of Electors appointed; and if no person have such majority, then from the persons having the highest numbers not exceeding three on the list of those voted for as President, the House of Representatives shall choose immediately, by ballot, the President. But in choosing the President, the votes shall be taken by States, the representation from each State having one vote; a quorum for this purpose shall consist of a member or members from two-thirds of the States, and a majority of all the States shall be necessary to a choice. And if the House of Representatives shall not choose a President whenever the right of choice shall devolve upon them, [before the fourth day of March next following,] Altered by 20th Amendment then the Vice-President shall act as President, as in case of the death or other constitutional disability of the President. The person having the greatest number of votes as Vice-President, shall be the Vice-President, if such numbers be a majority of the whole number of electors appointed, and if no person have a majority, then from the two highest numbers on the list, the Senate shall choose the Vice-President; a quorum for the purpose shall consist of two-thirds of the whole number of Senators, and a majority of the whole number shall be necessary to a choice. But no person constitutionally ineligible to the office of President shall be eligible to that of Vice-President of the United States.

AMENDMENT XIII

Section 1. Neither slavery nor involuntary servitude, except as a punishment for crime whereof the party shall have been duly convicted, shall exist within the United States, or any place subject to their jurisdiction.

Section 2. Congress shall have power to enforce this article by appropriate legislation.

AMENDMENT XIV

Section 1. All persons born or naturalized in the United States, and subject to the jurisdiction thereof, are citizens of the United States and of the State wherein they reside. No State shall make or enforce any law which shall abridge the privileges or immunities of citizens of the United States; nor shall any State deprive any person of life, liberty, or property, without due process of law; nor to deny to any person within its jurisdiction the equal protection of the laws.

Section 2 Representatives shall be apportioned among the several States according to their respective numbers, counting the whole number of persons in each State, excluding Indians not taxed. But when the right to vote at any election for the choice of Electors for President and Vice-President of the United States, Representatives in Congress, the executive and judicial officers of a State, or the members of the Legislature thereof, is denied to any of the male inhabitants of such State, being twenty-one years of age, and citizens of the United States, or in any way abridged, except for participation in rebellion, or other crime, the basis of representation therein shall be reduced in the proportion which the number of such male citizens shall bear to the whole number of male citizens twenty-one years of age in such State.

Section 3. No person shall be a Senator or Representative in Congress, or Elector of President and Vice-President, or hold any office, civil or military, under the United States, or under any State, who, having previously taken an oath, as a member of Congress, or as an officer of the United States, or as a member of any State Legislature, or as an executive or judicial officer of any State, to support the Constitution of the United States, shall have engaged in insurrection or rebellion against the same, or given aid or comfort to the enemies thereof. But Congress may by a vote of two-thirds of each House, remove such disability.

Section 4. The validity of the public debt of the United States, authorized by law, including debts incurred for payment of pensions and bounties for services in suppressing insurrection or rebellion, shall not be questioned. But neither the United States nor any State shall assume or pay any debt or obligation incurred in aid of insurrection or rebellion against the United States, or any claim for the loss or emancipation of any slave; but all such debts, obligations and claims shall be held illegal and void.

Section 5. The Congress shall have the power to enforce, by appropriate legislation, the provisions of this article.

AMENDMENT XV

Section 1. The right of citizens of the United States to vote shall not be denied or abridged by the United States or by any State on account of race, color, or previous condition of servitude.

Section 2. The Congress shall have the power to enforce this article by appropriate legislation.

AMENDMENT XVI

The Congress shall have power to lay and collect taxes on incomes, from whatever sources derived, without apportionment among the several States, and without regard to any census or enumeration.

AMENDMENT XVII

The Senate of the United States shall be composed of two Senators from each State, elected by the people thereof, for six years; and each Senator shall have one vote. The electors in each State shall have the qualifications requisite for electors of the most numerous branch of the State Legislatures.

When vacancies happen in the representation of any State in the Senate, the executive authority of such State shall issue writs of election to fill such vacancies: Provided, That the Legislature of any State may empower the Executive thereof to make temporary appointments until the people fill the vacancies by election as the Legislature may direct.

This amendment shall not be so construed as to affect the election or term of any Senator chosen before it becomes valid as part of the Constitution.

AMENDMENT XVIII

After one year from the ratification of this article the manufacture, sale, or transportation of intoxicating liquors within, the importation thereof into, or the exportation thereof from the United States and all territory subject to the jurisdiction thereof for beverage purposes is hereby prohibited.

The Congress and the several States shall have concurrent power to enforce this article by appropriate legislation.

This article shall be inoperative unless it shall have been ratified as an amendment to the Constitution by the Legislatures of the several States, as provided in the Constitution, within seven years from the date of the submission hereof to the States by the Congress.

AMENDMENT XIX

The right of citizens of the United States to vote shall not be denied or abridged by the United States or by any State on account of sex. Congress shall have power to enforce this article by appropriate legislation.

AMENDMENT XX

Section 1. The terms of the President and the Vice-President shall end at noon on the 20th day of January, and the terms of Senators and Representatives at noon on the 3rd day of January, of the years in which such terms would have ended if this article had not been ratified; and the terms of their successors shall then begin.

Section 2. The Congress shall assemble at least once in every year, and such meeting shall begin at noon on the 3rd day of January, unless they shall by law appoint a different day.

Section 3. If, at the time fixed for the beginning of the term of the President, the President elect shall have died, the Vice-President elect shall become President. If a President shall not have been chosen before the time fixed for the beginning of his term, or if the President elect shall have failed to qualify, then the Vice-President elect shall act as President until a President shall have qualified; and the Congress may by law provide for the case wherein neither a President elect nor a Vice-President shall have qualified, declaring who shall then act as President, or the manner in which one who is to act shall be selected, and such person shall act accordingly until a President or Vice-President shall have qualified.

Section 4. The Congress may by law provide for the case of the death of any of the persons from whom the House of representatives may choose a President whenever the right of choice shall have devolved upon them, and for the case of the death of any of the persons from whom the Senate may choose a Vice-President whenever the right of choice shall have devolved upon them.

Section 5. Sections 1 and 2 shall take effect on the 15th day of October following the ratification of this article (October 1933).

Section 6. This article shall be inoperative unless it shall have been ratified as an amendment to the Constitution by the Legislatures of three-fourths of the several States within seven years from the date of its submission.

AMENDMENT XXI

Section 1. The Eighteenth article of amendment to the Constitution of the United States is hereby repealed.

Section 2. The transportation or importation into any State, Territory, or Possession of the United States for delivery or use therein of intoxicating liquors, in violation of the laws thereof, is hereby prohibited.

Section 3. This article shall be inoperative unless it shall have been ratified as an amendment to the Constitution by conventions in the several States, as provided in the Constitution, within seven years from the date of the submission hereof to the States by the Congress.

AMENDMENT XXII

No person shall be elected to the office of the President more than twice, and no person who has held the office of President, or acted as President, for more that two years of a term to which some other person was elected President shall be elected to the office of President more that once.

But this Article shall not apply to any person holding the office of President when this Article was proposed by Congress, and shall not prevent any person who may be holding the office of President, or acting as President, during the term the term within which this Article becomes operative from holding the office of President or acting as President during the remainder of such term.

This article shall be inoperative unless it shall have been ratified as an amendment to the Constitution by the Legislatures of three-fourths of the several States within seven years from the date of its submission to the States by the Congress.

AMENDMENT XXIII

Section 1. The District constituting the seat of Government of the United States shall appoint in such manner as Congress may direct:

A number of electors of President and Vice President equal to the whole number of Senators and Representatives in Congress to which the District would be entitled if it were a State, but in no event more than the least populous State; they shall be in addition to those appointed by the States, but they shall be considered, for the purposes of the election of President and Vice President, to be electors appointed by a State; and they shall meet in the District and preform such duties as provided by the twelfth article of amendment.

Section 2. The Congress shall have power to enforce this article by appropriate legislation.

AMENDMENT XXIV

Section 1. The right of citizens of the United States to vote in any primary or other election for President or Vice President, for electors for President or Vice President, or for Senator or Representative in Congress, shall not be denied or abridged by the United States or any State by reason of failure to pay poll tax or any other tax.

Section 2. Congress shall have power to enforce this article by appropriate legislation.

AMENDMENT XXV

Section 1. In case of the removal of the President from office or of his death or resignation, the Vice President shall become President.

Section 2. Whenever there is a vacancy in the office of the Vice President, the President shall nominate a Vice President who shall take the office upon confirmation by a majority vote of both houses of Congress.

Section 3. Whenever the President transmits to the President Pro tempore of the Senate and the Speaker of the House of Representatives his written declaration that he is unable to discharge the powers and duties of his office, and until he transmits to them a written declaration to the contrary, such powers and duties shall be discharged by the Vice President as Acting President.

Section 4. Whenever the Vice President and a majority of either the principal officers of the executive departments or of such other body as Congress may by law provide, transmits to the President Pro tempore of the Senate and the Speaker of the House of Representatives their written declaration that the President is unable to discharge the powers and duties of his office, the Vice President shall immediately assume the powers and duties of the office as Acting President.

Thereafter, when the President transmits to the President Pro tempore of the Senate and the Speaker of the House of Representatives his written declaration that no inability exists, he shall resume the powers and duties of his office unless the Vice President and a majority of either the principal officers of the executive departments or of such other body as Congress may by law provide, transmits within four days to the President Pro tempore of the Senate and the Speaker of the House of Representatives their written declaration that the President is unable to discharge the powers and duties of his office. Thereupon Congress shall decide the issue, assembling within forty-eight hours for that purpose if not in session. If the Congress, within twenty-one days after receipt of the latter written declaration, or, if Congress is not in session within twenty-one days after Congress is required to assemble, determines by two-thirds vote of both houses that the President is unable to discharge the powers and duties of his office, the Vice President shall continue to discharge the same as Acting President; otherwise, the President shall resume the powers and duties of his office.

AMENDMENT XXVI

Section 1. The right of citizens of the United States, who are 18 years of age or older, to vote shall not be denied or abridged by the United States or any state on account of age.

Section 2. The Congress shall have power to enforce this article by appropriate legislation.

AMENDMENT XXVII

No law, varying the compensation for the services of the Senators and Representatives, shall take effect, until an election of Representaties shall have intervened.

Index

Second Plenary Council, 326; Third Plenary Council, 326-327; First Provisional Council, 325.

County system, 96-97.

Crusades, 3-4.

Davis, Jefferson, 287-289.

Declaration of Independence, 120-122; text of, 612-614.

De Kalb, 131.

De la Warr, Lord, 32.

Delaware, 57-58 .

Demers, Father, 259-261.

Depression of 1929, 446-450.

De Smet, Father Peter, 260-261.

Desegregation, 540-541

Dewey, Commodore George, 394.

Diaz, Porfirio, 407.

Dongan, Governor Thomas, 93.

Douglas, Stephen A., 279, 282-284.

Dred Scott Decision, 280, 283.

Drexel, Mother Katherine, 322.

Edison, Thomas A., 336-338.

Eisenhower, General Dwight D., 475-476, 482, 484, 519-528.

Election reforms, 360.

Emancipation Proclamation, 297-298, 300.

Embargo Act, 206-207, 268.

Endicott, John, 45.

England, John, Bishop of Charleston, 319, 325.

"Era of Good Feeling," 218, 219.

Eric the Red, 2.

Ericson, Leif, 2.

Erie Canal, 201-202.

Farragut, Commodore, 299.

Federal reserve system, 369-370, 452-453.

Federalists, 154, 172-173, 180, 184, 218, 234.

Field, Cyrus W., 333.

Fitzgerald, John, 132.

FitzSimons, Thomas, 132.

Foch, Marshal Ferdinand, 425-426.

Fourteen Points, 428, 431.

Franklin, Benjamin, 88, 102, 119-120, 148-149.

French and Indian War, 61-68, 99, 116, 190.

French Revolution, 173-174, 227.

Frobisher, Martin, 25-26.

Fundamental Orders of Connecticut, 49, 95.

Gadsden Purchase, 257.

Garfield, James A., 358-359.

Garrison, William Lloyd, 272-273.

Genet, Citizen, 173-175.

Georgia, establishment of, 39-40.

Gettysburg, Battle of, 302-303.

Gettysburg Address, 303-304.

Gibault, Father Pierre, 133-134, 159.

Gibbons, James, Cardinal, 326, 377-383.

Gilbert, Sir Humphrey, 26-27.

Gold Rush, 258, 344-345.

Good Neighbor Policy, 410-411.

ANSWER KEY

CHAPTER 1

1. Leif Ericson
2. to rescue the Holy Land from the Muslims.
3. During his travels in Asia Marco Polo saw the wealth and culture there. Many copies were made of the book he wrote about his travels, which caused increased interest in the Far East.
4. the compass and the astrolabe
5. The capture of Constantinople made it more difficult and expensive to transport goods over land. Hence it became important to look for an all-water route which would solve the problems of transportation and reduce the cost of delivering the goods. The search for water routes led to the discovery of America.
6. because he was so enthusiastic about exploration and navigation
7. Portugal.
8. geography, astronomy, and travel
9. Amerigo Vespucci was an Italian who made voyages across the Atlantic to the new world. He wrote a letter about the lands he had seen and expressed his belief that this was a new world. A German mapmaker called this new land "America" in honor of the man he thought discovered it.
10. October 12, 1492. Columbus called the land San Salvador.

CHAPTER 2

1. the land to its south was, as Vespucci had claimed, a separate continent.
2. one of his five ships, the *Victoria*, was the first to sail around the world.
3. Hernan Cortes
4. the names of their "gods" and the scale on which they practiced human sacrifice
5. Francisco Pizzaro
6. In 1551, the University of San Marcos was founded in Lima, Peru. Two years later, the University of Mexico City was founded.
7. Giovanni Verrazano
8. Samuel de Champlain
9. In 1608 the first permanent French settlement was established at Quebec.
10. John Cabot and his son Sebastian
11. Religious troubles
12. Henry Hudson

CHAPTER 3

1. 1607 in Jamestown
2. Captain John Smith made a rule: "He that will not work shall not eat," and saw to it that the rule was kept. Through his leadership, the colonists went to work.
3. Slavery started in Virginia in 1619 when the Dutch ship the *White Lion* arrived there carrying twenty

African slaves. The English needed workers and the Dutch needed supplies, so the Africans were traded to the English tobacco growers, who used them to work on their plantations.

4. The House of Burgesses was the name of the first self-governing legislature in Virginia.

5. George Calvert, the first Lord Baltimore.

6. St. Mary's

7. a law stating that all Christians should enjoy religious freedom.

8. the populations came from different places and the occupations also differed.

9. as a buffer against the Spanish Catholics in Florida, and as a refuge for inmates of the English debtor prisons.

CHAPTER 4

1. Because of religious persecution, some English went to Holland, but when they saw their children acquiring Dutch customs, they became alarmed, since they wanted them to remain English. They came to America to preserve their English customs and to enjoy religious freedom.

2. The Pilgrims landed at Plymouth in Massachusetts.

3. The Mayflower Compact was the Pilgrims' plan of government, in which the Pilgrims pledged themselves to enact and obey "just and equal laws" for the general good of the colony. Their government was to depend upon the will of the people.

4. Rhode Island and Connecticut.

5. Roger Williams and Anne Hutchinson

6. Thomas Hooker

7. protection against the Indians and against the threat of the French and the Dutch

8. in 1664 when it passed from Dutch to English control

9. Kateri Tekakwitha

10. William Penn. The Society of Friends, or Quakers.

11. The Dutch made the first settlement in Delaware; however, after it was destroyed by Indians, the Swedes created the first permanent settlement.

CHAPTER 5

1. England, France, Holland, Sweden, and Spain.

2. it was the gateway to Louisiana

3. The French and English both claimed the same lands in North America. The war lasted from 1754 until 1763.

4. George Washington acted as a messenger for Governor Dinwiddie of Virginia. He also built forts and fought the French.

5. It gave England control of Canada and ended French power in the New World.

6. General Montcalm of France and General Wolf of England

7. It was the only place they could go to receive the sacraments

8. a) Fr. Margil was a missionary from Mexico City who came to the Texas territory early in the eighteenth century to preach the Gospel, at the age of sixty. He walked from

the jungles of Costa Rica to the east of Texas, founding hundreds of missions along the way. He preached the Gospel to thousands of natives, and is called the Apostle of New Spain and Texas. b) Fr. Eusebio Kino was a missionary to Baja California and the Southwestern U.S. especially Arizona. He founded many missions during his life. c) Fr. Juan de Padilla was a Franciscan missionary from Spain who came to New Mexico, laboring for the conversion of the Indians living in the border territory. He was attacked and killed by savages after crossing the Rio Grande and making his way onto the plains. d) On the morning of December 9, 1531, Juan Diego, a Mexican, saw a vision of the Blessed Mother on the slopes of Tepeyac hill outside of Mexico City. She asked him to build a church on the site, and told Juan to gather flowers there in the dead of winter as a miraculous sign to prove her claim. When Juan gathered them and presented the roses to the bishop, the image of Our Lady had miraculously appeared on his tilma. Juan Diego was canonized in 2002.

9. the apparition of Our Lady of Guadalupe.

10. Pedro Menendez de Aviles and Fr. Francisco Lopez.

Chapter 6

1. Germany
2. Farming, fishing, shipbuilding, and manufacturing
3. Tobacco
4. Slave owners, whites who did not own slaves, the "poor whites," and slaves.
5. There were few good roads. In general, roads were narrow Indian trails. At first, the only method of travel was by horseback or by boat.
6. Benjamin Franklin.
7. Catholics could own land or engage in business.
8. The Ursuline Nuns opened Ursuline Academy in 1727 in New Orleans.
9. Harvard College
10. The House of Burgesses.
11. New England had the township system, the South used a county system, and the middle colonies had the township-county system.

Chapter 7

1. a. all colonial trade be carried on English or colonial ships which passed through English ports and paid duty; and b. the colonies should not manufacture goods that were being produced in England.
2. By enforcing the Laws, England had two goals. First, England hoped to compel the colonies to share in the payment of her war debts. Second, England wanted to protect her shipping industry from foreign competition.
3. The colonial merchants: enforcement of the Navigation Laws could seriously injure their business. The colonial manufacturer: financial ruin.
4. Blank search warrants that allowed customs officers to enter any house or board any ship to search for smuggled goods.
5. A tax levied on them by a

parliament in which they had no representatives.

6. The Stamp Act Congress marks the first united action of the colonies against England.

7. a. Boston's port be closed to trade until the town paid for the tea that had been destroyed; b. the people be deprived of all voice in their government and placed directly under officers appointed by the king; c. new troops be quartered in the colony; d. king's officers accused by the colonists be tried in England instead of in the colonies; and e. Massachusetts, Connecticut, Virginia, and New York be deprived of their western land claims, which would be made part of Quebec.

8. September 5, 1774 in Philadelphia.

9. The most influential man in Massachusetts. He led the protest of the Stamp Act there and represented Massachusetts at the First Continental Congress.

10. Patrick Henry

CHAPTER 8

1. a. they were fighting on their own ground, while the English were three thousand miles away from home. b. France had long been England's enemy and might be counted on by the colonies as an ally. c. The colonies had one of the best generals of the time in George Washington. d. The colonists had more at stake because they were fighting for their homes and families while many of the English soldiers were tired of war and fighting only as a job.

2. It showed the English could be defeated. This gave the colonists hope and made many ready to resist England.

3. a group of soldiers from Vermont lead by Ethan Allen who captured Fort Ticonderoga

4. It is almost entirely the work of Thomas Jefferson, with minor changes suggested by John Adams and Benjamin Franklin.

5. It changed the purpose of the war from a fight for the rights of Englishmen to a war for independence. It was the birth of the U.S..

6. In order to cut New England off from the rest of the colonies, the British could then control the middle colonies with an army of occupation and prevent the southern colonies from sending food and supplies to New England.

7. This victory convinced the British that the war was not over, and more importantly, it restored the U.S. army's morale.

8. It meant the end of Burgoyne's plan to seize the Hudson Valley and caused France to enter the War on the side of the U.S.

9. France wanted to avenge itself against Britain for its losses in the French and Indian War.

10. By borrowing money from France, Spain, and Holland. Also, some individuals gave money to the colonies.

11. The Marquis de Lafayette from France, De Kalb from Bavaria, Count Pulaski and Thaddeus Kosciusko from Poland, Baron von

Steuben from Prussia, and John Barry from Ireland.

12. Charles Carroll of Carrollton, John Fitzgerald, Stephen Moylan, Thomas Fitzsimons, and Joseph Orono.

13. a Virginian who captured Kaskaskia and Vincennes and succeeded in driving the British out of the land south of the Great Lakes. As a result, the U.S. obtained the Northwest Territory at the end of the war.

14. a. Great Britain recognized the independence of the U.S. b. the Mississippi River was fixed as the western boundary of the U.S. c. Florida, which then extended to the Mississippi, was returned to Spain. d. the Continental Congress was to recommend that the various states return the property taken from English subjects and loyalists.

15. First, the distance of the U.S. colonies from England made it difficult for England to fight the war. Second, it was impossible to blockade all of the ports along a thousand mile coastline, so the British could not completely cut off U.S. trade. Third, the colonists had a vast country into which to retreat. Finally, the English were greatly hampered by the lack of familiarity with the territory in which they were fighting.

CHAPTER 9

1. they feared that it would interfere with their liberties and would become as tyrannical as the British government had been

2. a dispute over the ownership of western lands

3. Seven states claimed huge stretches of land beyond the Appalachian Mountains based on their colonial charters.

4. It lacked power in four specific areas. First, it could not raise money by taxation. Second, it did not have the sole power to coin money, for each state also retained that right. Third, it could not regulate interstate commerce. Last, it could not call out troops to enforce law and order.

5. At the end of the war, Congress had paid each soldier a bonus of five years wages. However this payment was made in Continental currency, or paper money, which was practically worthless because Congress had no gold to back up its value, and was helpless to collect gold. To make matters worse, states were issuing their own currency which was only good in the state it was issued. These conditions caused frustration and desperation among the people, and especially ex-soldiers such as Daniel Shays, who had been a captain in the Continental Army.

6. The Northwest Ordinance of 1787 organized the Northwest Territory – the region from the Ohio River to the Great Lakes and from New York and Pennsylvania to the Mississippi River. First, the Ordinance said that between 3 and 5 states were to be made from this territory. Second, these states were to be admitted to the Union on an equal basis with the original states. Third, religious

freedom was guaranteed to all. Fourth, slavery was forbidden in the region. Fifth, free public education was provided. Sixth, trial by jury was guaranteed to the inhabitants.

7. James Madison.

8. Washington, Hamilton, and Madison.

9. 1. There would be two houses in the Congress: the Senate and the House of Representatives which each provided a different proportion. 2. Three-fifths of slaves be counted for both representation and taxation. 3. Congress was empowered to regulate trade but could not abolish the slave trade before 1808.

10. Each of the three branches of government has the power to check and balance the other two branches. A further check to the power of the national government was the power of the states.

11. 1789

12. A series of articles written by Madison, Hamilton, and John Jay that explain every part of the U.S. Constitution and argue for its adoption. It helped a great deal in securing the acceptance of the new plan of government, and is still considered the best authority on the nature of the Constitution.

13. James Madison, Alexander Hamilton, and John Jay

CHAPTER 10

1. St. Augustine, Florida

2. Unlike other colonies, Catholic priests were welcome to do their work there. In 1686 there was a Catholic chapel in Philadelphia. In 1730 Fr. Joseph Greaton became the first resident missionary in that city. In 1733, the Jesuits founded Old St. Joseph's Roman Catholic Church.

3. Fr. Junipero Serra, with a band of well-trained companions, established a number of missions from San Diego to San Francisco. Fr. Serra baptized and confirmed some 6,000 Indians and translated a catechism into one of the Indian languages.

4. The missionaries helped raise the Indian's standard of living. Among the missionaries were engineers, doctors, and men versed in almost every skill known at the time. They shared their skills, teaching the Indians how to farm and how to build.

5. During the debates preceding the adoption of the Constitution, Father Carroll went to Philadelphia. He pleaded before the convention delegates for the rights of his fellow Catholics. His words had much to do with the adoption of Article VI of the Constitution, which abolishes all religious tests for any public office.

6. Bishop Carroll sought to unify the work of his priests and people. He organized schools, promoted higher education, and constantly urged toleration for all religions.

CHAPTER 11

1. On April 30, 1789, (on the balcony of) Federal Hall in New York City

2. Thomas Jefferson, Alexander Hamilton, Henry Knox, and Edmund Randolph.

3. The first ten amendments to the Constitution intended to protect the rights of the people.

4. Among them are: a) freedom of religion, speech and the press. b) The right to bear arms. c) Protection against unreasonable searches of one's home by the police. d) Guarantee jury trial and protection from having to testify against oneself. e) Prohibit cruel or unusual punishments. f) They recognize there are human rights beyond those mentioned in the Constitution. g) They declare that the states and people retain the powers not specifically given to the national government or prohibited to the states.

5. Alexander Hamilton proposed that: a. the national debt be paid in full; b. that the national government take over the unpaid state debts; and c. that the government redeem the Continental paper money at face value.

6. Congress passed a tax on distilled liquors and other goods called an "excise tax." Along the frontier, this tax was violently resented by the backwoods farmers, who found transporting grain over the mountains too expensive and had begun distilling their grain into whisky, which was easier to transport and sell. Government officials who tried to enforce the tax in western Pennsylvania met with resistance from organized bands of frontiersmen. The uprising against the excise tax on distilled liquors was called the Whisky Rebellion.

7. a. Hamilton and his followers, known as the Federalists, favored a broad interpretation of the Constitution. They favored a strong federal government that was insulated from the changing opinions of the U.S. people, which they felt would be a protection against the danger of "mob rule." They said that the national government had implied powers in addition to those specifically granted by the Constitution. b. Jefferson's camp, known as the Anti-Federalists, held that the federal government only had those powers that were specifically named in the Constitution. They felt the national government should not be given any power not specifically given to it by the Constitution. They did not believe in "implied powers," thus, became known as "strict constructionists." They were concerned that the federal government would become too strong and threaten the power of the states.

8. The Kentucky and Virginia Resolutions were drawn in opposition of the Naturalization, Alien and Sedition laws. They declared these laws null and void within their borders, as contrary to the letter and spirit of the Constitution.

9. In the 1800 presidential election there was an agreement not to repeat the earlier mistake of electing a President and a Vice-President of opposing parties. Yet, when the electoral votes were

counted, Congress found that Thomas Jefferson and Aaron Burr had tied for the highest place, John Adams was third. As the Constitution provided, those three were submitted to the House of Representatives, where a bitter fight over the election developed. Finally Alexander Hamilton convinced the House to elect Jefferson. To make sure that a tie vote would not occur again, the Twelfth Amendment was added to the Constitution in 1804. It said that each elector should name in one ballot the person voted for as President and in another distinct ballot the person voted for as Vice-President.

10. Thomas Jefferson

CHAPTER 12

1. The great border scout who cut a wagon trail from the Cumberland Gap to Boonesboro in Kentucky. Eventually the restless Boone moved on to Missouri after numerous settlements were established where he lived.

2. Virginia and the Carolinas
3. 1787
4. Ohio, Indiana, Illinois, Michigan, and Wisconsin.
5. Tecumseh was the chief of the Shawnees. He went from tribe to tribe, urging the Indians to unite and defend themselves against the invasion of the white settlers.
6. in order to prevent France from closing the Mississippi to western trade
7. Napoleon desperately needed money to continue his war; also, when war

with England resumed, the English navy might seize New Orleans anyway.

8. Jefferson believed in a strict construction of the Constitution. He had always insisted that the national government had only the powers specifically given it by the Constitution. There was no mention in the Constitution about the right to purchase foreign land. Also, he was not sure the Senate would ratify the treaty.

9. To explore the Louisiana Territory and discover its value

10. She secured Indian guides and directed the explorers through the mountain passes to the upper part of the Snake River and on to the source of the Columbia River.

11. central Illinois

12. They could travel with greater speed and safety.

13. To allow for cheaper and easier transportation for trade

14. The Hudson River and Lake Erie

CHAPTER 13

1. Tripoli, Algiers, Tunis, and Morocco

2. To protect our ships from pirate raids

3. The Napoleonic wars created a large demand for U.S. goods. The U.S. built up a thriving export trade, particularly New England. But both England and France interfered with U.S. trade. Both nations seized U.S. cargoes, captured ships, and denied the freedom of the seas to U.S. ships. Both nations issued decrees against U.S. shipping, and

claimed the right to seize U.S. ships to prevent trade with the other country. Not being able to trade with Europe caused U.S. merchants to lose a great deal of money.

4. The Embargo Act forbade U.S. vessels to set sail for any foreign port and closed our harbors to European ships. This Act was later repealed and replaced with the Nonintercourse Act, which forbade only trade with England and France.

5. a. the impressment of U.S. seamen and b. the strong influence of the "War Hawks" and their followers, who blamed England for Indian uprisings and insults to America.

6. They were reaping the benefits of a prosperous trade with the countries abroad.

7. "Old Ironsides"

8. the victor of the Battle of Lake Erie

9. The Federalists were accused of being unpatriotic and they never attained national power again.

10. 1789

11. Baltimore, New York, Philadelphia, Boston, and Bardstown.

12. Elizabeth Ann Seton, Rose Duchesne, and Anne-Thérèse Guérin

CHAPTER 14

1. The protective tariff, the banking system, and slavery.

2. Property and religious qualifications

3. Jackson received the highest number of votes but none of the candidates had received a majority, so in accordance with the Constitution, the election went to the House.

Because of Henry Clay's influence in the House, Adams became the sixth president of the U.S..

4. Able and experienced workers were replaced with inexperienced and often unqualified political supporters.

5. He removed them from the land east of the Mississippi to land west of the great river.

6. The Nullification Act declared that after February 1, 1833, the tariff law of the U.S. would be null and void in South Carolina.

7. Jackson immediately issued a proclamation declaring that no state had the power to annul a law of the U.S..

8. Henry Clay and others put a Compromise Tariff Act through Congress that met the objections of South Carolina and was acceptable to the North.

9. Jackson ordered the Secretary of the Treasury to withdraw all the U.S. funds from the National Bank. Hostile newspapers called the banks where government money was transferred Jackson's "pet banks."

10. Martin Van Buren

11. William Henry Harrison, the hero of the Battle of Tippecanoe, and for his Vice-President, John Tyler

12. Harrison died within a month of taking office, and so, John Tyler became president.

CHAPTER 15

1. The Americans in Texas mistrusted Santa Anna, Mexico's President, and set up their own government. Santa Anna, with an army of more

than 4,000 men, came into Texas to restore Mexican control. He laid siege to the Alamo, an old mission in San Antonio used as a fort by the Texans. After a siege of thirteen days, he took the Alamo and killed all its defenders.

2. General Santa Anna
3. Sam Houston
4. The Northern States opposed admitting Texas to the Union because Texas was a slave state, and thus, would give the slaveholders more influence in Congress. There was concern that allowing Texas to join the Union would lead to war with Mexico.
5. a. the discovery and exploration of the Columbia River by Robert Gray, a Boston sea captain, in 1792; b. the explorations of Lewis and Clark; c. the establishment of a fur trading post called Astoria, at the mouth of the Columbia River, by John Jacob Astor in 1811
6. "Fifty-four forty" referred to the southern boundary of Alaska. Thus the slogan meant that the U.S. was laying claim to all of Oregon.
7. May 1846; with the capture of Mexico City by General Winfield Scott.
8. The U.S. agreed to withdraw all its troops from Mexico. Mexico sold the U.S. all the lands north of the Gila River and the Rio Grande for $15 million. The U.S. also agreed to pay all claims of U.S. citizens against Mexico.
9. In 1848 gold was discovered in California. Thousands of fortune hunters came to California. In one year it swelled from a few thousand to nearly a hundred thousand. This fast growth allowed California to be admitted to the Union.

10. John McLoughlin
11. Fr. Blanchet
12. Fr. Peter de Smet
13. Many U.S. Protestants believed that a person could not be both a good American and a good Catholic. The U.S. tradition of individualism and democracy made many Americans distrustful of strong religious authority. The growing feeling of nationalism made some Americans wary of any non-U.S. influence, like a pope in Europe.
14. Charleston, MA, in 1834
15. It was an anti-Catholic movement that occurred mostly in the Northeast U.S. from the 1830s to the 1850s, mainly because of the increase in Irish Catholic immigration.

CHAPTER 16

1. Cotton was the leading crop in the South. Growing, picking, and cleaning cotton were types of unskilled labor that the untrained slaves could do easily. There was no need for slaves in the industrial North because thousands of European immigrants provided the factories with a constant supply of cheap labor.
2. It made growing cotton a very profitable business and increased slave labor. The cotton gin ensured that the South would remain agricultural while the North remained industrial.

3. Washington, Jefferson, Henry, and Madison.

4. England outlawed slavery in the British West Indies in 1833. The government paid the slave owners almost a hundred million dollars to compensate for their lost "property."

5. The South pointed out that if the slaves were freed, there would be no one to look after their welfare. They argued that the slaves on the plantation had a happier life than the poorly paid factory workers in the North. They also believed that freedom for the slaves would be a danger to white society.

6. Those in the early 19th century who called for the abolition of slavery

7. Harriet Beecher Stowe was the author of *Uncle Tom's Cabin*.

8. Because at that time there were an equal number of slave and free states in the Union. The North had a large majority in the House where representation was by population. However, in the Senate, there were two Senators from each state, so the South had equal representation. It was important whether Missouri would be slave or free.

9. This compromise gave both sides some things they wanted. The North gained the abolition of the slave trade in the District of Columbia and saw California admitted as a free state. The South gained a new fugitive slave law, which provided that federal officers return runaway slaves to their masters.

10. Aware of the northerners' anti-slavery intentions, groups of pro-slavery settlers poured into Kansas from Missouri. Whichever group could produce the most votes would determine the issue. Kansas soon became a battleground between pro-slave and anti-slave settlers.

11. 1. A slave had no right to sue 2. Living in a free territory did not make a slave free 3. A slaveholder could take his property anywhere in the Union 4. The Missouri Compromise was unconstitutional.

12. To support the Union and to work for the gradual elimination of slavery.

13. A radical Abolitionist who had been active in the struggle to make Kansas a free state. He had been the leader of several bloody raids on pro-slavery settlements. He led an attack on Harper's Ferry in the hopes of starting a slave uprising.

14. Abraham Lincoln.

CHAPTER 17

1. Fort Sumter on April 12, 1861.

2. 1. It protected the rights of the individual states. 2. It specifically protected slavery. 3. It prohibited all tariffs.

3. The western part of Virginia broke away from Virginia and became a state in 1863.

4. The Union had more men, money, factories, supplies and railroads. There were twenty-three states on the Union side when the war began, with a population of about twenty-two million. The Confederacy had only eleven states with a population of about nine million, more than a third of whom were slaves.

However, the Confederacy had good generals so its armies were in good hands.

5. General Robert E. Lee, who was the best general in North America at the time.

6. The South felt it could win the war because it has always been easier to defend against an invasion than to invade a country. Fighting on its home ground, the South knew the land better than the North and could count on local support. Their few railroads actually meant Northerners would have a harder time getting supplies. The South felt certain that they could fight a defensive war until the North became tired of the loss of men and money, and gave up.

7. First, it would cut the South off from European trade. Second, the North would prevent the South from fighting as a unit, by seizing the Mississippi and important railroad centers of the South. Third, the Union would attempt to capture Richmond, destroying the seat of government of the Confederacy.

8. a. Bull Run: the first major battle of the war. Both sides realized that the war would be longer and more brutal than they had thought. b. Antietam: Union victory that halted Lee's invasion of the North. C. Chancellorsville: Major victory for General Lee. Union suffers its worst defeat however General Jackson is killed by his own men. D. Vicksburg: The Union is able to cut the Confederacy in two by taking control of the Mississippi River.

9. The USS Monitor won the battle because the Merrimac was driven off and was unable to return to fight the next day.

10. First, an attack on the North would threaten Philadelphia, Boston and Washington. Second, Virginia had almost been destroyed, and its starving people needed a break from the war. Lee's troops could live off the bounty of the Northern farms. Finally, the growing peace movement in the North meant to Lee that an attack into the North would "bring the war home."

11. they saw the battle as a setback and not a disaster

12. It was a warning to the South to stop fighting. It also increased public support for the war in the Union states and it kept England and France from joining the Confederacy.

13. Union General Sherman marched from southern Tennessee to the coast of Georgia destroying everything in its path.

14. April 9, 1865 at Appomattox Courthouse in Virginia.

15. It preserved the Union, it abolished slavery, and it determined that a state could not secede from the Union.

CHAPTER 18

1. Destruction, bankruptcy, desolation, and poverty were in the South; the terrible suffering of the people; the wounded and crippled troops; many had no homes to return to. The war had completely destroyed the plantation

system, agriculture and trade were paralyzed, and money was worthless.

2. The task of rebuilding the South after the terrible damage of the Civil War.

3. Lincoln's plan was opposite from the radical Republicans who wanted vengeance. Lincoln had no thought of punishing the Southern states or their leaders.

4. The man-power of the North had not been exhausted by war. The factories and farms had continued to operate. In the North, there was general prosperity. The soldier, who returned and found his job gone, went to the West. The widows, orphans and cripples made dependent by the war were supported by a system of government pensions.

5. Lincoln wanted the Southern states to resume their place in the Union. He realized there could be no reunion if the South was subject to brutal occupation. The Radical Republicans wanted both the states and their leaders punished.

6. Congress felt that the authority to re-admit the South into the Union belonged to Congress and not to the President. Congress resented what seemed an infringement on its power and refused to recognize the reconstruction state governments set up at the President's direction.

7. Carpetbaggers were Northerners who rushed to the South to obtain political positions and steal public funds. Called carpetbaggers because they carried all their possessions in carpetbags, traveling bags made of carpet. Scalawags were Southerners who qualified for public office by swearing that they had not fought against the Union. They were mostly just dishonest politicians.

8. The 13th amendment abolished slavery.

9. To grant citizenship to blacks; it reduced representation in Congress of any state which denied blacks the right to vote; it disqualified as officeholders the leaders of the Confederacy; it forbade payment of the Confederate war debt or reimbursement for loss of slaves.

10. This meant government by the old white leadership of the South. They passed laws that prevented blacks from voting.

11. After the slaves were freed, new emphasis was placed on promoting their conversion. The freedom after the war had a very bad effect on their Catholic Faith. Once freed, the blacks tended to fall away from their Catholic Faith. There were no black parishes to take over from the religious influence of their Catholic masters. Then Protestantism came in and spread fast among the blacks.

12. Bishop John Neumann was the 4th Bishop of Philadelphia. He built many schools and churches. When he became Bishop, Philadelphia had two schools, and after he died, it had 100. He was canonized by Pope Paul VI in 1977, the first male citizen of the U.S. to be so honored.

13. 1. It stressed the importance of the founding of a Catholic University

in the U.S.. 2. It decreed there are 6 Holy Days of Obligation. 3. It appointed a commission to prepare a catechism for schools (which became the Baltimore Catechism). 4. It prepared the Church in the U.S. for the move from a missionary land to a country ready to provide for its own support.

1. the term used to describe the changes created by mechanical inventions. These inventions completely altered the life of America and the Western world.

2. The Civil War and the emancipation of blacks. War and heavy taxes impoverished the planters. They did not have enough money to hire workers. Many freed slaves did not want to return to their former owners. They preferred to rent a little patch of ground or to buy it on an installment plan and thereby enjoy their freedom. Many plantations, therefore, were broken up into small farms and sold or rented on the share system. In this way, small farms came into existence in the South.

3. Improving Southern farming, the development of more than 300 products from the peanut, and the development of more than 100 products from the sweet potato.

4. The South was not as developed as in the North before the Civil War. However, with the breakup of the plantation system, many of the leaders and laborers gave up

on agriculture. They went to the cities and devoted themselves to industry and commerce. Industry was developed by building major railroads and tapping the rich natural resources of the South.

5. Miners, ranchers and farmers.

6. The time when gold was discovered in any place which lured thousands of treasure hunters to rush to the gold.

7. The Homestead Act of 1862; the building of railroads west of the Mississippi; and inventions that helped to solve the problems of farming in that fertile country.

8. Mining, cattle raising, farming, fishing, and lumbering.

9. The two cultures were so dramatically different. The Native Americans believed that all the land belonged to everyone and so they could travel anywhere on the land, while the white people believed in private ownership of the land as the source of their income and lived on the land they owned.

10. it united the East and West and made the U.S. a continental power.

11. Promontory Point near Ogden, Utah in 1869.

12. Thomas Edison.

13. The founder of the U.S. Federation of Labor in 1886 and for years was its guiding spirit.

14. Several separate businesses combined into one large company.

15. a leader in black education

16. Born a slave he became an agricultural scientist of international fame.

1. After the Civil War, dishonest men controlled the political process in many city and state governments. These men made all the appointments to city and state offices. One of these men was named William M. Tweed of New York City. He and his associates were called the "Tweed Ring." They stole millions of dollars of city money.

2. It was an example of the dishonesty that crept into the national government, particularly while Grant was President.

3. 20 votes were in dispute on the day of the election. To settle the dispute, Congress appointed an electoral commission of 15 members. The commission was made up of 8 Republicans and 7 Democrats. The 8 Republicans voted to count the 20 disputed votes for Hayes. Thus Hayes was elected President.

4. Not to trust politicians.

5. He was assassinated.

6. It was corrupt. Voters were often forced to vote as the boss directed. A voter could sell his vote.

7. Australia.

8. The means by which the individual voter is given more voice in choosing party candidates. Any member of a party may run for nomination. The party holds an election to see who will run for the party. Every member of the party is allowed to vote for the person he wants to run for office. Thus, the party's nominees are chosen by popular vote.

9. "The Initiative" gives the voter the power to initiate, or propose laws. The voter needs to obtain the signatures of a certain number of voters favoring the proposed law. Any voter may then demand that such a proposed law be voted upon either by the state legislature or by the people at the polls. If the proposed bill receives a majority vote, it becomes a law. "The Referendum" gives voters the right to vote upon certain laws enacted by the state legislature. The voter follows the same protocol as with the initiative. "The Recall" strengthens the control of voters over elected officials. It provides that if the required number of signatures to a petition is secured, an official may be forced to stand for a new election during his term. If at this special election a majority of the votes are in favor of the official, he retains his office. If they are not, he is recalled, or removed. These are three important powers because they increase the voter's influence in the government.

10. A teacher and a reformer. She proposed that the Constitution be amended to grant women the right to vote.

11. Wyoming in 1869.

12. 19th amendment

13. Republicans favored the tariff because they originally gained most of their support from the business interests of the North and the East. The tariffs protected these interests from foreign competition. Democrats opposed the tariff

because their support came from the South and the West. The South and the West did not like the tariff because it generally meant they paid higher prices for goods.

14. 16th amendment

15. It made it possible to ease many financial difficulties, such as shortage of currency, and it put great economic power in the hands of a semi-governmental organization.

CHAPTER 21

1. Western farmers began to complain in the late 1860's

2. The Grangers

3. It was the first step taken by the national government toward the regulation of U.S. business. Previously, such a regulation would have been left to the states. As a result, almost all commerce is now regulated by the national government.

4. A combination of firms in the same industry.

5. A trust could eliminate competition; refuse to sell to all rival companies; and set prices as high as it chose.

6. If a trust became a monopoly it crossed over many states and the law of one state might not be the same in another state.

7. The Act declared as illegal any "contract, combination…or conspiracy" that had as its purpose "the restraint of trade." It was enacted in 1890.

8. President Theodore Roosevelt

9. Child labor, the number of hours an employee could be required to work in a day or week, and laws regarding health and safety.

10. 1. Pure Food and Drug Act which required the truthful labeling of all foods and drugs. 2. Meat Inspection Act which required that meat packing houses be inspected by the government and meat had to be approved by a federal inspector before being shipped from one state to another.

11. Most U.S. Catholic workers were poor and worked in factories. They experienced long hours, meager wages, little security, unhealthy and dangerous working conditions, and a lack of leisure time.

12. He worked to help labor. In 1887, Gibbons met with the Pope on behalf of the Knights of Labor. As a result of Cardinal Gibbon's defense, the Holy Father decided that it was not necessary to prohibit membership in the Knights.

13. *Rerum Novarum*

14. Under Cardinal Gibbon's leadership, the Third Plenary Council of Baltimore was held. He resolved disputes between Catholics of different nationalities, between bishops, and between U.S. bishops and Rome. He was a best-selling author. His book entitled, *The Faith of Our Fathers*, is a simply written explanation of Catholic doctrine and practice. It helped bring thousands of converts into the Church. In addition, every President during his time looked to him for counsel and advice.

15. Helping others is an important part of the Faith. From the time

of the Apostles, the Church has been concerned not only with the spiritual, but also the physical welfare of all people.

CHAPTER 22

1. The U.S. bought Alaska from Russia.

2. The government was severely criticized for buying what was considered a barren arctic wasteland. Critics called it "Seward's Icebox" after Secretary of State William H. Seward who had agreed to the deal.

3. Good. Alaska is rich in natural resources, especially oil. The U.S. has gotten its money back many times over.

4. He was suspicious about the revolt that had occurred in 1893. The number and power of Americans had grown so large they successfully led a revolt against Hawaii's queen, Liliuokalani. President Cleveland sent someone to Hawaii to investigate the situation. He learned that the Americans in Hawaii had deposed the queen and requested annexation. As a result, Cleveland had dropped the idea of annexation.

5. When William McKinley became President in 1897, the Hawaiians urged the U.S. to annex the islands. McKinley liked the idea, so he drew up a treaty, and in 1898, Hawaii was annexed.

6. At the end of the Spanish-American War, Spain sold the Philippines to the U.S. In 1934, Congress passed an act granting the Philippines independence in ten years. Meanwhile, the islands governed themselves except in foreign affairs. Due to WWII and the invasion of the islands by Japan, independence was delayed until July 4, 1946.

7. a. the stories heard by Americans about the mistreatment of Cubans by the Spanish. b. the explosion in Havana harbor of the battleship the *USS Maine*

8. John Frank Stevens, Colonel George W. Goethals, and Colonel William C. Gorgas.

9. The policy of allowing all nations to trade with China on equal terms.

10. Initiated by President Herbert Hoover who decided that our relations with Latin America needed to improve. As President, he made a good will tour of Latin America and began a policy of cooperation with Mexico. Soon after he took office, he withdrew the Marines from Latin America. The policy was carried on by President Franklin Roosevelt who in his first inaugural address said he would "dedicate this nation to the policy of the good neighbor."

11. A Chinese society known as the "Boxers" began a movement to rid China of "foreign devils." A series of uprisings followed. Bloody attacks were made on missionaries and government representatives and their families.

12. A priest martyred by the Communists when they ruled Mexico. Thousands were killed for the Faith.

13. William Howard Taft

14. a. Guam: Acquired in 1898 as a naval base. b. Puerto Rico: A U.S. force took possession of this during the Spanish-American War. As a result of the war the U.S. acquired it. c. The Virgin Islands: sold to the U.S by Denmark.

15. The U.S. had declared war on Spain.

16. Reporting that makes no attempt to provide balanced or accurate reporting but instead uses eye-catching headlines to sell more newspapers. Techniques include exaggeration of news events and sensationalism.

CHAPTER 23

1. a) Nationalism. Nationalism was the belief that an individual nation had to stress its superiority over other nations. b) Since there was a lack of trust established because of Nationalism, this leads to the next cause, which was the need each nation felt to fortify its borders. Each nation felt it needed to build its military, develop a spy system, and train constantly to be prepared for war. This was called Militarism. c) The next cause is built on the idea of Militarism. Since each nation needed to be better protected against neighboring nations, there developed alliances. The two most important alliances were the Central Powers and the Allied Powers.

2. The assassination of the heir to the Austrian throne, Archduke Franz Ferdinand and his wife, Sophie.

3. Germany and Austria-Hungary (and Italy)

4. England, France, and Russia.

5. it was bound by ties of language and culture to every nation in Europe. Millions of Americans had been born in one of the warring nations and they identified with them.

6. Britain violated the international law of the sea by preventing U.S. trade with neutral countries and blockading neutral ports. Germany violated the law of the sea by attempting to blockade with submarines. The submarine could not observe the international law of providing safety for passengers and crew. Also, submarines generally attacked without warning, so passengers have no time to evacuate.

7. President Wilson said that the U.S. must fight not only to uphold the freedom of the seas, but also to make the world safe for democracy.

8. The government raised taxes and issued war stamps. People purchased war bonds. Various welfare organizations raised large sums of money.

9. by passing the Selective Service Act, or the draft law

10. with men and money

11. the commander of the Allied troops

12. WWI began on July 28, 1914 and ended on November 11, 1918.

13. Germany was to surrender all her colonies, practically all of her navy, all of her artillery, and most of her railway equipment. An Allied army was to occupy German territory along the Rhine River. Germany also had to surrender all prisoners of war, military stores, and submarines.

14. England, France, Italy and the U.S. Represented by David Lloyd George, Georges Clemenceau, Vittorio Orlando and Woodrow Wilson.
15. The man who began Communism. He was a German philosopher who wrote *The Communist Manifesto* in 1848. He believed that government should be controlled by a small group of people, the Communists.
16. The Bolshevik Leader, who had been in exile and was transported back to Russia, in April 1917, in an attempt to destabilize Russia. By November 1917, Lenin had seized control of the Russian government and made a separate peace treaty with Germany. He ordered the Czar and his family killed. He planted the seeds of Communism in Russia.
17. Union of Soviet Socialists Republics
18. It created a huge resentment among the German people and destroyed the German economy
19. The establishment of Communism in the Soviet Union
20. General John Pershing

CHAPTER 24

1. The nations who signed it renounced war as an instrument of state policy. They resolved to settle disputes by peaceful means.
2. all worked to reduce government spending; to increase the tariff and decrease taxes; and to reduce government borrowing
3. he was Catholic and he wanted to repeal the 18th amendment, which banned alcohol

4. because Americans were more happy and prosperous than ever and they did not want to do anything that might change that
5. They were a new way to reach consumers; the popularity of movies made Hollywood a leading cultural influence. The national nature of movies and radio broke down regional differences. Americans began to develop a national culture led by Hollywood and New York.
6. The time period during which the manufacture, sale, and transportation of alcohol was outlawed, according to the 18th Amendment.
7. Many Americans had believed that government could solve the problem of drunkenness.
8. The worst stock market crash in U.S. history. Stock market prices dropped suddenly and everyone started to sell their stocks. On October 29, 1929, more than 16 millions shares were sold on the market for anything they could bring.
9. The Crash of 1929; bank failures; families stopped buying; decrease in foreign trade, increase in unemployment; a decrease in wages and hours; and the "Dust Bowl."
10. by trying to restore the confidence of the American people in the U.S. economic system by various means
11. Franklin D. Roosevelt. He is considered controversial because of the significant changes to America that he made during his term in office.

1. The "bank holiday" closed all the banks in the nation. The purpose was to give the federal government time to determine which banks were sound and which were not. Only those banks that were found to be solid were allowed to reopen. Eventually confidence in the banks was restored and people stopped withdrawing money.

2. 1. The Agricultural Adjustment Administration (AAA) – the chief purpose of this act was to raise the price of farm crops by cutting production. Farmers who cut the production of certain crops, such as, cotton, corn, rice, and tobacco, were given benefit payments. This act was later declared unconstitutional. 2. Soil Conservation Act – farmers were paid for planting crops that would conserve natural resources rather than paying them to not plant anything at all. Under this act, many activities formerly carried on under the AAA were continued. 3. Farmers Mortgage Foreclosure Act - this was to prevent farmers from losing their farms because they could not pay their mortgages. 4. Farm Tenancy Act – provided farmers with money to buy farms. It established the Farm Security Administration which allowed for needy tenant farmers a chance to get small loans for the purchase of work animals and equipment. 5. Farm Mortgage Refinancing Act – provided money for refinancing farm mortgages at low interest

3. Through the establishment of the Home Owners' Loan Corporation (HOLC). Through this, homeowners could obtain long-term mortgage loans to save their homes from being lost. In addition, the Federal Housing Administration was set up to make it possible for a greater number of people to own their own homes. The FHA insures banks and loan associations against some of the loss that they might suffer if the people to whom they have loaned the money cannot repay the loan.

4. 1. National Industrial Recovery Act (NIRA) – this act gave the federal government control over industry for two years. This was later declared unconstitutional. 2. National Labor Relations Act – this was in response to the previous one and was actually more favorable to labor and within the powers of Congress to pass. 3. Fair Labor Standards Act (FLSA) – was also called the Wages and Hours Law. The purpose of the law was to create jobs. The idea was that the employer would hire two workers rather than pay one worker time and half. This law also established minimum wage and prohibited child labor in interstate industries.

5. generating and selling electricity at a very low rate

6. The Roosevelt administration wished to enact a permanent social program that would prevent similar disasters like the Depression.

7. Provides security for the aged, the handicapped, the unemployed, and needy children.

8. a large increase in our exports and

improve friendly relations with other nations.

9. It gave the President the right to lend or lease weapons and war materials to any government whose defense he considered important to our country. FDR considered it important to help England, so we lent them goods instead of money, since England could not pay cash for her purchases because she was going bankrupt.

10. FDR's plan to enlarge the Supreme Court, so that he could add more Justices to the Court who favored his proposals.

CHAPTER 26

1. He became the leader of the National Socialist Party or the Nazi party. Hitler promised to restore Germany's greatness. Many Germans responded to Hitler's promises and increased his popularity. As a result, he was elected Chancellor of Germany in 1933. He set up a military dictatorship.

2. Austria and Czechoslovakia.

3. The bombing of Pearl Harbor on December 7, 1941.

4. Japan was able to conquer many islands and gained much needed supplies and military bases in doing so. She also inflicted much damage on the U.S. fleet.

5. Fought from June 4-7, 1942, the U.S. lost one aircraft carrier and the Japanese lost all four carriers they had in the battle. The US victory of this battle ended the possibility of a Japanese invasion of Hawaii and the West Coast.

6. An air conflict which lasted from July 10 to October 31, 1940. Considered a turning point in the war. Hitler knew that his navy could not defeat the British navy so he began a massive air attack that he hoped would make England surrender. At the start of the war, Germany's air force was better than the British air force; however, Hitler underestimated the daring of British pilots. Hitler's attempt to force surrender was unsuccessful.

7. Communist dictator of the Soviet Union. Stalin became an ally of Britain and the U.S. because Hitler was more of an immediate threat than Stalin.

8. The Soviets were needed to win the war against Hitler who was more of an immediate threat than Stalin was.

9. To drive the Axis forces out of Africa thus gaining bases for an invasion of Europe from the South.

10. A victory that delivered a crippling blow to the Nazis in the East. Hitler refused to allow his army to retreat from the Soviet Union; because of this, his huge army was killed or captured.

11. The invasion of Normandy on June 6, 1944.

12. Initially commanded the U.S. army that landed on the coast of French North Africa. He later prepared his forces to invade and recapture Italy. Also, he was the commander of the invasion of Normandy.

13. The Prime Minister of Great Britain during the time of WWII and one

of the greatest anti-Communists of the century.

14. Allied victory that gave General MacArthur control over the seas around the Philippines and spelled the end of the Japanese Navy.

15. Because Roosevelt died in office. Harry Truman was his Vice President.

16. Hiroshima and Nagasaki.

17. It provided bases from which to carry out the final defeat of Japan.

18. His advisors told him that it would take 18 months and cost a million Allied lives to conquer Japan. It would cost countless civilian lives as well.

19. On board the *USS Missouri* in Tokyo Bay.

Chapter 27

1. May 14, 1948.
2. The U.S.
3. the forced return of refugees to Stalin
4. By force and deceit
5. the protection of Greece
6. 1. To stop Soviet expansion 2. To weaken Communist influence around the world and 3. To encourage democracy.
7. The Western Allies flew supplies into Berlin for almost a year after the city was blockaded by the Communists. It was needed because Stalin established a blockade of the city. By cutting off rail, water, and road traffic, the Soviets were giving the Western powers notice to leave or to let Berlin starve.
8. When the Soviet army entered the war against Japan, there was a Japanese army of about one million men in China. When Japan surrendered, much of these arms ended up in the hands of the Soviet army. All of the captured arms and equipment were given to the Chinese Communists.

9. to create lasting peace and work to avoid another world war

10. Chiang felt that the only way to win was to launch an offensive to destroy the Chinese Communists while he still had the strength. He felt that America was forcing him to fight a purely defensive war.

11. The Nationalists experienced acute shortages in their supplies and weapons, while the Communists still received supplies and weapons from the Soviet Union. The military balance shifted decisively in favor of the Communists.

12. The man running against Truman in the election, Thomas Dewey, promised large-scale aid to China if he won.

13. a military alliance for mutual defense among Western Europe, Canada, and the U.S.

14. Mao Tse-tung

15. The Marshall Plan was an attempt by the U.S. to restore the economic health of Europe. It was a success because it reduced the threat of Communism in Europe and it helped to re-establish Europe's faith in America.

16. Stalin hated the plan and retaliated by forming a bloc of Communist nations.

1. Previously, Korea had been ruled by Japan. After the defeat of Japan in WWII, Korea was divided into two sections, North Korea and South Korea. North Korea was run by the Soviet Union and South Korea was run by America. The Soviet Union refused to establish a unified government between the two and set up a Communist government while America set up a democratic government. In June 1949, America and the Soviet Union removed their forces from Korea and on June 25, 1950 North Koreans invaded South Korea. The Soviet Union and China supported the aggression of North Korea.

2. The site of a major battle that occurred in 1950 during the Korean War. The Chinese army fought against the First Marine Division. The Chinese stopped the northward advance of U.S. troops; but, the Chinese suffered many casualties losing eight divisions. The Marines were forced down to the sea, evacuated and transferred back to Allied lines in the south.

3. President Truman felt MacArthur had gone too far in publicly criticizing him.

4. Dien Bien Phu fell to the Communists. The French withdrew from Vietnam. The country was broken up into two parts. The Communists controlled the North and the anti-Communists controlled the South.

5. In order to obtain the good will of the new President of Egypt, Gamel Abdel Nasser, the U.S. and the Soviet Union offered him aid for various projects. The U.S. offered to help build a dam. The Soviets offered to trade weapons for Egyptian cotton. As Nasser became friendlier with the Soviets, the U.S. withdrew its support. In return, Nasser seized control of the Suez Canal and declared that Israeli ships were not allowed to use the Canal. France and Britain feared that they would be prohibited as well. These countries asked the U.S. for help and the U.S. refused.

6. Lacking UN support for their attack of Egypt, they had to withdraw their forces. This issue caused resentment which lasted for years.

7. Most of the focus was on the Suez Canal Crisis which was occurring at the same time and President Eisenhower was focused on his presidential campaign.

8. Through the U.S. media and the negligence of U.S. politicians.

9. A U.S. spy plane called a U-2 was shot down inside Soviet territory. At first the U.S. denied that it was a spy mission; however, finally admitted that it was a spy plane sent to take pictures of Soviet nuclear facilities. This was an embarrassment for America because she was caught spying on another country and then lied about it.

10. The U.S. failed attempt to overthrow Fidel Castro by supporting an invasion of Cuba at the Bay of Pigs by a group of Cuban exiles. However, JFK decided to

withdraw air support without telling the exiles.

11. Hungarian Cardinal arrested as a spy for protesting the Communist takeover of Catholic schools. He was tortured and forced to sign a false confession. In 1949, the Communists imprisoned him for life. He eventually was able to take refuge in the U.S. embassy during which time he became a symbol of the resistance against communism. He died in Vienna, Austria in 1975.

12. a) Claus Fuchs: Communist spy who worked on the Manhattan Project. He provided the Soviet Union with information regarding the atomic bomb. b) Alger Hiss: U.S. government official charged with being a Communist spy. Identified by Whittaker Chambers as an American Communist. Hiss had been an influential assistant to the Secretary of State. He had also been present at Yalta and had been a leader in setting up the United Nations. After being investigated by the House Un-American Activities Committee, Hiss was convicted of perjury and sent to prison. c) Whittaker Chambers: former Communist who use to work with Alger Hiss as a spy, and who later converted to Christianity. After his conversion, he provided the government with the identities of a number of U.S. Communists. d) Joseph McCarthy: Catholic elected as Senator from Wisconsin 1946. A leader who attempted to uncover Communist spies and Communist influence in the government. Over time he began to lose support.

1. he was a war hero awarded for his bravery

2. He gave a speech in Texas during his Presidential campaign in which he said that his Faith would not be the basis for his policies.

3. JFK ordered a naval blockade of Cuba; he demanded that the Soviets remove the missiles that were already there; he placed the U.S. military on full alert. The crisis was resolved by Khrushchev and Kennedy negotiating. Khrushchev agreed to remove the missiles if the U.S. agreed not to overthrow Castro.

4. A Buddhist priest and a former member of the Communist Party; because of his actions that the world falsely believed that there was a terrible persecution going on in South Vietnam.

5. in order to stop East Germans from escaping to the West and freedom

6. Lyndon Johnson, the Vice-President, became President

7. the belief that a Communist victory in a particular country, such as Vietnam, would lead to the fall of every other country in the region

8. Alan Shepherd

9. John Glenn

10. the effort of black Americans to gain equal treatment under the law and overcome segregation and discrimination

11. Boycotts during the Civil Rights movement. In December 1955,

Montgomery, Alabama, a black woman named Rosa Parks refused to give up her seat to a white man on the bus. She was arrested and put in jail. After this, several thousand black people began to boycott the city buses.

12. A black Baptist Minister who became the leader of the Civil Rights movement. He became well known for his use of direct action and non-violent methods, such as sit-ins and boycotts. He was killed in 1968 in Memphis, Tennessee.

13. "Separate but equal" referred to the segregation of blacks and whites in public places. According to the 14th Amendment everyone had to be treated equally under the law. In 1896, in Plessy v. Ferguson, the Supreme Court decided that this meant that facilities for blacks and whites could be "separate" as long as they were "equal."

14. Lee Harvey Oswald

15. President Johnson's social policies

16. The Resolution that gave the President the power to take the steps that he felt were needed to prevent further attacks against the forces of the U.S.. This resolution was passed as a result of the North Vietnamese attack on *USS Maddox*.

17. A countrywide attack in Vietnam against American troops by the Communist Vietnamese. The attack occurred on the Vietnamese New Year's Holiday, called Tet. The Tet Offensive was a major military victory for the U.S. and the South Vietnamese. However, the Communists won a psychological

victory. The fact that North Vietnam could launch such a large scale attack convinced many that the end of the war was not in sight as the government had said it was. The U.S. media said that the war could not be won.

18. In January 1968, the *USS Pueblo* was seized by North Koreans who claimed that the ship was spying in North Korean waters. 82 U.S. sailors were held hostage for nearly a year while the U.S. negotiated for their release. The hostages were finally released; but the ship was never returned.

19. He was assassinated.

20. Richard Nixon

CHAPTER 30

1. With an "honorable peace." He was determined to get U.S. troops out of Vietnam and to save South Vietnam from Communism in the process.

2. North Vietnam reacted violently by launching their largest military attack.

3. America would withdraw all of her forces from Vietnam if the North promised not to attack anymore. There would be no withdrawal of North Vietnamese troops from the large areas of the South that they now controlled. America would withdraw and get virtually nothing in return.

4. If the U.S. forces left and the Communist forces remained, then it was only a matter of time before the Communists seized the rest of the country.

5. Nixon told Thieu that, whether he

accepted the truce or not, the U.S. would sign the treaty and withdraw.

6. Millions of unborn babies have died

7. A political scandal that began during the 1972 presidential campaign between Democrat George McGovern and Republican Richard Nixon. The scandal grew out of a break-in at the Democratic Party headquarters at the Watergate hotel in Washington, D.C. This crime was committed by some of Nixon's aides and covered up by President Nixon himself. After Congressional hearings, the scandal was concluded by the resignation of President Nixon in 1974.

8. in order to prevent dissension among the U.S. people that would have arisen from the prosecution of Nixon. Americans were beginning to put the scandal behind them and Ford wanted the "long national nightmare" to end.

9. First, the failure of the secret rescue of the Americans taken hostage. This failure occurred when two U.S. aircraft collided in the Iranian desert. Second, this failure insured that the hostage crisis would continue to embarrass Carter for the entire 1980 presidential campaign.

10. They resulted in a peace agreement between Egypt and Israel, which had been a major concern for the U.S.

11. a) George McGovern: the 1972 Democratic Presidential Nominee. b) Anwar Sadat: President of Egypt who stunned the world when he flew to Jerusalem to speak with the Prime Minister of Israel, Menachem Begin. Sadat was the first Arab leader to recognize the nation of Israel. He called for diplomatic relations and a peace treaty.

12. There was substantial opposition to the Communists and the Soviets wanted to put an end to the revolts that were going on there.

13. economic sanctions; an embargo on all U.S. sales grain to the Soviets; a boycott of the 1980 Olympics that were held in Moscow; weapons to the anti-Communist resistance

CHAPTER 31

1. 1) cut taxes; 2) cut spending; 3) oppose Communism; 4) return America to her Christian roots and values.

2. as governor of California. He was already known for being a strong anti-Communist, and then became known for his support of Christian moral values.

3. a poor economy and the weakness of America overseas during his presidency. President Carter had also been weakened by a serious challenge in his own party by Edward Kennedy who argued that Carter had not provided the leadership the nation needed.

4. cutting taxes which he believed allowed for more money to stay in private business which would then help the economy to grow. As the economy grew, government income from taxation would also increase.

5. Reagan's policy toward Communism: The U.S. would no longer be content merely to assist countries seeking to avoid

Communist takeover. America would actively support anti-Communists who sought to oppose existing Communist governments.

6. He believed that nothing could be gained by negotiating with a foreign country from a position of weakness.

7. An independent labor union of Polish workers. It was the first of its kind created in a Communist world in September 1980.

8. It was faced with a united Western opposition lead by President Reagan. The Holy Father, Pope John Paul II, warned the Soviets that he would return to Poland and personally stand before the invading Soviet tanks.

9. a) It appeared that the Soviets and the Cubans hoped to establish an air base on that island. b) The people of Grenada asked for help. c) A U.S. medical school on the island became threatened.

10. Members of President Reagan's staff secretly were selling arms to Iran, which was at war with Iraq. The profits of these sales were used to support the Contras, a group of freedom fighters trying to overthrow the Communist government of Nicaragua.

11. From 1985, he was the Communist leader of the Soviet Union but believed in reform.

12. Literally means "restructuring" in Russian. Gorbachev hoped to restructure the Soviet Union's economy and political system on a democratic, free enterprise model.

13. With the increase in free enterprise came an atmosphere of more open discussion about political life. This discussion, or criticism, of government inefficiency had not previously been allowed in the Soviet Union. This "openness" was called glasnost.

14. a) destruction of the Berlin Wall and the collapse of Communist regimes. b) Massive demonstrations in East Germany. c) free travel between East and West Germany. d). the Communists take down the Berlin wall. e) in Romania, the Communist dictator Nicolae Ceausescu is removed from power after the people revolt.

15. 1991

16. A reformer who was elected President of the Russian Republic in 1990.

17. President Ronald Reagan, Pope John Paul II, and Mikhail Gorbachev

CHAPTER 32

1. George H. W. Bush

2. A U.S. soldier was shot by Panamanian forces in December 1989. Bush's goal was to remove Noriega from power.

3. 1. Iraq had to withdraw from Kuwait; 2. Kuwait's legitimate government would be restored; 3. Security and stability of the Persian Gulf had to be assured; 4. U.S. citizens abroad had to be protected.

4. General Norman Schwarzkopf

5. George Bush, William (Bill) Clinton, and H. Ross Perot

6. NAFTA is the North U.S. Free Trade Agreement that was ratified

in 1993. NAFTA's goal was to eliminate trade restrictions between the U.S., Canada and Mexico.

7. When two U.S. helicopters were shot down in Somolia (Africa) in 1993. A rescue mission was sent to extract the U.S. soldiers who were trapped behind enemy lines.

8. Bill Clinton

9. He was charged with perjury during a case in which he was being charged with misconduct during his time as Governor of Arkansas.

10. During the 9/11 attacks, two planes destroyed the World Trade Center's Twin Towers in New York City. A third plane was flown into the Pentagon. A fourth plane was supposed to crash into the White House or the Capital; however, the passengers overpowered the terrorists and prevented the crash into one of the buildings.

11. President Bush asked the Taliban to hand over Osama Bin Laden who was believed to be in hiding in Afghanistan. When, the Taliban did not hand over Bin Laden, the U.S. and allied forces began a bombing campaign against terrorist bases in Afghanistan.

12. President Bush gave Saddam Hussein forty-eight hours to leave Iraq. If he did not, then the U.S. would force him from power. Hussein refused. Intelligence

reports indicated that Hussein intended to re-start Iraq's nuclear weapons program and he was not getting rid of his weapons of mass destruction. President Bush also believed that Hussein was supporting the Al-Qaeda terror network.

13. President Bush said that North Korea, Iran and Iraq were the "Axis of Evil."

14. the Kurds, a minority group in Iraq.

15. Catholic Senator John Kerry

16. New Orleans, Louisiana because it is located below sea level and needs levees or dikes to keep the city from flooding; but, these levees were not built to withstand the strength of a hurricane like Katrina so New Orleans flooded after they failed.

17. Stem cells are cells whose future type has not yet been determined; they have the ability to develop into another kind of cell. Stem cell research involves injecting these kinds of cells into a human or animal in order to determine if these cells would revive damaged organs.

18. a) He did not want federal money to be used for research where stem cells are derived from the destruction of a human embryo. b). None.

19. Barack Obama